Tucson Was a Railroad Town
The Days of Steam in the Big Burg on the Main Line
by
William D. Kalt III

To Andrew and Sue,
We feel so fortunate
to have met such wonderful
British friends
All the best,
Bill

VTD Rail Publishing
3604 220th Pl SW
Mountlake Terrace WA 98043
http://www.vtd.net

Printed in the United States of America by
Gorham Printing, Centralia WA

ISBN 978-0-9719915-4-5

Library of Congress Control Number 2006934320

Editors: James Ayres, W. Eugene Caywood, Dave Devine, Richard Dick, Richard Hughes, Sharon Hunt, Benjamin E. Kalt, Tom Kerby, Dr. James B. Klein, and James Reel.

Cover:
Black and white portion AHS #B32380
Color portion Kalt Collection

Generous thanks and appreciation to the wonderful men and women who shared their railroad stories, pictures, and lives with the people of Tucson.

Those known to have passed away at the time of publication, including Charles Babers, Carl A. Ball Jr., David Bear, Eddie Caballero Sr., Ralph Coltrin, Sandra Heidel, Harold Jackson, Gordon Manning, C. R. McGowan Jr., Floyd Roberts, Annie Sabala, Harlan Payne, and Helen Starliper.

Special appreciation to rails and family members, including Edith Auslander, Elgin and Mary Ball, Eugene Ball, James A. Barnes, Arnold Bays, Rudy Benitez, T. Herman Blythe, Lovell Bonnie, Emily and William Bradley, Judith Britt, Eleanor Brundick, Jason Burke, Nicholas Lowell Burke, Robert Bushnell, Carolina Butler, David Butler, Aurelia V. Caballero, Ralph Coltrin Jr., Bettie and Al Crawford, Randy Curtin, Joe Datri, Robert and Louise DeHart, Katie Dusenberry, James W. Elwood, Dorothy Fitzpatrick, Tim Flood, Manuel Gallardo, Elizabeth Garigan, Lee Goerke, Judith Hall, Jacob Harris, Jean Heidel, Alice Hinton, Hazel Hook, Hazel Houston, A.E. Huffman, Tom Kerby, Harvey Lang, Nyle Leatham, Raymond and Louise Lee, A.T. Lewis, George Lundquist, Geraldine Mackaben, Ruth Manning, Harlin Marlar, Robert McClelland, Frank Mendez, Mrs. C. W. McKissick, Ruben and Irma Moreno, C.D. Murtaugh, Julia Peters Newman, Norma Nibblet, Betty Nowell, Kathy Nugent, Armando Pain, Eddie Pecktol, George Perkins, Susan Peters, James and Sylvia Pfersdorf, Cara Randall, Johnny Rhoades, Dale Romero, A. Martin "Marty" Ronstadt, Hamilton Salsbury, Barbara Salyer, Federico Sayre, Sid Showalter, Clifton Smith, Leon Speer, Richard Stapp Sr., Lloyd Stead, Betty Stein, Charles Stoddard, Maria Thim, J.J. Tierney, E.C. Webster, Lovell Gunter Welsh, Dona Genevieve Whelan, Charles Wherry, William H. White Jr.

Words do not express my heartfelt appreciation to my sweet wife, Gail, for her love, strength, honesty, and endless re-reading. Special thanks also to the Tucson-Pima Historical Commission for their generous financial support, to James W Nugent for being my "grandpa," to Bonnie Henry for reminding me there was "Another Tucson," to Norma Nibblet for her steadfast confidence and steel-strong support, and to David Devine for his remarkable generosity of spirit, fine eye, and abundance of good humor. Many thanks also to Amec Infrastructure, Arizona Historical Society Tucson and Yuma, Laura Caywood Barker, Dr. John Bret Harte, Carol Brooks, Leslie Broughton, Chrystal Carpenter Burke, California State Railroad Museum, Sister Alberta Cammack, Burel Carney-El Zaribah Shrine Temple, Rudy Casillas of KUAT-TV, Peggy Castillo, W. Eugene Caywood, Cincinnati Museum-Historical Society Library, Colossal Cave Mountain Park Research Library & Archives, Robert Conrad, Jan Davis, Kristy K. Dial, James H. Ebert, Gerald W. Emert, Kim Frontz, Gaylon Grodt, Gus Gustafson, Richard G.Guthrie, Pete Guzman, Ellen Halteman, Wanda Hammonds, Jacob Harris, Dr. Bill Hendricks, Charles H. Herner, Huntington Library & Gardens, Imperial Valley Irrigation District, Ken Jolly, Laraine Daly Jones, Damon J. Kalt, Esq., Dr. Joseph P. Kalt, Dr. Kenneth Karrels, Doug Kupel, Robet LeBaron, Dan Lewis, Ph.D., Ray Lund Family, L.E. Maucher, Jill McCleary, Debbie Newman, Ernesto Portillo Jr., Cara Randall, Ed Rzewnicki, Annie Shellberg, Leslie A. Shellie, Sherman Library & Gardens, Ruby Spurgeon, Dave Tackenberg, Theresa Taylor, Lynda Thomas, Jill Thrasher, Lynda G. Trimm, University of Arizona Special Collections, Jenni Van Brocklin, Harold York

Fortune smiled the day I teamed with most professional, skilled, positive, tenacious Mr. Thomas White, who designed the cover and book, and served as producer, technical adviser, project manger, and all-around ass-kicker.

TUCSON
Was a Railroad Town

"Take them as a class and they are the most intelligent citizens found anywhere. Their duties make them so. The engineer is the most keen, courageous, self-reliant man of any calling. Conductors are the very best class of citizens. The firemen must be men above the average for their responsibility, and the brakemen likewise. All of them must be high-grade men. Take the mechanics of the company; machinists, boilermakers, blacksmiths, car and other builders—all artisans must be. They are a superior class of men. They are the bone and sinew of Tucson."

Arizona Daily Star, *October 20, 1898*

Tom Davenport (right) stood among the bone and sinew of Tucson. Tom worked his first engine on the Tucson Division July 4, 1890 and his last on the same day forty-eight years later. The son-in-law of fabled Arizona pioneer Capt. J.H. Tevis grabbed his oilcan when he stepped off No. 4302 on his final run. (Maude and Al Hammonds Collection)

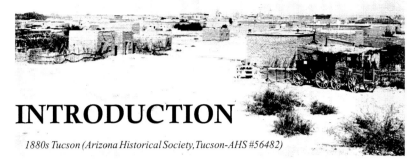

INTRODUCTION

1880s Tucson (Arizona Historical Society, Tucson-AHS #56482)

Thundering, snorting fire she came—massive stallion of steel, rupturing the silence of the desert and the history of its people. Penetrating, permeating—the age of the steam locomotive crashed forward into Arizona. Across her southern deserts, the Southern Pacific Railroad (SP) laid tracks that would bind the nation's eastern and western regions. All knew life would change forever; few could imagine how much.

Tucson stood as the metropolis of the territory when engineer J. W. "Jack" Bruce brought the first SP train into the city during March 1880. Former SP railroad worker, city councilman, and Southern Arizona Bank president John C. Etchells remembered his father took him to "Nine-Mile Water Hole," north of town, to see construction of the new rail line. "The train rolled [rocked] as it ran along the tracks because the roadbed was uneven and not packed very firm," Etchells said. "One day, I peeked into a coach on the train and saw a cage with a bird in it. It was a canary, the first one I ever seen."

Sam Hughes, who arrived in Arizona in 1858, remembered that one Sunday he and Dr. John Handy rode to the *arroyo* at the north end of Meyer Street to watch grading crews prepare the roadbed for Tucson's first train. "The engine of the work train puffed and snorted," Hughes recalled. "Dr. Handy had left his horse standing and the animal became frightened as were many people by the panting and the snorting of the iron horse." SP agent T.M. Cash declared that Tucson parents should "caution their children from playing on the track," or "a fatal accident will certainly happen."

The March 20 arrival of a special train carrying Charles Crocker and other SP officials inspired frolicsome revelry. The *Phoenix Enterprise* crowed: "There was rejoicing in Arizona last night. The iron horse panted into Tucson and with its neigh gave notice that a new order of things was about to be established. The horrors of that Sahara, which stretches for many leagues beyond Yuma, are hereafter to be but themes of jest; the heart of Arizona has been moved up within two days ride of the port of San Francisco; the modern Evangel—the locomotive has gone to carry comfort and joy to that Territory." Tucsonan Leonard E. Romero witnessed the city's pivotal moment and remembered citizens partied with fervor. "People don't celebrate like we did in the old days," Romero recalled seventy-five years later. "These days they just get tired too quick, I guess."

Dust clouds rose above the din of industry as sixty men graded the grounds for a passenger depot and freight house

River boats provided transportation and carried freight before SP trains arrived in Yuma. These boats continued their work after the railroad began operations in Arizona in 1877. (AHS #25126)

The SP used coal-burning locomotives when it began operations at Tucson in 1880. Arizona's "most ancient and honorable pueblo" boasted being the sole U.S. town to sell Mexico $5 million in goods, and the only one with a population of 8,000 people and 10,000 dogs. Not a single concert or theatrical performance graced the adobe settlement that year. (AHS #41568)

one-half mile east of Tucson that week. The company's large turntable sat ready for use while crews laid sidetracks and switches. Canvas tents soon sprang up, housing the Branch Hotel, Pioneer's Rest, Excelsior Saloon & Restaurant, and Head Light Saloon. Well-known merchant Joseph Sresovich announced he would receive "fresh fish and fresh fruits such as one seldom finds in Arizona," by express train. The *Arizona Daily Star* noted, "Such is the effect of enterprise and capital; it is the magic wand which transforms the desert into a teeming field of busy life."

The SP established its local office in Manuel Vasquez's former room, next door to long-time merchandisers Lord & Williams on Congress Street. Early the following month, forty to sixty passengers entered the city by train each night, and total receipts reached almost $5,000 a day. Teams of mules stood waiting at the depot site to carry away the tons of arriving materials and goods. Soon, a lack of cars and service personnel held up traffic. The *Los Angeles Herald* reported the company would double crews on its passenger trains between Tucson and the coast. Railroad workers over-filled freight cars designed to carry ten tons, with twelve to sixteen tons of merchandise to meet shippers' demands. In mid-April, lack of clerical supplies forced agent A.J. Finlay to close his freight office for two days and SP agent T.M. Cash declared, "The [passenger] depot now being built will not be large enough for Tucson."

Arizonans had agitated for a railroad before 1860, with no success. In his *Pioneer Days of Arizona*, Dr. F.C. Lockwood explained: "In reality, Arizona was such a lone, alien, orphan thing that her need was only an atom in the larger urgency felt by her highborn sisters, East and West, for a transcontinental railroad route. At the time, Arizona's fate stirred little interest; she was merely an infant crying in the night and with no answer but a cry. Like many other hardy and forlorn infants, Arizona had been deposited at the right spot and was traversed at a fairly early date by two of the chief Pacific coast routes [SP and Santa Fe]."

The Southern Pacific bestowed great things upon southern Arizona. Foremost, the railroad helped bring to an end the enduring Apache Indian wars that had terrorized the southwest since the late 1600s. The train's rapid movement of increased numbers of U.S. Cavalry troops and supplies shifted the balance of military advantage. Ever the wily foe, native warriors found their circle of freedom tighten at greater and greater cost. Attacks diminished in southern Arizona, and the cavalry brought the final Apache fighters to ground in the mid-1880s. Though occasional raids continued, southern Arizonans sighed in relief as the violence abated at last. In the

Two Apache warriors "posed" in shackles for this photograph. Fierce native shaman Geronimo declared that, because the Great Spirit did not interest himself in the petty quarrels of men, warriors should seek their own revenge. For forty years Geronimo exacted retribution on both American and Mexican people for the slaughter of his wife and small children when he was just twenty years old. After the Spanish-American War, he enjoyed the fact that the United States had defeated Spain in a few weeks but could not subdue his small band of fighters over many years. (AHS #B94656)

The railroad opened the region to mining as never before. Moving heavy equipment and ore on trains made mining operations more profitable. Branch lines emerged off the SP main line to connect the most productive mines with smelting operations and assay offices. The SP developed cattle markets and hauled Arizona's herds to buyers nationwide. It took the lead in reclaiming arid lands by digging wells across the desert to provide water for its steam process, employees, and customers. Steam locomotives lugged trainloads of furniture, lumber, wagons, paints, windows, and countless other goods into the adobe village, quicker and at less cost than by freight wagon. Though a brickyard existed in Tucson as early as 1879, many declared local clay and pressing techniques less than adequate. The railroad delivered better quality lumber and allowed Tucsonans to import El Paso pressed brick, initiating the broader use of materials other than adobe in construction.

Tucson consumers benefited from the railroad, but it wrought mayhem in the city's business community. Businesses encumbered by existing freighting and merchandising contracts could not compete with those that paid lower railroad shipping rates and receved their goods much qucker. Freighters Tully & Ochoa, Lord & Williams, and other established concerns collapsed under the burden. Firms such as Leo Goldschmidt's furniture store adapted and survived while other ventures sprouted anew.

SP trains also delivered people by the carload, from all parts of the world. The swifter, more comfortable ride brought individuals and troupes of entertainers with greater variety and talent. Ideas and conversations, inventions and concoctions made their way in greater haste to the desert borough after 1880.

Over the next two decades, the railroad employed, supplied, bonded, entertained, thrilled, aggravated, and mystified Tucsonans as did no other entity. Despite

safer climate, both Anglo and Mexican businessmen and citizens focused on commercial development.

Their fates interwoven in a complex web of economic, social, political, and spiritual mutuality, the influence of the SP surfaced in Tucson and across southern Arizona in many other ways. The SP reduced the trip to Los Angeles from five days to less than one, and its $100 cost by two-thirds. Freight shipments that previously took three months now arrived in four or five days, while freight charges dropped to one tenth that of steamer or wagon transportation.

Travelers arriving by Southern Pacific rail enjoyed this view looking east from their passenger coach in 1892. Across the tracks lay adobe houses, the city's largest hobo encampment, and in the distance, the Tucson Indian School (back center) and Old Main (far right) on the University of Arizona campus. (University of Arizona Special Collections-UASC)

advances, however, the community's hopes for growth and prosperity met a brutal reality. Tucson remained a rough, remote, unsanitary mud pueblo. Uneven streets and few sidewalks meant always walking at a tilt, through either dust or thick mud. In summer's prostrating heat, the rank stench of open cesspools (privies) became intolerable in some parts of the city. Prostitutes hung from open windows and doors with

Local "man-of-all-work," "Frying Pan" Charles Alzamora reigned as one of Tucson's most unique nineteenth century characters. Frying Pan ran drinks and sandwiches to the players and operators at roulette wheels and faro tables in the city's several gambling establishments. Almazora knew all the killers and irresponsible characters by their first names. In 1937, Albert Steinfeld remembered, "He associated with the roughest and the most lawless men of the city, and he survived. He has probably seen more gunfights than any pioneer still around Tucson."

impunity, and opium dens graced the area around Pearl Street. Fistfights settled minor brush-ups in the city's streets and saloons, while pistols remained within reach. Geographic isolation and cultural incivility, combined with whimsical fluctuations in the national economy, caused local business to lag and the city's population to decline. With no free mail delivery, a water system that relied on river water and gravity, and no "sewerage" works, pilgrims found more than a bit of the Wild West in the Old Pueblo.

Railroad workers, called "rails," built communities like Tucson across the United States. Their unwavering character, large numbers, and regular paydays lent stability to otherwise transient towns. The size and power of rail equipment made danger railroaders' constant companion, and their work demanded safety, accuracy, and industry. The company chose reliable, honest, and trustworthy men, shunning the alcoholic, slacker, and "hanger-on." Conductors, engineers, telegraphers, station agents, master car repairman, dispatchers, switchmen, baggagemen, and machinists began to appear on Tucson streets. As in the California Gold Rush earlier in the century, businesses emerged to supply rail families and to share in the prosperity of the railroad's mega-scheme.

Through time, work around the daily comings and goings of trains became ritualized and romanticized, fostering a nationwide rail culture. Railroad songs and legends fed a powerful mystique spun about the great steam trains. In Tucson, the SP and its employees influenced all aspects of city life, forming the collective spirit of a railroad town. Early folk heroes, railroad workers dispensed nicknames and built enduring camaraderie. Earning respect from their fellow citizens, rails became key players in Tucson's economic, political, and social structure. Many used their steady employment and ready transportation as a springboard to other enterprises. These are the stories of an SP railroad town during the steam epoch.

Near the heart of Arizona's metropolis, the corner of Main Avenue and Ott Street hardly looked urban in 1893. The names of several city streets derived from Tucsonan's pivotal role in the Apache Wars. City fathers honored early rancher E.G. Pennington and U.S. Cavalry officers Colonel John Finkle Stone and Lieutenant Howard Cushing for giving their lives in combat against the native raiders. Simpson, Kennedy, Scott, and Jackson streets also acknowledge men killed in Apache battles. (AHS #46703)

"Rails" predominated in Tucson after the railroad's arrival. The local SP shops bred strong, tough men who posed for this photograph ca. 1890. (AHS #9229)

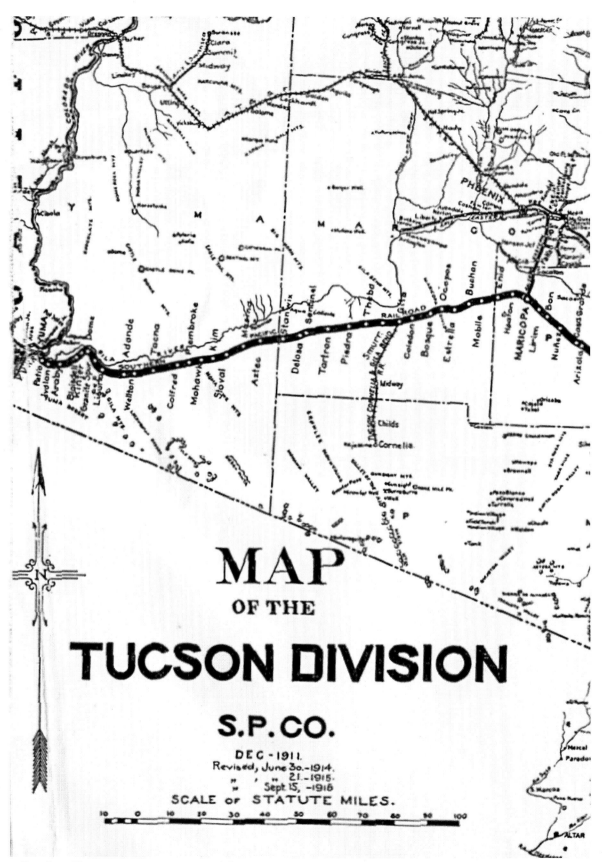

East from Yuma, across Arizona to Lordsburg, New Mexico, the Tucson Division provided an important link in SP's southern transcontinental route. At times, the division extended to El Paso and Tucumcari, New Mexico.

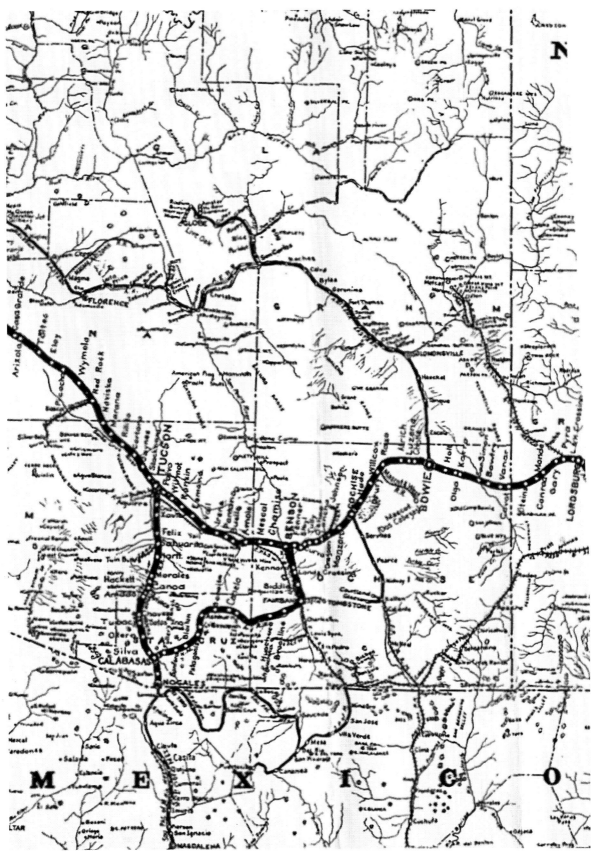

The company took over the line south from Benson to Nogales and on to Guaymas, Sonora in 1898 and the line through Calabasas in 1910. The division point rested at Lordsburg in 2006. (Kalt Collection)

The Southern Pacific's San Xavier Hotel sits at the top right in this 1891 photograph (above). The hotel stood north of the passenger depot, far from the center of town, with little but desert between it and the University of Arizona's Old Main (center in distance). (AHS #2924)

Charles Rivers Drake (left) sat on the Tucson city council when it granted the SP its local reserve August 21, 1879. Drake's instrumental role in bringing SP trains to the adobe pueblo goes largely unheralded. (AHS #B13508)

Engineer Joe Oman (left) began on the local division in 1887 and ran steam locomotives for forty-nine years. Oman paused while oiling his straight stack 4-4-0 engine at Steins, New Mexico ca. 1900. (AHS # 21413)

Table of Contents

Chapter 1

*Fire in the Pueblo and Tucson's
Renaissance of 1898*

The mouthwatering bouquet of roasting *carne* (meat) nestled within the crisp, earthy smell of burning *mesquite*, saturating the early morning air around Hillside Park, near present-day Stone Avenue and Speedway Boulevard. Vicente Valenzuela had begun digging several holes for Sunday's *asada* (barbeque) the night before. Laying stones in the bottom, he built a fire in each. When the flames died and only the glowing coals of the hard desert wood remained, Vicente secured several steers' heads inside each hole overnight.

This aging image of an early Tucson barbeque captures stylish revelers in a dusty desert land. Tucson enjoyed a reputation as a metropolis of "high-sounding 'whereas' resolutions and mass meetings" in 1898. (Ray Hanson Collection)

Streaks of orange and scarlet battled for a piece of the eastern sky as Valenzuela's beef broiled in its own juices, indenturing to it a special *sabor asada* (roasted flavor). When his treasure burst forth, *el asador* (cook) peeled back each skull's hide to fall upon its succulent, meaty mother-lode. Several gallons of *menudo* (a traditional Mexican stew containing tripe, hominy, chiles, and vegetables), bread, but-

ter, and coffee "made to the Queen's taste" completed a juicy feast for the families of Henry Meyers, railroad shopman Ed Hale, and Vicente Cordova. Thus stood the "ancient and honorable" pueblo of Tucson, Arizona, in 1898.

The remote southwestern town had joined the United States with the signing of the Gadsden Purchase forty-four years earlier. The culture of her people, however, continued to reflect Mexican roots. The railroad brought more people of European heritage, called "the Americans" in local newspapers, to the city. By 1898, one-half of the Old Pueblo's residents claimed Mexican heritage. Tucson's distinctive essence included Chinese, African-Americans (called Negroes during the steam age), Jewish pioneers, Tohono O'odham (Papago) or "Desert People," and later, the Yaqui people, in a toothsome blend of cultures.

"Policy" was the money game and the roulette player's favorite number 17 during the year Tucson's story took a most dramatic turn. Arizona's role in the national scene intersected with favorable financial and social factors in 1898. Increased investment in building, mining, and municipal development, and the rudiments of a social consciousness, formed the upshot near the banks of the Santa Cruz River. Unprecedented economic, social, cultural, and infrastructure development signaled the inception of the late pioneer period in the city's history, and that year marks an appropriate point for beginning this tale.

The Southern Pacific Railroad (SP) provided most of the jobs in Tucson in 1898 and paid the largest share of local taxes. Its men and women formed the city's core, as the *Arizona Daily Star* explained: "Take them as a class and they are the most intelligent citizens found anywhere. Their duties make them so. The engineer is the most keen, courageous, self-reliant man of any calling. Conductors are the very best class

Southern Pacific provided the most jobs and paid the largest share of local taxes, and its employees formed the city's core throughout the steam era. (Maude and Al Hammonds Collection)

of citizens. The firemen must be men above the average for their responsibility, and the brakemen likewise. All of them must be high-grade men. Take the mechanics of the company; machinists, boilermakers, blacksmiths, car and other builders, all artisans must be. They are a superior class of men. They are the bone and sinew of Tucson."

SP rails (railroad workers) saved the city from fire more than once in 1898. Tucsonan's greatest fear since the cessation of Apache depredations, flame occupied a special place in the mind of every resident. The city faced a three-fold problem. Flammable wooden fronts and awnings adorned many city buildings and provided ready fuel. A gravity-flow water system produced a stream that reached no higher than the awnings of one-story buildings, and a demoralized city volunteer fire department lay in shambles. Despite good intentions, Tucson had dawdled in its own defense.

The city had purchased "The Chemical," a shiny new fire engine, for $1,984 the previous fall. Designed to respond quickly and spray chemicals on a fire until men could establish a water stream, the new fire engine symbolized great hopes for the future of Tucson's volunteer department.

Wooden awnings added to Tucson's flammable construction. (Left: Kalt Collection, Above: AHS #13370)

City firemen pulled the Chemical to local blazes by hand, but one businesswoman loaned them a pair of horses to pull the engine in the 1898 Fourth of July parade. Sitting on the seat left to right are E.E. Johnson, Arnold Smith, and John Francis; Bill Martin, sitting on the hose reel, L. Corea standing on back step, Mr. Santa Cruz standing beside reel; John Stockhalm, beside the horses; and William Katzenstein, standing beside the wheel. Early policemen came from the ranks of the volunteer fire department. In July 1902, assassin Teodoro Elias shot Katzenstein while he performed his police duties. Today, he is honored as the second policeman killed in the line of duty. (AHS #B94484)

D.J. "Jack" Boleyn sits atop a high-wheeled livery wagon in turn-of-the-twentieth century Tucson. The frustrated fire chief blasted the mayor and council for its failure to fund a salaried steward. Elected officials deserved the blame for his department's woes, said the rough and tumble Vermont native, not his 'fireladdies.' (AHS top, #48105; right, #60094 Boleyn)

Sadly, not a single man had full training in its operation. In January 1898, Fire Chief J.D. "Jack" Boleyn explained: "I can take the average ten-year-old boy, which has any intelligence and teach him the working of the Chemical in ten minutes. The whole trouble is everybody is afraid of it." Exasperated, Mayor Henry Buehman lamented, "While our chemical engine is a thing of beauty, it fails to be a joy forever, for the poor thing has not had the smell of smoke since it made its appearance." In addition, lack of a harness team of horses meant firemen had to drag the contraption to fires by hand.

No regular steward had manned the city fire department's engine house to sound the alarm or tend the equipment during the previous six months. When volunteers sounded a false alarm, criticism of the department mounted. Chief Boleyn blasted the mayor and city council for failing to fund a salaried steward. Blame for his sagging department's woes rested on elected officials, said the chief, not with his "fireladdies."

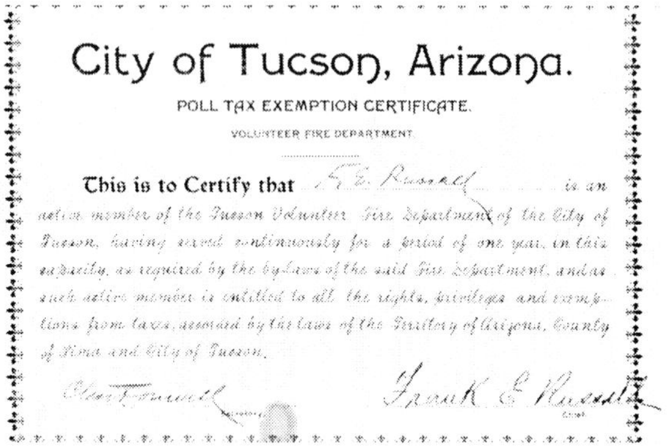
City of Tucson, Arizona.

POLL TAX EXEMPTION CERTIFICATE.

VOLUNTEER FIRE DEPARTMENT

This is to Certify that F. E. Russell is an active member of the Tucson Volunteer Fire Department of the City of Tucson, having served continuously for a period of one year in this capacity, as required by the by-laws of the said Fire Department, and as such active member is entitled to all the rights, privileges and exemptions from taxes, accorded by the laws of the Territory of Arizona, County of Pima and City of Tucson.

Frank E. Russell

Chief

Though denied the exemptions granted to city fireman, shopmen continued to answer the alarm. (F.E. Russell Papers, AHS)

A blaze in Boleyn's own sheds and corrals, on Eleventh Street (now Broadway Boulevard) near the SP shops, destroyed $3,900 in hay, buildings, wagons, buggies, and harnesses near the end of February 1898. When flames threatened to engulf rail superintendent Epes Randolph's house at 70 S. Fifth Avenue, men from the railroad shops formed a bucket brigade and saved it. City volunteers pulled the Chemical to the fire but it "didn't scare the flames a bit and water there was none until the connection was made with the railroad," reported the *Citizen*.

The men of the railroad shops had fought before at the front of Tucson's attack on fire. In a conflagration at the large brick schoolhouse on Military Plaza, "the Southern Pacific Company's water supply saved large amounts of property of both the city and private citizens from destruction," reported the *Star*. Master mechanic L.S. Pratt and his foreman, C. O'Keefe, organized company machinists into the SP Fire Brigade in March 1898. The valiant crew included Chief O'Keefe; foreman O.R. Hale; first assistant foreman Charles Strauss; second assistant foreman S.R. Russell; nozzlemen R.W. Vail and George Burns; hydrantmen John Simpson and P.O. Boyers; and hosemen W.W. Cooper, W.C. Kitt, George Giles, and Jack Rice. Well-drilled and fighting fit, the twelve-to-fifteen-man unit stood ready to tackle the beast of blaze.

SP shopmen raced down Congress Street from the local depot toward the Santa Cruz River to a fire at Dickinson's Furniture Store on September 16, 1898. Rails hurried to get a water stream on the inferno, but flames destroyed the building and its contents. The shopmen's sterling efforts again drew commendation from the *Star*: "Had it not been for the heroic work of the SP shop fire brigade and the SP water supply, the fire would have no doubt swept down Congress Street, doing a vast amount of damage. Too much can not be said in praise of the railroad boys and the water supply they furnished, for it is an admitted fact that had they not come to the rescue, the Tucson fire department with their equipment could not have stopped the fire in the entire block."

Railroad machinists wrestled Tucson's nastiest fire the very next morning. Around 10:30 a.m. Sunday, September 17, 1898, fire started in the L.G Radulovich block at the northeast corner of Congress Street and Stone Avenue. A symbol of progress in pioneer Tucson, the Radulovich Building hopped with activity on most days. Now fire had its way with the city's most attractive and distinctive structure. Many still in their church clothes, members of the city fire department showed up first but failed to produce a water stream more

L.G. Radulovich's busy "block" (building) sat on the northeast corner of Congress and Stone prior to its searing demise. Just before the "great fire," W.F. Kitt worked stocking his new dry goods store and Wells Fargo agents hustled to keep up with the city's growing express shipping business. Proprietor Radulovich displayed a large stock of pottery and housewares, while those with a sweet tooth stopped at ex-SP engineer P.B. Ziegler's Candy Kitchen, to sample his brother Albert's latest "sponge" candy. C.F. Hoff's Sunset Telephone & Telegraph Company kept residents and visitors in touch with each other and the world, while doctors Mark A. Jones and F.A. Odermatt shuffled patients through their third-floor offices. (AHS #24402)

than fifteen feet high. Railroad firefighters arrived to find huge tongues of flame shooting through the grand building's roof.

Rails worked to get a water stream on the flames as gawkers watched in transfixed horror. "Streaked with black smoke and shooting high in the air, now a vast sheet of flame, again rising in jagged peaks and streamers, the spectacle was awe inspiring," the morning newspaper later reported. "The heat was terrific and again and again the crowd was driven back by it only to surge forward yet again in fascination." Machinist firefighters recognized the

futility in their fight to save Radulovich's block and sought to protect nearby buildings. Blasted by the fire's intense heat, rails kept water and wet blankets on the Koehler Block across Congress to the south and Fred Fleishman's drugstore to its west. Their paint blistered and windows broken out by the firestorm, both structures endured.

The Radulovich fire raged out of control for three hours and smoldered for days. The owner's losses totaled almost $50,000, while his insurance covered just $10,000. SP telegraphers provided Tuc-

Luke G. Radulovich

PLUMBER AND TINNER,

Importer and Dealer in

Queensware, Stoneware,

Crockery, China Glassware, Tinware, &c.

son's sole communication because the inferno ruined Chas. F. Hoff's Sunset Telephone and Telegraph office. Two weeks later, manager Hoff continued to push a crew of ten men to restore telephone service. Hoff used insurance money to order a top-of-the-line metallic switchboard and promised upgraded service. The fire also consumed more than 80 percent of University of Arizona chancellor Colonel William F. Herring's eighteen-hundred-book library, as well as many irreplaceable documents and papers. "Incomparably the best in Arizona," mourned the *Star*. Remembered for years afterwards as "the great fire," the Radulovich blaze brought the city's water predicament into sharp relief.

A "Good Lesson for the City," screamed the *Citizen*. The fire proved "the utter worthlessness of the so-called water supply...and the utter helplessness in which the city would find itself in another conflagration. Had it not been for the

prompt and noble attendance of the railroad boys with their matchless stream, perhaps a good part of the city would be in ashes today." With the morale of the volunteer fire department crushed and its membership at just six men, the city council disbanded the unit within the month.

Early in October, SP division freight and passenger agent Charles M. Burkhalter chaired a meeting to form a new volunteer fire department. Thirty men met at the Church Street engine house and formed a fifteen-man chemical company, a hook and ladder team, and a six-man hose company. To spur performance, the city council resolved to pay $2.50 to the first team responding to an alarm, $1.50 to all crews who answered a false alarm, and an extra $1.00 to the first group to take out the hook and ladder truck.

Two weeks later, a fire at F. J. Villaescusa's wagon shop brought twenty-five city volunteers running "at the first tap of the bell." The Chemical "got the credit for showing greater efficiency than on any previous occasion," said the *Citizen*. "Keep up the good work boys, and Tucson will have a department worthy of praise and unequaled in the territory." Though denied the exemptions granted to all city firemen from Tucson's $25 poll tax and jury duty, the men of the SP shop brigade continued to answer fire alarms. The following year, the city

The Radulovich fire smoldered for days. (AHS #633)

The 1901 Revised Statutes of Arizona provided that seven years service entitled this volunteer fire -fighter to exemption from military service in times of peace and from payment of poll, road, and street taxes. (F.E. Russell Papers, AHS-T)

made the railroad contingent a separate division of its fire department with full exemption privileges.

Lack of a pressurized city water system stood as an unconscionable obstacle to Tucson's civic advancement. The *Citizen* declared: "Tucson is not a 'fire town' but as each new building goes up it advances one more step in that direction. When a fire does come, and misses the adobes, it demonstrates how utterly helpless the city is." First sold in goatskin bags from springs along the Santa Cruz River and later for 5¢ a five-gallon bucket, early Tucson water flowed through *acequias* (ditches), and from two or three wells in Elysian Grove that bore a dreadful saline taste. Sylvester "Sly" Watts and H.A. Lawton bought Bob Leatherwood's franchise and built the first municipal water system in the territory in 1881. Watts's simple gravity flow arrangement provided Tucson with water at a good rate for domestic and agricultural uses, but one inadequate for fire fighting. The SP water system gave Tucson its only water pressure sufficient for fire protection, just as it did in many towns across the west.

SP dug a well north of town at its Stockham Station, now near Prince Road and Interstate 10, and four more near the depot to pipe water to its facilities.

High-pressure steam pumps in the SP shops provided water to run company operations and fight fires. During 1898, after years of discussion, a radical difference of opinion emerged regarding the vital liquid's city-wide provision. The SP's sizeable investment in Tucson and its future prompted the company to pursue a timely solution.

Local SP superintendent Epes Randolph proposed that the railroad provide all of Tucson's municipal water and protect the city against fire around the clock for 30¢ per thousand gallons. "Our condition is deplorable in the extreme," said Randolph. "No man in town knows when he goes to bed at night whether he will have a roof over him the next morning, besides this our citizens are paying $30,000 annually to insurance companies." He also

Epes Randolph outlined the railroad's plan for the city's water system in a letter to the city council. A tenacious diplomat, Randolph kept a .38-caliber handgun secreted in his private car, the Pocahontas, for hard times and tough characters. (Huntington Library)

pointed out that residents east of the Military Plaza had to "drive," drill, their own wells, lay pipes for domestic uses, and pay SP for fire protection. The Tucson School district also paid the SP $15 per month for water. Randolph assured city officials he could deliver water "within fifteen minutes after the closing of a contract."

Harangues rang out on the city's Court Plaza against Sly Watts and his water company, while big-hitters in the community weighed in on the issue through the daily newspapers. Merchant Albert Steinfeld favored the SP plan, worried that if the city owned the water plant the tax rate would increase and drive off investors. Tucson pioneer Sam Hughes supported city ownership of the waterworks through bond sales, saying, "I do not believe in building a furnace and letting the other fellow own the bellows. Make the bonds payable in fifty years and let those who come after us foot the bill." Insurance man H.D. Underwood proclaimed that a pressurized city water system would reduce rates by one-third for businesses and by one-half for Tucson home owners.

Tucson's Board of Trade (called the Chamber of Commerce after March 1902) lent hearty endorsement to the SP plan, but city council members cast aside the railroad's water proposal in favor of remaining with Watts & Co. The SP continued to develop its own extensive water system beneath city streets, replacing six-inch lines into town with ten-inch mains and doubling the capacity of the Stockham pumping plant, to 100,000 gallons per day.

Despite its water problems and lack of a sewer system, affluence and its attendant amenities rolled into Tucson on SP rails. In his 1982 volume *Tucson: the Life and Times of an American City*, former editor of the *Journal of Arizona History* and noted author C.L. Sonnichsen proclaimed, "In 1898, Arizona moved closer to the rest of the United States." Sonnichsen pinpointed the Spanish-American War as a key to the transformation of Arizona that year.

A bomb exploded aboard the battleship Maine on February 15, 1898. While the nation pondered cause and consequence, several of Tucson's young men enlisted Orndorff Hotel clerk Eugene W. Waterbury to write Lieutenant Alexander Brodie and express their eagerness to join his nascent territorial militia. The *Star* trumpeted: "None but...men who are known to be stayers, good shots, and cool when under fire will be accepted. Tucson's Kirt L. Hart is one of the best shots in the Territory and just the man to choose men for the company."

Led by Captain Kirt Hart, men lived on bacon, beans, and hard tack at Camp McCord, named in honor of Arizona governor Myron H. McCord, on the flat near Eagle Mills at 70 S. Main Avenue. Volunteers boarded trains at the SP depot and Tucson's young women dressed up to bid them farewell during the first week of July 1898. The Palace Saloon posted regular war bulletins and a sign above one door at the depot read, "Boys, old Tucson bids you God's speed and safe return. Remember the Maine, our country, our flag, humanity, and victory." (AHS #63550)

The Elks Club incorporated in late March 1898, purchased land for $5,000 from Paddy Woods, and began building an impressive clubhouse west of the courthouse on Ott Street between Pennington and Court streets. In addition, cattleman R. G. Brady, hotelman C.E. Lowe, and Catholic Bishop Peter Bouregarde remodeled the abandoned San Augustine Cathedral into a traveler's inn, flushing rumored ghosts from the building when it opened at the start of October 1898. (Gaylon Grodt Collection)

Phoenix Republican cheered: "These quick movements have brought Arizona the recognition of the United States."

The nasty Spanish conflict brought the light of national acclaim to Arizona. That her men— cowboys, miners, and pioneers—rose shoulder-to-shoulder with bankers, professional men, and the "flower of aristocracy of eastern cities" sparked pride across the territory. "The people of Arizona are all shouting for our American heroes," cried the *Star*. Many felt that statehood, and the investor confidence it would create, stood just around the corner. Alas, politics dictated another fourteen years of stubborn wrangling before statehood became a reality.

When reports of small bands of Spanish sympathizers crossing into the United States surfaced, the U.S. Army shipped 300 stands of arms to Bisbee. In addition, a company of U.S. Seventh Cavalry troops from Fort Huachuca took up patrol along the border with Mexico. However, no large-scale attacks on the United States originated in Mexico during the three months and twenty-two days of vicious Cuban warfare.

Arizona shone in the short but brutal Spanish-American War. Prescott's William O. "Buckey" O'Neill led the territory's fighters into national wartime service. Arizona filled its quota of volunteers first, and her men arrived first at the rendezvous of troops in San Antonio, Texas. Arizonans joined the initial wave of troops on the front lines of battle and Governor Myron H. McCord resigned to lead a Western fighting regiment. Arizona boys hoisted the first U.S. flag over El Caney in Cuba, and the

Nationally, panic had ripped through Wall Street in 1893, casting a blanket of gloom over the entire economy. Business volume fell off and tumbling freight rates forced many railroads into receivership. Finally, as 1898 started, brighter times shimmered on the national horizon. New York's *Bradstreet's* affirmed, "After a series of years of alternate panic and stagnation and a slow and painful revival," the previous six months had "presented a large volume of business."

Awakening commerce across the United States soon made its way into southern Arizona. After several years of declining fortunes, mining spirits rose in Pima County when farming brothers Warren and Frank Allison struck a "gold bonanza" near Fresnal Canyon south of Tucson. Local newspapers reported that

John Heidel (in center, wearing white apron) worked in his brother-in-law, Ed Bohn's, Cactus Saloon in 1898 and purchased the establishment the following year. Heidel's nickel beer and Bohn's quarter sandwiches made the trip west across Toole Avenue from the SP depot worthwhile for turn-of the century travelers. (John Heidel Collection)

1898. By fall, agents of capitalists roamed Pima County looking to invest in good mines.

The monetary credit necessary for investment and building rose from a discounted value to more than par value in the territory that year. "Foreign" investors, those with money from outside of Arizona, expressed new confidence in territorial securities. Backers grew more comfortable in Pima County, with good reason. Tucson Savings & Loan brought its stock to maturity in less time than any other association in the country. Consolidated National Bank and Arizona National Bank, the two strongest banks in the territory, amassed a record three-quarter million dollars in gold reserves during 1898. In addition, the city of Tucson carried no floating debt during the three previous years, and Pima County had dropped taxes by 25 percent during the two preceding years.

Renovation and construction followed money into Tucson during 1898. Near the end of January, ten cars of lumber and machinery arrived for the new Tucson Ice and Cold Storage plant, one block east of Stone Avenue on the south side of the railroad tracks. Wholly owned by Tucsonans N.W. and A.C. Bernard, George Pusch, John Zellweger, and Fred Pistor, the ice plant opened that March as the largest in Arizona.

Tucsonans treasured ice. Since Cosmopolitan Hotel proprietor Paul Moroney first provided the frosty delight years earlier, it symbolized civility and sanity in the

the pair removed "amazingly rich ore," and that their mines might be a half-million-dollar cluster. Within months the Commonwealth group of investors bought one-fourth interest from the Allisons. Company officials believed the new mines might rival their famous Commonwealth Mine, in Cochise County, as a gold producer.

In combination with J. George Hilzinger's book, *Treasure Land*, published the previous fall, the gold found near the Fresnal generated increased interest in local mines. The University of Arizona recruited students for its tuition-free mining course to fill jobs across the territory. To mark the fiftieth anniversary of the discovery of gold in California, Arizona governor Myron H. McCord called the territory's miners to their first convention on January 25, 1898. Several hundred miners attended, electing Tucsonan M.G. Samaniego the group's first chairman. After sitting closed for two years, the Tucson Sampling Works assay office reopened in August of

baking Arizona desert. Twice-a-day ice delivery at 75¢ per one hundred pounds, with a guarantee not to weigh tongs and hands, busied the company's fifteen employees. The plant's large capacity allowed the railroad to use cranes to fill its incoming "reefers" (refrigerator cars) with large blocks of ice.

A new sixteen-hundred-square-foot cold storage facility opened that April, with sixteen-inch walls and a one-inch space filled with "rosin tar" that the company deemed "perfect insulation for cold storage purposes." The SP laid new rails to the

The F. Ronstadt Co.
Cor Acath & Broadway

F. Ronstadt and Co. incorporated in 1898 and finished a two-story blacksmith and wagon shop on the southeast corner of Broadway Boulevard and Scott Avenue. That August, the Star reported: "A party of railroaders held down the corner of Congress Street and Church Avenue for an hour yesterday. Their laughter could be heard a block away. The yarns are not on record." (AHS #2878)

facility for daily deliveries of beer, butter, eggs, poultry, game, and all kind of fruits and vegetables. Exciting times prevailed in the city's hearts, minds, and kitchens. Now, more families could enjoy ice and cold-storage products, at more reasonable prices than they paid for shipments from California. The *Star* noted the significance of the new enterprise on the Tucson economy: "Every dollar is home capital. It will keep at home the many thousands of dollars sent out annually for ice." The Old Pueblo now became a more desirable place to live for both natives and highly sought-after "foreigners" from outside the territory.

With a vision of New Tucson emerging, the city council ordered condemnation of the city's infamous "Wedge" in 1898. Neither aesthetically appealing nor functionally efficient, the area provided a distasteful reminder of an adobe age that Tucsonans longed to abandon. A wild conglomeration of disheveled buildings lay jammed one upon the other from Stone

Avenue to Meyer Street between Congress Street and Maiden Lane. Demolition began in May 1902 and the *Star* remembered, "The city wanted to become more up-to-date, wanted to shake off the old pueblo idea and be able to say Nueva [sic] Pueblo, greater Tucson."

Business bustled and citizens built, as several key enterprises began or expanded in 1898. Locals reported the first hard-fired brick building north of the tracks went up at 629 East Ninth Street that year. Tucson Electric Company signed a contract to install new lamps throughout the city and completed modern buildings to house their new steam engines for producing electricity. To meet thriving demand, the company doubled its steam capacity by fall and provided new poles and wires for 1,200 new lights. The Natatorium, a swimming and recreation facility large enough to host gatherings of fraternal and social groups at the southeast corner of Main Avenue and Alameda Street, incorporated. In addition, SP engineer W.G. Riggs built a five-room house northeast of the tracks in Buell's Addition, fast becoming known as the "little city of railroad cottages."

The Arizona Press Association held its annual meeting in Tucson that spring, and journalists visited the SP shops, south of the depot. Superintendent Colonel Epes Randolph and master mechanic L.M. Pratt showcased the "compressed air lifting machines"; the "great lathe used to turn the steel wheel rims"; the "splendid trip hammer"; and the tube welding process. Following the impressive industrial display, Randolph "wined and dined" the scribes in his inimitable southern style at his fashionable home on South Fifth Avenue.

Chas. F. Hoff's horse-and-mule-drawn street railway added an exciting new dimension to emergent Tucson in mid-May 1898. Ten cents bought patrons a four-mile round trip and manager Hoff made tickets available at Sam Drachman's cigar shop and from his brother, Gustav A. Hoff. In her book *Old Tucson: a Hop, Skip, and a Jump from 1539 Indian Settlement to New and Greater Tucson*, Estelle M. Buehman observed, "Its plodding motive

The Santa Catalina Mountains loom behind one of Tucson's ten early streetcars. The Prescott Courier cheered, "They do say Tucson, with its sleepy record and cobwebs of the centuries, has taken a new lease on life." Sadly, voters' rejection of tax funds for local schools in 1898 cast a dark pall over the city's progressive image. (UASC #22153)

power—not at all responsible for its grizzled appearance—was a big step in transportation facilities for the social set of Tucson."

Hoff asked that customers bring "any inattentiveness of employees" to his personal attention, but the new conveyance often ran late. "Seldom could it be caught for the return trip as darkness often settled before it made an appearance," explained Buehman. "If the conductor saw, across the plaza, a prospective passenger frantically waving her hands, the kind-hearted man would wait a full ten minutes." Many a man "resorted to the biped trail" rather than waiting for "the car," but he could lose his way and "find himself in the arroya" (sic) under the Stone Avenue Bridge. "Why mock the mules, even though they are the city's joke?" asked Buehman.

Running from the SP passenger depot on Toole Avenue, north on Stone Avenue, and east on Third Street to the University of Arizona, the novel transportation facilitated copious early-morning flirtation. Tucson's young men could reach their ROTC drill grounds at the University of Arizona on foot. Yet, many chose to "take the car" and chat-up the city's comely coeds, bound for home science class. When the mules "lost their equanimity" and pulled the slow ride off its track, the "fun-loving yet good-natured boys" jumped off and, "putting shoulder to the wheels," lifted the car "girls and all" back on the track, said Buehman. The exuberant chaps would then "cheer the mules on, as sort of an apology, and to make up for lost time." What a gay time those early-morning sojourns to the university campus must have been.

National gold reserves reached an all-time high of $225 million that summer. The country's soaring financial fortunes prompted Henry Clews to predict in the August issue of *Weekly Market*: "The half of the year 1898, say July to January, will beyond doubt mark the highest notes of prosperity which the country has attained in its history." In awakening Tucson, thoughts turned to the upcoming winter tourist season. The *Star* proposed that the Tucson Board of Trade hire a man "with suave manners; a man who knows how to introduce the matter of climate and its advantages" to ensure the good word of Tucson's healthful climate went "well distributed in the northern watering places." In July 1898, the Board of Trade hired T. Seddon Bruce to direct its Bureau of Information.

The city had struggled with a shortage of housing, especially small, three-to-five-room apartments. "Tucson is a heavy loser each year by reason of not being able to accommodate...tourists and prospective permanent residents," noted the *Star*. That fall, visitor accommodations grew by 25 percent. With rents half of those in Phoenix, Tucson awaited tourists with eager anticipation. Information Bureau Chief Bruce prepared and mailed four thousand twelve-page folders describing Tucson amenities and reasons to immigrate to the big burg. The search for new visitors, residents, and investors now began in earnest.

> SP carpenter Walter Vipond made the city's most bizarre contribution in late December 1898. Feeling less than his best, Vipond purchased one dollar's worth of Capt. G.W. Smith's W.W.W. medicine, at the elevated platform in Church Plaza. The *Citizen* reported that Capt. Smith's elixir loosed a "monster tapeworm, 75 feet long" from Vipond's innards. The ghastly creature wiggled around for "several hours in a large glass vessel of warm water," at the corner of Church Avenue and Congress Street.

Despite the presence of the SP depot east of town for almost twenty years, locals laughed at the idea of the area becoming Tucson's business center. Entrepreneurs George Pusch, Fred Fleishman, and L.G. Radulovich began creating a new perception during the late 1890s. When well-known grocer John Ivancovich started construction of his attractive Oriental Block on east Congress Street in July 1898, Tucson's eastward commercial shift gained momentum. Built of native pink and grey stone and El Paso pressed brick, the structure inspired the *Citizen* to proclaim, "This will be the first [in all its details] really modern, up-to-date block in the city; and the first to depart from the hand-made brick and frame fronts so commonly found here." Ivancovich's masterpiece established yet another pillar in the robust push toward New Tucson.

With business and building a-boom, Republican mayor Henry Buehman pushed Tucson ahead on the civic front. The city continued its new street-grading and sidewalk program and required clear posting of house numbers, to ready the Old Pueblo for free mail delivery during the coming spring. One ordinance required that businesses suspend their signs nine feet or higher and their awnings higher than eight feet above the ground. "No one thing will improve our streets so much as the enforcement of this ordinance to the letter," predicted the morning newspaper. Enforcement proved lax, however, and five years later, city leaders continued to threaten scofflaws.

Open cesspools faced regulation, and, to stem the spread of tuberculosis, Ordinance No. 112 established penalties for spitting on sidewalks and in public places. Though not strictly enforced, the edict raised the bar on community comportment, highlighting Tucson's intention toward refinement, good manners, and culture. Another regulation demanded that prostitutes no longer hang from open doors and windows, and mandated putting doors and curtains on houses of prostitution.

"It becomes no less our duty to care for Tucson's moral well being and prosperity," Mayor Buehman declared. "On all sides I hear complaints that the moral tone of the city is indecent. Many eastern people coming west with their families...will undoubtedly look into our existing moral conditions before deciding on a home."

Buehman and the city council, which included SP passenger and freight agent Charles M. Burkhalter, also banned cock-fighting and badger brawls. The *Star* cheered: "Tucson can never reach that proud distinction which her many unrivaled tributary resources entitle her, until her people unite in making a community, which demands those social and moral conditions common to all communities of settled and fixed notions on morality, religion and simple decency."

Under construction above, Eagle Mills stood for years as the city's tallest building. Each day the whistle calling its workers to the flourworks reminded citizens of Tucson's prosperity. (AHS #29140)

Arizona Territory's spirited involvement in the Spanish-American War, along with improving national and local economies, and what the *Star* called an "underlying spirit of progressive conservatism," combined to initiate a new era for the city in 1898. SP provided the economic foundation for Tucsonans to build a "civilized" new city. The mayor applied his own moral stamp, and the city council voted its support. Citizens responded well, as evidenced by the frequency of daily police reports with few or no violators. Police Chief George Oaks noted: "Tucson has never been in a more peaceful mood. Why, the two men under me have to keep walking nights to remain awake. Fact. Great town is Tucson."

As the landmark year wound down, long-time community stalwart Leo Goldschmidt and partners neared completion of their new Eagle Flour Mills. The thirty-thousand-square-foot plant opened the following April two blocks northwest of the depot, between the railroad tracks and Toole Avenue. For decades, the sun glinting off the golden eagle flying atop the mill presented one of Tucson's most rousing sights and defined its skyline.

Forty-five years later, Mountain States Telephone Company explained the phenomenon many called "New Tucson": "As the frontier isolation of the town faded, the populace grew more stabilized. Men of substance began to raise families and to establish businesses of a permanent nature. Literary societies flourished; the library did a rushing business; teas and other functions common to a genteel and organized society became news items in the local press."

To be sure, the city remained an adobe town of dusty and muddy streets, gambling, and prostitution, but more and more of its denizens envisioned a cosmopolitan metroplex in the Arizona Sonoran Desert. In sharp contrast with the preceding year's summary, the morning paper reflected: "The year which has gone into eternity [1898] was the most inspiring and hopeful in many respects of any year of the [nineteenth] century."

Chapter 2

The Legend of Pay Car Curve and the Forward Thrust of a Railroad in a City on the Move

SP acquired the rail lines south from Benson to Nogales and Guaymas, Sonora in 1898. Later, the company pushed its line toward Guadalajara, Jalisco until the Mexican Revolution ended construction in 1912. (South-ern Pacific Bulletin, *Vol. 10. No. 1, October, 1921)*

"The advance of a railroad into any region is tantamount to the advance of progress and civilization," the *Arizona Daily Star* once proclaimed. "Pulled by a mighty locomotive shining, glittering, straining and roaring, [a train] is a tremen-dous power in opening the mind's eye, enlarging the vision of the beholder."

As it had for the city of Tucson, the year 1898 proved pivotal for the Southern Pacific Railroad (SP). That April, the com-pany issued a cost-cutting edict that forever changed engine service. Early engineers ran their personal locomotives, caring for and pampering them as one would a fine racehorse. Henceforth, the SP mandated that engineers take out the first available motive power unit or engine. Though old heads among the engineer force found ways around it, the decree rendered the company substantial savings.

That same year, SP magnate Collis P. Huntington followed the advice of local superintendent Colonel Epes Randolph and acquired the New Mexico & Arizona Railroad through Benson to Nogales, and the Sonoran line south to Guaymas, Sonora. To circumvent Mexican law, the SP entered into a reciprocal lease on July 15, 1898, which extended joint-use rights to the Santa Fe Railroad on SP's Needles-Mohave line. The SP spent almost $50,000 building up its Benson facilities to handle increased traffic on its new line.

The November 30, 1898 completion of the Globe, Gila Valley & Northern Railroad (GGV&N) line into Globe also brought greater main-line traffic. Seeking an agreement giving the railroad right-of-way through the San Carlos Apache Reservation west of Geronimo, Arizona, GGV&N President William S. Garland and SP chief engineer William C. Hood partied with more than three thousand Apache people in mid-February 1898. Fifteen beeves (cattle), abundant coffee, flour, sugar, and tobacco fueled an all-night feast. Chief engineer Hood "inveigled into the jollifications and figured quite prominently," reported the *Globe Silver Belt*. Two "buxom" Apache women "took the dignified chief engineer's hand and put him through his paces in a most approved manner," the paper chuckled. "Mr. Hood danced, you bet he did; he cavorted, and brought down the house." The next afternoon, eligible tribal members voted to grant the railroad right-of-way across their lands.

When the GGV&N lines entered Globe, it ended almost twenty years of waiting for the people of Gila County. Incorpo-

rated as a separate operation but run to the desire of the SP, the company built its new line to block incursion by the dreaded Santa Fe into the Gila River Valley's rich and profitable market. "People of every age and color were there viewing this miracle of American progress, the railroad," sang the *Globe Times*. "The old hills seemed to frown at the invasion of their ancient seclusion, but every citizen of every calling, and even the tired out freight horses seemed to welcome the sight with joy."

In rail towns like Globe, and many others throughout the West, the words "railroad payday" rang with a special wonder during the age of steam. At first, bringing gold but once a month, the pay car or "running of the ghost" brightened every corner. Tucson newspapers announced the coming of the pay car several days in advance, igniting anticipation citywide. On the day the "gold wagon" arrived, a monetary sigh of relief echoed from house to house, fostering an unparalleled quickening of the local heartbeat. Rails stood a little taller, filled with the certainty that all their labors had been worth it; that the wait for precious necessities, or that rare luxury, had finally ended.

SP paydays became grand social events during the steam era. The streets filled with *la gente* (the people), and Tucson came alive again! Of all ages and heritage, people mingled downtown, enjoying the society and bustle. Dressed in their best, Tucsonans strolled city streets to pay their phone, electric, and other bills. Rail families settled accounts at the *carniceria* (butcher's), the *tienda* (mercantile), and the *panaderia* (bakery), while storeowners collected on outstanding accounts to fill their tills for the coming week's purchases. Bars and saloons made up for the preceding days' "dryness" as brakemen and dispatchers, clerks, and machinists, found liquid escape from railroad rigors.

Railroad paydays never failed to "happify the railroad boys, and incidentally the merchants and many others who will

Dressed "to-the-nines," roundhouse foreman Al Hammonds and his wife, Maude, glide down Congress Street ca. 1941. Former boilermaker's apprentice and "SP Rails" centerfielder "Nicho" Elias remembered that as late as the 1950s, "There wasn't that much to do around here and small pleasures satisfied us. Going downtown was our lives, our fun." (Albert and Maude Hammonds Collection)

get a whack at the coin before it passes into the vault of the millionaire," the *Citizen* once explained. Not to be outdone, the *Star* declared, "The ever welcome pay car...arrived yesterday. In a word, everybody is happy, down to the baby and the favorite canine."

Saturday, July 28, 1898 proved one of those inspiring paydays in the Old Pueblo. When the pay car arrived at four that afternoon, the uplift of human spirit must surely have been conspicuous. Paymaster Charles J. Robinson paid local railroad employees and then turned his attention to enjoying a night in the big burg on the main line. Early the next morning, the money car rumbled out of Tucson as the

only coach behind engineer William W. Walker's locomotive. In its safe, $42,700, designated for wages down the Nogales line and east toward El Paso. Walker worked his engine and its precious "consist" (car in the train) uphill out of Tucson, through Esmond, Vail, and Pantano. Over the Mescal summit, the well-liked engineer pressed his train into the San Pedro River Valley. There, two miles of steep grade and tight, unforgiving curves challenged every engineer to control his speed. Slicing round the first sharp, seven-tenths-of-a-mile arc near milepost 1028, engineer Walker's zipping rail missile flew from the track with brutish indifference.

Spitting a blaze of rocks and dirt, the mighty locomotive chewed turf, yanking its valuable cargo in tow. Back in the pay wagon, the crew had been chatting as breakfast sizzled over a gasoline cookstove. Following a stiff jolt, the pay car rolled and bounced, scrambling breakfast, the cook, the stove, paymaster Robinson, a guard, and two clerks into one fine muddle. The stunned pay squad scurried to safety and watched in awe as fuel from the cookstove soaked the coach's interior and flames consumed it. Rushing toward the engine, the men located conductor C.W. Crowder in the weeds beside the wreckage, his left arm and four ribs broken. Crushed beneath the locomotive's boiler lay thirty-two-year-old fireman A.J. Taylor. Sadness gripped Tucson as word of fireman Taylor's violent death reached the city. Men from the Brotherhood of Locomotive Firemen Cactus Lodge No. 94 took charge of solemnities for the respected father of four small children.

SP investigators found engineer Walker's speed the tragedy's culprit. "Pulled badly scalded, burned and bleeding from the tangle of metal," engineer Walker moaned, "I've gone in that ditch once and I probably will again," reported the *Citizen*. Not alone in his troubles at the devilish curve, the injured rail recovered and soon returned to service.

The SP straightened "Pay Car Curve" after Walker's crash, but it continued as the division's most dangerous stretch to enter at high speeds. The SP stopped paying employees in gold and cash and issued paychecks that first arrived in Tucson July 28, 1903. The change created "uncertainty amongst the employees as to how they should get their money," reported the *Star*. Consolidated Bank soon agreed to cash rails' checks.

Just before Christmas 1909, another speeding locomotive pulling the mail and pay warrants took wing above the tricky curve. Free of its steel confines, the big engine ploughed through the ground for seventy feet before plunging into a six-foot gully and tumbling over.

The wreck killed the train's engineer and fireman, hurling them forty to fifty feet from the cab. "Trainmen raced to the engine to lend aid but could only doff their caps in somber silence upon seeing the fate of the two enginemen," reported the *Star*. The payroll car splintered and telescoped into a bundle. Approaching trainmen heard a low moan from the demolished car. Fearing the worst for four postal and payroll employees trapped inside, the men began frantic efforts to rescue their rail brethren. Two men staggered out swollen and bruised, and fainted in pain. Rescuers located the other two pinned beneath piles of debris and pulled them to safety.

Passengers in the train's observation car and two Pullman tourist sleepers flew from their beds, many sustaining cuts and black eyes. "Dressed in only their nightclothes, some [passengers were] unconscious, some groaning, others calling for help, desperate from pain and fright and danger and fighting wildly to escape," reported the *Star*. One rail raced into Benson where yardmaster Lord put together a relief train. A yard switch engine pulled a diner and baggage car as hospital facilities to carry doctors and a crew of men to the scene. Superintendent Epes Randolph and SP physicians H. W. Fenner and A.W.

Olcott arrived from Tucson with blankets and hospital supplies around 4:30 a.m. The doctors established a triage location on a mesa near the track and began covering the wreck's survivors with blankets before evaluating and treating each. The SP rushed thirteen of the most critical patients to St. Mary's Hospital in Tucson while thirty to forty passengers went to Benson, received treatment, and continued their journey to points in Kansas and Oklahoma. Maggie Smith, the train's sole Tucsonan, suffered only bruises.

The 1909 wreck's intense congruity added fuel to the Legend of Pay Car Curve. For, taken along with his fireman William A. Bauer, lay prophetic speedster William W. Walker—the same man plucked from rubble in the pay car crash of 1898! "Yesterday, in the blackness that precedes the

Conductor Henry Stapp started on the division in 1915 and shared the Legend of Pay Car Curve with his son, Richard Stapp Sr. Richard found this early railroad smudge pot when his father took him to the infamous curve in the mid-1950s. (Kalt Collection)

morning's dawn, the time they call 'Death's Hour,' Walker's words came true," the *Star* reflected.

Other local SP rails flourished—in live performances, fraternal gatherings, sporting events, and artistic endeavors, fueling Tucson's budding cultural sophistication. Local conductor Barney M. Mariner proved one of the railroad's most generous souls. Using his own monies, Mariner bought instruments for a forty-piece brass band to train the city's musical youth. Boys, ages six to fifteen, paid $2.50 a month for semi-weekly instruction under the rail conductor's enthusiastic direction. The band gave its first concert in late April 1898, at A.V. Grosetta's "big opera house" at 51 E. Congress Street. The morning newspaper trumpeted, "Mariner's Juvenile Band covered themselves in glory and won a thousand commendations for their patient and indefatigable trainer, B.M. Mariner."

Word of Mariner's unique musical success reached both coasts. The *New York Journal* and the *San Francisco Examiner* sent photographers to Tucson for pictures of the youthful phenomenon. The unflagging SP conductor also built a small orchestra to include young women. Fierce pride in his twelve-year-old cornet player, Lizzie Dickinson, and nine-year-old first violinist, Warren Grosetta, drove Mariner to stand a $1,000 bet that both could out-play anyone their age in the United States. For his fabulous double bass

player, twelve-year-old Manuel Montijo Jr., he extended the challenge to all of Europe. Mariner's Juvenile Band played in bright red uniforms at the Republican office in Phoenix in December 1899. Mariner relinquished direction of the group in January 1900, when changes in the SP timetable forced its musical muse to lay over in Yuma, rather than in Tucson. To the city's great fortune, its Juvenile Band remained strong in the able hands of Albert Roletti and Dr. George Martin.

J.W. Small, SP master mechanic, and Dr. Mark A. Rodgers organized a "first-class brass band" in 1901, under a proviso in Arizona military code that allowed for a regimental band of thirty or more members.

Fred Ronstadt and J.D. Balderas's "Philharmonic Band" had wowed audi-

Mariner's Juvenile Band in 1898: top row (l-R). Allen Bernard, Jose Martin, Albert Roletti, Frank Crum, Kennedy boy, Edgar Paul and Manuel Montijo. Second row, Leo Goldtree, George Martin, Willis Buehman, unidentified, unidentified, Andy Martin, unidentified. Third row, Willie McFadden, Harvey Cake, Ned Bernard, Joe Clark, Emmett Ford, Alfred Tripple, Morris Copple, Louis Pellon. Fourth row: Fritz Bernard, Hiram "Hi" Corbett, Harry Burnett (?), Maurice Holladay, Willie McFadden (written twice on the photograph), and Leslie Hardy. Bottom row, Charles "Little" Hardy, Warren Grosetta, Del Anderson, Scotty Gray. (UASC)

ences in the 1890s. Financial woes ran down the popular group, however, and some envisioned Small and Rodgers's effort as its resurrection. As enticement to move to the desert and play in their band, the pair secured employment for prospective members at the SP shops. At the time, SP paid boilermakers 40¢, machinists 38¢, and helpers 25¢ per hour. The company gave preference to sober and industrious men with families. Rodgers and Small ran advertisements in the *New York Clipper* and asked local businessmen to notify them of job openings for incoming musicians.

By early September, three of the band's four members worked in the shops under master mechanic Small. The fledgling ensemble began Monday and Thursday evening practices in a small hall at the foot of west Congress Street on October 1, 1901. By the following January, the new group's members included band leader A. Schirman and Manuel Montijo Jr. on cornet; saxo-

phonists Manuel Galvez, Filiberto Baffert, Leo Goldtree, Luis Rodriquez, G. Bizarre, S.L. Rodgers, and Alex Barreda; snare drummer Tom Legarra; Manuel Montijo Sr., piccolo; clarinetists Pedro Grijalba and L. Holcomb: bass players Carlos Jácome and L. McKenna; W. F. Cooper, trombone; and Harry E. Sayre on bass drum and cymbals. The SP band favored Tucson with its honeyed rhythms into the 1940s, endearing its members to the community.

To encourage increased travel throughout southern Arizona, SP granted special rates for recreational, business, religious, commercial, fraternal, professional, and governmental events. These special fares ranged from "one-fare," the cost of a one-way ticket with the return trip being free, to "one and one-fifth fare" or more. The reduced rate allowed a larger segment of the population to travel for their entertainment. Local officials gave one-fare excursion rates for teacher con-

The SP Band performed ca. 1910. Beloved by the community for almost thirty years, Mexican musicians formed the majority of its members. Band leader Eugenio L. Esparza (seated front left) once performed as assistant director of Pancho Villa's band. His father, Antonio Sanchez, sits in the back row, third from left. (AHS #B41648)

ventions, political meetings, and other fa-vored groups. Filled with rails, however, the local Lodge of Free and Accepted Masons rode to their conventions free of charge.

Popular trips to ball games, rodeos, and bullfights formed a key component of Tucson's emerging social life. Though motivated by business interests, SP excursions to and from these events provided unique opportunities for fostering a strong sense of community pride and camaraderie. Just as pre-game "tailgate" parties enlivened the late twentieth century, great fun surrounded riding the train to sporting events, and such excursions became the "thing to do" in southern Arizona.

The SP often ran Sunday specials to bullfights south of the Mexican border. On February 1, 1902, a Mexican band regaled more than two hundred "Tucsonites" aboard three special coaches bound for Benson, then over the El Paso and Southwestern line to the new *plaza de toros* in Naco, Sonora. The train arrived two hours before the bullfight's three o'clock start, allowing time for enthusiasts to explore the Mexican mining town. Americans rained silver coins upon matador Refugio "Cuco" Hernandez as matadors killed four bulls and a bull killed one horse in the town's new bullring. Satiated by the bloody affair, the entire Tucson group nestled into their own beds by midnight.

Local rail photographer Norman Wallace recalled: "In those days, Tucson had all the road shows like Madam Schumann-Heink and Paderewski. People in Phoenix would 'get up a train'; the Southern Pacific would give them a passenger coach, or maybe two of them and an engine and they would go down there [to Tucson] in an evening and come back the same night, sometimes two o'clock in the morning before they would get back."

Athletics provided a real kick for early Tucsonans, and baseball proved the city's No. 1 gal. "Baseball was early Tucson's only major sport," local fixture Roy

Drachman avowed in 1999. Roy's father, team captain Emanuel Drachman, collected money to purchase Tucson's first catcher's mask for his "Bushwackers" club in the summer of 1890. The primitive mask reportedly required cutting holes in its face to allow the catcher to see. "It was the pride of the team," noted the *Tucson Daily Citizen*. "The up-to-datedness of the mask was heralded far and wide." Stories of Drachman sleeping with his treasured face protector to insure its safekeeping persisted decades later.

SP rails dominated Tucson's favorite sport. Early seamed-sphere contests dazzled locals and lent a semblance of civility to the city. Shopmen and other rails made up the core of the teams that represented Tucson in the twentieth century's first two decades. Regular Sunday baseball games provided weekend entertainment throughout the year rather than just in the summer. A mid-day game let fans chew over the contest's details with a robust post-game meal. Teams often played for a fixed dollar figure, or the manager distributed the gate receipts among his players. On occasion, teams paid to enter tournaments for a chance to split prize monies—$750, $350, and $250 to the top three teams in one early Tucson event.

SP freight and passenger agent Charles M. Burkhalter's Tucson Grays scored one of the greatest hardball victories in city history when they took two of three games in a home series with William Tyler's Los Angeles team in 1899. The ball club included SP stores department agent A.S. McKelligon, who started at the "hot corner," third base. The slow-footed McKelligon worked the leather "without a peer as a fielder," and enjoyed a reputation as "the prettiest slider of the entire lot," the *Star* later said.

Railroad stores department clerks the Redford brothers helped key Tucson's victory over the Angelinos. Wyndham "Little" Redford used speed to overcome his "handicap of being a lefty," while his

Photographer Joseph C. Parker (center, 11) set up a tent on Camp Street, later Broadway, to photograph the illustrious Tucson Grays (Aier & Zobel Grays) in game attire. The club included infielder Frank Levy (1), freight and passenger clerk and pitching star Frank "Rube" Armstrong (2), the father of Tucson baseball, catcher Emanuel Drachman (3), future head of the SP stores department, manager and infielder A.S. McKelligon (4), brakeman shortstop George Godfrey (5), store department clerks, outfielders Hennings (6) and Wyndham (7) Redford, SP clerk and sometime umpire Mose Kelly (8), infielder Gus Quickenstedt (9), and pitcher O.H.J. 'John' Johnson (10). Not pictured: blacksmith/pitcher/catcher H.S. "Happy" Woods, and pitcher/infielder W.E. "Fireballer" Farrow. (AHS #23931)

brother, Hennings Redford, prowled the outfield. The Grays's stirring win inspired G.H. Noyes to write a powerful tribute, entitled *Tucson's Triumph on Manuel Drachman's Colts.* "It was the team that brought the metropolis from obscurity in the sporting world to the very pinnacle of fame in the southwest," the *Star* remembered. "It was this team that fans were willing to go meal-less for an entire week to see when they met such cracks as Clifton, Morenci, Cananea, and El Paso."

The Tucson Grays reorganized under manager O.H.J. Johnson in January 1900, electing former Grays manager Burkhalter an honorary team member. Two months later, Edward F. Beuhring, rail superintendent Epes Randolph's private secretary, took over the city's team. Locals knew Beuhring as "an old time fan ...fond of genuine athletics that disdained anything that was not of high standard."

Beuhring made immediate changes. Levi H. Manning donated land just off Main Street, along with $800 to build a quality grandstand. Fans and Grays players leveled the playing field while the

Secretary to rail superintendent Epes Randolph, Edward Beuhring (right), and honorary captain, general freight and passenger agent C. M. Burkhalter (left) led the Tucson team in 1900. Son of Tucson patriarch Sam Hughes, David Hughes stands top left, next to W.R. Courtney, an unidentified player, and Mose Kelly. Herb Drachman sits to the left in the middle row while Emanuel Drachman holds an early catcher's mask in the center of the bottom row. (AHS #16534)

morning newspaper tooted: "The team must have generous support from the business men of their hometown. A ball team advertises a town and brings many visitors."

Local SP freight and passenger agent Frank R. "Rube" Armstrong took over a financially struggling Tucson team in November 1901. That month, Bisbee manager

Steam power chugged into Douglas behind the international border town's baseball diamond when the Tucson Grays and their fans visited in May 1901. Fan comforts proved scarce but the game attracted well-dressed hardball enthusiasts. (AHS #13567)

V.R. Stiles arranged the season's final tussle between his railroad boys and those from Tucson. The Arizona Eastern Railroad freight and passenger agent secured a $3 fare from the Cochise County mining town to the big burg. Armstrong hustled local businessmen for subscriptions to raise a $1,000 guarantee for the railroad. When less than half of the expected enthusiasts traveled from Bisbee, backers went bust. Demonstrating their lack of practice, the Tucson team fell apart after four innings in a six to four loss. Following the depressing performance, local baseball slipped away in silence.

By 1903, "love of the game" reigned again, but team loyalties meant little. Rails filled both lineups for a Thanksgiving Day battle at Carrillo Gardens, pitting the machinists' Crescents team against the Tucson Grays. Though the game's attendance fell victim to a traditional holiday football

Rapt baseball fans enjoyed an early twentieth century contest at Elysian Grove. (AHS #41608)

SP shop boys filled the Corbetts team, during the 1907 season, representing J. Knox Corbett Lumber Company. That June, brawny S.P. blacksmith Woods proved "seven-eighths of the cheese," spinning a four-hitter for a 6-5 win over the Groves, a local team formed by baseball enthusiast Emanuel Drachman. (AHS #B94395)

The view from the right field stands in the Cananea, Sonora ballfield ca. 1907. Railroad men played for the Corbett's when they visited Mexico that year. A pitcher's repertoire of "twists and benders" often baffled hitters before the sport's "modern era." (UASC)

game at the University of Arizona, baseball fans witnessed a thriller. Strikeout artist and manager Rube Armstrong "chucked the pale pellet" for the Grays, while his second baseman in the previous game, rail

W.E. "Fireballer" Farrow, "served the guts" for the Crescents.

Both teams filled the bases more than once, but home plate umpire, local SP clerk Mose Kelly, oversaw eight scoreless innings. In the top of the ninth, first baseman McGrew and machinist centerfielder Thomas Lane plated Crescent runs. Third baseman and car repairer A.G. Reynolds scored for the Grays in the last of the ninth, as the Crescents held on for a 2-1 victory. "The best game of baseball ever pulled off in Tucson," proclaimed the *Citizen*.

SP shop boys played for J. Knox Corbett Lumber Company during the 1907 season. That July, local "dyed-in-the-wool, blown-in the bottle" fans planned a trip to the tough mining camp of Cananea, Sonora for a rousing game of hardball. The SP asked $1,000 to ensure a profit for its special train and Arizona Board of Regents Chancellor M.P. Freeman persuaded nine other citizens to put up $100 each to advance the trip.

"When the aggregation hits Cananea, a roar will go up that is likely to jar loose several thousand nuggets of copper in the big camp," predicted pundits. "Never before in the history of the Old Pueblo has baseball enthusiasm been at so high a pitch. Bugles will blow, horns will toot and cheers will resound as the train pulls into the big copper camp."

"Suspenders," clothier Vic Hanny's white bulldog, played team mascot and good-luck charm that summer. Hanny made the prize pug a special coat, and it stood in one of Brannen & Hanny's display windows for several months, wearing a brass collar and growling at every dog that walked by. Three days before the Cananea trip, Hanny tied Suspenders to a post in front of his store to promote him. During a moment of lapsed vigilance, bold thieves made off with the popular pooch. A posse of eighty-four baseball enthusiasts combed the city all night, searching for Suspenders without success. "If the wicked party is found by irate fans he will stretch a rope on the nearest mulberry tree," railed the *Star*.

The distinctive sounds of Samuel J. Mansfeld and Harlan Richey's famous "Club 13" mandolin group spiced festivities at the depot on the morning of the Cananea excursion. Ordered to wear Tucson's "regulation uniform" of "auto caps and linen dusters," fans strolled among the cars at leisure. "Happy" Smith handed out whistles while Harry "Arizona" Drachman distributed "small scorers" so fans could record each inning's hits, runs, and outs. Fine fortune prevailed when Hanny appeared with Suspenders just in time to join the victory-bound contingent.

Shortly after 5:00 a.m., 293 fans amped up the noise and town spirit as veteran engineer Dennis Ryan highballed his huge "battleship" locomotive east toward Benson. Tucson Division's largest baseball special to date rumbled over the former Santa Fe line to Naco, Sonora and south to Cananea. As the rollicking party rolled into the Greene Consolidated Copper Co. mining camp, several thousand Mexican fans sent up cheer after cheer. Cananea's crack municipal band played its famous air, translated into English as "We'll Hand them a Package of Lemons." One Sonoran woman contended, "*Vinieron por coches dormitorio pero volverán en vagones de carga.*" [They came in sleepers but they will return in freight cars.]

Cananea rails delivered a 22-7 thrashing to the Old Pueblo boys that summer day. Disconsolate Tucson fans passed their merry whistles to the *muchachos* (young men) of Cananea as they boarded the train home. When the Corbett's furry mascot, Suspenders, fell down the grandstand, broke his leg, and a Cananea policeman shot and killed him, local baseball fortunes hit bedrock.

Connie Mack brought his Philadelphia A's ball club to the Old Pueblo for an exhibition game during 1909. Major League players acted "huffy" when just 150 fans showed up, a smaller crowd than regu-larly attended Grays games. Despite the snub, Mack deemed Tucson's climate "the finest in the world." The all-time career leader with more than 3,700 managerial wins added, "Mark Tucson down as a place to train for professional baseball players." Mack's vision came true when the Cleveland Indians began training in Tucson during 1947. The Tribe returned for forty-seven years. In 2007, the Arizona Diamondbacks, Colorado Rockies, and Chicago White Sox enjoyed the city's warm spring days.

America's "national disease" found another local low mark during the fall of 1910. Forced to play without pay due to low attendance, Tucson men balked when asked to pony up their share of the opposing players' expense money. A game against a team from Douglas, Arizona met financial doom in early October and forced Tucson players to settle accounts from their own pockets. Unwilling to continue absorbing costs, local diamond dandies laid the game to rest in the once-proud hardball burg.

The *Citizen* reported, "Baseball is officially declared dead and there will be no funeral services." Manager and left fielder Fred Sullinger announced the cancellation of scheduled local games, vowing, "If the city ever cares to see baseball, and will help us keep up the games, we will furnish games." Within the month, never-say-die local supporters developed a brand-new proposal for reviving their special sport. Organizers asked baseball aficionados to donate a fixed, monthly amount to insure sufficient funds for visiting teams' expense money. In exchange, contributors received a different colored ribbon each month as their "passport" to upcoming games.

The SP maintained Eagle Field, its hardball diamond near Sixteenth Street and Second Avenue, as local baseball fortunes ebbed and flowed. Weeds dotted the dirt pasture, and a row of mulberry trees lining its western edge did little to stop swirling "dust devils," but at least the boys had a ball yard. No suitable city-maintained baseball ground existed in Tucson by fall 1920, forcing local teams to play all their games on the road. Under the direction of Judge Charles Blenman, the Tucson Baseball Association formed and purchased three acres on Simpson Street north of Elysian Grove for $4,200. The group sold stock to baseball "cranks," avid enthusiasts, and Blenman Park became a reality in 1921.

Fans saw Tucson's "classiest battery" battle the railroad team during the 1921 season. Ottomar Pfersdorf, a left-handed pitcher and imminent locomotive engineer, hurled to catcher and future engineman's instructor Jim Pfersdorf. "Local fans have seen both in action in high school circles and they stood head and shoulders above everything else that showed locally," explained the afternoon newspaper. "The boys look to be the best prospects locally and with proper prepping

should put Tucson on the baseball map." Both ballplayers enjoyed sterling careers on the diamond and the Tucson railroad.

"Crash of willow against horsehide" rang again during mid-January 1922, filling Tucson baseball hearts with expectant joy. Local shop foreman and team skipper Mike Robles drilled his Ess Pee White Sox at Blenman Park and announced two strong additions to his already powerful club. "Tucson's hope for the big leagues," Chili Francis, donned the catcher's equipment, and a rail newcomer from the Imperial Valley named Gonzales "fired the pea" from atop the "hill," or pitcher's mound.

In perhaps the nastiest baseball series ever played in Tucson, the Ess Pee White Sox shop team squared off for the city championship against the SP Motive Power Club in August 1922. Hard play in the first-ever series between the two rail squads got out of hand when the engineers'

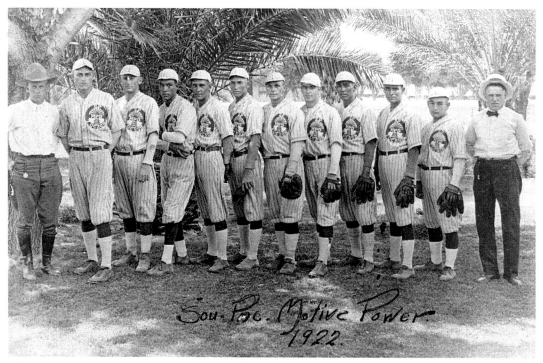

The 1922 SP Motive Power team included (l-r) Clarence E. Brimmer (master mechanic's chief clerk), Benny Smith, Marty or Williams (as written on photograph), Rafael McCormick, Teddy Sonoqui, Ramon Scott, unidentified, Frank Hall, Gilo Mejias, Jesus Olivas, Charles "Shorty" Pellon, and Herb A, "Porky" Patten, manager and locomotive engineer. The SP often rewarded local schoolboy stars with jobs to play baseball on company teams. (AHS #48104)

team prevailed in the opener, 10 to 3, and again when the White Sox won 5 to 2. The fierce series knotted at one game apiece, shopmen sent R. Fito Aros to the mound in the rubber game, chucking to catcher "Dizzy" Carrillo. Motive Power squared off with its own powerful battery, proven lefty Young McCormick hurling to slugger M. "Phat" Padilla. Shopmen took a 2-1 lead into the bottom of the fifth inning when the Motive Power squad exploded for eight runs enroute to a 10-2 victory. "The game

Family fun followed fierce railroad baseball at Randolph Park during the late 1930s and the umps always stunk. Roundhouse foreman Al Hammonds (third from right first row) played for this SP machinists' baseball club in 1937, along with Claude Loving (fourth from right, second row), future Democratic city councilman Fred D. Lee (second from right, first row), and Jim Flaherty (far right, first row). (Albert and Maude Hammonds Collection)

was marred by dirty baseball, Olivas being badly spiked on one play and several other players being gashed in the course of the combat," reported the *Citizen*. "Statements made prior to the game that both teams were out for blood proved absolutely correct in every way."

Local rails kept baseball kicking yet again in 1926. The *Southern Pacific Bulletin* published a "vote of thanks" from the *Citizen* that November: "The Southern Pacific team has well represented Tucson on the diamond this season, being the nucleus around which baseball interest has centered. Its players are entitled to thanks for keeping alive baseball interest and conserving the sport until such time as the city is prepared to support a league club."

Native Tucsonan and long-time educator Geraldine "Maudie" Hammonds Mackaben remembered that the sport thrived during the late 1930s. "In 1937-1938, they played at Randolph Park on Sunday afternoons," said Mackaben. "The firemen had a team, the engineers, boilermakers, and the machinists all had

teams." Hard-fought contests turned to post-game friendship as rails relaxed with their families. "After the games, everyone would go to the Mission Swimming Pool or Wetmore Pool for a barbeque," Mackaben recalled. "Oh, those barbeques were so good! They'd have a pit barbeque of beef, pinto beans, tortillas, and *pico de gallo* or *salsa fresca* to die for! Of course, they drank a keg of beer, maybe more. I don't know how anybody got home safely. The umpires were always rotten, though, ha, ha."

Former SP engineer Peter B. Ziegler provided the venue for another Tucson recreational favorite. Credited with running the second passenger train into Tucson in March 1880, Ziegler acquired considerable local real estate. Along with several homes near the corner of Ninth Street and First Avenue, a confectionery shop, and bottling works, Ziegler owned the Union Race Track. Located southeast of the corner at Park Avenue (then called "C" Avenue) and Twenty-Second Street (then Kings Highway), the half-mile, dirt oval played host to the Tucson Driving Association (also called

Sired by famed Kansas trotter Robert McGregor, Creaceus proved the fastest among a baker's dozen horses to gain notoriety out of Robert Lee Ives Prairie Dell Farm in Shawnee County. (Arizona Daily Citizen, December 18, 1901)

the Jockey Club) and showcased some of the Southwest's best horseracing.

Excitement whistled round the depot one mid-December morning in 1901. At about 9:30 a.m., a large crowd gathered to meet the No. 10 train bringing Creaceus, "King of Trotters." The magical horse arrived in his special express car, along with four other handsome equine wonders owned by George H. Ketcham. Induced into town by racing enthusiast J. D. Moore, Ketcham proclaimed, "Almost everyone who knows or cares about God's greatest creation in the brute world knows Creaceus and his accomplishments on the turf." Mike the Tramp, his pace-horse, also ran a fine race, added the guest of Tucson lumberman J. Knox Corbett.

"Nothing appeals to the visibilities of man like a good horse," noted the *Citizen* as race day neared. "We are glad

to note that the railroad has given a special rate into town for the event." In an affair called "epochal in the equine history of the territory," Creaceus upheld his reputation on a "poor track, deep in dust." Trotted over the oval by his owner Ketcham, the great stallion "paced" the mile in 2:14 2/5 pulling a twenty-nine-pound sulky, to capture the event's silver cup.

Several local rails owned horses for sport and pleasure during the early twentieth century. In Tucson's milder evenings, Colonel Epes Randolph and his wife, Eleanor, could often be seen riding city streets behind two grand Kentucky stallions. James B. Finley, territorial councilman and SP master car repairman, trotted his handsome bay gelding, Hilltop. Nanela, SP detective Colonel Wm. Breakenridge's double-gaited mare, paced the mile in 2:17 while Judge William H. Barnes's brown gelding, Roydello, held the 1902 territorial record, pacing the mile in 2:12 1/4. Union Park proprietor Ziegler's fine trotter, Fancy, always ran a good race, and University of Arizona Chancellor M.P. Freeman owned an excellent Kentucky trotter. Joseph B. Corbett, territorial legislator and locomotive engineer, also proved himself a

Carriages continued in popularity long after the first automobile arrived in Tucson. Entrepreneur John Heidel (rear left) stands with his family and a carriage at their 727 N. Seventh Avenue home ca. 1915. (John Heidel Collection)

skilled driver during Tucson's glory days of trotter racing.

Not everyone in the city enjoyed the track's Sunday racing schedule. A letter to the evening newspaper by "An Arizonan" in late February 1903 warned that "injurious effects and dangers of the sport" stood as "an evident peril to the young..., which all the years of correction and parent's remorse cannot remedy."

A trotting circle east of the tracks near Second Avenue and Sixteenth Street provided local rail superintendents escape from their constant responsibilities. Known for wearing large scarves in warm weather, William W. Wilson often enjoyed a brisk scamper during the late 1930s. "Superintendent Wilson owned a trotter and a trotting cart," remembered Geraldine Mackaben. "Mr. Wilson was a nice man and his trotter was his hobby. I can still see him,

Superintendent Wm. Wilson (left) greets conductor Adam Schuh in 1934. Wilson enjoyed a good trot, but no evidence exists that he ever raced in competition. In 2004, Kim's Lass held the world record for trotting horses over the mile at 1:52.1. (AHS #10635)

sitting there, white-haired, with his toes up and his feet out on his trotting cart."

Tucson rails always enjoyed a good party, and car-shop foreman Phillip T. "Irish" Garigan proved the right man to host festivities. Born October 13, 1881, Phil and his dynamic wife, Mary Annabelle Garigan, hold a special place in Tucson railroad lore. Beginning on the division in 1911 and promoted to car inspector foreman by 1916, Phil's Irish heritage bent him toward a jolly-good time. In mid-May 1921, Garigan spearheaded merriment on Sonoita Creek at Flux, about four miles south of Patagonia down the Benson-Nogales line. Fifteen hundred strong, local rails and their families filled twenty-two passenger coaches in two trains bound for the SP's annual employee picnic.

Garigan arranged for two boxcars filled with lunch baskets, cake, and other delights. After securing their wives and children under suitable arbor, rails worked to lay a pre-constructed dance pavilion at the remote siding. Chappie Homer took charge of the floor, and rail families, young and old, danced a flurry to the scintillating strains of the SP band. Tucson newspapers reported that local superintendent William W. Wilson left conductor C.A. Owens "wheezing along the track as he romped nimbly to the finish line" to seize the trophy in the "fat man's race."

The Garigans endeared themselves to countless southern Arizonans during Phil's long railroad career, none more so than the day he and Mary rushed goat's milk to a sick baby from their ranch on east Broadway Boulevard, near present-day Sarnoff Drive. When Mary reached downtown Tucson with the lactic treasure, SP's eastbound Argonaut local passenger train had already left the depot. The Golden State Limited arrived fifteen minutes later. Its conductor took charge of the precious goat's milk and the dispatcher held the Argonaut at Mescal to await the Golden State Limited. The Golden State Limited made a short unscheduled stop there, and the Argonaut's conductor hurried "the medicine" to a grateful mother and child. The generous act typified this hardy western rail couple.

A nationwide shop strike terrorized railroads during the summer of 1922, firing local tensions. Big-hearted Phil Garigan lightened the load for rails with the SP Entertainment Club. Railroaders loved a good "mill" or boxing match, so he and shop man Mike Robles featured several four-round skirmishes on Friday nights. When "Fistic Thrills" entertained a large crowd in late August, almost half the fighters in the Garigan/Robles show wore the moniker "Kid," but Coyote Lee and Bombard Edwards helped round out the boxing card. The Dixie Quartet treated fans to "Jelly Roll," "All by Myself," and other tunes between bouts. Then, after Professor E. Castro sang his solo, the *Citizen* reported, "Kid Mesa and Kid Leon crossed leather at 128 pounds. There has not been a fight for many months that produced so much enthusiasm from the spectators as did this mill." During the early 1950s, Phil and Mary Garigan's ranch provided Tucsonans with weekly rodeos, another entertainment staple of the American West. Complete with wild mule riding and prize money, Garigan's rodeos enlivened childhood for east side Tucson "baby boomers."

Together, railroaders comprised a formidable array of collegial unity and individual accomplishment when steam locomotives ran the local division. SP rails played as hard as they worked, providing fun-filled entertainment in a desert town whose residents hungered for "something to do." In addition to their musical, athletic, and entertainment gifts to the city, SP rails founded labor brotherhoods such as the Brotherhood of Locomotive Firemen and Engineers and the

Order of Railway Conductors. Rails also led Tucson's fraternal organizations such as the Elks, Masons, Shriners, and Knights of Pythias.

Phillip Garigan, SP general shop foreman, held down left field when the division's married men faced its single fellows in August 1922. The married man team captain, Superintendent Wm. Wilson, claimed he played baseball in Ireland and turned down offers to play in the major leagues. The stout Wilson "smashed his way into Tucson's hall of fame" with his bases-clearing drive into a centerfield gap during the contest. (Mary Annabelle Garigan Collection)

Mary Garigan and her husband, Phil, posed in front of their home at 808 E. Sixth Street. The couple built near Broadway and Sarnoff in 1928. Mary wrote directly to Eleanor Roosevelt because the Garigans had no phone service and the family boasted a working phone within the month. Their children, Donald, Byron, and Charlotte "Chat" Garigan, each enjoyed long SP careers. Fellow rails called Byron "the epitome of a railroader," after he was killed when his engine collided with a yard engine at Yuma in June 1987. (Mary Annabelle Garigan Collection).

Athlete, sportsman, and division engineman's instructor Jim Pfersdorf (second from left) poses with (l-r) E.T. "Happy" Houston, Ben Padgett, and Carl Ball Sr. on the Circle Diamond Four Hunting Club's annual horseback trip to the Rincon Mountains east of Tucson. Composed of engineers, the group began living the pioneer days of hunting during 1927 and continued for decades. Pfersdorf starred at Tucson High in football, track, and baseball and pitched for the University of Arizona before his career at the SP. The white-tail buck deer Jim took from the Rincon Mountains stood as an Arizona record for many years. (Jim Pfersdorf Collection)

Tucsonans held "mid-winter cowboy tournaments," forerunners of the modern-day rodeos, early in the twentieth century. During 1933, the SP promoted the city's Fiesta de Los Vaqueros rodeo on the cover of its dining car menus. "One of the outstanding rodeos of America," the company explained. "Cowboys and girls, prospectors from the hills, and ranchers from the valleys come to Tucson to enjoy a week of western fun." Locals also found a rousing good time at Garigan's Rodeo (above) ca. 1952. (Mary Annabelle Garigan Collection)

The SP and its employees formed Tucson's foundation at the inception of the twentieth century. Over the next five decades, they would provide the city's wage and tax base, transportation, sweet music, good entertainment, and a well-fought game of sport, all components of a SP railroad town in the nation's southwest corner.

Chapter 3

I'll Meet You in the Cornfield: The Tragic Train Wreck of 1903

Outstanding baseball player and SP fireman George McGrath presaged catastrophe of unimaginable magnitude. A Los Angeles woman also reported her premonition of the rail accident at Esmond. (AHS #48200)

George McGrath was bursting with joy that winter day, late January 1903. On Sunday, February 1, he would marry his true love. At age twenty-five, his life lay splendidly before him. Good looks, admirable character, and a secure job as a fireman on Southern Pacific Railroad's (SP) famed Sunset Limited made him a great catch for his bride, "a well-known young lady in Tucson." But a dark cloud loomed over George's bliss that day.

To his fiancée, McGrath confided his terrifying *sueño* (dream) of the previous night. In it, he saw SP engineer J.W. "Jack" Bruce and himself in a head-on collision, called a "corn-field meet" by railroaders. Earlier, McGrath told his landlady that if he was "brought [in] on a stretcher she would know it was on account of a careless dispatcher." Although his fiancée pleaded with him to lay off, George refused.

Cycles of train wrecks had plagued the nation for several years. Just two years earlier, rail accidents had injured more than fifty thousand people and killed almost eight thousand. Renewed economic prosperity had substantially increased both the shipments of goods and the number of rail passengers beginning in 1897-1898. The increased demand strained resources on many lines, including the SP. To keep cars moving, the company ran some trains too long, and many times two or three sections or groups of cars traveled under the same identifying number. In addition, the SP ran scores of extra trains to handle the augmented business. The matter had engendered much discussion in the press and the *Los Angeles Times* screamed, "Traveling has become so dangerous that an accident policy is a necessity and should be attached to every through ticket."

	TUCSON SUBDIVISION															
Eastward	FROM SAN FRANCISCO															TOWA
	SECOND CLASS					FIRST CLASS				Time Table No. 83				FIRST CLASS		
	92	244	412	418	426	110	4	102		October 1, 1920				109	101	1
	Los Angeles Manifest Freight	San Francisco Manifest Freight	Freight	Local Freight	Freight	Sunset Express	Golden State Limited	Sunset Limited			STATIONS			Sunset Express	Sunset Limited	California
	Leave Daily	Leave Daily	Leave Daily	Leave Daily Ex. Sunday	Leave Daily	Leave Daily	Leave Daily	Leave Daily						Arrive Daily	Arrive Daily	Arrive Daily
	10.15PM	2.20PM	8.40AM	6.40AM	2.15AM	10.35AM	1.40AM	12.01AM	983.9	DN-R TUCSON		164.4	3.15AM	7.10AM	6.20PM
										T. A N. R. R. JCT.					
	10.30	2.50	9.10	7.02	2.30	f10.43	1.48	12.08	987.7	DNR POLVO		160.6	3.07	7.02	f 6.10
	10.40	3.12	9.32	7.14	2.40	f10.50	1.55	12.13	990.7	WILMOT		157.6	3.02	6.57	f 6.05
	10.50	3.30	9.50	7.26	2.57	f10.57	2.02	12.18	993.8	RANKIN		154.5	2.57	6.52	f 6.00
	11.05	4.07	10.10	7.44	3.15	f11.06	2.11	12.26	998.6	ESMOND		149.7	2.50	6.44	f 5.52
	11.25	4.17	10.30	8.02	4.00	f11.16	2.20	12.33	1003	VAIL		145.0	f 2.42	6.36	f 5.43
	11.45PM	4.33	10.55	8.20	4.30	f11.27	2.31	12		IR		9.8	2.31	6.25	f 5.30
	12.01AM	4.44	11.15	8.35	4.50	f11.37	2			PAN		18		6.17	f 5.20
	12.35	5.12	11.29	8.50	5.10	f11								6.12
	1.05	5.30	11.53AM	9.05	5.25									5.55
	1.50	5.50	12.30PM	9.20										

These examples are typical of the timetable and train orders used in the era of the Esmond wreck. Overlooking or misreading a single piece of paper could result in disaster, as it did at Esmond. Telegraph operator Clough violated rules intended to prevent such errors. The conductor was required to sign each order he received. Clough telegraphed the "signature" of conductor Parker to the dispatcher before the train arrived. The dispatcher transmitted a second order. Parker left without the first order, which had already been "delivered and acknowledged".

(Timetable: Kalt Collection, Train Orders: Thomas White Collection)

With the increased traffic, trains moving on established timetables often ran late, invalidating the timetable. In such cases, the dispatcher issued train orders specifying where and for what period of time the train should take a sidetrack to insure its safe movement. Late-running trains created tremendous stress for conductors, telegraph operators, and dispatchers who worked under constant pressure to push their trains ahead as quickly as possible. Some took risky chances to avoid the wrath of a railroad superior.

Maintaining safety on a single-track railroad that relied on train orders always proved daunting. The safe movement of trains rested solely on the keen judgment of the individual dispatcher and the vigilant adherence to the rules by the line's multitude of telegraph operators, conductors, and engineers. A lack of signal lights to control train movement made the Tucson Division even more perilous. Rails referred to it as "dark territory," and the company imposed strict regulations to ensure the safe operation of its trains. When a station telegraph operator received orders, he completed a "flimsy," or train order form, in duplicate. SP rules called for him to hand one form directly to the conductor, who signed the orders and read them aloud while the operator verified them against his copy. If everything checked out correctly, the operator issued a clearance order allowing the train to proceed.

Forty-eight-year-old John W. "Jack" Bruce sat in the hoghead's, or engineer's, seat on the westbound No. 7 Sunset

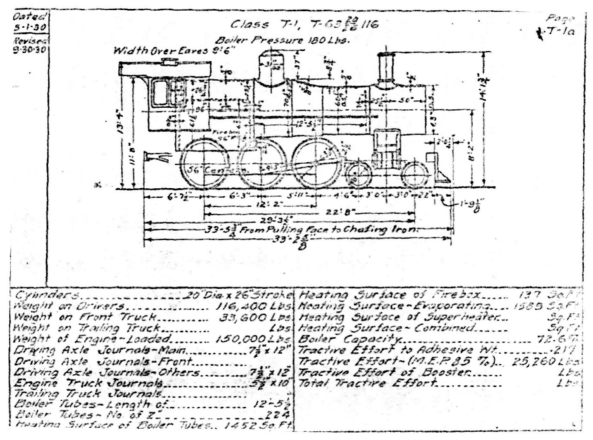

This type of locomotive was involved in the Esmond wreck. (Arnold Bays Collection)

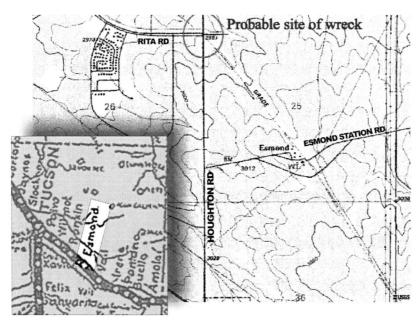

(Large map, USGS; inset, Southern Pacific Company Timetable, Kalt Collection)

Limited early on the morning of January 28, 1903. The thirty-year rail veteran, a native of Altoona, Pennsylvania, had run SP's first train into Tucson in March 1880 and represented Pima County in the 1893 Territorial Legislature. After picking up the order at Vail to pass an eastbound freight at Wilmot siding, the Sunset Limited came hurtling downhill into Tucson from the east. Almost twelve hours behind schedule, "the flyer" entered the sharp curve just west of the Esmond siding, fourteen miles east of Tucson,

Jack Bruce (holding baby) rented rooms in his house at 316 E. 12th Avenue to fellow engineers (l-r) Jim Guthrie, Neil McGinnis, Johnny Clancy, Johnny Tull, and Chief Shop Foreman Drew. In addition to bringing the first SP train into Tucson, Bruce ran the first train over the Tehachapi summit in California. (AHS #12833)

Coffins lay beside the track in anticipation. (AHS #24858)

at about forty-five miles per hour. At the same time, the eastbound No. 8 Crescent City Express chugged its way up the hill at approximately twenty-five miles per hour. As his train rounded the curve, engineer Eugene R. "Bob" Wilkie spotted the headlamp of the oncoming Sunset Limited. Wilkie pulled hard on the long emergency brake lever, called "throwing it into the big hole" by rails, and yelled to his fireman, W. S. Gilbert, "Jump! Save your life! I will hold to the throttle."

In a terrifying instant the monster steam locomotives slammed together. Fireman Gilbert vaulted from the cab and tumbled into the early-morning darkness. Badly cut, with a broken shoulder and leg, and unable to speak for several days, Gilbert survived to recount the story of "his heroic chieftain." In the train's day coach, conductor Otis H. Scriven had not quite finished collecting all of his tickets when the blow came. Just as Scriven reached for the whistle cord, to signal for passing the flyer at Esmond siding, his coach began to cave in as the car behind climbed over its back. Managing to keep his balance, Scriven

Youthful R.M. De Lamaters stands atop the pilot of locomotive No. 2275 in Lordsburg during 1901. Fireman McGrath (standing left) and engineer Bruce (standing center) receive their train orders just over a year before they perished in the Esmond tragedy during January 1903. (AHS Transportation-Railroad-Wrecks-Esmond)

jumped to the ground with his passengers close behind.

The crash staggered conductor G.W. Parker aboard the Sunset Limited. Gathering himself, Parker leapt to the ground and dashed forward to the crumpled heap that had been the locomotives of the two trains. There, he located engineer Bruce's burning body, almost beneath the train's oil tank. Next to Bruce lay prophetic fireman George McGrath, who "would have been living today if he had heeded the premonitions and the advice of his sweetheart," the *Star* later reflected. Realizing he could not help the two enginemen, Parker raced ahead to the Crescent City Express, where he found the train's first two cars engulfed in flame. Ordering all the able passengers off the train and away from the blaze, Parker began working to free the injured. Returning again and again to the burning cars, the veteran conductor finally collapsed to the ground, bleeding and exhausted.

Fire raged. Fuel oil saturated much of the wreckage, forming streams down each side of the track and torching a line of burning cars on both trains. Chaos and panic reigned as the screams of the dying and wounded mixed with the smell of burning flesh. Witnesses told of seeing the flames from miles away, with smoke visible from Tucson. "The scene beggared description," reported the *Phoenix Enterprise.* "The night air was filled with cries of the injured who were pinned in the wreckage and cried for relief from the rapidly approaching flames." The *Citizen* reported that rescue workers could not approach the wreckage for several hours because "the

(Arizona Daily Star, *January 28, 1903)*

ironwork of the cars was red hot."

A brakeman off the rear of the Crescent City Express ran on foot to Vail to notify headquarters in Tucson of the wreck. The *Star* reported that twenty-one-year-old night telegraph operator E. Frank Clough asked the brakeman: "Is anyone killed? I don't care so much about the cars being destroyed, but I am sorry I killed anybody."

Back at the wreck, the carnage defied comprehension. A *Citizen* reporter spotted "several spots of pure white ashes" and "innumerable small bones" lying about the scene that many believed were human remains. Coffins lined the track in anticipation as investigators battled the odds to secure positive identifications. Survivors described many grizzly sights. Among the grimmest, a group of consumptives traveling west, clustered along a nearby fence and coughing uncontrollably in the cold morning air.

Moments before the wreck, Tim Donahue, a railroad fireman and sometime news butcher, who sold passengers candy, cigarettes, newspapers, and sundries, had been enjoying a smoke in the eastbound Crescent City Express's smoker car with Oscar Marion Stewart, a Mormon farmer who spent three months in the territorial prison at Yuma for polygamy. At impact, the smoker rolled on its side as burning fuel oil drenched it. Donahue fought to free himself from the fiery tomb. Then, remembering the door at the top of the car, he quickly flung it open and struggled out.

His clothes aflame and gasping for breath, Donahue felt Stewart's hands grab

Oscar Marion Stewart hurried to Bisbee to comfort his daughter, whose husband, engineer William Cherry, had died earlier the same week, in an EP&SW train wreck near Forrest Station, east of Bisbee. The Mormon farmer from present-day Chandler talked with Tim Donahue in the luxury of the eastbound train's smoker when the crash came. Donahue waged a bitter battle to save his traveling comrade. (Nyle Leatham Collection)

at his feet and fought desperately to save his fellow passenger. Finally, as fire devoured the entire coach, he resolutely kicked himself free and dropped to the ground. W.B. Kelly, editor of the *Bisbee Review*, threw his coat over Donahue and smothered the fire. Savagely seared, Donahue lived to recount the hideous scene but died several days later at St. Mary's Hospital in Tucson.

Prior to the crash J. M. Hilton had been conversing with a Mr. Glidden of Cambridge, Massachusetts. The collision hurled Glidden through the train car's window, slamming the eastern capitalist to the earth. Hilton regained his composure and hurried to help Glidden, only to find the man pinned beneath the flaming mass of mangled metal. He watched helplessly as Glidden burned to death. A hobo from Benson named Jack Dwyer described how he and three "pards" had hitched a ride on the Crescent City Express's engine tender. The collision

with the Sunset Limited had thrown Dwyer to the ground and crushed his less-fortunate friends.

Passengers banded together to move a Pullman sleeper at the rear of the Crescent City Express away from flaming cars. Soon, they lost control of the Pullman car and it began to roll west, back downhill toward Tucson. Inside, an unidentified Negro porter assigned to apply the brake realized that he was powerless to stop the moving car. Thinking quickly, he piled the sleeper's mattresses to form a breastwork, or padded wall, at the head of the runaway sleeper. Then, wrapping himself in blankets, he held on tight and waited for the

Fire destroyed cars on both trains. (AHS #MS1207f25A)

The SP sent section workers to the wreck site to clear debris and build a shoo-fly that allowed rail business to continue. One hundred years later, a strut from the cow catcher on one of the locomotives still lay on the earth's surface near Rita and Houghton roads. (AHS #24860)

wild, careening ride's inevitable abrupt conclusion. In Tucson, officials at the SP yard ordered a wrecking train to the crash site. Just as that locomotive entered the mainline, the escaped Pullman smashed into and climbed atop it. The petrified porter emerged ashen faced but unhurt to tell of the awful accident up the line. Years later, then-sixteen-year-old fireman, Maynard Flood, recalled being catapulted back onto the locomotive's tender, when the maverick Pullman slammed into his engine that fateful morning.

A relief train carrying M.D.s H.W. Fenner, W.B Purcell, and W.V. Whitmore along with SP superintendent C.C. Sroufe arrived around 4:00 a.m. Workers began loading the most

seriously injured for transport to St. Mary's Hospital, while the others went to the San Xavier Hotel to rest and recover. Rails erected a shoo-fly, or temporary track, and diverted rail traffic around the mass of wreckage by early afternoon. Meanwhile, fear whipped through the streets of Tucson, as rumors circulated that as many as fifty people had been killed. One railroad employee cautioned that fire charred many bodies beyond recognition and that a full listing of the dead might never be compiled.

Tucson shuddered under the weight of the tragedy. Nearly everyone in town knew someone who had been either killed, maimed, or had just escaped the conflagration. Dr. James Collier Norton, Arizona territorial veterinarian (1891-1912), rode the eastbound train that horrible morning. One hundred years later, Norton's granddaughter, former Pima County Supervisor Katie Dusenberry, remembered: "In his role as the territory's veterinarian my grandfather made numerous trips annu-

The cataclysmic rail accident occurred about one mile west of Esmond Station (above), initially called Papago Station. In the spring of 1907, George Hessick drilled several wells at Esmond Station, including one to 625 feet. Harry Lundquist, who worked as a pumper at the remote desert location, named his son, Harry Esmond, in honor of the station and took this 1912 photograph. (George Lundquist Collection)

ally to inspect the territory's cattle herds. On several occasions he would take my dad, Oakley, along. They were on the eastbound train that day."

The "James Boys" traveling performance troupe lost an entire boxcar of instruments and stage props. (AHS #2999)

Visiting the wreck became fashionable in the first days following the crash. Women wore attractive dresses and carried parasols to Esmond, while vigorous men rode their "wheels" (bicycles) fourteen miles through the desert to search the mangled wreckage for victims' belongings. News of the accident reached engineer Jack Bruce's family late that morning. Fifty years later, his son, George Bruce, recalled that "Judge" William Angus came to their door saying, "There's been trouble down the line...don't know much about it yet." George never went to the wreck site but remembered, "It seemed like every horse and buggy in Tucson did."

Several factors combined to exacerbate the disaster: the downhill grade upon which the Sunset Limited came flying; volatile fuel oil that soaked both people and materials; the lack of water at the wreck site; the darkness of the early morning hours; the absence of any way to call for help; and, as subsequent testimony would show, a veteran conductor and a young telegraph operator at Vail Station who violated company rules.

A hard-working young man, Frank Clough had taken up his duties at Vail Station only a week prior to the accident. He had established a good record during approximately four years working the telegraph key with other lines. Witnesses reported that although he felt very badly about the collision, he did not act overly nervous or excited. The conscientious rail worked until noon, answering almost sixty telegrams. Then, maintaining his innocence, Clough boarded the No. 11 train for Tucson.

When questioned about the events of January 28, Clough explained that Tucson dispatcher Charles F. Gray sent two orders to the Vail station early that morning. The first instructed the westbound Sunset Limited to wait at Wilmot for an eastbound freight train. The second, sent ten minutes later, called for the Limited to pull out at Esmond siding and allow the Crescent City Express to pass. Telegraph operator Clough later acknowledged the receipt of both telegrams, the final order arriving twenty-one minutes before the Sunset Limited reached Vail Station.

The young man claimed that when the flyer "tied up," or stopped, at Vail station, he placed the two train orders on the counter and hurried outside to load the mail and express on board the train. Returning to his office, Clough discovered that conductor Parker had taken only the top order and yelled out, "Parker, you have left one of your orders on the counter." The conductor did not respond, quickly boarding

Young Herman Bonorden cuts a distinguished figure in this family photo. By 1903, Bonorden served as Tucson's chief dispatcher. (Eleanor Bonorden Brundick Collection)

his train and signaling the engineer to proceed. Clough maintained that Parker violated company rules by not reading the orders aloud for verification.

At 2:50 a.m., Clough telegraphed Tucson saying that he was unsure whether conductor Parker had picked up both of his train orders from the station's counter. About five minutes later, Clough notified headquarters that a "large sheet of flame" had flashed on the track west of Vail, and he "believed there was a wreck."

At least one anonymous SP employee believed Clough's story. He said the man appeared "calm and sincere when he talked to him and did not betray any excitement." Judging him a "truthful and conscientious young man," the unnamed rail declared: "You will not see Clough in this part for a long while; there is no use of the coroners waiting for him to come and testify, for he will not come." The telegrapher did report to his SP superiors, however. The *Citizen* reported, "Clough arrived on Wednesday afternoon, and went immediately to H. G. Bonorden, the chief dispatcher in Tucson, asking for his voucher, so that he could get his pay and leave."

That afternoon, local SP superintendent C.C. Sroufe called a conference of all surviving employees involved in the fatal collision. According to the *Arizona Re-*

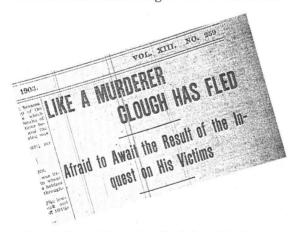

Rumors floated that a friend had slipped the fugitive telegraph operator a roll of bills as he skedaddled for Mexico. (Arizona Republican, January 31, 1903)

publican, Clough "came into the meeting with some display of bravado" but soon broke down and admitted his responsibility. Ordered to appear before a company inquest the following day, Frank Clough was never seen in Tucson, Arizona again. City streets buzzed with discussions of Clough's disappearance, and coroner W.H Culver ordered deputy constables Refugio Pacheco and Robert Frazier to search the city for "a large, heavy-set man, above medium height, with a smooth face and a good general appearance." The *Citizen* accused the railroad of aiding and abetting in the escape. "Clough's deliberate absence is accepted as a plea of guilt," the newspaper blared. "The policy of the company is plainly obscurantism." Clough should have been "taken into custody at once." Instead, with the sly wink of his employers, he "simply took a train to the international line" and disappeared.

Confusion over the wreck's casualties ran wild as people poured into Tucson to search for nearest and dearest. O.C. Parker attended to the remains of engineers Bruce and Wilkie and fireman McGrath at his funeral home. Curious crowds gathered to view the bodies of the dead rails while friends kept family members at home to spare them the anguish of hearing gruesome details. Reilly's Mortuary cared for the corpses of eleven passengers, though conjecture ran to many additional dead. Some people listed as deceased turned up in other locations. The inscription on a sterling-silver pocketknife found under the hand of a man burned beyond recognition read "Eugene P. Willard." Investigators assumed the San Francisco cigar maker and his wife had perished in the flaming wreckage. The couple, close friends of cigar-store owner Sam Drachman and his family, happily turned up in Jerome, Arizona. Willard reportedly "derived some amusement over the persistent reports that were made to establish his death in the wreck."

(San Francisco Chronicle)

When a *Citizen* reporter requested a passenger list, SP officials explained that people traveling west turned their tickets in at El Paso and that the company kept no record of passengers eastbound from Los Angeles. An exact documentation of the dead would never be compiled. Several young boys did a brisk business selling high-quality photographs of the destruction to passersby downtown. Fortunate survivors of the crash proved to be their best customers. The day following the wreck, Vail Station agent H.A. Mann received a telegram from Mrs. Ethlyn P. Clough intended for her son. It read: "IT IS HORRIBLE. BE BRAVE FOR MY SAKE. EVERYTHING WILL COME OUT ALL RIGHT."

The devastating train crash fueled a battle *royale* between Tucson's daily newspapers. The *Citizen* charged SP with murder, claiming that the company had crammed as many as five bodies into a sin-

gle coffin to hide the number killed in the collision. "The railroad company will attempt to cover up the facts," the newspaper predicted. "This is but natural. . . . It is not the fault of the tired and over-worked employee. It is the fault of the improperly managed system." The *Star* jumped to the SP's defense. "It seems they [the *Citizen*] want the responsible head of the Southern Pacific executed, quartered, and cremated as partial atonement for the terrible disaster," said the paper. "There is nothing to be gained...by exciting acrimonious feelings on such occasions simply to gratify an abnormal appetite which fattens on the abuse of corporations."

Ceremonies honoring the dead filled the city over the next few days. J.W. "Jack" Bruce, the Sunset Limited engineer and former territorial legislator, left a wife and five children. Fellow rails remembered engineer R. W. "Bob" Wilkie of the Crescent City Express as a good Mason and a reliable railroad man. A procession of Masons and thirty men from the local Brotherhood of Locomotive Firemen escorted George McGrath's remains to the depot for shipment to his Connecticut home. The brother of passenger John E. Cassidy buried his body in Tucson. "It was useless to take his remains home as he could not be recognized," explained the grieving Texan.

In the midst of the suffering, a row erupted over jurisdiction in assessing responsibility for the tragedy. "A squabble, in which is instilled no little bitterness, has arisen between the two justices of the peace W.H. Culver and O. T. Richey, as to which has the power to act as coroner in this case," the *Citizen* said. Culver prevailed, and his jury conducted its investigation and soon announced its findings. It placed blame for the collision squarely on telegrapher Frank Clough, but identified only three corpses, engineers Bruce and Wilkie, and fireman McGrath. The jury listed the remaining dead as "eleven unknown supposed male bodies."

Judge Richey's "rump jury" finally rendered a wordy decision on February 9, 1903. It concluded: "fourteen bodies [were] recovered; that there were others killed but the number is not ascertained." Richey's jury also found Clough at fault in the disaster and went on to chastise railroad officials for not providing guards over the wreckage. The flood of visitors "made off with all sorts of matter and articles of value," avowed jurors.

Conductor Parker admitted under oath that he broke the rules by not reading the order to pull out on the Esmond siding back to Clough. Although the SP conceded that Parker's violation had been "of a purely technical nature," they nonetheless fired the well-liked conductor. In a "semi-official" statement to the *Star*, the company explained that his release proved necessary "to maintain the rigid discipline in the army of employees." Parker quickly found work with the El Paso & Southwestern Railroad.

On February 10, the *Star* published a long letter from Mrs. Clough defending her son's sudden departure from Tucson. Conductor Parker stood "as much or more to blame than Frank," said the distraught mother. "He is an older man, had been many years with the company and knew the rules better than Frank." Mrs. Clough wrote again the following month claiming to have indisputable proof of her son's innocence. She refused, however, to reveal his whereabouts.

Two ironic epilogues circulated among Tucson Division rails throughout the month of February. One told how SP fired a brakemen for standing at the rear of the eastbound Crescent City Express, rather than at his assigned position on the "head end" or front of the train, where he surely would have been killed. The other story celebrated the fortuity of M.F. Ingham. For the third time, the lucky engineer avoided an accident, by laying off from his daily run.

The wreck generated at least one legal skirmish and it was a corker. Twenty-eight-year-old Hugh Mackenzie, a wealthy and "finely educated" Australian mining engineer, reportedly boarded the Crescent City Express in Los Angeles, heading east to claim his inheritance of an immense estate in Aberdeen, Scotland. When Hugh failed to arrive, the youthful capitalist's wealthy parents spared no expense looking for him. After ten full months of desperate searching, the Mackenzies reached an obvious conclusion. Their son had been incinerated in the rail debacle near Esmond.

O.M. Stewart posed for this early photo with one of his families. A century later, his descendants remember Stewart as a loyal father and husband of two families. (Nyle Leatham Collection)

The SP took a starkly different view. Company investigators declared they possessed no record of Hugh Mackenzie ever boarding the train. Neither his body, his brass-bound trunk, nor any of the pieces of his valuable jewelry had been recovered. Ten months after the Esmond wreck, unable to probate either the Scottish estate or his Australian properties without conclusive proof of Hugh's death, the family filed a $5,000 suit against SP for misplacing their young aristocrat. Both the outcome of the lawsuit and the ultimate fate of Hugh Mackenzie remain a mystery. With less contention, the SP tendered a $2,000 settlement to the two families of polygamist Oscar Marion Stewart. During the ensuing years, Stewart's survivors fought bitterly over its distribution.

The Esmond rail disaster poignantly highlighted the need for an improved system of communication and traffic control on the rails. It also helped change the face of railroading in Arizona and across the entire SP system. One of the most horrific of four serious crashes in the nation within a twenty-four-hour period, the Esmond wreck sparked discussion about how to prevent such accidents on editorial pages from the *New York Times* to the *Los Angeles Times*.

As the SP hustled to put the finishing touches on a new edition of the company's bible, its *Book of Rules*, Tucson railroad superintendent Sroufe called his division assistants together to discuss ideas for preventing similar wrecks. The group faulted the seniority system that kept more competent men from assuming responsible posts simply because they lacked years of service. Their suggestions included no longer requiring conductors to sign orders that had "died" several hours

WHAT SEEMS TO BE NEEDED

The Los Angeles Times suggested a patented, asbestos-lined, pipe-proof wreck protector.

S. P. TRAIN AGENTS RELIEVE CONDUCTORS

NEW DEPARTURE ON PASSENGER IN EFFECT MAY FIRST.

CONDUCTORS AFFORDED TIME TO MANAGE TRAINS AND FOLLOW ORDERS—BRAKEMEN AND BAGGAGEMEN FAVORED.

(Arizona Daily Star, April 9, 1903)

earlier and demanding that dispatchers regularly remove train orders from their often cluttered desks.

Sroufe carried the division's views to a meeting with company officials in San Francisco. The SP took quick and decisive action. In April, the railroad issued a new schedule that called for passenger trains to proceed at a slower pace in hopes that trains could run closer to the printed timetable. The next month, SP created the position of Train Agent on all passenger trains. Drawn from the baggage and brakemen's corps, these assistants to the conductor collected tickets and fares. The change reduced the duties of conductors, allowing them to focus fully on train management and following train orders.

Captain J.H. Tevis of Bowie Station had studied the railroad safety problem for years. Just days after the Esmond tragedy, Tevis met with local rail leaders at the San Xavier Hotel to describe his invention. Tevis proposed erecting a dynamo at every pumping station along the Tucson Division and stringing electric wires to illuminate bulbs on every second or third telegraph pole. Any agent who detected an error in handling orders could press a button signaling every train affected to stop and proceed slowly until the railroad cleared the trouble. Tevis applied for patent protection

Esmond station lay unprotected and deteriorating 100 years after the nearby rail wreck. Thanksgiving night 2004, men from the city's southernmost fire station fought in vain to save the Stormy's last train order station, after vandals ignited the historic white fir structure. (Kalt Collection)

of his idea, though no record exists of its having been granted. Within six years, a block signal system similar to that proposed by Tevis protected the Tucson Division for more than two hundred miles. However, noted G.A. Parkyns, SP assistant general freight and passenger agent, "Plainly, as long as railroads must depend upon the human agency to perform a great part of the work, then there shall be accidents."

The *Star* captured the essence of the Esmond heartbreak: "Out on the desert is the charred and smoking mass of debris which marks the spot of the fearful wreck of Wednesday morning. The wreck of Esmond will never be forgotten. On the tablets of memory, anguish, suffering and death has been written ineffacably the horrors of the worst railroad disaster that has ever occurred in the Territory of Arizona."

Echoes of the 1903 train wreck that forever changed lives and families in Arizona continue to reverberate across the state. In December 2004, Nyle Leatham, retired *Arizona Republic* journalist and amateur historian, drove his motor home south from Mesa to stand at the scene of his great

uncle Oscar Marion Stewart's death. The first member of his Mormon family to visit the crash site, Leatham explained, "No one in our family understood why our records showed Oscar Marion Stewart died in Vail, Arizona. We couldn't understand why a farmer from present-day Chandler would be in that area. Just recently, we found out about the train wreck near Esmond. Oscar Marion Stewart had gone to Bisbee to be with his daughter whose husband, William Cherry, was killed in a train wreck four days earlier, at Forrest Station near Bisbee. It cleared up a lot of mystery surrounding his demise."

Today the story of southern Arizona's horrific cornfield meet lies buried in local archives. The site of the Esmond disaster at Rita and Houghton roads in incorporated Tucson remained all but forgotten for more than a century. In June 2005, historian of the West Lewis Wagner, the Boy Scouts of America, and other hard-working volunteers dedicated a plaque at Pyramid Credit Union on that intersection's southeast corner in honor of those families touched by the Esmond tragedy.

Nyle Leatham reflected on the spiritual connection he made during his 2004 visit to the scene of his great-uncle Oscar Marion Stewart's demise in the long-ago Esmond nightmare. (Kalt Collection)

Chapter 4
A Railroad Is as a Railroad Does: Full Steam Ahead

W.H. Whalen (back row sixth from right in black bowler hat) towers over his staff in this 1910 photograph. Hand-lettered identification recorded most of the roster for posterity. Note, director of water operations Robert Benzie (7), and future division superintendent Wm. W. Wilson (31). (AHS #62346)

The thunderous explosion ruptured the peace of a warm and windy Tucson night, June 18, 1909. Reverberating through the city with frightening force, the concussion shattered windows in several nearby buildings. At first, many thought a steam locomotive had blown up in the Southern Pacific (SP) rail yard. "Police galloped through the various streets, while those afoot ran to the various banks and business houses and inspected doors and windows," the *Arizona Daily Star* later reported.

Slammed against the wall by the blast, Tucson Division superintendent W.H. Whalen and his wife lay dazed amid the wreckage in their rooftop cupola at 70 South Fifth Avenue. Fighting to clear his head, the massive "old man" searched the rubble for a route to fresh air. In his house behind the superintendent's home, D.J. "Jack" Boleyn, former Tucson fire chief, saw a sheet of flame burst from his neighbor's house and rain sparks down upon its roof. Grabbing his ladder and racing to the building, Boleyn scrambled atop to find a shocked Mrs. Whalen whom he carried to safety, while her burly husband descended unaided.

Aground, the always-expansive Whalen put forth his version of the incident: "My wife and I were asleep in the cupola on the house at the time of the explosion. My wife was hurled out of bed

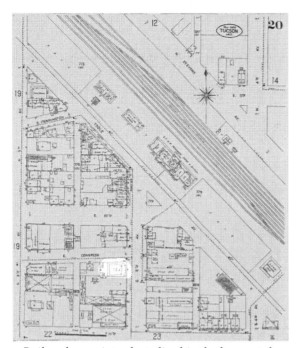

Railroad superintendents lived in the home at the southwest corner of Congress Street and Fifth Avenue (highlighted) until felons dynamited the house and the company began housing the division superintendent on South Third Avenue. Southern Pacific formed a separate corporation to build a transcontinental rail route through southern Arizona and Tucson in accordance with Arizona law on September 20, 1878. The Southern Pacific Railroad of Arizona operated through the southern half of the territory until it merged with the Southern Pacific Railroad of California and of New Mexico in late-February 1902. (Sanborn Insurance Company)

and so was I. As I weigh 252 pounds, some idea may be had of the force of the explosion. Twice I heard a sizzling noise but paid little attention to it as I had not the slightest idea that an attempt was being made to blow up the house. I would judge that the first two attempts at firing the charge were made about midnight. It was 2:22 o'clock by my watch when the explosion occurred." Friends took a nerve-wracked Mrs. Whalen to SP physician Dr. H.W. Fenner's home. Meanwhile, her husband continued to maintain composure, discussing the event with all who would listen.

Led by SP master car repairman E.M. Dickerman, investigators found that evil-doers had ignited dynamite at the top of the stairway leading to the home's cupola. The Whalens' salvation lay in the fact that, while black powder's typical lateral burst might have accomplished the perpetrators' deadly goal, dynamite always caused a downward thrust. By good fortune, the first-floor bedroom, often used by the couple's son W.T. or daughter Marie, lay dark and empty when the blast obliterated it.

Scoundrels chose a most secluded spot to do their nasty business that summer night. The seldom-used alley between Fifth and Sixth avenues dead-ended into a large embankment of dirt. Dickerman concluded that nefarious novices had positioned the explosives, explaining that a "skillfully placed" charge would have blown the house to pieces and wrecked adjoining buildings.

Anger over the dynamiting escalated. Calling it the "most dastardly and cowardly crime in the history of Tucson," the *Citizen* raged: "Dynamiting is the most hellish form of murder. There is no other crime more damnable." Thugs had "callously disregarded" the life of Mrs. Whalen,

$250. REWARD

The Tucson Chamber of Commerce offers a reward of $250.00 for information leading to the arrest and conviction of the person or persons who wrecked the home of Superintendent W. H. Whalen, in this city, on the morning of June 18, 1909. By order of
THE BOARD OF DIRECTORS.

$500. REWARD

BY AUTHORITY OF THE BOARD OF SUPERVISORS OF PIMA COUNTY, ARIZ., I hereby offer a reward of $500.00 for information leading to the arrest and conviction of the person or persons who wrecked the home of Superintendent W. H. Whalen, in this city, with dynamite or other explosive, on the morning of June 18, 1909.
Tucson, Ariz., June 18th, 1909.
JOHN NELSON,
Sheriff of Pima Co.

Rewards totaled $1,250 within twenty-four hours. (Arizona Daily Star, June 19, 1909)

Master car repairman E.M Dickerman (top row center) joined a powerful cadre of SP officials in Tucson during 1914, including (back row) night chief dispatcher H.W. Cassidy, storekeeper J. H. Collins, Dickerman, trainmaster Chas. M. Murphy, general shop foreman Jas. McChestney; (middle row) day chief dispatcher Wm. Wilson, chief clerk J. E. Lovejoy, master mechanic Wm. C. Petersen, assistant superintendent T.H. Kruttschnitt, superintendent J.H. Dyer, assistant superintendent Geo. L. Hickey, division engineer J.R. Matthews; (front) station supervisor C.O. Leslie, and trainmaster Percy Slater. (AHS #26,903)

who "could be in no wise [sic] be involved in any affairs with men of that stripe."

Tucson mayor Ben Heney lamented, "It is appalling to think that this city harbors a dynamite fiend. May the dastardly perpetrator be speedily caught and quickly receive his just deserts." By day's end, posted rewards for a capture and conviction totaled $1,250, and SP chief special agent M.T. Bowler arrived from Los Angeles. Known as one of the most skilled detectives in the Southwest, Bowler seized command of local operations and "vague clews" began to emerge.

A dairyman driving down Fifth Avenue reported seeing three "well-dressed" men run from the scene that morning. Fuzzy descriptions pointed to one "short

and rather heavy," and two "tall and slender" felons. Judge O.T. Rouse's wife, whose home shared the alley with the Whalens, reported hearing men "talking in a low tone and somewhat excited" before the explosion. Barber G.D. Morris spoke of "suspicious actions" by two men "lurking" about the superintendent's house just prior to the detonation. Expressing confidence that he could identify the culprits, Morris temporarily laid aside his job and devoted himself to "running to earth the would-be assassins."

Isidore "Isaac" Neustatter, Pima County deputy sheriff, arrested local telephone employee John Desmond on charges of "suspicion" the next day. Other policemen combed the city for a "hard character with an unsavory record" who had "shrunk at the sight" of railroad detective Guy E. Walters. The SP appointed master car repairman E.M. Dickerman to investigate the damage. Dickerman declared the Whalen home, valued between $12,000 and $15,000 dollars, a total loss. Authorities stationed a guard at the demolished house to protect the Whalens' belongings. In a disappointing turn, police soon released prime suspect Desmond. Rushing to stem a growing tide of civic indignation and anxiety, authorities arrested two former SP employees the following day, ex-conductor Ben Klink and popular former brakeman Tom Northern. Prosecutors soon dropped charges against Klink but sticky circumstances confronted Northern. After twice being fired within the last few months, he had approached superintendent Whalen seeking reinstatement without success. Witnesses said the rebuffed rail left the local yard "in an ugly state of mind."

Rail detective Guy Walters placed Northern at the scene. SP watchman Henry Pacheco reported seeing a man matching Northern's description standing in front of the Whalen home following the dynamiting. Friends of the accused posted a $2,000 cash bail and joined a large group of spectators, who jammed the courtroom and overflowed into the streets. Legal fervor faded when evidence failed to stand judicial test

Railroad and city policemen scoured the streets, including Toole Avenue, for the vicious dynamiters. Entrepreneur John Heidel bought property across Toole Avenue from the SP depot from L.G. Radulovich in February 1902. Heidel built his hotel (above) five years later. (John Heidel Collection)

George W. Bragg cut hair in a barbershop near the depot when he became the subject of concerted efforts to convict him of attempted murder. Completed just three months prior to this December 1907 photo, the new Tucson depot brightened the city. (UASC)

and the court released Northern. Police officials next arrested Patrick Collins of Benson but soon set him free. Baffled investigators returned to their search devoid of leads.

Three months after the dynamiting, prosecutors began proceedings against another presumed malefactor. This time the spotlight sparkled on George W. Bragg, a Negro tonsorial artist in the SP Barbershop near the depot, at 48 N. Fifth Avenue. Familiar to local lawmen, Bragg faced Justice of the Peace John E. Dufton for the second time in a year. The previous July, Negro bartender E.W. Walker went "a little too strong" in demanding Bragg pay his bar tab at the Legal Tender Saloon.

The *Star* reported the truculent barber "sent his fist crashing against one of Walker's optics on Congress Street and drew steel [a knife], compelling Walker to hike the tall and uncut, despite the pain and humiliation brought on by the jolt from Bragg's fist." Four well-known Tucsonans posted Bragg's $5,000 bond, and Justice Dufton fined him just $20. "Had I known that you was goin' to fine me $20, I would have beaten him up for $40 worth," Bragg told the judge.

Several parties conspired to control Bragg's trial for the attempted murder of Whalen. Aggrieved barkeep Walker invoked his revenge on the bad-tempered barber. He swore Bragg had cursed the SP superintendent and declared Whalen ought to be killed for firing two of his best customers. Bragg told him, "they had blown up that [censored] of a superintendent" but "could not get the stick [of dynamite] where they wanted because the [censored] coughed," said Walker.

Miss Nellie Hazel Turner also came forward with an incriminating story. Turner claimed she saw Bragg talking with two white men only a few hundred feet from the Whalen

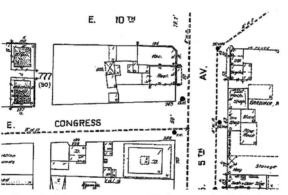

Detail of the map on page 57 showing the Fifth Avenue and Congress location of the superintendent's house (Stan Benjamin Collection)

residence until 1:30 a.m. the night before the blast. Miss Nellie's story withered when the Texas belle confessed that "Cyclone Bill" Beck and two other men brought her into town to give false testimony in order to collect the large reward. Turner then charged Bragg's mother, Minnie L. Pierce, with trying to bribe her by paying all her expenses to clear out of the country and not testify against her son. Authorities soon arrested the chagrined mother Pierce.

Bragg testified he had no involvement in the heinous crime and denied saying Whalen should be killed. Bragg further stated that he used dynamite only when

working his mining claims. The hair-cutter's statement earned his acquittal, but Bragg, "broke down utterly and gave full vent to his disappointment and despair," when guards escorted him to his cell to gather personal items. Confused jailers soon learned that, entangled in a legal web of "whereas and therefores," Bragg believed himself convicted and being returned to his cell to await sentencing. Finally convinced of his acquittal, Bragg's cries turned to those of happiness, concluding one of Arizona's more bizarre trials.

No record of further prosecution exists in the case of Tucson's despicable dynamiting. The SP refurbished the superintendent's house and moved it to "Officers' Row" south of Twelfth Street on Third Avenue. The home's property, 120 feet fronting Congress and 68 feet along Fifth Avenue, went on sale for almost $8,000. Superintendent Whalen maintained he had not "a single enemy" who wanted to kill him. Local rails told a far different story, however. Former railroad draftsman and photographer Norman Wallace recalled: "Old man Whalen was the guy that used to get the conductors and engineers on the carpet and wanted to know why they did this and that. If they didn't answer right he would hit them in the jaw!"

Other SP rail operations proved more inspirational. The company's San Xavier Hotel, west of the local passenger depot, began providing comfort and cuisine for both the traveling public and locals in 1881 as the Porter Hotel. The SP leased its hotels for a nominal fee, to proprietors who ran them to the company's desires. Along with the New Orndorff, the Hall House, the Occidental, and the "new" the San Augustine Hotel, the San Xavier represented Tuc-

Norman Wallace at Lomas, Sonora in August 1908. Wallace shared the story rails told about W.H. Whalen along with a vast collection of archival papers and photographs. (AHS #PC180f208_d)

son's high-end accommodations as the twentieth century began.

Wise to native survival techniques, the SP built a second roof, three feet above the San Xavier building. This created the shade needed to inspire desert breezes and combat Tucson's summer heat. The company also used this roof style on its "barracks" at the northeast corner of Second Avenue and Sixteenth Street, and several other buildings along the division. A heat test one June day demonstrated an outside temperature of 105 degrees beaten back to an enjoyable 78 degrees inside the San Xavier's elegant dining room. Captain J.H. Tevis took over as "mine host" (manager) in charge of the hotel's operation in 1898. The fabled Arizona pioneer introduced "the most painstaking, polite, good-looking and accommodating young lady waiters" to his restaurant staff, noted the *Citizen*. "Just now there is not a more inviting spot in Arizona than the Depot Park and lawn surrounding Hotel San Xavier."

L.J.F. Iaeger bought the San Xavier Hotel franchise from SP physician Dr. George Goodfellow in December 1901 for $13,000. The "Iaeger system" of hotels included the Campbell House in Bowie, the SP Hotel in Yuma, and the Montezuma Hotel in Nogales. With walls and ceilings

freshly repainted and roof repairs complete, Iaeger made plans to put a lunch counter and an all-night bar in his new Tucson operation. That same month, the SP contracted for fourteen dining cars and began serving à la carte meals. The move cut eighteen hours off the SP's run from New Orleans to San Francisco. It also did away with travelers rushing to eat their meals in ten or fifteen minutes, as the company's system of dining rooms forced them to do. Within two years, the addition of dining cars reduced Iaeger's food business to only those who got off the train for a cup of coffee. The once glorious San Xavier Hotel served primarily as a boarding house for single rails, no longer the luxurious, commodious traveler's inn of its salad days.

Sunday, June 28, 1903, began as did so many summer Sundays in the Sonoran Desert—in torpid lethargy. The hotel dining room closed at its regular 9:00 a.m. hour, after several railroad boarders and ten out-of-town guests finished breakfast. Minutes later, smoke's vicious cousin leaped into the ceiling above the San Xavier's kitchen range. The hotel's two-story wooden frame proved no match for the fire devil coursing through its rafters to the roof.

Reminiscent of the "great" Radulovich conflagration five years earlier, the blaze brought city volunteers and the railroad fire brigade, but neither could render aid to the burning SP landmark. Caught by a northeast wind, fire engulfed the San Xavier end-to-end in twenty minutes. "One of the quickest fires on record almost completely wiped out the San Xavier Hotel," said the *Star*.

Railroad personnel rallied with remarkable haste, however. "Ready hands" joined chief clerk Frank "Rube" Armstrong in removing valuables from division freight and passenger agent Charles M. Burkhalter's office in the San Xavier's southeast wing. Other rails saved the barbershop of E.G. Sparks, while the hotel's safe emerged intact. And, as if by miracle, prompt action

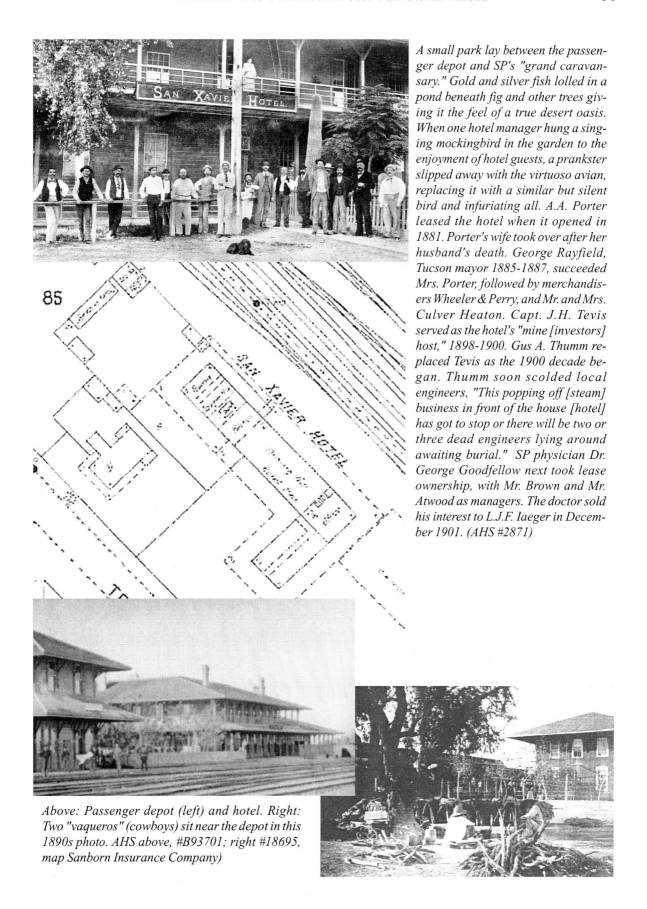

A small park lay between the passenger depot and SP's "grand caravansary." Gold and silver fish lolled in a pond beneath fig and other trees giving it the feel of a true desert oasis. When one hotel manager hung a singing mockingbird in the garden to the enjoyment of hotel guests, a prankster slipped away with the virtuoso avian, replacing it with a similar but silent bird and infuriating all. A.A. Porter leased the hotel when it opened in 1881. Porter's wife took over after her husband's death. George Rayfield, Tucson mayor 1885-1887, succeeded Mrs. Porter, followed by merchandisers Wheeler & Perry, and Mr. and Mrs. Culver Heaton. Capt. J.H. Tevis served as the hotel's "mine [investors] host," 1898-1900. Gus A. Thumm replaced Tevis as the 1900 decade began. Thumm soon scolded local engineers, "This popping off [steam] business in front of the house [hotel] has got to stop or there will be two or three dead engineers lying around awaiting burial." SP physician Dr. George Goodfellow next took lease ownership, with Mr. Brown and Mr. Atwood as managers. The doctor sold his interest to L.J.F. Iaeger in December 1901. (AHS #2871)

Above: Passenger depot (left) and hotel. Right: Two "vaqueros" (cowboys) sit near the depot in this 1890s photo. AHS above, #B93701; right #18695, map Sanborn Insurance Company)

salvaged the dining room's elegant wooden bar.

Pushed by the morning's ill wind, the roaring pyre of San Xavier took dead aim on Tucson's wooden passenger depot to the east. Winds swirled across the hotel's mass of glowing embers, sending cinders sailing above the city. Inside the rail depot, freight and passenger agent Robert Lowrie and his men guarded baggage and official papers. Wells Fargo express agent E.C. Hutchinson loaded the day's express onto trucks for a rapid retreat, should the morning's combustion take more permanent root. Upstairs, Irving McAvoy's men removed all of the instruments and important papers from resident engineer F.A. Bordwell's office. Firebrands ignited several small blazes on the roof. Firefighters used trees in a garden east of the hotel to buffer the blistering heat and rained water streams on the passenger depot's west end, saving it and trainmaster J.G. Lindsay's house to the west.

By that afternoon, several lonely fireplace stacks stood lifeless lookout above the blackened heap of hotel. In the wink of the fleeting fire, all the San Xavier's guests had evacuated uninjured, though several lost baggage and belongings. Auditor and cashier George Michelson escaped with his important business documents and a good suit of clothes. Alex Rossi agreed to accept meal tickets at his Columbus Café from those displaced by the fire. Soon, H.G. Ross led a crew of forty men in clearing debris from the former hotel site and leveling the ground. The *Citizen* reported that hotel operator Iaeger, "a prince of good fellows," paid off his twenty-seven employees and "seemed to take the situation good humoredly but later on began to consider it more seriously."

The SP fared well in the fiery demise of its aging San Xavier Hotel. With both local rail superintendent C.C. Sroufe and San Xavier proprietor Iaeger out of town that morning, and a "blanket policy" covering the SP-estimated $15,000-$20,000 loss, opportunity lay ripe for purposeful collection of a handsome insurance settlement. Its old lumber frame a liability, the hotel had outlived its attractiveness and its usefulness to the railroad. Decreased business in the company's dining rooms, following the introduction of dining cars, and few traveling guests occupying its sleeping rooms on most nights, had reduced the need for such accommodations. In addition, the SP needed more space for offices and passenger services.

Existing records and accounts support the veracity and integrity of all the principal men involved in the San Xavier Hotel fire. Yet, be it the circumspection of the modern mind, or circumstances of the day gone by, suspicion persists. In the drift of more than a century, however, conjecture strains at reality's doorstep. With only long-removed souls to testify, speculation becomes but the fleeting plaything of a wistful observer.

Local railroad and business interests had long pushed for a modern, high-class hotel on Tucson's Military Plaza. The former site of Camp Lowell had been a dusty eyesore since the U.S. Army abandoned it in favor of Fort Lowell seven miles east of the city in 1873. Fine accommodations in Tucson's "eastern quarter" promised to infuse vigor into the city's tourist trade and enhance local rail traffic. During 1900, two Tucson city councilmen, SP machinist George Angus and conductor Thomas O. Clark, had encouraged the sale of lots in the plaza to generate funds for a

Businessman Alex Rossi's restaurant at 15 W. Congress. (UASC)

posh caravansary. Supporters envisioned natty and updated features.

Not everyone stood eager to jump aboard the SP's highballing hotel special. Mayor C.F. Schumacher garnered a one-day delay to study the plan and "guard the city's interests before railroading." Following a series of legal battles, the city council sold Los Angeles developer R.H. Raphael land to build the hotel for $1, with the stipulation that the builder invest at least $25,000 in the first year. Raphael employed contractor J.V. McNeil, who began building during the summer of 1902. Construction lagged, however, after Raphael depleted his funds.

Levi H. Manning, who built a fortune selling commissary items to the SP, took over financing the Santa Rita Hotel in March 1903, along with Colonel Epes Randolph, wagon builder Fred Ronstadt, and merchant Julius Goldbaum. Charles

M. Shannon assumed the public role and the morning paper crowed: "As the *Star* has frequently stated, the opening of this hotel will be the next most important event to that of the coming of the Southern Pacific railroad. A new era will open for Tucson on February next. Keep this in mind, because it will be a fact."

Jubilant crowds opened the Santa Rita Hotel on February 1, 1904, but the *Star* noted, "The small boy and his father will meet with a disappointment in the loss of the Military Plaza as a site for a circus tent or a dog and pony show." The Santa Rita's "initial luster did not last long as the Downtown area began developing west of Stone Avenue and business and prestige followed the newer buildings," said Tom Peterson, former director of the Arizona Historical Historical Society's southern division museum. "The Santa Rita didn't have enough prestige to carry its own area."

Stone Avenue runs in the foreground in this Ben Gross view of Tucson looking east from the court house ca. 1891. Legal battles over the disposition Military Plaza (top) led to Dr. George Martin erecting a "castle" on the plaza's northwest corner in 1900. When the sheriff rode his horse into the plaza to evict the squatting pharmacist, Martin refused to leave. Mayor Gustav A. Hoff fired the lawman, leaving the city without its means of enforcement, but relented as the ex-sheriff rode off. "Yanked out of his boots and jammed right back in them," laughed the Star. (AHS #12644)

Levi H. Manning and his grandson William Manning Gunter share a tender moment in this early family portrait. Manning purchased the contract to supply the local SP stores department from C.R. Drake in 1900. By 1923, said former mayor Gustav A. Hoff, "If you knew his net profits...it would stagger you." That year, Manning worked preparing 25,000 acres of pasture on the Canoa Ranch, north of Nogales, for his son Howell. One of Tucson's most dynamic businessmen, Levi also built a luxurious home on Paseo Redondo in the city's "Snob Hollow" neighborhood. (Lovell Gunter Welsh Collection)

This early image of the Santa Rita Hotel belies its regal splendor. By the 1930s, Tucson's "No. 1 Howdy Man" Nick Hall, whose "flamboyance flowed over his new ward like a bottle of champagne over a pound of aspirin," and Barney Goodman inspired flush times at the Santa Rita. Six-foot-four and more than two hundred pounds, the "garrulous" Hall ran his hotel with "unmitigated informality" that made it "synonymous with Western hospitality," explained the Star. "A western hotel's gotta be western," Hall once said. "I don't go for those high-fallutin' places with no genuine atmosphere." Rodeo clowns fed their mules and Gregory Peck once rode his horse in the hotel lobby, lending authenticity to Hall's declaration, "I'm just naturally informal and if the boys cut up once in a while it was just in good fun." (AHS #41442)

Dining at the Santa Rita Hotel (AHS #72550)

The SP faced no such problems. Collis P. Huntington, Charles Crocker, Leland Stanford, and Mark Hopkins, the "Flonzaley Quartet of shoestring promotion," as *Fortune Magazine* once called them, had incorporated the SP in Kentucky in 1868. Led by Huntington, the railroad built furiously to gain hegemony over rail competitors during the corporation's early years, eight thousand miles of track from Portland, Oregon, south to Guaymas, Mexico, and east to New Orleans, Louisiana. In its rush to gain business footholds across the nation, the company neglected maintenance of roadway, facilities, and equipment.

After Huntington died in August 1900, Edward H. Harriman, Union Pacific Railroad chief executive officer, wrested full control of SP operations from Huntington family interests. Harriman began an expensive and time-consuming rehabilitation of SP rail operations. With chief engineer William C. Hood, the dynamic rail wizard completed $240 million in infrastructure improvement on the Harriman System.

SP constructed its Tucson plant more than one-half mile east of the center of town when it arrived in 1880. Bisected by the train tracks, SP's local railroad reserve ran south along Third Avenue from its intersection with Toole Avenue to Sixteenth Street, east to Park Avenue, north to Tenth Street, and west to Stevens Avenue. From there the line ran northwest along Stevens to Eighth Street, west to Sixth Avenue, and south along Toole Avenue to Sixteenth Street. Tucson's twenty-four-car roundhouse went up near the rail yard's eastern end as the first trains arrived. Shop workers serviced the railroad's steam locomotives inside the predominantly wooden

A "pin-up" calendar graces the wall behind playful looking stores department workers. Fusees to shovels, faceplates to flags, the department provided it. Initially under the master mechanic, stores became a separate department in March 1902. (AHS #62328)

building. Local officials expanded the roundhouse to twenty-five stalls in 1901.

The SP began construction of a new thirty-stall brick and steel roundhouse during May 1904. Extending in a half circle, the facility housed a modern 70-foot turntable and stalls built to handle two of the "mammoth" engines of the day. This advancement proved invaluable as locomotives grew larger during ensuing decades. In the railroad shops, south and west of the new roundhouse, blacksmiths, boilermakers, machinists, and other craftsmen completed every task needed to keep trains on the road.

East of the shops, the storekeeper's department stood at the eastern head of Fourteenth Street. The division storekeeper provided all the parts, tools, and equipment needed by the maintenance-of-way and motive-power departments. The SP completed the storekeeper's large main building No. 1 to house its office staff and supply depot in 1906. Storeroom No. 2 followed for the car department; No. 3 for the commissary, where clerks requisitioned materials; and sheds No. 4 and No. 5 for maintenance-of-way supplies.

West of the storekeeper's buildings, four material tracks serviced the yard and a storeroom for coal, coke, cement, and charcoal. The railroad drew oil from two 55,000-gallon tanks, positioned between

Shop workers pause in the Tucson yard ca. 1918. The SP purchased a forty acre tract east of the roundhouse, toward the rail neighborhood of Barrio Millville, in 1900. A large force of men graded the land to erect a new freight depot, but those plans never materialized. The company moved its stockyards from the eastern "head" of Tenth Street to the new parcel the next spring. (Ray Hanson Collection)

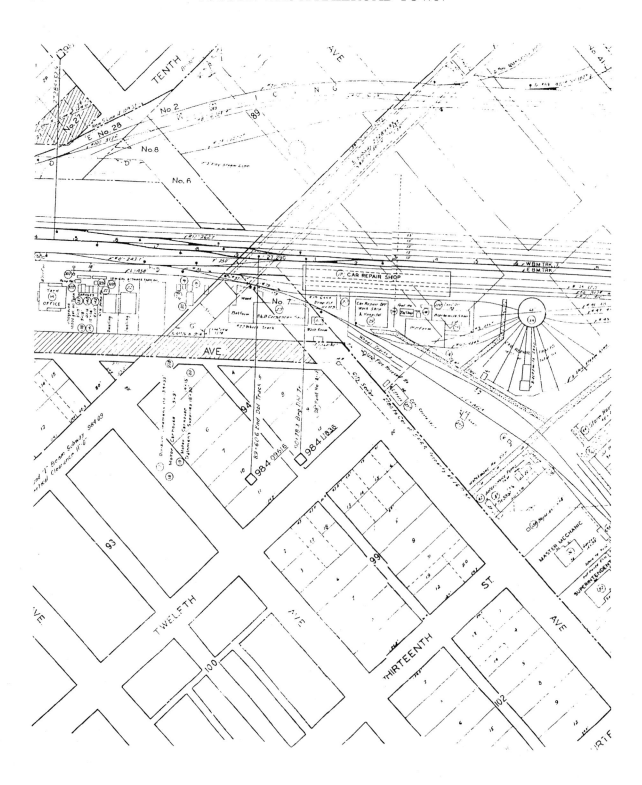

the main line and Pacific Fruit Express re-icing platform to the north, to fill smaller tanks for a variety of uses around the yard. A 350,000-gallon, steel water tank stood to the west of the oil tanks.

The railroad made substantial upgrades in Tucson between 1904 and 1907, altering local business dynamics in the process. The company built a new $10,000 employee clubhouse and reading room near

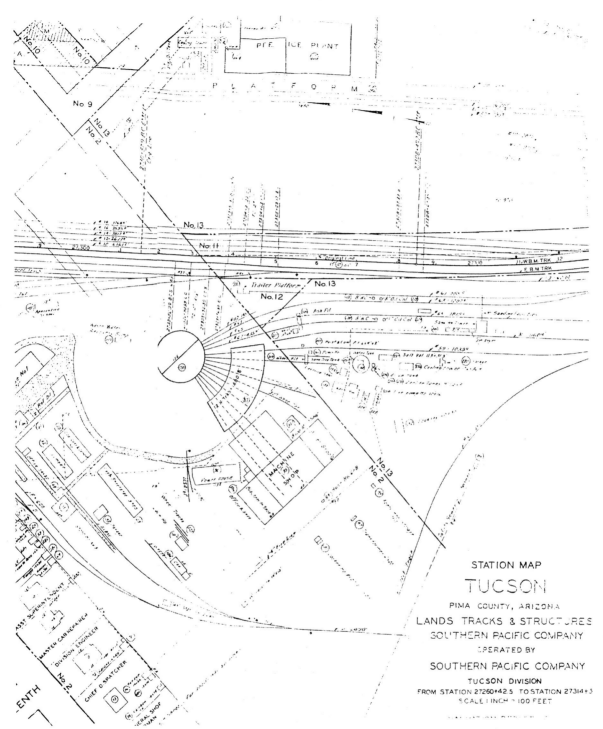

(Left and above) Adjoining segments of a large map of SP facilities in Tucson. (James W. Nugent Collection)

the corner of Tenth Street, Hoff Avenue, and Stevens Avenue in 1906. SP turned the former employee's facility into the local yard office. Six bathrooms, a billiard room, card room, and music room made the build-

ing a prime gathering spot for local rails. In addition, two thousand "well-selected books and all the latest periodicals" offered cultural stimulation and relaxation.

Curious Tucsonans gathered in front of the original SP clubhouse when the company re-roofed the building. (AHS #93046)

This photo shows the 1906 SP clubhouse prior to landscaping. At least once a year, talented rails "monopolized the entire building for songs, gaiety, and terpsichorean divertisement," noted the Citizen. *The SP clubhouse remained popular with employees, but lack of a restaurant or other source of income caused it to lose money. The company closed the Tucson clubhouse, along with the one at Gila Bend in May 1922. Later the SP remodeled this building for use as the local yard office. (AHS #29405)*

In April 1906, an earthquake demolished San Francisco. SP's original headquarters and countless irreplaceable company documents burned in the catastrophe. Already battling Imperial Valley floods, the oft-maligned railroad lent unprecedented aid to the ravaged Bay Area city. On the day after the quake, SP trains carried more than one thousand carloads of refugees out of the broken metropolis. Over the next thirty-five days, the company hauled 224,000 passengers free of charge and brought in more than 1,600 carloads of relief supplies. The SP also opened its sheds to homeless citizens and lent city authorities heavy equipment to clear debris. "A large fraction of the city's populace was, for a considerable period, dependent for their very lives on the course pursued by the Southern Pacific," declared the *New York Times*.

The company rented offices at 870 South Market Street and remained there for more than a decade. Construction finally began on an eleven-story operational headquarters at 65 Market Street in 1917. Designed in accordance with ancient Chinese *feng shui* principles, SP's new rail temple's plain, peach-yellow exterior hid an "old fashioned and utterly masculine" heart, explained *Fortune Magazine*. "You first enter a marble lobby, but the lobby is somewhat tarnished and the air smells faintly of cigars." Upstairs brown woodwork and "plush green carpet reminiscent of the day coaches of the twenties; and desks and partitions of golden oak," highlighted the building's classy interior.

In Tucson, contractor Quintus Monier's crews worked building a modern brick Mission-style passenger depot north of its aged wooden predecessor during 1907. Transfer of the telegraph operator's offices and those of resident engineer F.A Bordwell completed the move of almost seventy employees on August 20. Bordwell's maintenance-of-way department stored all the old depot's doors, windows, and other usable material. "The company does not throw away much if loss can be prevented," said Irving McAvoy. There would not be enough left "to build a hen house" when they completed the job, added the likeable assistant resident engineer. Soon, crew

Construction materials remained (right foreground) as workers completed Tucson's new depot in August of 1907. (AHS #41440)

chief Jack Angus and his men hauled away the rubbish using Tucson Transfer mule teams.

Finish work continued on the $65,000 facility into early September. Chief decorator A.E. Wocker and two assistants completed a dark frieze in the depot's smoking room, bearing a shield for each of the states and territories through which the SP ran. Painters applied a buff tint to the depot's exterior. *Sunset Magazine* artist Maynard Dixon also came to Tucson. Copying the "rich rare colors" he found during a visit to San Xavier Mission, Dixon painted four oil-on-canvas half-moon-shaped panels, called lunettes, for the building's west vestibule. "It [the mission] offers more to the lover of old paintings than can be found anywhere in the United States," the celebrated San Francisco artist explained.

Each of Dixon's lunettes represented an Arizona feature. *The Apache* depicted a mounted native warrior keeping a watchful eye over his family and horses in mescal country like that found in Cochise County, southeast of Tucson. *The Prospector* portrayed a miner examining a piece of ore in the state's rich mineral country. A mounted cowboy pushes his cattle across the desert in *The Cattleman*, and a farmer hoes corn in *Irrigation*. "The town took kindly to my work," Dixon later recalled. "The Americans, they heard it was the proper thing. The first breeze I got from one [of] these was the question, 'Are they all hand-painted?' The ones who really took to my work were the Mexicans. My fine knowledge of Spanish perhaps saved me some embarrassment."

The SP paid Louis Zeckendorf $11,500 for his property at the corner of Stone Avenue and Franklin Street, and began constructing a new division freight house in May 1906. Workmen hauled in thousands of cubic yards of dirt to build up

Criminal destruction put lives in peril on the Benson and Sonora roads during 1904. Perpetrators destroyed bridges, ran two trains into the ditch, destroyed freight cars, and burned the Nogales depot and other rail buildings at a cost of more than $75,000. When banditos fired several shots into a moving passenger coach in mid-June, the Star *growled: "This is so evidently malicious that there is reason to believe that there is a set purpose to damage the interest of the SP Company in any and every conceivable way." (AHS #BN109331)*

These are the three remaining oil-on-canvas lunettes Maynard Dixon created in 1907 for the new depot. Prints of the Dixon masterpieces will soon hang in Tucson's Historic Depot. See page 334. (Photos by Al Mida)

the grade beneath the almost 6,800-square-foot structure. Stabilizing the roadbed and raising the platforms to car height also required extensive fill work before construction began at the start of December 1907. Built to increase freight-handling efficiency, the new depot utilized four platforms for mule and horse teams to load and unload on its south side. Two rail tracks served a fifteen-foot-wide platform to the north. Sixty-five-foot-wide cement and "asphaltum" floors extended eighty feet along the building's east and west ends.

Business began to slow as 1907 ended, and the railroad scaled back its operations. The SP cut trainmen off their jobs and asked new job applicants to provide a "personal record" of their employment history along with their application. Capital projects continued, however. The company installed an alkali removing and water-softening plant at Tucson for $6,500. Other upgrades included $7,000 for additions to the master car repairer's shop; repairs to the old roundhouse; $7,000 for a Wells Fargo branch depot; and beautifying the depot grounds at Toole Avenue and Sixth Avenue.

Few could disagree when the morning newspaper proclaimed, "Every piece of property in this city has appreciated in value as the result of the SP improvements." Growth in local railroad facilities forced the SP to move long-time merchants off its railroad reserve, precipitating the blossoming of Tucson's warehouse district. Bail & Heineman Bottling Company built a new warehouse on North Stone Avenue at

The foundation of this huge rock crusher remains on the hillside above Steins Pass today. (AHS #29682)

the tracks, while merchants Wheeler and Perry moved into the Tucson Ice and Cold Storage plant near North Stone Avenue, between Toole Avenue and the tracks. Albert Steinfeld relocated his warehouse to Ninth Avenue, north of Franklin Street; and the Estill, Windsor, and Skinner Lumber Company built sheds, yards, and an office at 275 North Ninth Avenue. Tucson Warehouse & Transfer Company also began construction on Toole Avenue east of Franklin and Stone. "The north side, that section north of Council and Miltenberg, will show a marked change in 1907," predicted the *Star*. "Watch Tucson grow, especially in the warehouse district."

The company opened a large rock-crushing plant at Steins, New Mexico, during its construction campaign. Twenty-seven feet high, the impressive crusher utilized a "grizzly" to crack rock into five-inch pieces, and a smaller unit to break it into two-inch fragments for ballast beneath its railroad tracks. Tucson Division superintendent W.H. Whalen supervised the southwest's largest blast for creating ballast material on May 14, 1909.

Over the previous three months, workmen had excavated four, four-by-six-foot tunnels about one hundred feet apart and buttressed their openings with concrete. Then, wearing burlap covers on their shoes to prevent sparks, workmen loaded each hole with fifty to sixty tons of

During 1907, the SP took an aggressive approach to charges that it hid the facts in railroad wrecks such as the one near Esmond Station four years earlier. Julius Kruttschnitt, Harriman's maintenance and operations manager, suggested that the rail boss order division superintendents to publish all the details of accidents along his Harriman lines in local newspapers. Despite the bold effort to forestall popular censure and legislative scrutiny, SP continued to antagonize many.

Champion black powder. DuPont Powder Company's A.H. Crane positioned himself behind a small mountain about a quarter mile away and, using an electric blasting machine connected to each tunnel by copper wire, ignited a tremendous explosion. The concussion blew the front off Stein's mountain and the entire hillside fell to earth in a shattered mass. Three days later, rock crushing began for renewing the ballast beneath 180 miles of main line.

Back in Tucson, the railroad added a home for the division's chief dispatcher to those of the superintendent, his assistant, the master mechanic, master car repairer, and division engineer, on south Third Avenue. The SP also built two "box car homes" for general roadmaster W.F. Monahan and chief clerk A.C. Guthrie on Toole Avenue between Third and Fourth avenues. The company placed two boxcars side-by-side, with room for a hallway between, and covered the affair with a roof. Painted cream-colored, with a porch on the front and rear, each dwelling had gas lights, baths, and plumbing that gave it a modern feel.

SP announced plans to build a $10,000, eight-foot-by-eight-foot subway under the local rail yard during July 1910. Designed for walkers and bicyclists, but not vehicles, the planned passageway would align with Fourth Avenue to establish "easy communication between the main part of town and the northeast section." The SP promised electric lights and an air-circulation system inside the tube to sweeten its proposition. P.N. Jacobus, the city's mayor, defended SP's decision not to build the subway wide enough to accommodate vehicles and ac-

In 1901, community pillar John Heidel (above) greeted passers-by on Congress Street "like King Solomon in all his glory," aboard a brilliantly painted E.M.F. touring car, one of the city's early automobiles, reported the Star. *(John Heidel Collection)*

cepted the company's offer with grace. The railroad scuttled the plan when a destructive fire destroyed the local shops just two months later.

Across Toole Avenue from the passenger depot, hotelier John Heidel kept pace with the city's fabled Santa Rita Hotel. Heidel's bellhops dressed in "gaudy uniforms of scarlet [with] gold buttons," his great-granddaughter, Sandra Heidel, reported years later. To carry guests from the depot to his hotel and about town, Heidel ran a six-seated carriage "with two prancing horses and a driver in a silk hat and a gay uniform." Arguably Tucson's first "man of leisure," the ever-up-to-date Missouri native leased out his Hotel Heidel in 1910. He invested wisely, and spent most of his afternoons on golf courses in Tucson or southern California. Sadly, John's son, SP brakeman Charles J. Heidel, succumbed to intestinal problems in 1924; however, his grandson John Heidel enjoyed a fifteen-year career as a pipefitter with the SP.

As the first decade of the twentieth century wound down, a familiar scare rattled local business minds when Gila Valley, Globe & Northern right-of way agent C.D. Reppy proclaimed that SP planned to build a line through the Box Canyon of the Gila River that would "open the way to elimination of heavy traffic over the Tucson Division between Bowie and Tucson." SP officials disavowed any plans to build a railroad so "deadly parallel to the Tucson division," reported the *Star*. "Phoenix will have to wait a little longer for the road they think will cause the 'sidetracking' of Tucson—Arizona's metropolis."

Tucson's distasteful reminder of the adobe age it longed to forget, the Wedge included blocks 202, 206, and 207 on the city plat. Between Maiden Lane on the north and Congress on the south and from Stone Avenue to Meyer Street, buildings of crumbling adobe and rotting wood lay jammed together in a disgusting pock of dishonor upon the city.

Tucson's renewal focused on Block 207 of the city plat map, the upper wedge. Against the resolute opposition of Mayor C.F. Schumacher and city attorney Roscoe Dale, discussions of the Wedge's elimination finally produced an ordinance to proceed with its removal. The dictum gave tenants and landowners ten days to vacate. On May 3, 1902, federal Judge George R. Davis gave possession of the upper wedge to the city of Tucson.

Three days later, city councilman and local contractor O.M. Anderson led a crew of thirty men with picks, axes, and other tools in the assault on the unsightly source of local shame. In a stroke of irony, Tucson tackled the upper wedge on the day Arizona's governor, N.O. Murphy, resigned under accusations of wrongdoing.

The crowd cheered as workers smashed the first mud walls and the city orchestra played the "Star Spangled Banner." Smart-alecks wrapped the first two adobe blocks removed in paper for judges O.T. Rouse and D.F. Glidden, as souvenirs of their "gallant but useless fight to prevent the removal of the wedge." Some tenants proved slow to the step as the area's "big four barbers" hurried out just in time. Tailor G.K. Smith continued working on the suit of a prospective groom, however, and retreated only "as light began to shine in among the rafters."

At 7:30 p.m. Mariner's Juvenile Band marched down Congress Street to the head of the Wedge and played several tunes. Bonfires dotted the streets along with hundreds of Roman candles and fireworks. A large wagon was set in the street from which Royal A. Johnson and others spoke. Fifteen and one-half hours after picks and shovels first struck, the upper wedge's final partition tumbled. "A smile was on everybody's face yesterday," said the Star. "All were glad that the old wedge had seen its last day."

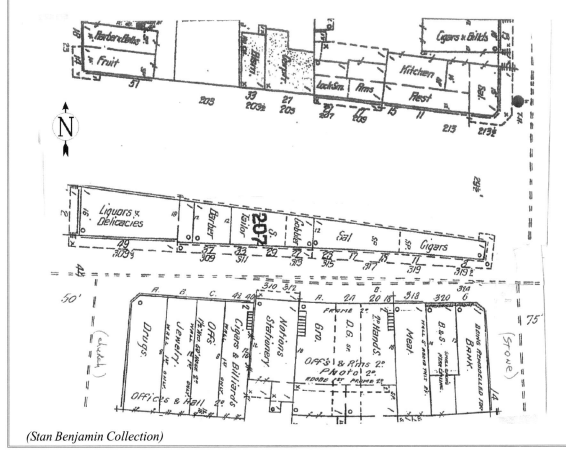

(Stan Benjamin Collection)

Chapter 5

Inventors, Wandering Willies, and Unique Souls: Something in the Desert Air

(AHS #41591)

Tucson has long enjoyed a reputation for sheltering creative genius, eccentric expression, and authentic, free-thinking spirits. Indeed, across the Southwestern frontier, the freedom to pursue a new existence and experiment with so many aspects of life drew inspired, inquisitive souls. People who looked through the obvious to the possible came to Arizona. These individuals thrived in a region that demanded easier, faster, and cheaper solutions to physical challenges.

During the early twentieth century, several southern Arizona inventors designed features that furthered rail operations and made money. "There must be something inspiring in the climate of Tuc-son which excites the inventive genius of the searchers of hidden secrets of nature," trumpeted the *Star* in December 1903. "Tucson can claim several important inventions which some day will create not only much interest but will make fortunes for the discoverers."

One of these talented inventors, Southern Pacific Railroad (SP) freight conductor M.B. Bulla, held the El Paso to Tucson run in 1902. That year, company officials granted Bulla unrestricted access to shops in Los Angeles to perfect his new electrical appliance for signaling engineers on passenger trains. The apparatus provided a far superior communication system to the bell cord and air whistle system. The SP conducted a successful trial of Bulla's unit on a train between Los Angeles and Santa Monica. The company reportedly gave serious consideration to buying enough of Bulla's devices to equip its entire passenger fleet. Record of such a purchase has not been located.

Rugged Arizona pioneer Capt. J.H. Tevis filled his Arizona in the 50's with tales of mid-1800s life at Apache Pass Stage Station, and in the mountains of southwestern New Mexico. (AHS#11586)

The creative brilliance of Captain J.H. Tevis sought countless outlets. He invented a windmill, learned the Chiricahua Apache language from Chief Esconela, protected the citizens of Pinos Altos, New Mexico, as a captain with the Arizona Scouts, and served in the Sixteenth Arizona Territorial Legislature. In 1903, Tevis applied for a patent on a signal device to warn trains of problems on the track ahead, though no record of its issuance exists.

William Stump Kengla (right) and his brother settled along the Rillito Creek near the U.S. Army's Ft. Lowell when they arrived in Tucson during 1883. Kengla's granddaughter, Dorthy Fitzpatrick, explained, "When William's sister married Bernabe Robles, two of southern Arizona's pioneer families came together." (Dorothy Fitzpatrick Collection)

When he suggested that Arizona close its territorial prison at Yuma by hanging the worst criminals and treating the rest to the whipping post, however, the Cochise County free spirit found little support.

Born in the nation's capital during September 1862, one-time division car inspector William S. Kengla studied at George Washington University until the age of eighteen. Striking Arizona in 1883, Kengla opened a saddle and harness "manufactory" in Tucson. He began to tan leather using the *cana aigre* root's rich acid, found in abundance across the southern portion of Arizona and northern Sonora, Mexico. Native peoples had used the root in curing animal hides for centuries, but the resourceful Kengla sought to patent the process and formed the Southern Tanning Company. With success imminent, he sold his interest and returned to making saddles and harnesses.

In 1903, Kengla invented an apparatus for reducing the cost of running oil-burning locomotives. Earlier burners required building a great deal of steam to spray atomized oil into the firebox. The Kengla invention used air rather than steam to atomize the burner's oil, thus lowering fuel consumption. In addition, the in-

vention threw flame almost 20 feet beneath the boiler, rather than the short distance of earlier burners. After several months of successful performance, experts calculated the new "appliance" reduced fuel consumption by 15 to 25 percent. "Local Man's Invention Will Prove Big Thing of the Century," proclaimed the *Star*. "Success for 'Billy' means new enterprise for Tucson and it is well to support all such endeavors." The paper predicted: "It is only a matter of time when the Kengla crude oil burner will be used on stationary as well as locomotive boilers, on account of its superiority in generating steam as well as in controlling the flames. Score another one for Tucson's inventor." The following January, the Electric Light & Power Company of Tucson equipped its stationary boiler with a Kengla crude-oil burner.

William S. Kengla died tragically in 1906, when he tumbled into a copper vat at

The Citizen *opened its 1890 New Year's edition with a feature on William Kengla, including a beautiful pointillist sketch. The story detailed Kengla's life to that point and explained his most ingenious cana aigre tanning process. Later, Kengla inspired Tucsonans with his new oil burner for steam locomotives. (Dorothy Fitzpatrick Collection)*

Greene Consolidated Copper Mines in Cananea, while working with his eldest sons, Bernard and Henry. Ninety-six years later, William's granddaughter Dorothy Kengla Fitzpatrick remembered that the accident savaged his loving wife and six children. "My father, Herman Kengla, went to work at the SP when he was quite young to help his mother make ends meet after his father's sudden death," Fitzpatrick recalled in her gorgeous midtown home. "He eventually rose to auditor for the Southern Pacific of Mexico and traveled extensively in that capacity for the company."

Making steam on the Tucson Division's west end proved difficult because high alkali content in the region's water caused it to froth in the boiler. Veteran division engineer and Twenty-Second Arizona Territorial Legislature council member Joseph B. Corbett introduced a compound designed to neutralize alkali in water during June 1904. Decades later, division engineers continued to use Corbett's solution. "It worked okay," Jim Nugent recalled. "You'd take a couple of balls, about the size of tennis balls, and toss 'em in the water tank on the tender. However, the company still had to take water elsewhere to be able to run their engines."

The SP took a creative approach in its ongoing battle to make steam at Yuma, using water from

the muddy Colorado River. The river's fine silt made filtering and cleansing its water for steam production tedious and interminable. Between 1879 and 1893, the SP built a four-compartment settling tank on a

Pioneer inventor W. S. Kengla's photograph hangs on the wall behind his distraught family following his tragic 1906 death. (Dorothy Fitzpatrick Collection)

SP's water settling tanks provided clean water for making steam at Yuma. When diesel engines replaced steam the railroad abandoned the tanks. Graffiti covered their inside walls during Amec Infrastructure's 1998 engineering study, which recommended their eventual demolition. (Amec Infrastructure)

Demands for potable water prompted H.W. Blaisdell to design and patent a washing apparatus to clean Colorado River silt out of his sand filters. Today the unique machine sits near the Yuma County River Crossing Park. Blaisdell installed Yuma's first water system in 1892. The eccentric Massachusetts native pumped water from the Colorado through a two-mile-long redwood stave to a reservoir at Fifth Avenue and Fourteenth Place. Along its path, Blaisdell planted orange, pepper, and palm trees, which he watered with taps placed along the line, marked today by the name "Orange Avenue." (Kalt Collection)

kept the railroad's great idea flowing during the tumultuous fall of 1904. With the river on the rise in the middle of October, basin tender Young reported the water "extremely muddy" but "settled fairly well." Washing out the basins proved difficult, however, due to "no pressure on hose." Within a couple of days, the basins began settling "nine inches of partly clear water" in four hours. The next day, however, tenders could settle no clean water. That evening the night man closed off the incoming water at his basins in order to furnish passenger train No. 9 with clear water. Soon, so little water reached the basins that it became impossible to wash them out. SP used City of Yuma pumping equipment in emergencies, but when that proved insufficient to meet the needs of his trains, basin tender Young turned to another southern Arizona inventor, water-filtering wizard H.W. Blaisdell. The crusty inventor, investor, and entrepreneur, who supplied water to the city of Yuma, responded that he did not feel compelled to provide any "sudden amount" to the railroad and that Young should exercise patience.

ridge above the Colorado's south bank. Directly west of the SP bridge, the brick reservoir stood 8 feet high, 40 feet wide, and 120 feet long. The company pumped river water into the holding basins, allowed the silt to settle to the bottom, then ran the clean water downhill through a 6-inch wooden main to tanks in the SP yard on Madison Avenue between Fourth and Fifth streets. The railroad also sold water to one Yuma school and a few citizens.

Quixotic water levels and catastrophic floods hampered struggles to settle the river's silt and supply good water for passing locomotives. The number of hours required to settle the silt depended upon the sometimes-hourly whims of the Colorado. In addition, silt clogged the bulkheads, filters, pipes, and basins, requiring vigilant cleaning and maintenance.

The SP Water Basin Tender's log provides a look into the lives of the men who

Water continued to flow slowly from Yuma's city pump into the cement tanks. Because he could get no clear water, Young began adding alum to each basin to aid in settling the silt. Clear, steam-making water finally arrived from Blaisdell six days after Young's request. The next day, the basin tender reported the water "very muddy but settling good" at two feet an hour.

Brilliance took many forms at the SP in the early twentieth century. Son of pumper J.D. 'Jack' Peggs, accountant Joseph M. Peggs (center) held dominion over figures. Joseph graduated from Safford School in 1906 and attended Preparatory at the University of Arizona. He paused from the numbers grind in this photo of the division's accounting department ca. 1910. Peggs earned certification as the state's fifty-third accountant and Mojave County citizens elected him to the eleventh state legislature in 1932. Subsequently, the roly-poly, jolly Tucsonan served as the state tax commissioner and wrote much of Arizona's initial revenue tax code. At big Joe's death in 1959, the Arizona Republic *dubbed him the "father of pari-mutual wagering" in Arizona. (Kalt Collection)*

Though troublesome and without end, the maintenance of the Yuma water-settling basins provided clear water that kept S.P trains moving during the steam era.

Most patents issued during the first three decades of the twentieth century emanated from Eastern and Midwestern cities such as Brooklyn, Baltimore, Chicago, and Newark, New Jersey. However, in 1906, B.F. Wooding founded the Wooding Railway Warning Device Company in partnership with former University of Arizona chancellor William F. Herring and other investors. With their principal place of business Tucson, the company built and marketed automatic electric warning and signaling devices for railroads. Wooding secured a patent in 1908, on his first train signaling device for grade crossings. Wooding

invented train-signaling devices for twenty years, including one that called for installing a five-foot "road magnet" at crossings, which rang a gong mounted in automobiles to signal the driver when a train approached. "Many in Washington believe it is more valuable than train control," Wooding explained to stockholders. "Probably five thousand are killed and three times that many are injured annually at crossings."

In later years, the prolific inventor moved operations to Montclair, New Jersey but always fought against "the large financial companies that are on the inside with the railroads." Wooding explained, "While our appliance has maintained a lead in simplicity, though denied installation, it is constantly being improved." One stockholder cried that after eighteen years of fruitless investments, "to the extent of Millions of dollars, the Wooding seems to have fallen out!"

Other ventures proved more successful. Son of an SP engineer, Tucsonan Steven P. Miller built and sold what may have been the first evaporative coolers in Arizona. Miller grew up hearing tales of rails who beat the baking heat in Yuma by hanging wet burlap over their bunks to catch a breeze. While attending Tucson High School, he began building wooden frames in which he enclosed excelsior shavings in chicken wire. Then, he hung his contraption in an open window. Running water through a copper tube to the excelsior, the young inventor used a fan to pull air across the wet affair and into the house. Miller sold his coolers for $18 each, bringing relief to a scalding state. Later, he worked as a service technician for Glover and Clark Air Conditioning and rose to president of the company, which eventually bore his name.

Along with talented inventors, the other exceptional brethren of the railroad, its free riders, spiced life in Tucson. The eccentricity of the technologically creative minds found its parallel among the matchless characters who rode the rails in nomadic foray across the Tucson Division. Much of the wherefores and few of the whys fill the tales of these "wandering willies" who chose itinerant lives. In "hobo jungles" across the nation, a culture grew among the mostly male travelers, complete with a code of honor.

Riding trains without a ticket began with the inception of rail transportation. Be it circumstances or volition, some individuals saw jumping a freight train as the "only way to ride." Lack of a regular job, a dwelling to call their own, and a guiding purpose in their lives defined this loose-knit group of railroad ramblers. Hobos, tramps, freeloaders, they had several names, each denoting their lifestyle. The public used the terms interchangeably, but to men of the "freight car literati," a hobo rode the trains

The term "bindlestiff" arose from the German word meaning bundle and denoted a hobo, especially one who carried a bedroll. "Wandering Willies" arrived with the first SP trains, and smallpox joined them, prompting local rail officials to issue occasional orders requiring that all employees provide proof of their vaccination. (Kalt Collection)

while tramps walked railroad right-of ways. Both took pride in exchanging work for a meal and looked down upon the common freeloader.

Two days before the official SP train arrived in the city in March 1880, the *Arizona Citizen* exclaimed: "So far Tucson has been spared the affliction of that detestable evil known as the city tramp. One may walk the streets of a night without being stopped at every corner by some fat, dirty, impertinent vagabond asking in a whining tone for 'a little assistance'." Soon the same newspaper lamented, "Three weeks ago a tramping beggar was almost unknown in Tucson and

Bread and water greeted hobos and tramps in Tucson when pranksters staged this "hold-up" at John Heidel's (far left behind bar) Cactus Saloon across from the Tucson depot ca. 1900. Heidel built a classy hotel north of the saloon in 1907, which hosted the first meeting of the Tucson Greyhound Association November 9, 1909. Principals named Heidel treasurer and Emanuel Drachman president. (John Heidel Collection)

themselves and developed reputations. Dubbed "Silverlocks" by the *Star*, one such vagabond appeared in Tucson during the fall of 1898. Deaf and unable to speak, the fellow caught the city's fancy. Local newspapers took an interest in the hirsute wanderer and reported his adventures. When he showed up at the Fashion Saloon in late January 1899, a *Citizen* reporter learned more of Silverlocks's story, when he wrote on a pad he always carried with him.

now one cannot walk down Meyer Street of an evening without being stopped by them."

Within the year, hobos established the city's first "jungle" called "Isla De Cuba." East of Third Avenue where Ninth Street crosses Railroad Arroyo, now Arroyo Chico, transients built a permanent campsite that endured for more than a decade. Wieland's Beer Depot, just to the west, helped fuel hobo festivities and earned the area a notorious reputation. When a large wagon bridge went up across the arroyo in 1892, hobos cleared out and the SP built a company bunkhouse on the site near present-day 120-128 North Hoff Avenue.

From "harmless bindlestiff" to "hard-boiled gaycat," men tramped or rode division rails gratis from here-to-there-to-nowhere during the steam days. Some showed streaks of noble character that earned them respect and even admiration among Tucsonans. A few made names for

H.V. Siedenberg, forty-four, had journeyed west with an opera troupe that went bust in Seattle, Washington. He worked setting type for a "big metropolitan daily" until linotype came along and his eyes failed him at age twenty-two, changing "the whole aspect of affairs." Now, he tried to work his way home to Houston, Texas, by performing impersonations and sleight of hand. Preferring to be called "Brick the Advertiser," Silverlocks told of his travels with a circus and of his acting exploits. To earn his way, Brick developed a "scheme" for street advertising, generally for traveling shows. "I have several characters I impersonate," he wrote. "My specialty is a country girl. I expect to use it here next week." The *Star* explained that the "big boy who wore his hair at an unusual length because it assisted him in his 'make-up' as a maiden fair, just dropped into Tucson as hundreds of others do." One reporter "pitied

"Hardboiled" or "harmless," hobos and tramps proliferated during the steam days. (Kalt Collection)

the misfortune of the man and espied a noble trait that prompted one to rustle so hard for self support. A helping hand to an unfortunate creature may not make some of us any poorer."

Brick the Advertiser first promoted a local bargain sale. "Yesterday, in his masque," said the reporter, "he was the object of the special attention and merriment of the town as he rambled around advertising Felix's dry goods store." Soon, Sam Hall, proprietor of a poultry and oyster house called the Wave, befriended Brick, and he exchanged work for his room and board. Hall often used a young burro in his business. The hobo hit it off with the four- footed creature right away, eventually purchasing it from his benefactor.

Silverlocks decided to walk to El Paso along the SP tracks in late February 1899. Bankrolled by several Tucson friends, the healthy, long-haired tramp started east one step at a time, with his six-month-old burro, "Tucson," at his side. He planned to use the animal to carry his possessions and then ride it after it matured. He trained the animal to his whim and, ignoring warnings that he would starve to death and not make it ten miles a day with a burro, the Advertiser did reach El Paso. In a letter to the *Citizen*, Brick explained that he had struggled to communicate with the many Mexican people he met who could not read English. On his first day, Brick did not find any water until 6:00 p.m. Though unfit to drink, the foul liquid left man and burro no choice.

At Pantano, a pump man fixing an irrigation ditch fed the ravenous tramp and his equine sidekick, then put Brick up in his chicken coop for the chilly night. In Bowie, his 50¢ bought him a room, and on the trek to San Simon, he "gave the burro a good whipping," Brick explained. "You would think that burro actually cried, for the tears streamed down her face. Henceforth the burro would not keep at it and kept getting between the tracks. About four miles from Gage, a fast freight ended the burro. I be-

Silverlocks met charity at Pantano Station on his trek to El Paso. (George Lundquist Collection)

lieve that burro actually committed suicide because she ran before the train for a little ways and then laid down with her head on the track." By April 1899, Brick the Advertiser had returned to Tucson and alerted authorities that he discovered that hobos planned to sabotage a railroad trestle on the Tucson Division.

Prior to the Tucson Division's wholesale conversion to oil-burning engines, athletic hobos sometimes "passed coal," shoveling the hard fuel from bins into the trains' tenders in exchange for a ride. "The company loses nothing by the operation as these men would beat the trains by riding the rods or otherwise," declared the *Citizen* in the spring of 1899. Hobos also collected the large amount of coal that lay scattered along the roadbed from normal operations. Scrambling down into a nearby wash, they built fires with the wayward coal to fight off the desert's cold winter nights.

Early on the morning of April 21, 1899, one such fire burned near Ligurta, twenty-six miles east of Yuma. Winds whipped the fire into a blaze, igniting the railroad bridge's support trestle. For nine hours no train passed the bridge until a "mammoth" 110-ton locomotive, pulling three or four heavily loaded freight cars, crossed over its fire-weakened wooden timbers, dove off the track, and collapsed into the arroyo in a steel heap. "The big engine…turned in the twinkling of an eye into a fearful agent of destruction, stood upright in the wash…with its nose jammed into the opposite bank," reported the *Citizen*. Freight cars following the engine off the track burst into flames, killing fireman J.H. Courtney, conductor W.O. Dovey, and two tramps. Doctors sent engineer Mark H. Adams to the SP hospital in Tucson with severe scalding on his head, shoulders, and arms.

Hobos could render a brakeman's life torturous. The *Citizen* noted: "If the brakemen on the SP trains did not have the tramps to look after, their work would be light and agreeable, but no, it is arduous and exasperating. The persistence with which the hobos stick to the trains often calls for the exercise of a great deal of forbearance." When an 1892 city ordinance allowed officials to assign vagrants to work details, they greeted railroad free riders with a breakfast of bread and water and put them on a chain gang cleaning up around the courthouse. Though later city ordinances called for up to 30 days in jail, lawmen often gave the wandering crew "twenty minutes to get out of town," if they promised not to return.

Hobos almost overran Tucson during the winter of 1900. Local jails filled with tramps, and police blamed transients for a large fire at Tucson Lumber. Amid the hobo proliferation, the afternoon newspaper went to bat for one road ranger that February. "Said to be the best type of the real tramp article," the chap presented "a chance for someone who has some old clothes to do a kindly act and set McLean out on the road prepared for the cold," said the *Citizen*.

In *Tales of the Iron Road: My Life as King of the Hobos*, Maury "Steam Train" Graham explained that many came to accept the term hobo as a badge of honor. "As impressive as a graduate degree from a respected college or university," said Graham. "They strove to make the title one that carried with it a high degree of pride. The hobo and the tramp lived their unorthodox lifestyle out of pure choice, unlike transients, bums, winos and dopeheads."

Hobos, generally, kept their camps clean and wore good-quality black or dark blue suits, "many times with a white shirt and neckerchief, and many times a necktie," said Graham. "They selected dark clothing to make it more difficult for railroad police to spot them at night. There were very strict rules of etiquette that I knew must be observed when in a hobo jungle. You walked up to the first cook fire and introduced yourself or made some pleasantry, then you waited for an invitation to join in the meal. If none came, you moved on and repeated it at the next fire. This ritual was not conducted out of lack of hospitality or unkindness but rather simple economics. They couldn't invite someone to sit down if there wasn't enough to share, so they just wouldn't."

Spurred by the Depression of 1893, hoboing reached its peak as the nineteenth century ended. Between 1870 and 1902, the tramp population in the United States rose at a rate almost four times greater than the general population, to almost 57,000. Hobo "Professor" John J. McCook estimated that ticketless travel had risen 235.4 percent since 1870, costing rail companies $11 million annually. McCook decried the nation's erratic and inconsistent policy toward hobos. Many towns continued to adhere to a policy of "move along," he said, while others instituted local regulations so "fierce and panicky" that they no longer enforced them after a year or two. Officials should remand younger tramps to reformatories, suggested McCook, because the institutions had demonstrated 75 percent effectiveness with ordinary felons.

The "Champion of the Tramps" rode into Tucson on the brake beams, support braces located beneath each car, of the Golden State on February 19, 1902. F.C. Welch, "Penn the Rapid Rambler," explained that he had bummed around the world five times, covering 530,000 miles. Sunday supplements and magazines frequently wrote him up as the "idle tramp," he declared. The *Citizen* fanned the flames of this queer character's legend, saying: "He is just a plain hobo bent on bumming and hating work. Yet he has a 'divine spark' in some way. If he hadn't elected to be a hobo he might have made his mark in the world. 'Penn' is just as much a champion hobo as Jack Johnson is the champion prize fighter." The newspaper warned, "Tucson household-

ers without a woodpile who meet a gent looking for a little help should be careful not to offend the famous 'Penn' by calling the police." Soon, the illustrious vagabond headed off for his first visit to Mexico City.

Standing SP policy called for railroad "bulls," or policemen, and brakemen to remove all hobos from company property. Some took to the task with bright-faced vigor and clubs, unleashing merciless violence on the ticketless travelers. Stories of beatings, shootings, and hobos' bodies found brutalized along the railroad tracks encouraged creative strategies for avoiding the furor of hell-bent pursuers. Experienced hobos reported the harshest treatment between Lordsburg and El Paso, on what was then the Tucson Division. Brakemen could not be "subsidized with a little cash," often making riders get off as the train slowed on an uphill grade, sometimes many miles from a station. Others claimed Willcox held the reputation as the worst place to loiter around the rail yard or go begging at houses for food. The Sulfur Springs Valley cattle town boasted a very strict marshal who ran a street cleaning gang when he had enough men.

In the spring of 1903, hobo F. Hunter rode a series of trains west from Philadelphia with a colleague named Casey. When an SP brakeman discovered the pair near Sentinel, Arizona, he ordered them off the train. Following a heated exchange, the brakeman slipped into his ca-

Hobos called Willcox the toughest town on the Tucson Division, when future road foreman of engines, or "traveling engineer," fireman Carl Ball Sr. (left) and engineer Jim Williams ran the helper engine from San Simon, Arizona to Steins Pass, New Mexico ca. 1919. (Elgin Ball Collection)

Bullets sizzled around passengers at the Sentinel depot, when an SP brakeman opened fire on hobo F. Hunter during the spring of 1903. By 1916, trespassing on the tracks accounted for forty-nine percent of the year's total railroad fatalities, noted one Southern Pacific Bulletin. (Kalt Collection)

boose and grabbed a gun. In a flash, he fired three shots. One whistled past a woman standing on the Sentinel station platform, eliciting screams of terror from waiting passengers. The final bullet ripped off one of Hunter's fingers and lodged in his right groin. The wounded hobo begged rails to take him to a hospital, but trainmen refused, leaving him instead at the Gila Bend depot. Rails there dressed his wounds and put Hunter on a train to Phoenix, where they dumped him at the SP depot. Dr. Henry A. Hughes, Maricopa County Hospital superintendent, told bewildered rail officials that the hospital would not admit Hunter without a permit. Railroad workers loaded the wounded man into a hospital wagon in the Phoenix yard and pushed him onto a sidetrack. The SP, at last, obtained the required permit and hospital personnel came for him, but Hunter could not be found. When workers discovered him late that evening, Hughes reported, "the chances are against his recovery."

Enraged, Dr. Hughes chastised the SP for neglecting to seek medical care for Hunter. He said the railroad should take injured men into their company hospital at Tucson or make arrangements for the admission of its victims to the county hospital rather than just dump them at various depots. Disgusted by the company's indifference, the *Phoenix Republican* shouted, "This is the third man that the Southern Pacific has caused to be sent to the hospital in this informal way."

Tucson peace officers went on frequent "tramp crusades." In December 1903, police set out to provide local "heroes of the legalized 'vags union'" with a stay at city marshal J.S. Hopley's "Hotel Hopley." Unbeknownst to the police, a large group of hobos lay bent on making the holiday roundup particularly exciting. The *Citizen* reported that a tough "gaycat" named Harris convinced his fellow tramps they had sufficient numbers to commandeer an SP train. Under Harris's leadership, twenty men boarded the eastbound No. 9 train of conductor Ezra Shelley at Casa Grande and claimed a free ride into Tucson as their right.

In an instant, "the 'bos took full control," reported the *Star*. "In fact, they seemed to hold the whip hand on the train crew and the train conductor." Conductor Shelley wired ahead to trainmaster W.H. Averell, the nephew of SP head Edward H.

Harriman, in Tucson. Averell quickly organized a group of SP men to jump aboard the eastbound train at Jaynes Station, north of the city. Rails surrounded the hijacked hobo wagon and forced the entire pack of rail mutineers into the caboose. Sheriff Frank E. Murphy met the train as it pulled into the Tucson depot. Murphy released nine of the rail pirates and took eleven others "to the place where food and shelter is cheerfully given," chuckled the *Star*. Judge O.T. Richey sentenced the insurrectionists' leader, Harris, to fifty days and six of his followers to twenty-five days each.

Dignity, nevertheless, grew among hobos. Tales circulated of great feats by individuals, and "rambling roadies" adopted a code of ethics and behavior. They also developed high-level skills. The *San Francisco Chronicle* once noted: "Hobos seem to know intuitively which freight cars contain the champagne and which the cigars. Hobos and tramps never break into a car unless there is something inside worth having. Whenever a freight car with unstealable goods is broken into, you may be positive it is the work of some novice." Hobos also read a great deal. "There was a saying that you could easily tell a hobo from a bum," said famous Hobo King Steam Train Graham. "While they both lined their coats and jackets with insulating newspapers, the hobo read his first."

Many "box car gentry" proclaimed themselves "King of the Hobos." Famous Tramp King "Dr." Ben L. Reitman bounced off a train that arrived in Tucson from Chicago during mid-July 1907, full of venom. Calling himself The King, Ivan Stepanoff, stood tall and well built for his sixty years. His flowing white beard and distinguished manner lent "more the appearance of a well-to-do artisan or minor official than a beggar," said the *Star*.

Arrested forty times in Arizona, Reitman led off by complaining about the "unsanitary condition" of Arizona jails. In addition, the territory's "unjust" vagrancy law allowed "the constable, judge, and

jailer to make a tidy sum," while using tramps as "the medium of exchange." Calling Bowie the worst place for the traveling man that he had ever seen, Reitman said, "The constable and judge down there are getting rich picking up tramps on the fee system."

The "vast army of tramps" could be eliminated if authorities would lend "a helping hand instead of kicking them further down the ladder of life," the errant king explained. Under the motto "Kindness and No Red Tape," Reitman's Brotherhood Welfare Association proposed to "give the tramp a square deal; help him over the rough places; get him in shape to work by providing him with clean collars, with socks, etc., and a meal ticket and get him a job." Reitman advised putting arrested tramps to work at 50¢ a day plus board. When a bum completed his sentenced time, he could use the money he earned to buy a suit of clothes and a ticket to a new locale. Reitman expressed confidence that his plan would be cheaper for communities in the end, declaring that his "labors for the hobo fraternity would yet be crowned with success."

Few stories of free rail travel ended in success. The sorrowful tale of Charles E. Drumgold spoke of a hobo gone mad for lost love. On his very first railroad trip, Drumgold "misplaced" his wife and children. Irreparably crazed, he set out on foot from El Paso in search of his family. Every railroad man from El Paso to Colton, California, knew Drumgold as "Desert Charlie." The *Citizen* reported that he wore "scant clothing...tattered and torn, his shirt sleeves in shreds leaving his arms to bake and blister in the desert sun."

Desert Charlie plodded his love-lost heart back and forth across the desolate southern Arizona and California deserts, refusing always to ride the trains that raced beside him. A small amount of money from his well-heeled brother, a San Francisco jeweler, fueled the tireless quest. As he moved, Charlie asked rails along the

The railroad kids of Barrio Millville had nothing to fear when hobos frequented their neighborhood. The gang gathered at the home of locomotive engineer James B. Sheffield for this mid-1920s photo. (l-r)(1) future division timekeeper Elgin Ball, (2) Perelis Wallmark, (3)Eva Mae Sheffield, (4) Genola McGuffin, (5) Myrtle Hopkins, (6) Bernice Keeling, (7) and (8) unidentified, (9) Jimmy Sheffield, (10) Henry L. "Bill" Sheffield, (11) Elizabeth Granger, (12) Zona Kleinhenz, (13) Esther Sheffield, (14) Hannah Wallmark, and future Pima County Sports Hall of Fame member (15) Buddy Granger. (Elgin Ball Collection)

way for tidings of his loved ones. The "kind-hearted knights of the rail passed the word on from one to another to look out for him," noted the *Star*. "The decrepit, demented old man imagines he is paid to watch the railroad track and prevent wrecks." On occasion, brakemen and other rails slipped him a little money, which he accepted as part of his "salary." In January 1908, Drumgold's brother placed the beloved desert drifter into a private asylum. Shortly afterwards, reports of Desert Charlie's death circulated on the Tucson Division. Rails mourned his passing, sure that "another strange waif of the desert had passed into history."

Yuma rail Jack Heyl threatened to "throw a fit and swear that he would change his brand" when he saw Desert Charlie crawl out from under a freight car the following year. Debunking stories of his rumored demise, Charlie jumped to his feet and shook the startled Heyl's hand "as if he had never been reported dead and buried for lo, these many days," reported the *Star*. Good news for the SP, because in the millions of steps and countless miles that he trod through the years, Desert Charlie came upon many potential rail accidents. Designating himself a trackwalker for the SP, Charlie saved "the Southern Pacific thousands of dollars through his news of washouts, obstructions, etc.," said the newspaper.

Under the title "Pestiferous American Hobo in Old Mexico" the *Star* explained a unique tequila phenomenon in May 1909: "A Mexican can handle tequila to a mild extent. It has cost centuries of application and constant practice to bring him to this state of perfection, but an American, never! Each ounce is guaranteed to contain six disputes, three fights, two headaches, and a jail sentence. Pulque when distilled is known as mescal. A whiskey glass of this dynamite and the tramp wants to go out to the bull ring and show the toreros some new stunts; two of them and he starts to remodel Don Porfirio's government; three and he'll head a revolutionary party for Central America; and four, the finish, lands him in the *comisaria* [jai]."

Circuses often brought a rough bunch of hobos into Tucson. "Dips" cruised the crowd and "lifted" pocketbooks. The "hold-up man" waited in the city's outlying areas to accost people as they came and went from the circus, while burglars preyed on their homes as they enjoyed the performance. Though the SP resented hauling circus troupes because government officials forced the company to transport them at low rates, such ensembles delighted entertainment-starved Tucsonans.

The city's population almost doubled when a well-known troupe came into town during September 1910. Circus trains held priority over passenger trains, so No. 2 waited at the Sixth Avenue switch until flat cars carrying circus horses and wagons passed. Schools closed and local students joined several hundred gawkers to watch the great circus unload. Soon, the train's second section arrived, bringing acrobats and other entertainers.

Men erected large tents on the regular circus grounds near Third Avenue south of the roundhouse as other workers prepared for the spectacular parade of circus delights that preceded all shows. With youngsters skipping along beside, the pageant strutted west from the railroad grounds on Fifteenth Street to Main Avenue, then, north to Congress Street, before returning east to the SP reserve. The parade was filled with "a multitude of horses and wild animals" and "a small army of pets dressed like farmers, bands, good herds of elephants and camels and at the end the inevitable calliope," smiled the *Citizen*. Concerned police chief Frank Murphy ordered his officers to arrest "all suspicious characters who cannot give accounts of themselves." The chief asked residents to lock their doors, unheard of in Tucson until the 1960s, and call the police upon seeing "dangerous looking or acting individuals."

Hobos slept near towns, out of reach of the law in hobo jungles, panhandling, trapping game, and working in exchange for food. While some "swiped" their meals, many found help among Tucson's working class. Families fed hungry men in exchange for a bit of labor, or from the kindness of their heart. Carl A. Ball Jr. grew up in Barrio Millville, along south Park Avenue near the tracks. The dynamic former SP vice president of labor relations remembered: "It was a completely different feeling toward hobos, back then. They'd come off the trains and sleep near the railroad. In the morning, they'd wake up and walk around our neighborhood's dusty streets looking to cut some weeds, stack some wood, or do some other job.

"These men were not like the ones that you see today," declared Ball in April 2002. "These guys were real hobos, headed for San Francisco, or Los Angeles, or Bakersfield. The attitude of the residents in Millville was, 'Feed 'em!' My mother would usually find something for them to do and then make them a couple of sandwiches, fry a couple of eggs, or give them some stew. They'd never come into the house, always sitting in the yard to eat. Then, they'd slowly move on. I never recall one hobo causing any trouble."

SP police set a record on the Tucson Division in September 1921, arresting

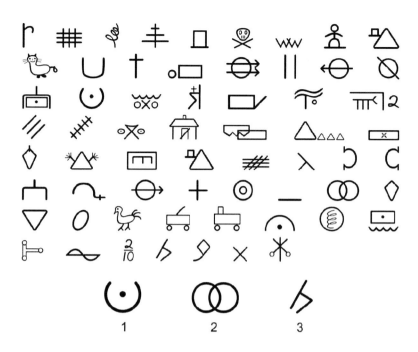

1   2   3

Hobos employed an elaborate sign language to let their brethren know the score in each town along the division. Chalked messages on fences, walls, or water tanks indicated houses and businesses where a hobo might find an 'easy touch' for a meal or a day's work. Sign number 1, for example, signified that the neighborhood was not hostile and sign number 2 alerted 'bos to watch out for unfriendly police. All the smart "rail royalty" hurried out of town when they saw sign number 3, sure of hostility toward their crowd. (created with Tech-M Hobo Symbols font)

3,373 tramps. Bowie led the way with 1,280 apprehended, followed by Lordsburg with 596, Yuma with 541, and Gila Bend with 477. Officers made only 10 percent of their arrests in the Old Pueblo because Tucson's chain gang had become a "bugaboo" in hoboland. SP Chief of Police Joe Kelly explained that bums usually "dropped off" the train before they reached the Tucson rail yard and walked around the city before rejoining the line outside of town.

Hobos rode the "blind baggage," between the locomotive tender and baggage car, on the "rods" underneath freight cars, or on the "bumpers" or open tops of passenger trains. Following World War I, the practice of 'bos separating cars by stepping on the patented uncoupling device between them became a common rail danger. "The rider of the brake beam is a menace to the

safety of others," screamed the *Citizen* in the fall of 1921. "He is an expense to the railroad and to the communities along the road." The county generally picked up the expense of any injuries that resulted because of an accident.

By Thanksgiving 1921, more than fifty hobos jumped to the ground in Tucson each day. Tucson police chief Dallas Ford announced a "novel" campaign to rid the city of wandering willies. To help curb petty theft and robbery in the city, police began rounding up and arresting local bums. Tramps who could give no logical reason for being in the city or show visible means of support had twenty minutes to clear the city limits or face assignment to the chain gang. The *Star* stated that such a campaign would be successful in ridding the city of its "floating population" because "news of such municipal action travels fast in the jungles and soon tramps and hobos throughout the entire country will know that Tucson police are not to be imposed upon."

Geraldine "Maudie" Hammonds Mackaben grew up in the SP "barracks" at the corner of Sixteenth Street and Second Avenue. Her father, Albert Hammonds, worked as roundhouse foreman, just north of the duplex-type housing. Maudie recalled that the drifting men of the road played a regular part in everyday life during her childhood years. "There was a sizeable hobo camp between the company housing and the railroad tracks," she said.

"I always rode my bicycle right though their camp on the way to school and again on the way home. We never thought twice about it, no one ever bothered us or said an ugly word to us. Mostly, they seemed like nice fellows who had just had a run of bad luck. My friend, Emily Rinkleib Bradley, the daughter of former engineer Bernard Rinkleib, says she remembers that hobos marked X on the outside of our gate to signify where they could get a meal."

While most hobos maintained friendly relations with the public, SP bulls sometimes faced violent attack. Special Officer Robert E. Echols found trouble at the Pacific Fruit Express near Broadway Bou-

Tucson educator Geraldine "Maudie" Hammonds Mackaben shows off Bud DeSpain's pedal-car in the yard at SP housing on the northeast corner of Sixteenth Street and Second Avenue during 1928. Maudie grew up riding her bicycle to school through the large "hobo jungle" near Sixteenth Street and Park Avenue without trepidation. (Albert and Maude Hammonds Collection)

levard during July 1934. When Echols ordered five hobos loitering near the plant to leave, the quintet pulled knives and jumped him. In the melee, one transient hurled a brick, striking the policeman in the head and knocking him to the ground. Captured later by Tucson police, one "plenty tough" hobo declared, "It's a good thing I haven't got a machine gun or I'd cut you birds down."

George A. Bays, former division superintendent, recalled one hobo who earned a place of honor among the railroad's free riders. Pulling out of San Carlos, Arizona, one day, Bays's secretary discovered a huge Apache man riding on the observation platform of the private car, "Tucson." After explaining that he was headed for a beer bust in Globe, the gentle native giant amused the rail leader with a litany of reservation jokes. Bays deemed the fellow "the only hobo who ever hitched a ride on the railroad superintendent's private car."

Hobo Joe Bentley earned a place in the division's hall of fame through his heroic actions after the 1946 explosion of engine No. 5037 near Bosque, about ten miles east of Gila Bend. From the diesel helper engine, added to increase power uphill to Estrella, brakeman Ted B. Holaway credited Gila Bend drugstore owner Jimmy Nash with saving his life. Nash deflected the praise to Bentley, who had raced forward from about twenty cars behind the blast to pull fireman Frank X. Bouglas from the diesel engine's cab. Hobo Joe used his own blankets to wrap Bouglas, then rushed to lend aid to Holaway and J.E. Rhoades, the other diesel engineman.

The names and faces of the rail lines' eccentric and exotic characters changed through the years, but their collective mystique endured. Eighty-one-year-old SP switchman and rail photographer Sid Showalter began on the division in 1951 and recalled: "There were always lots of hobos. You'd see 'em goin' west and a few days later you'd see 'em goin' the other way.

Hobo Joe Bentley's heroism earned him belated praise when locomotive No. 5037 exploded in 1946. Curious rails examined the terrible wreckage near Bosque siding. (Jason Burke in T. Herman Blythe Collection)

We had a hobo that hung around the railroad named Maxwell, but everybody called him 'Sundown.' He was an honest-to-goodness, real hobo. Sundown was not a very big man but a friendly guy. He had been educated and spoke real well, but he had an alcohol problem. When he ran out of money, he'd ask a switchman for 50¢ and tell ya right out that it was for a bottle of wine. I'd give him 50¢ and wouldn't see him again for three weeks and when he saw me he'd come over and pay me. Sundown got me for 50¢, though, and died owin' it to me."

The number of authentic hobos dwindled as the steam era came to a close, but a non-paying rail ride remained a prized commodity for old-timers. "In my day," Showalter said, "You'd see 'J.B. King, Esq.' written on the side of cars quite often. It was not uncommon to see it four or five times a week on different cars. We had no idea where he lived or even if he was a real person or not. Sometimes it looked like guys tried to imitate him."

Showalter photographed a Hobo Honor Roll while switching cars one day. Inscribed in chalk on the side of an aging caboose by renowned hobo historian "Hood River Blackie," the makeshift ledger spoke of hundreds of years riding brakebeams. Blackie recorded the demise of hobos like Maricopa Red, Fat Oscar, and Sheepherder

Charlie; and listed "real" hobos left on the road like Slow Motion Shorty, Cotton Harry, and Main Line John. "Probably the most brilliant hobo I ever knew was Ralph Gooding whose road name was 'Hood River Blackie,'" said Steam Train Graham. "He started on the rails at age fourteen after his stepfather angrily hurled a pitchfork at him. Blackie was tested at a university and found to possess an IQ of 146, a near genius. Along the road, he collected 610 hobo biographies and published some in a book, *The Passing of the Hobo*."

Tucsonan Francisco "Frank" Mendez's grandfather, Robert Frazier, chased down hobos as a city constable for several years around the turn of the century. Frank grew up near the Tucson rail

History lover and former SP switchman Sid Showalter built a superb collection of date nails used by the SP to record the laying of new ties, along with rail photographs and vivid memories of his days on the SP in Tucson. (Kalt Collection)

Remember These old Time Hoboes Who are gone now
Bughouse McCann - Died in "62" in Idaho age 74
old Joe Bennett - Run over by train in "64" Everette Wash. age 71
Amboy Fats - heart attack in jungle at Butte. age 17 in 55
Fat Oscar - Died in his sleep July "73" - Yakima age 76
Tex Medders - Died of cancer "67" Weimar Calif. age 77
Maricopa Red - vanished - his fate is unknown
Montana Blackie - Run over by train - Wenatchee "73" age 62
Sheepherder Charly - Died in oroville Cal from gas stove 1969 - age 64
Austrian Mike - Died of pneumonia at Reno 1954 age 70
Frank Sherrock - fell dead id ogwood Calif 1969 age 80
Panama Kid - Died of stroke yub City 1968 age 85
Whitey Olson - Died in Rest home at Wenatchee "70" age 73
These men were my good Friends.   Hood River Blackie the hobo Historian

"Hood River Blackie," Ralph Gooding, recorded the history of some "classic hobos" on the side of this boxcar in 1979. Blackie got his name because he once picked apples and pears in Hood River, Oregon and sported a full head of coal-black hair. Gooding died at age 59 in 1984. (Sid Showalter Collection)

Hobos still on the Road.
Oklahoma Fats   Palisade Joe
Cotton Henry   Texas Jack
Whistling Jack   Montana Red
Tanker Whitey   Big Town Gorman
Big Red   Slow Motion Shorty
Florida Slim   there are only about
Radio Jake   50 real Hoboes Left
Overcoat Dan   in America.
Denver George   See them at The
Main Line John   Hobo Convention in Brit
Steam Train Graham   Iowa Aug 10 1974
Green Curley
Hood River Blackie The Hobo Historian 34 yrs on the road
See my Life Story in Harpers Magazine Soon. also a film about me will be made in april by me & Sunya Film Corp.

Along with those who passed beyond, Hood River Blackie listed hobos still on the road. From attire, to custom, and code of honor; men lived countless hobo manifestations, each bearing a colorful moniker that told of their individual story. (Sid Showalter Collection)

yard in Barrio San Antonio. Near the end of June 2002, in his comfortable midtown home, Mendez reminisced about those bygone days. "The hobos would work for a sandwich, a *burrito de frijoles*, whatever," Frank recalled. "You'd see 'em every day. People would sleep with their doors wide open or sleep outside and not have a worry at all. It was an altogether different Tucson then, really. You felt safe any place you went. I used to walk through the long Broadway subway and never worried. There were hobos and tramps there to get out of the weather, but they wouldn't bother you."

In the local rail yard, the sand house held sand for cleaning engines' flues and for applying to the rails for increased traction. Former roundhouse foreman T. Herman Blythe recalled: "The sand house had steam pipes runnin' through it to keep the sand dry. It was always hot, and in the winter, there'd always be five or six hobos layin' around on the sand to stay warm. That's where they slept."

Eccentricity and creativity proved Tucson's strong suit during the age of steam. From the odd to the brilliant, quirkiness found a home on the Tucson Division. As the era faded, conductors M.R. "Mack" McCann and Harold Wallace continued the tradition of distinctive expression among Tucson rails. The ingenious wordsmiths penned poetry that brought to life the people and the work on the division. In unique style, each spun a tale, described a funny situation, or executed a pinpoint jab at another rail's most glaring foible. With the help of talented artist and local engineer Dale Romero, the free-spirited Wallace left every rail wondering if he'd be the next victim of his "poison pen."

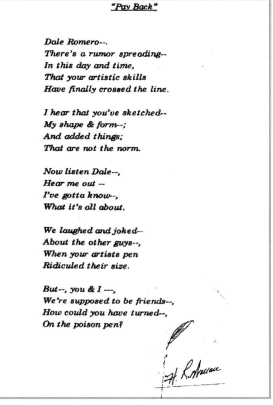

"Pay Back"

Dale Romero--.
There's a rumor spreading--
In this day and time,
That your artistic skills
Have finally crossed the line.

I hear that you've sketched--
My shape & form--;
And added things;
That are not the norm.

Now listen Dale--,
Hear me out --
I've gotta know--,
What it's all about.

We laughed and joked--
About the other guys--,
When your artists pen
Ridiculed their size.

But--, you & I ---,
We're supposed to be friends--,
How could you have turned--,
On the poison pen?

(Poem by Harold Wallace)

One trick fooled them all. For, everywhere Harold Wallace went, "someone" placed rocks atop fence posts all along the division. Though none could say for sure who made the magic, Engineer/artist Dale Romero remembered, "One ol' conductor climbed down onto his knees to look under a moving train and catch Harold, but even he had no luck!"

Wrote Wallace,

"One thing puzzles
Me the most:
Countless rocks
On the old fence posts...

Rumors abound-
Speculation is rife,
The stacker of rocks
Leads a double life.

It may never be known
Who placed those rocks on high-
An even greater mystery
is: Why?

Chapter 6

Colonel Epes Randolph: Dynamic Railroad Man of the Southwest

Where in the world was the Colonel? Many Tucsonans had noticed his private car, the Pocahontas, in the local rail yard throughout the day, but Colonel Epes Randolph was nowhere to be found! The city's Cinco de Mayo committee gathered on May 10, 1910 to present him with a silver "loving cup," as a gesture of appreciation for personally influencing the Southern Pacific Railroad (SP) to complete its Twin Buttes line through Calabasas to Nogales.

Befitting his style, Randolph "harmlessly hoodwinked" the committee's efforts, leaving the shiny silver cup sadly wanting. The *Star* reported that despite being overheard to mumble something about a "hasty trip to California... every day Colonel Randolph had been visible on the streets." Friends called him "afraid of that ceremonial" and "shy of facing that committee and being addressed in eulogisms."

Finally cornered in his office two weeks later, Randolph accepted the silver cup as "evidence of the goodwill of the community... [and] because of his energies in the up-building and in fostering the indus-

"History, Carlyle said, is the biography of great men. The history of the southwest is the story of its great men—those staunch, far-visioned, intrepid men that blazed the trail of Western Progress. Such a man was Epes Randolph—a Randolph worthy of the Randolphs."

Arizona Daily Star, *August 24, 1921.*
(Photo:Imperial Valley Irrigation District)

tries of the community [Tucson]." This conspicuous display of self-effacing modesty belied Epes Randolph's stature and importance. As the nineteenth century became the twentieth, few men could claim wider admiration in Arizona and throughout the West than the stylish railroad man and capitalist. Possessed of astounding foresight and vision, exceeded only by his drive and ability, Randolph accomplished great feats in the face of often incapacitating illness. Buried beneath time's passage and the state's growth, Randolph's legacy endures almost a century later.

Born to William Eston Randolph and Sarah Lavinia Epes on August 16, 1856, young Epes called Lunenburg County, Virginia, home. Randolph completed his public school and technical education at eastern institutes and began his railroad career on the Alabama Great Southern Railroad at the age of twenty. He soon joined Collis P. Huntington's Chesapeake & Ohio rail system. Over the next decade, Epes worked in rail construction and maintenance, securing the dynamic rail

baron's trust. In 1885, Randolph took over as chief engineer on his Kentucky Central Railroad.

Huntington held his young Virginian in remarkable esteem. Once, when he overheard an underling grousing, Huntington whirled on the unsuspecting whiner and snapped, "I understand you mean that I object to these things while I wink at my pet, Epes Randolph, playing poker. Now, when you can do as big work as Epes Randolph, you may play poker, too."

Epes took to his rail and engineering endeavors with a special vigor. He also took to Eleanor "Ellie" Taylor, ten years his junior, and made her his bride in January 1886. The following year, Huntington named the thirty-one-year-old Randolph

The C&O Bridge (under construction in this photograph) spanned the Ohio River between Covington, Kentucky, and Cincinnati, Ohio. C.P. Huntington admitted to Randolph, "It is true that I did at one time say to you through Mr. H.E. Huntington that I would turn over my Kentucky and Ohio bridge charter to you." When Randolph failed to accept the offer promptly, the senior Huntington presumed it refused. (Cincinnati Museum-Historical Society Library)

his chief engineer of construction for the C. & O. Bridge over the Ohio River between Covington, Kentucky, and Cincinnati, Ohio. The ambitious project created the longest center span and most expensive bridge, per foot, in the world at the time.

As work began on the $5 million bridge project, Collis wrote to his nephew, H.E. "Edwards" Huntington, "If the question should arise, let it be distinctly understood that Epes Randolph is the chief engineer of the Bridge and that it is to be constructed under his supervision and inspection." One of Huntington's cadre of bright, talented lieutenants that included his nephew Edwards, William F. Herrin, Julius Kruttschnitt, and William Sproule, Randolph jumped to task. Despite profound confidence in his young project manager, the railroad magnate reminded Epes of the bridge project's importance, through company treasurer E.G. John: "As you know, much depends on your own care and vigilance and we are relying largely upon your discretion and ability. Keep the work well in hand and crowd it all that can possibly be done to advance it."

After Ohio River floods destroyed it, Randolph's rapid reconstruction of Cincinnati's C & O Bridge earned him national acclaim. Never an "employee," the brilliant engineer maintained a semi-autonomous relationship with rail industry kingpins. (Cincinnati Museum-Historical Society Library)

Begrudging with plaudits, the elder Huntington extended Randolph high praise in early August 1888. "You have done well, and I suggest that you never tire in well doing," wrote the autocratic rail head. Later that same month, raging Ohio River floodwaters ripped away the bridge's falsework, or temporary construction frame, and destroyed its "traveler," the rolling crane used during building. The devastating collapse of his special project spurred chief engineer Randolph to "press the work" even harder. George Lewis, another Huntington leader, later recalled: "New timber was obtained, the false work and traveler rebuilt, seven hundred thousand pounds of the floor system re-rolled, and the Channel Span swung [ready for business] twenty-six days after the wash out. This was a noteworthy achievement, and greatly to the credit of Mr. Randolph and his organization." Edwards Huntington recalled that Randolph, "his swarthy complexion aglow," sat among the dignitaries of the first train to cross the C. & O. Bridge on Christmas Day 1888.

His reputation established, Epes conducted business as an independent financier, contractor, and engineering consultant. Utilizing his civil engineering skills and business acumen, he solicited contracts from the elder Huntington and other bridge-building concerns. In 1891, backed by "strong Cincinnati parties," Randolph successfully bid to do the masonry and earthwork on the approaches to "old man" Huntington's bridge at Evansville, Indiana. "If the parties are strong, the bridge bonds will be as good or better than money, after the bridge is built," concluded Huntington. The next year Randolph undertook construction of the Licking River Bridge linking Newport and Covington, Kentucky. Shortly before eleven o'clock on the morning of June 16, 1892, the bridge collapsed, killing twenty-five workmen. Investigation revealed that the building contractor, and not Randolph, had neglected warnings regarding the perilous state of its false work. Later reports indicated that Randolph severely and permanently damaged his lungs after diving under heavy pressure constructing the C&O Bridge. In light of its timing, it is more likely that, if he sustained an injury, it occurred during the Licking River Bridge tragedy.

This poor quality image captured a young Epes Randolph. (Kalt Collection)

That Randolph contracted tuberculosis seems more likely. During 1894, vicious pulmonary hemorrhages wracked Randolph's bedridden body. The bleeding came when it wished, driving Epes to his knees. His only chance of surviving the insidious lung condition lay in his removal to a dry climate. Driven to work through his infirmity, Randolph continued to consult on several bridge projects in both the United States and Mexico from his sickbed. Collis Huntington assured him that any position in his vast system, where the climate fit Randolph's needs, would be his. When he was well enough to travel, Epes and Ellie made for the West's healing, desiccated atmosphere. The couple went first to Indio, California where Epes had to be carried off the train on a stretcher. It soon became clear that the California desert town did not feel right. Randolph next accepted the superintendent's job on Huntington's Aransas Pass line in San Antonio, Texas.

Things took a strange twist in that historic town when Randolph met furious resistance upon his arrival. Word of his relationship with Collis P. Huntington had run the line ahead of him. Randolph confided to his amigo, Edwards Huntington, that local officials "feared having a man in their midst who shared such close ties" to the famous rail chief. "They will not have, if they can prevent it, one who owes his first allegiance to Mr. Huntington," he explained. "They do not want a man here with modern and conservative ideas [or] anything that would bring the Atlantic and the Pacific systems (of the SP) together." Edwards would be "astonished and disgusted" at the "undignified and childish" manner in which the men in San Antonio "gave vent" to their feelings, Randolph declared. Accustomed to respect and acceptance by those he worked with, Randolph pleaded, "It surely could not be anything that I have done as these men do not know me."

Recognizing the futility of winning over the men of the San Antonio force, Randolph opted to explore the rail superintendent's job in Tucson. The fit proved perfect, and on September 1, 1895, he took over the Tucson and Yuma divisions of the Southern Pacific of Arizona and New Mexico Railroad. Epes and Ellie Randolph would grow to love Tucson mightily.

His friend, community pillar Mose Drachman, explained, "It [living in the desert] enabled him to live twenty-five [more] years of crowded, glorious life." The love affair was mutual as Tucsonans quickly warmed to the thirty-nine-year-old southerner. As his health improved, Randolph gathered around him a group of loyal and impressive friends. Drachman recalled: "There was some quality in the man which made one long to serve him in some way. He was a wonderfully fascinating, attractive, magnetic gentleman." Arizona governor Myron H. McCord named Randolph paymaster general of the Arizona militia, with the rank of colonel, on August 27, 1897. Thereafter, local newspapers often referred to him as "the Colonel" and he soon developed political wallop without equal.

As local SP superintendent, Randolph controlled free passes on the only

H.E. "Edwards" Huntington and Epes Randolph forged a friendship that endured for more than three decades. Through their years together, Edwards came to rely on Randolph for solid engineering and business decisions and the two became fast friends. The friendship between the two rail wizards transcended business, however.

Frequent combatants around a game of rummy, Randolph teased his pal, "Dearest Eduardo," when he finally learned some new card tricks. "Your old ones, had long ago become so thin that a blind man could easily see thorough them," needled Epes. "In all modesty, I confess right here [the old tricks are] the reason why I always beat you."

As Edwards Huntington prepared to marry his uncle Collis's former wife, Arabella, in Paris during July 1913, Epes Randolph wrote the happy couple: "I'll be on hand to bid God's speed and au revoir to the sweetest lady friend in all the wide world and the best and dearest old chum [barring R.U.M.] of my life. I know my dear; your life is now one ceaseless song of happiness. I unite you both in one loving embrace of sincerest friendship. Ever your same 'old sport', Randolph."

Randolph took a fatherly interest in Edwards' son from his first marriage, Howard E. Huntington, while directing the young man's internship in the engineering department at Tucson. Howard re-joined his mentor in southern California after completing his Harvard education in 1903. Randolph told the Los Angeles Examiner, "I have had my eye on Howard a long time for he is a strong man and I want him to work for me here."

When his friend died before him, Edwards Huntington wrote, "I was terribly grieved by Randolph's death and never knew how much I loved him until he passed away." Huntington built a fabulous collection of art and literature, founding the Huntington Library, Art Gallery, and Botanical Gardens on August 30,1919. Today, the breathtaking facility accepts researching scholars and tourists in San Marino, California. (Imperial Valley Irrigation District)

rail line in and out of Tucson. In addition, he had the resources and connections necessary to jump forthwith into the region's most substantial business deals. Using the pulpit of the press and his secretive "personal counsel," Randolph held sway over bankers, investors, politicians, and the general public. General Levi H. Manning, Randolph, and Eugene S. Ives formed one of Tucson's most dynamic triads. Years after their passing, Judge Gerald Jones recalled that the three were "pioneer prophets" and "oracles of the desert...daring, distinguished men—all, willing to take a chance." Of the three, Jones remembered being most in awe of Randolph. "He was courteous, like a colonel from Virginia," said Jones. "I remember him as a very dignified, handsome and impressive man. He was a fine Southern gentleman and took a great deal of pride in the fact that he was a descendant of Pocahontas. When I first arrived in Tucson, Randolph was the 'man about town.'"

Levi H. Manning (left) and his wife, Gussie, enjoy a peaceful moment in the lush garden behind their mansion west of Main Avenue on El Paseo Redondo. Manning, Randolph, and Eugene S. Ives formed a formidable Tucson trio during the early twentieth century. (Lovell Gunter Welsh Collection)

The Colonel found great challenges in Arizona. In 1895, Frank M. Murphy, backed by money from the "Diamond Joe" Reynolds estate, built a line south from the Santa Fe Railroad at Ash Fork into Phoenix. Randolph recognized trouble when citizens of the capital city raised $5,000 to extend the rails south from Phoenix. He convinced Collis Huntington that a competitor's railroad slicing directly through the center of Arizona to the tidewater seaport of Guaymas, Sonora, posed a serious threat to Southern Pacific commercial dominance. To block such a line, the SP granted rights to the Santa Fe over its Tehachapi Loop line in southern California during July 1898. In exchange, the SP took control of the "burro," New Mexico & Arizona Railroad's winding line with heavy grades between Benson and Nogales, and the Sonoran road to Guaymas. Randolph soon changed the order of business in southern Arizona, by running passenger trains all the way through into Tucson. "Before that, all passengers to the territory from Sonora had to stop over in Benson," remembered Drachman. "Sonora began to open up in a business way with the result that the road began to pay. This was a great benefit to Tucson."

Randolph invested heavily in the business of the region and began speaking out on public issues. In March 1898, he exposed his politics and a bit of his personal style. When the question of Tucson's water system arose, Randolph proclaimed: "I don't think there is any better way to discuss questions of public policy than in the press. Let the people know what is going on. If you throw light on subjects and give taxpayers a chance, they are very apt to reach sound conclusions. Every man can get his paper, read what is said and form his own conclusions. When you get a lot of people together in a hall, one or two men will do all the talking and some eloquent attorney, working for a fee, is very apt to out talk a dozen men who make their living by the sweat of their brow rather than by the wag of the tongues."

With gray-blue eyes, a mustache, and his hair parted in the middle, Randolph enjoyed a "boiled shirt and starched collar" reputation. A prominent nose and sharp cheekbones reflected his Native American bloodlines. Randolph learned the Spanish language and the hard truths of living in his adopted desert homeland. In his *Reminiscences*, former city councilman and Arbuckle Coffee salesman Mose Drachman recalled that Randolph possessed a "keen sense of humor and delighted in telling ridiculous incidents and anecdotes." One of the Colonel's favorite stories involved the death of a leading Tucson politician for whom he held little fondness. The man's widow felt obliged to inform Randolph of her husband's death, but delivery of her collect telegram required a series of horsemen traveling deep into Mexico, far from civilization. "The cost was $50!" recalled Drachman. "He used to say to me, with a twinkle in his eye, 'You know, Mose, I wasn't that glad!'"

Collis P. Huntington died August 13, 1900, and the railroad worlds of Edwards Huntington and Epes Randolph split wide open. Through their years together, Edwards had come to rely on Randolph for solid engineering and business decisions, and the two had become fast friends. Both men assumed that when Collis died, Edwards would ascend to the SP presidency and, then vault Randolph into one of the company's highest positions. Asked earlier who would succeed him, the senior Huntington assured reporters: "Why, there is Ed [Edwards Huntington]. No better boy ever lived. He's been with me twenty-eight years and knows a thing or two about railroads. I'll trust him."

New York moneyed interests took control of the SP, however, and named their own president. Edward H. Harriman soon bought almost $40 million in SP stock and seized command of the railroad. Shaking off his disappointment, Edwards Huntington made for California and bade his amigo and trusted civil engineer join him. Epes Randolph resigned as superintendent of the SP Tucson Division effective January 1, 1902 and joined Edwards in building the Los Angeles Inter-Urban Railway and the Pacific Electric Railway systems.

Huntington formed a syndicate with banker I.W. Hellman and moved swiftly to control the electric streetcar business in the Los Angeles basin. SP head Harriman had designs on the same commercial plum, however, and a war of moguls blazed. "Randolph was happy; he certainly liked to fight," remembered Drachman. "He spent tremendous sums of money on [furthering] the enterprise." One day, Hellman approached Randolph at the famous California Club, asking if he knew that his account at the bank was $150,000 overdrawn. "Oh, Mr. Hellman, you are mistaken," Randolph answered. "According to my books it's $350,000!"

By 1904, Huntington and his general manager, vice-president, and cartographer Randolph had located and built almost seven hundred miles of electric rail lines in and around Los Angeles. His hand-drawn map of the company's Southern Division lines demonstrated keen appreciation of the area's topography and far-sighted vision of its future population centers and remains in existence today. "Randolph contributed as much as any man to the phenomenal growth of Los An-

Oneonta Park in Pasadena honors Edwards Huntington's birthplace of Oneonta, New York. Electric railway officials named the southern California village of Randolph in tribute to Epes in 1903. The town struggled when water and a streetcar right-of-way proved difficult to obtain. George E. Pillsbury, W.J. Hole, and Tucson's colonel planned mansions in the area but built nothing. In 1911, the towns of Randolph and Olinda consolidated into Brea, California. (Charles Wherry collection)

This postcard depicts Congress Street during the early 1900s. Colonel Randolph set up headquarters in the Cameron Block, on the northwest corner of Broadway and Stone Avenue, when he returned in May 1904, and hired Charles E. Walker as his personal secretary. (UASC)

"Mesopotamian Monarch" E.H Harriman amassed an incredible fortune through his "Associated" rail lines. The demanding rail ruler also founded and sustained the Boys Club of America, and funded a major scientific exploration of Alaska. (Imperial Valley Irrigation District)

geles," wrote Nat McKelvey, in his July 1950 article, "The Indomitable Epes Randolph," in *Trains Magazine.*

The potent pair next hatched a plan to build an electrified streetcar line from Los Angeles to San Francisco. While Huntington went east to secure a $150 million loan, Randolph began hunting for hydroelectric power sites along the California coast. Edwards returned with guarantees of funding for the massive project, but "the bugs," as he called his brutal pulmonary bleeding, slammed Randolph to his sickbed once again. He consulted the premier pulmonary specialist in the world, who told Randolph that if he wished to prolong his life he needed to return to Tucson. Randolph returned to the desert in May 1904.

Born through grand projects, Edwards Huntington's confidence in Randolph's engineering legerdemain endured. For the rest of the Colonel's life, Huntington gave him $10,000 a year and paid for his private secretary, in exchange for consultation and advice on railroad and engineering problems. A letter from Pacific Electric General Manager and engineer J. McMillan, written five years after Randolph's departure from Los Angeles, illustrates the arrangement. "Mr. [H. E.] Huntington...did not want to authorize work...until you have personally approved those plans," McMillan informed Randolph. "I will be obliged if you will look them over at once, and if satisfactory, write in red ink somewhere on the face of the blueprint 'Approved, Epes Randolph.' As

soon as these drawings have been received back with your approval, Mr. Huntington has authorized the letting of the contract."

His disease now full-blown tuberculosis, Randolph returned to Tucson and joined E. H. Harriman's SP team. National City Bank president Frank A. Vanderlip, himself a former director of several railroads, remembered: "Out of a host of men important in Harriman's service who clamor for recognition, I find myself fixing my mind on Epes Randolph. Mr. Randolph was a grand man, one who was particularly loveable. I am sure you might find a thousand men who would be as fully aware as I of his endearing qualities."

Epes set up headquarters in the Cameron Block, in the northwest corner of Broadway and Stone Avenue, and hired Charles E. Walker as his personal secretary. Randolph turned his efforts to the SP's subsidiary rail lines in Mexico and to the melding of five separate roads into the Arizona Eastern Railroad's "Randolph Lines." Fate, however, delivered his greatest challenge during the summer of 1905.

In the deep Southwest, just below the border with Mexico, the Colorado River coursed 387 feet above the Salton Sea's ancient bed to its west. The California Development Company (CDC) seized upon this gift of nature and cut an "intake" opening in the Colorado's western bank to run water through a canal to the barren lands in California's Salton Sink. Euphemistically marketed as the "Imperial Valley," the newly tillable lands began to fill with settlers, 10,000 by 1904.

Then, "El Toro Colorado" (the Red Bull) raged! Seething floodwaters of the Colorado River burst through the intake opening in 1905, inundating a hundred thousand acres and completely submerging the New Liverpool Salt Company. Late that June, as a condition of Harriman's $200,000 loan, the CDC named Epes Randolph its president. The Colonel called upon Professor H.T. Cory to serve as his chief engineer. By mid-July, two-thirds of the Colorado River had left its channel and gushed westward into the primordial sink.

Roiling floodwaters crash and swirl through the breach in the Colorado River. (Imperial Valley Irrigation District)

As the opening in the riverbank grew, many of the nation's most renowned engineers presented ideas on how to divert the river back into its original channel. "Undaunted Promoter of the Imperial Valley" C.R. Rockwood built a piling-brush-sandbag gate across the opening that worked well for months, until it buckled and the river swept it away. When the earth shook and San Francisco burned in April of 1906, Harriman sent Randolph to the ravaged California port city to lend aid. Amid the San Francisco devastation and the ruins of SP corporate headquarters,

Randolph persuaded Harriman to forward another $250,000 toward saving the Imperial Valley from Colorado River floodwaters. "That was the really remarkable thing in a whole chain of extraordinary happenings," remembered Professor Cory. The San Francisco tragedy proved but a short-lived distraction.

That summer, floods widened the Colorado's two-hundred-yard breach into a crevasse more than a half-mile wide. A broad sheet of water stood four feet deep at Calexico, California, and adjacent Mexicali, Baja California del Norte, Mexico. Damage to the CDC's Imperial Valley water system left 30,000 cultivated acres without water and unfit to live on for a year and a half.

Over a nine-month period, the Colorado deposited four times the soil excavated during the building of the Panama Canal. "Very rarely, if ever before, has it been possible to see a geologic agency effect, in a few months, a change which usually requires centuries," engineer Cory observed.

None of the almost fifty celebrated engineers who visited the site could agree on which plan offered the greatest chance of closing the river's breach. "At one point there seemed to be accord, namely, that the situation was a desperate one and without engineering parallel," Cory recalled. Many experts believed that unless workers first laid down a mattress of brush, the silty bottom of the Colorado would swallow up everything that workmen dropped into it. With the stakes in their river battle inordinately high, Cory asked Randolph if convening a board of engineers might be advisable. "He answered [that] he would regard a hundred feet of good, strong brush mattress, in place on the river's bottom, as more valuable," Cory recalled.

When his men could find very little brush nearby, Randolph decided on building a progression of rock dams without laying the recommended brush foundation. "Practically every engineer, and they included many of established national and in-

Epes Randolph employed 600 Pima, Tohono O'odham, Maricopa, Cocopa, Yuma, and Diegueno Indians to fill the Colorado's wound. Men brought their families to a camp nearby, creating a large community during damming operations on the river.

Men survey progress on the dam in this photo taken just one week before the final sealing of the Colorado River's breach.

Workers sit like "birds on a wire" above the Colorado during 1906 flooding. (Photos: Imperial Valley Irrigation District)

ternational reputation... considered a rock barrier dam unworthy of consideration," Cory recalled. Nonetheless, by "throwing very ordinary railroad trestles across the break and...making rock filled dams in series," they sealed the rupture in early November 1906.

Unfortunately, the solution again proved temporary as the rock barriers gave way and floodwaters choked off rail traffic and threatened national commerce. President Theodore Roosevelt telegraphed Harriman, imploring him to close the river's break. "It will be a matter of such importance that I wish to repeat there is not the slightest excuse for the company (SP) waiting an hour for the action of the government," said Roosevelt. "It is their duty to meet the present danger immediately and then this government will take it up."

With losses to the railroad projected at $1 million a month, Harriman agreed to help. The SP advanced funds to the development company, and Randolph called in Tucson Division resident engineer C.K. Clarke to lead the next attack on the problematic river. In the end, Randolph's deci-

siveness won the day. When companies working on both sides of the international border to close the break began to struggle financially, Randolph furnished money for materials and supplies to the company in Mexico, as independent agent for the SP. In the United States, "the operations were exclusively under the name Epes Randolph, Agent, SP Co.," Cory recalled. During the next seven months, the Colonel handled two-thirds of all the cars of gravel used to build levees along the Colorado, receiving 42¢ per car and netting $3,867 for his trouble.

Crews dumped ton upon ton of rock into the opening, faster than the river could wash it away. The work disrupted normal operations over 1,200 miles of SP main line for fifteen days. Randolph's men completed the job, at last, on February 10, 1907, and a grateful nation shuddered in relief.

Years later, Randolph lamented assigning Professor Cory to write the history of their momentous success. His "young friend," he said, "waited so long and worked in so much technical stuff that very few people read it, and it is now ancient history."

Nelson Rhoades Jr., vice-president and manager of the Sinaloa Land Company, offered perspective on the amazing feat: "The returning of the Colorado to its channel constituted one of the most remarkable civil engineering feats of the twentieth century. And this after renowned civil engineers of the day had declared the task impossible and one or more had tried to no avail."

Through it all, a vision burned within Epes Randolph's heart. More than once, he propounded, "Give the West Coast of Mexico ten years of uninterrupted peace and development, tapped by a railway that will give it means of sending its products out, and in that time it will prove richer than Southern California." A man of action, Randolph began sending crews of engineers down the Mexican coast to collect preliminary data for selecting the optimum route. With Harriman's backing, and Mexican permission to proceed, construction of company headquarters and extensive shops in Empalme, Sonora, began in 1905.

The *Ferrocarril del Sud-Pacífico de México* (Southern Pacific of Mexico) incorporated in June 1909. From its inception, the company faced incredible obstacles. Construction crews pushed their way through some of the roughest country in the Northern Hemisphere. With the outbreak of the Mexican Revolution in 1910, workers dodged bullets and bridge trestles burned, seventy-five torched during one month alone, and building stopped in 1912. During the next twelve years of the Mexican civil war, the railroad ran for only five months on the eight hundred kilometers between Guaymas and Tepic.

At the same time, Randolph coordinated the operations of Arizona's railroads serving Phoenix, Globe, Bowie, Cochise, and the Salt River Valley, the Harriman lines. Known locally as the "Randolph lines," the companies consolidated into the Arizona Eastern Railroad in 1910. *The Legislative Blue Book of Arizona* noted in 1913 that Randolph "took charge of several small

roads which might have been termed 'tracks of rust' with poor equipment and merged them under one head as subsidiary lines of the Southern Pacific company and brought them to a high state of efficiency."

Workers filled refrigerator cars at the Empalme ice deck during the mid-1920s. (Stanley M. Houston Collection)

Bright white uniforms and large ice tongs festoon this Empalme ice house crew during the mid-1920s. (Stanley M. Houston Collection)

Women carry water to outfit cars, a part of daily life on construction crews. (Stanley M. Houston Collection)

SP de Mexico's *engine house at Empalme. (Stanley M. Houston Collection)*

The SP de Mexico spent more than $1.5 million on its concrete and steel facilities in Empalme. (Stanley M. Houston Collection)

SP's venture into Mexico proved tumultuous during the twentieth century's first two decades. Stanley M. Houston (human on right) later headed the SP de Mexico's locomotive power division. (Stanley M. Houston Collection)

(UASC)

Even churches suffered from the violence that wracked Mexico during its revolutionary period. (Stanley M. Houston Collection)

Stanley M. Houston (above) rose to Globe master mechanic. By the end of the steam era, Houston reigned as company assistant superintendent of motive power. Locals Charles Babers and Carl A. Ball Jr. also scaled company heights to a chair in San Francisco during their careers. (Stanley M. Houston collection)

In addition to running international railroads, Tucson's dynamo interested himself financially in several major enterprises. Randolph served as vice president of Consolidated Bank and president of Consolidated Telephone and Telegraph. He also held an interest in the Sonora Hotel and the Roadside Mine. Ever expanding his reach, Colonel Randolph joined William E. Parker and Mose Drachman in filing articles of incorporation for Tucson Realty in March 1905. The Colonel took personal interest in and maintained constant vigil over all. While maintaining his entrepreneurial whirlwind, Randolph socialized heartily. He served on the Elks Club Corporation when the Benevolent and Protective Order of Elks built its first clubhouse and as president of the Old Pueblo Club.

Word had it that during the first two decades of the twentieth century, all the first-rate mines in Arizona ought first be proposed for possible investment to Epes Randolph. Chief among them was the King of Arizona (KofA) mine, forty-five miles north of Mohawk Summit, east of Yuma. Randolph

and Ives purchased the interests of O.E. Eichelberger, who discovered gold there in 1897. After a series of acrimonious legal wrangles, the title finally resolved in favor of the Tucson pair. They engaged expert waterman H.W. Blaisdell, of Yuma County, to find water. Blaisdell soon located the liquid grace five miles south of the KofA mine. Company president Randolph ordered pipe laid across the desert floor, water flowed, and the operation took off running. Along with the Copper Queen Mine in Bisbee, the KofA mine paid the highest wage in the Territory, $3.50 per day. Two dividends paid in 1906 totaled almost $45,000, all but $6 going to the company's two principal investors, Randolph and Ives. It would become one of the largest gold mining operations in Arizona territory before it "played out" in September 1910.

Not everything Randolph touched turned to gold and he made his share of enemies. One fall, well-known mining experts Lycurgus Lindsay and Henry F. Mackay approached Randolph with a mining proposition in Mexico. The two, whose "opinion had great weight," showed him a prospectus for a fabulously rich ore body. The *Los Angeles Times* stated that some said the mine "would seriously disturb the position of gold as the great circulating medium of

Arizona Eastern's roundhouse at Globe, Arizona ca. 1920. (Stanley M. Houston Collection)

the business world." Based on the sparkling reports, Randolph bought into the mine and organized the Llanos de Oro Mining & Milling Company with Lindsay.

Within a few months, investors "of great shrewdness offered to purchase the entire operation and double stockholder's money," reported the same Los Angeles newspaper. In the glare of great expectations, Randolph's group refused the offer. One year later, the newspaper noted, "This apparently very rich mine looks, at the present time, as if it would result in an absolute failure." The biggest loser in the fiasco at $150,000, the Colonel issued a circular to shareholders saying, "Mr. Lindsay and myself are arranging to provide personally for the indebtedness in Mexico" (about $35,000). As might be expected, a series of legal battles erupted between the two, further souring the deal.

It is the nature of power that the real heavyweights, those with pervasive control, often avoid exposure and unwanted attention. Such men are vigilant in denying the weight of their influence. Their business is conducted outside the scrutiny of both the public and the press. A broker of clout on the Arizona frontier, Randolph vigorously pursued his privacy, so that the citizenry might never understand the full weight of his command.

Perhaps for this reason, Epes Randolph's personal files remain elusive.

The letters of his associates, however, provide glimpses behind this turn-of-the-century capitalist's screen of secrecy. The industrious Arizonan frequently relied on "cypher telegrams" to communicate the particulars of important transactions to his colleagues. When Randolph and attorney Ives organized the Arizona Eastern Railroad Company in 1904, confidentiality was especially crucial. Ives explained, "When this road was originally incorporated it was deemed advisable not to divulge who was back of it. For this reason Randolph was not a charter member." Ives published the required notice of incorporation at the legal deadline, telling Randolph he had delayed "in order to obscure the line's ownership. Assuming that was your intention." To further conceal their actions from competition, Frank M. and N. Oakes Murphy and the Santa Fe Railroad, the pair appointed a little-known desert health-seeker, William A. Grauten, company president.

Prior to turn-of-the-century anti-trust enforcement, monopoly was the name of the game, and all the smart folks with money played. Most markets in the burgeoning West were too small to hope for business success by claiming only a portion of the existing commerce. To ensure sufficient volume and profit, it often became necessary to corral all the trade in a particular region. The Colonel shed light on his business approach in the *El Paso Times* during October 1910: "We couldn't if we would and we wouldn't if we could, explain our position with reference to keeping additional railroads out of Tucson."

Well-schooled in the Collis P. Huntington model, Randolph pursued aggressive expansion through debt financing and reorganization of his acquisitions. Requiring a sizable floating debt at any given time, the game's success was predi-

```
Chagre a/o E.S.I.
                                    Tucson Ariz. Feby. 5,1902

Epes Randolph
          c/o Los Angeles Ry. Co.,
                    Los Angeles Calif

Enrichment New York conference with Greene arblasts Steinfeldt

Creditress dissonancy Goldschmidt ticement lumbago March first

Ballance mortgage recorded.  Will forward same.  Answer

quick.

                    E. S. Ives
```

Following C.P. Huntington's lead, Colonel Randolph and his associates used cypher telegrams to secret important details. (UASC)

Intimates of the Randolphs, Augusta "Gussie" Connell Manning (above) and Levi H. Manning often entertained in their luxurious home. During late October of 2005, Gussie Manning's granddaughter, Lovell Gunter Welsh remembered: "Mr. and Mrs. Randolph were a handsome, elderly, gray-haired couple. If they were in town at Christmas, they celebrated it with our family." After the Colonel's death, Mrs. Randolph spent many summers in the South with her family or in Paris, but always called Tucson home. "My grandmother often had Ella Randolph and her close friend Mrs. J.B. Breathitt as dinner guests, following Mr. Randolph's death. She was an elegantly dressed lady of quality and participated in many philanthropic projects." (Lovell Gunter Welsh Collection)

cated upon being in the correct location at the key moment to capitalize on one's expected gain.

In particular, Randolph understood that the Mexican government's practice of granting *concesiones* (franchises), which allowed American companies to do business in that country, lent itself to building an exclusive cartel. Randolph's association with the Pacific Smelting & Mining Company in 1910 exemplified both his covert style and

commercial strategy. Courtenay DeKalb, University of Missouri professor and internationally known mining expert, served as general manager of that company's smelting operation. Despite his position, said DeKalb, he "did not know for several years" that Randolph owned stock in the company." Nowhere within the venture's annual report could the Colonel's name be found. Yet, explained DeKalb, Randolph's $10,000 purchase of the Mexican custom smelting concession enabled the company to establish a monopoly in the port cities of Sonora. Its strategy sound, the enterprise prospered until, remembered DeKalb, the "lapse of concessions under the [Mexican] Revolutionary regime destroyed this combination and prevented the development of the enterprise as planned."

Early twentieth-century capitalists freely enjoyed serial conflicts of interest. The scrutiny of an Interstate Commerce Commission Subcommittee on Banking and Currency shone light upon the activities of such moneyed brokers in 1912, however. The committee determined that "inter-connectedness" among corporate directorships played a central role in developing a monopoly. Big money players sitting on each other's board of directors combined to create what many claimed amounted to a single financial interest. Progressive examiner Samuel Untermyer described the relationship as a "close understanding among the men who dominate the financial destinies of our country and who wield fabulous power." Committee investigators named 310 men throughout the nation who formed what they termed an "inter-locking directorate." Headed by J.P. Morgan, the list included W.K Vanderbilt, National City Bank president Frank Vanderlip, John David Rockefeller and William Rockefeller of Standard Oil, and Tucson's Epes Randolph.

Despite his position as a central power sachem in the Southwest and Mexico, Randolph viewed himself as a member of the great working class. E.J. Fenchurch, former general freight and passenger agent for the Arizona Eastern Railroad, explained: "Whatever his title, Colonel Randolph was always the idol of the rank and file. There was no trouble too small and at no time was he too busy to manifest a personal interest in their joys and sorrows. The world has seen few men like Colonel Randolph."

His philosophy and actions mirrored lessons absorbed during Randolph's years of association with Collis P. Huntington. "Labor is the basis of the arts and sciences, and civilization," the commanding rail captain once wrote. "The aristocracy of labor is my aristocracy." Randolph saw no conflict between his capitalist philosophy and his identification with the common man. Three days before his death he laid out his views in a letter to Arizona Congressman Carl Hayden. "Forty-five years I have labored," he averred. "The laboring man, whoever he may be and however he may labor, with head or hands, has my sincerest sympathies and utmost goodwill."

At the same time, the Colonel and Ellie enjoyed fineries of which working men could only dream. Tucson's transplanted southerner once remarked, "I am not in a class with you 'Nabobs,' but I like to 'trot in that class.'" Then, too, his portly friend, Eugene S. Ives, kept a constant stream of lobsters, turtles, other fine seafood, and magnums of champagne arriving at the local depot for the enjoyment of family and friends.

Randolph flashed his political fangs to Senator Hayden in his final communiqué. The railroad and mining industrialist told of baby *alacranes* (scorpions) in the desert that "immediately climb upon the body of the mother and subsist upon her until she is no more." Randolph reminded Hayden: "When Socialism first blossomed in this country, politicians imitated the baby alacrans [sic] and jumped on the Huntingtons and the [rail magnate James] Hills and sucked the life blood out of the railroads because these wicked fellows had

dared to amass fortunes. The work was quickly done but the doers forgot to stop when railroads no longer represented individual fortunes." Undeterred, Edward H. Harriman then "induced the investment of several hundred million dollars in the Southern Pacific and other western roads and thus gave to the people of this country the best transportation system the world has ever seen, and at the lowest rates for service," wrote Randolph. "His efforts caused this country to prosper as it had never prospered before."

Many a grand scheme had issued forth from Epes Randolph's fruitful mind through the years. But he had one more goal for the people of Arizona, and for himself. He proposed erecting a hydroelectric dam on the Colorado River, vowing that "Arizona would have 1,000,000 more acres of fertile land under cultivation than it now has, and other enterprises would be paying one-half of the amount for electrical energy that they are now paying." Randolph and his associates perfected plans and secured the $50 million in private capital necessary to proceed. A federal power commission approved a preliminary permit to develop 2.3-million horsepower plant, but before the project could be started, the federal government instituted a conservation plan that removed all available river sites from private enterprise. Disconsolate, Randolph advised Hayden that the imaginative project had been stopped "for politics only."

Prolific Western author Edward Hungerford remembered: "If Epes Randolph had been possessed of even ordinary health he would have gone even further as a railroad builder. I used to see him sometimes in his old upstairs office in Tucson; a mere wraith of a handsome man, sitting close to an ancient wood stove, a shawl gathered around his shoulders, a man dying by inches, living and still realizing his magnificent dreams."

A fiercely competitive and complex man, Randolph surely pressed his personal financial interests and amassed significant wealth. Elected by the Arizona Board of Regents as chancellor of the University of Arizona in 1919, he played hardball in the business and political worlds. Randolph fought flooding rivers, built bridges, and ran railroads at both edges of the continent. He held tight to his vision of the future for both Mexico and the American Southwest. Drachman saw a side of Randolph that he hid from others. "He was intensely human and very charitable," Drachman recalled. "His charities cost him thousands of dollars a year and no one ever knew anything about it. I handled giving away money for him several times. He was always doing something for somebody, particularly for sick people. Being sick himself he had great sympathy for other sufferers."

Tucson mayor Gustav Hoff lamented, "Yes, Col Randolph is with us no more. No longer will he direct large enterprises, neither will he be able to offer encouraging words that he so often extended to those who came to him for help, assistance, and encouragement." (El Zariba Shrine Temple-Phoenix)

Late in the steamy summer of 1921, a pall of incredible grief descended over the Old Pueblo. One of the Southwest's most influential pioneers was dead! Some of his 200 local employees draped black crepe over the three office buildings of Randolph's Arizona Eastern Railroad, in the 200 block of east Congress Street.

The flag in front of the SP depot hung "limp, lifeless at half-mast" reported the *Tucson Daily Citizen.* As word spread beyond the city, key figures in both nations that Randolph had come to love weighed in on their loss. Mexican president Alvaro Obregón learned the doleful news sitting in a card game, while rumbling through the countryside on a train.

Stricken, Obregón ordered, "*Caballeros bajen sus naipes. Acabo de perder a mi mejor amigo.*" (Gentlemen, put down the cards. Just now, I have lost my best friend.) The following week, the *Los Angeles Times* called Randolph "The most widely loved and respected American in Mexico by *la gente fina* (gentry)."

Near the beginning of June, Epes had gone to California for five weeks to build his strength. Friends said he returned healthier, and the ardent Arizona promoter put in "full working hours" on August 22. Gustav A. Hoff remembered stepping out of the Southern Arizona Bank and Trust Company about half past nine that morning and encountering the Colonel on his way to work. "He passed the time of day and I made the statement that he must surely have enjoyed his breakfast, since I never had the pleasure of seeing him so happy before," Hoff recalled. "He answered that he never felt as fine as he did this morning."

Feeling more vigorous than usual, Epes took Ellie on a short automobile ride that evening, before returning to their apartment at the Santa Rita Hotel. Later, instead of retiring with his wife, as was his custom, Randolph sat in the living room reading the newspaper. Suddenly, shortly after ten o'clock, blood erupted from Randolph's lungs. Following a brief rebound, Tucson's "Colonel from Virginia" died at age sixty-five.

Randolph's body lay in state at the elegant Scottish Rite Temple, 160 South Scott Avenue. Hundreds of mourners trudged by the open casket to pay final respects to a special man who would walk no more among them. Two services filled the temple on the pre-burial night. "The eight o'clock ceremony of the Knights of Templar was most impressively performed," remembered Hoff. The midnight services of the Scottish Rite, the first performed in Arizona, "must ever be remembered, owing to their beautiful language and impressive lessons conveyed."

Of Randolph's fight with tuberculosis, the *Star* noted: "He played the 'lone, long game' against the disease and won. Won such a flying victory that the best years of his life came after and not before the malady attacked him." The lesson in the Colonel's life, said the paper, "is not in the extent of his influence but in the spirit that made that influence possible. It was the spirit of Robert Louis Stevenson that rose above the disease; the spirit of Daniel Boone that surmounted the obstacles set by nature; the spirit of Jim Hill which carved a mighty railroad out of a wilderness."

More than seven hundred mourners filled the Masonic temple hall on the day of Epes Randolph's funeral. Autos packed the streets solid for blocks in every direction. The city called in extra policemen to handle the crowds that overflowed into the surrounding neighborhood. Tucson pillar Roy P. Drachman remembered, "When Epes Randolph died...there was no room inside, so hundreds of us had to stand outside: his funeral was, without a doubt the largest one held in Tucson for many years."

Most businesses closed at four in the afternoon. In a dramatic show of respect, all the wheels in all the shops and on all trains of the two SP railroads which Randolph directed stopped for one minute of silence at the five o'clock funeral hour. Only Collis P. Huntington had ever been accorded such an honor in the history of American railroading. In addition, Randolph's Consolidated Telephone offices held all local and toll calls for one minute.

Eloquent tributes flowed during the brief funeral service. SP president William Sproule recalled that his long-time colleague "loved his fellow men. Anything that attracted human sympathy in a personal and practical way interested and moved him. He had the quality of attracting to him men with a sentiment that was near akin to affection. He had that quality of personal identity, which would have made him a figure beloved in any community, even though he held no place of title or designated business distinction."

University of Arizona president Rufus B. von Klein Smid spoke of Randolph's contributions to education: "In the death of Chancellor Epes Randolph the University of Arizona loses one of its very best friends. No item of the University escaped his notice and no plan of progress existed that did not claim immediately his deepest interest and concern.... He possessed the prophetic vision of John Harvard and the practical wisdom of James Burrell Angell in looking forward to the type of university which the state of Arizona would demand and the organization of which could best fulfill those demands."

To the throbbing moan of Chopin's funeral dirge, pallbearers carried Randolph's casket out the Masonic temple doors and through a "gauntlet of adulation" formed by the Blue Lodge Masons. Torpidly, as if attempting by its dilatory pace to defy the inevitable finality, the funeral procession crept toward the burial ground. In appropriate serendipity, the Chicago Limited was stopped at the Stone Avenue railroad crossing No. 1 while the cortege moved past. At the Masonic plot, lengthy graveside rites were observed and then, as "bellies lurched with angst the remains were finally interred," noted the *Star*.

"Nearly prostrate from the shock," Ellie Randolph was "bearing up well under the grief," cared for by her dearest friend, Mrs. J.B. Breathitt. To her comfort, more than one hundred telegrams poured in from both sides of the international border. Described by friends as "quiet and retiring and [one who] took no part in social organizations," Ellie survived her husband by almost twenty-eight years.

Randolph Veterans chuckled as one member lit a match during their annual photograph ca. 1940. (AHS #MS0715,f24c)

Armed with letters of introduction to ambassadors and European royalty, she traveled extensively but always kept her room at the Santa Rita Hotel, where she died in 1948.

Arizona Eastern Railroad vice president L.H. Long assumed command of the Randolph lines as Arizonans adjusted to their loss. If the citizens of Tucson had been granted their wish, the memory of Epes Randolph might never have faded. Those who had known him honored Randolph. In the week following his funeral, members of the Tucson Business and Professional Women's Club who had worked for him, paid homage to their late employer.

Mose Drachman claimed that for the rest of his earthly days, each night before going to bed, he spoke aloud to Randolph's memory, sharing the day's events or a story that would have gotten a chuckle from his buddy. "There is no question but that Randolph was one of the greatest railroad geniuses that the United States has ever produced," Drachman reflected. "Had he kept his health, the Eastern part of this country would have been enriched by his power instead of the West, as it happened."

Eighteen months after Randolph's funeral, Masonic lodge members Peter E. Howell and Eric Monthan helped open the new Epes Randolph Lodge of Free and Accepted Masons No. 32 on February 14, 1923. In 1925, the city named the public park at Alvernon Way and Broadway Boulevard in Randolph's name. Then, almost two decades after his death, sixty-five former employees of the *Ferrocarril del Sud-Pacífico de México* and the Arizona Eastern railroads gathered to honor Colonel Randolph on the anniversary of his birth, in "the culmination of a collective impulse." The nostalgic group convened on August 16, 1939 at the Tucson Country Club near the southwest corner of Broadway Boulevard and Country Club Road, to honor their erstwhile leader.

That night, his men formed the Randolph Veterans Memorial Club, electing future Tucson Title Insurance Company head J.J. O'Dowd, president. Calling Randolph "one of us, but our superior," the group gathered annually over the next dozen years to share stories of their friend. The men organized the Randolph Veterans Association, and chapters sprang up in the Los Angeles and San Francisco areas. Along with many other leaders of industry and government, Arizona governors Robert T. Jones and Dan Garvey counted themselves among the group's alumni. Oney Anderson Jr., the association's historian, delightfully summarized the feelings of the men: "All the material things wrought in Arizona and Mexico by Epes Randolph have been practically destroyed, but that faith and love which he built in the hearts of his fellow men still lives. Those destroyers have been execrated, unpitied and unsung long ago, while his memory still lives, on and on. As yet no one in Tucson has taken his place as a leader. His many acts of charity (not Alms) are known to many of us, and it would be amiss for us to boast of them for he would not want it so."

Forgotten by most Tucsonans eighty-five years after his death, the material contributions of Epes Randolph endure today. In Cincinnati, Ohio, almost 350,000 cars buzz across the Clay Wade Bailey Bridge each month using the southern pier of Randolph's original C. & O. Bridge. In the Los Angeles basin, the communities of La Habra, Whittier, and Monrovia that grew up around the street railway lines designed by Randolph pulse to the rhythm of modernity. Mexican trains still run between Guaymas and Tepic along the right-of-way laid out by Randolph's engineers so long ago. In California's Imperial Valley, one-half million acres of irrigated land that Randolph's efforts rescued from inundation produce more than $1 billion in field, vegetable, and permanent crops annually. Each year, more than seven thousand carloads, much of it copper ore, rumble over the Globe branch of the Arizona Eastern Railroad line that Randolph developed between Globe and Bowie. Beneath the layers of time and tumbling of events, the strong hand of Tucson's adopted "Colonel" can still be seen in the commerce and daily lives of America.

A fierce guardian of his privacy, Randolph constructed, saved, and refurbished key infrastructure in the United States and Mexico. A "robber baron" capitalist to some, Randolph walked the streets of Tucson revered, during the first two decades of the twentieth century. Today, a mid-Tucson golf course and the tiny community of Randolph, near Eloy, publicly commemorate the man who once dominated the southwest's railroad, mining, investment, and political scene. The words of his friend Mose Drachman précis: "What a colorful life was his. Filled as it was with so many, many interesting chapters, it deserves a more powerful pen than mine, and I hope that some day, such a pen may depict its charm."

Fifty-seven years after the Colonel's death, the Tucson city council voted to rename Randolph Park in honor of venerable civic leader Gene C. Reid. Tucson sculptor Nicholas Lowell Burke created a stunning bust of Epes Randolph for a small park west of the mid-town golf course that still bears his name. Still in a rough patina here, the soulful piece now resonates with a glow reflecting its earthly inspiration. (Bronze Portrait Bust Nicholas Lowell Burke)

Chapter 7

And the Beat Goes On: Rail Competition, Humanity, and World War I

A muscular brakeman chuckles and pulls at his chin as he walks by a group of fellow rails. Each man steps away from the group and heads for his work station, sure that "Whiskers," the division superintendent, will soon walk by. Local leaders of every ilk held the "old man's" chair on the Tucson Division during more than seven decades of steam. The line of superintendents through southern Arizona began March 1, 1879 when the Southern Pacific Railroad (SP) named E.E. Hewitt, superintendent of the Los Angeles Division, head of the Arizona Division from Yuma to Stanwix. Because the railroad had yet to arrive in the big burg, the Tucson Division did not exist.

By the first day of 1881, W.G. Curtis held the reins on the Arizona Division, split into the SP of Arizona with the Gila Division from Yuma to Tucson, and the SP of Arizona & New Mexico, Tucson Division, east from Tucson to Deming, New Mexico. Inveterate political manipulator John A. Muir supervised the Gila and Tucson divisions by October 1, 1884. Muir held that position until March 1, 1888 when J.S. Noble replaced him. On September 1, 1895, Colonel Epes Randolph assumed the "old man's" chair for the Gila and Tucson divisions, and Noble left to take control of the Shasta Division in California. Randolph oversaw the Tucson Division until he departed for Los Angeles on January 1, 1902.

B. A. Worthington served just two months in Randolph's stead before future Arizona governor T.R. Jones replaced him. C.C. Sroufe took the head chair until November 1, 1904 when W.A. McGovern succeeded him. "Something of a surprise, even to Mr. McGovern," recalled the *Star*. W.H.

The office door for a succession of SP steam-era superintendents: Averell, Whalen, Dyer, Williams, Fitzgerald, Wilson, Fairbank, Lowe, Hughes, Bays, Kirk, McCann, and Coltrin. (Kalt Collection)

Averell, the thirty-two year-old nephew of SP head E.H. Harriman, assumed command June 1, 1907. Earlier, Averell had worked as Tucson trainmaster for two years. W.H. Whalen took the old-man's job on October 1, 1908. The decisive Whalen held the position until the SP named him superintendent of the Los Angeles Division in July 1911. Future company general manager Joseph H. Dyer succeeded Whalen and served for three years, later reigning as one of the SP's "Little Five" vice presidents who ran the company in San Francisco.

Thomas H. Williams, a director of the original Old Pueblo Club, took over in July 1914, followed in July 1916 by J.W. Fitzgerald, and by William W. Wilson in January of 1918. Wilson controlled the division for more than seven years. The *Southern Pacific Bulletin* credited him with starting the SP's construction of schools for its section workers, noting, "Wilson some time ago realized that in the Tucson terri-

tory...the need for Americanization work and educational facilities for the children was of great importance." In cooperation with county school boards, the company built schools at Mohawk and Sentinel, using a sunroof to cover two portable houses.

Wilson left the job to H.S. Fairbank in August 1925 but returned as division superintendent on January 1, 1929. Described as "young and soft-spoken" despite his twenty-seven years with the SP, A.A. Lowe took the division reins in 1939 and H.R. "Hard Rock" Hughes followed in 1940. George A. Bays began as superintendent in May 1944. D.R. Kirk followed Bays and then A.S. McCann. Ralph Coltrin replaced McCann when he succumbed to lung cancer, and was superintendent as the steam era ended. Arnold Bays, son of the former

Locomotive No. 3643, a 2-10-2 engine, sits in the Tucson yard ready for action ca. 1920. The SP faced challenges from the north and south in its bid to rule commerce in Arizona. Hoping to stop SP's march, the Santa Fe surveyed the southern part of the territory as early as 1878 but cast aside plans until the early 1900s. The Santa Fe reorganized under the leadership of President Edward P. Ripley and its general counsel, Harvard-educated Victor Morawetz in 1896. Over the next six years, the company doubled revenues to $60 million. "By 1901 Ripley had turned a derelict line into a major transportation artery," reported a 1989 Arizona State Historic Preservation Office study. (Ray Hanson Collection)

superintendent, served as division super-intendent from 1978 to 1980.

Coltrin held fond memories of the superintendent's private business car. "It was for entertaining in the interest of the SP," explained the genial Coltrin. "There was nice wood paneling throughout. It had windows along the back so I could sit inside or go out on the rear platform and make my inspections. It had three bedrooms and the cook's quarters. My colored cook, Ralph Smith, was tremendous. You pretty near had no choice but to eat when Ralph put one of his steaks down in front of you. We usu-ally used it three to four times a month, to entertain officials from the different un-ions. It was better to be on good terms with them than not."

D.R. Kirk (center) served a brief term as division superintendent and posed for a photo with Carl Ball Sr. (right) and Jr. in the summer of 1961. (Elgin Ball Collection)

Ralph Coltrin shakes hands with a rail in the Tuc-son yard ca. 1962. (Ralph Coltrin Collection)

The vast unsettled valleys of the West lay as a sumptuous feast before the fertile minds of late-nineteenth-century railroad moguls. Exacting large capital out-lay, rail lines into the West's bounty of min-eral, timber, and cattle promised immeasurable financial return. Compa-nies employed a dynamic mix of coopera-tion, collusion, competition, and combat to glean their flow of shekels.

Consumers rejoiced when competi-tors marched across SP's southern terri-tory. Built to serve Phelps Dodge's Copper Queen Consolidated Mine, the Arizona & South Eastern Railroad Company ran its first train into Bisbee from Fairbank and connection with the New Mexico & Arizona Railroad on February 1, 1889. The South-western Railroad of Arizona incorporated in October 1900 and far-sighted leader and philanthropist Dr. James S. Douglas built one hundred fifty-five miles of rail line west from Deming, New Mexico and east from the Arizona town of Don Luis, near the Mexican border.

The company established its divi-sion headquarters, including main tele-graph and business offices, in Douglas, Arizona and ran its first train from Deming to Don Luis in mid-February 1902. The rail-road opened its rail yard in Benson that spring and one El Paso newspaper soon ob-served: "The SP yards in Benson present a very vacant appearance to what they did a few months ago. A conservative estimate places the loss of receipts on the SP road at $100,000 per month." In June of 1902, the El Paso & Southwestern (EP&SW) pur-chased the two earlier railroads.

The SP locked horns with EP&SW in July 1907 over the right to build a rail-road across Dr. Douglas's land in Nacozari, Sonora. Superintendent of the Phelps Dodge Nacozari smelters, Douglas believed he held the exclusive railroad concession from the Mexican government for the Douglas to Nacozari branch line. Epes Randolph purported to control legal access across the same land and began purchasing

The Phelps Dodge-owned El Paso & Southwestern Railroad eased SP's stranglehold on southern Arizona consumers when the first train tied up in Tucson on November 20, 1912. (AHS #22135)

shacks owned by Mexican families along the disputed right-of-way. Randolph's group controlled all but eight of the forty to fifty lots in the area and had razed many of the houses. "To the Mexicans, we paid $5,000 and $6,000 and after tearing them down and gave the lumber back to them," said Randolph. He also tendered an offer for Douglas's Mexican concession. The eminent capitalist and southern Arizona benefactor declined the proposal, refusing to concede that Randolph possessed Mexican authorization. On July 17, 1907, three days after Douglas refused the overture, workmen began tearing down eight Phelps Dodge buildings. Attorneys converged from El Paso, Bisbee, and other points of the southwest, ready for a brutal legal brawl. By mid-September, however, the two rail giants had reached a truce in their Nacozari dispute.

Primarily a mine and smelter supply railroad, the EP&SW would not build into Tucson for another five years. The company's first train arrived to an enthusiastic welcome on November 20, 1912. After twelve years, the SP acquired the EP&SW through purchase at the start of November 1924. That same month, the SP promoted E.J. Fenchurch to head the railroad's freight and passenger offices. Fenchurch

announced that the SP would not relocate his staff to El Paso when it consolidated rail operations, easing anxieties among Tucsonans.

EP&SW owners took good care of their railroad. Prior to its sale, crews began

Smart visitors to the EP&SW passenger depot included local brakeman H.T. Stapp and his female companions ca. 1916. The elegant building hosted a series of restaurants in the late twentieth century. (Richard Stapp Sr. Collection)

The garden at the company's passenger depot on West Congress delighted locals and travelers for decades. (Richard Stapp Sr. Collection)

This cover adorned the Citizen's special Cinco de Mayo edition highlighting the new Tucson-Nogales line. (UASC)

adding four inches of crushed gravel to the roadbed and laid new track before closing its defunct Tucson freight station. Ninety-pound rail covered 105 miles west of El Paso, and block signals protected 313 miles of track. One hundred-ten coal locomotives, nine oil burners, 92 passenger cars, and more than 4,600 freight cars comprised the rolling stock. The company also had orders pending for three diners, three baggage buffet cars, and 400 forty-foot box cars. Four thousand new employees and 1,140 miles of track also joined the SP with the deal. SP closed the EP&SW passenger station on November 17, 1924. The company rerouted the daily No. 2 Rock Island eastbound to Chicago, and the No. 7 and 8 trains, between Tucson and El Paso, to the SP depot on Toole Avenue. In August 1930, the Whitman Metals Reduction Corporation leased the old EP&SW roundhouse on Twenty-Fifth Street from the SP, and opened its Cop-O-Lead plant with a ten-man workforce.

SP had expanded its operations when it dedicated a direct line from Tucson through Calabasas to Nogales on May 5, 1910. The day's Official Program for Celebration of the Tucson/Mexico connection

trumpeted: "Celebration of the opening of the Tucson, West Coast of Mexico Railroad marks an epoch in the business life of Tucson. Mining and agriculture in Pima County will receive an impetus from the construction of this road; and its commercial position, always strategic, will be greatly strengthened." The program further proclaimed: "That the close bonds uniting Northern Mexico and Southern Arizona will ever grow stronger and more cordial as the years pass by is a forgone conclusion. Tucson has excellent reasons for self-congratulations at this time. Existing conditions are highly satisfactory and her future commercial prosperity is assured."

Festivities kicked off with a parade by military and civic organizations at 10:00 a.m. Schoolchildren gathered for a flag-raising at Washington Park east of the

Spectators marvel as soldiers parade across the EP&SW station grounds during World War I. (AHS #B32189)

Carnegie Library on South Sixth Avenue. A free noontime barbeque followed at Elysian Grove near the Santa Cruz River. Games, pony races, and baseball filled the afternoon until 5:00 p.m., when Troops F & G of the U.S. Eighth Cavalry performed an exhibition drill. At 8:30 p.m., officials held a public reception and while the city's society women enjoyed an invitation-only card party at the Old Pueblo Club. While the ladies played cards, Tucson's gentlemen bought $5 tickets for a banquet at the Santa Rita Hotel, replete with a "canopy" (canapé) of anchovies, wild pigeon on toast, and a spectrum of cold meats including smoked tongue and lamb. The evening concluded with desserts of rum omelet, imported cheeses, and one's choice of cigars or cigarettes. Following the feast, all returned to Elysian Grove and danced the night away.

Six years later, workmen completed the Fourth Avenue vehicle underpass in 1916. The Tuscan-columned throughway penetrated the barrier to the city's northeast side formed by twelve sets of SP tracks. Two years later, World War I raged in Europe, challenging the nation's railroads. "To combine the purposes of war, of industry, and of finance," President Woodrow Wilson federalized control of the nation's railroads. Wilson named Treasury Secretary William G. McAdoo Director General of Railroads. "Every bad-order locomotive is a Prussian soldier, every idle locomotive is working for the Kaiser," proclaimed McAdoo.

The European conflict taxed the nation's railroad labor force and most rail lines suffered severe losses during government control. "Hundreds of miles of military railroads in France are being operated...by men drawn from the ranks of the skilled officers and employees of the railroads of this country," explained McAdoo. "It is the patriotic duty of the men who are considered necessary for the operation of the (U.S.) railroads to claim deferred classification." Men from the Apache, Hopi, Navajo, and Pima tribes joined SP work crews across the company's Pacific System.

The Director General attacked railroad corporations in February of 1918, claiming many rail officials had not loyally responded to government control. That September, McAdoo specified minimum wages for railroad employees, strapping the coffers of many rail companies. Thereafter, unskilled workers earned 32¢ an hour, with many shop workers making 55¢ an hour. Freight car-body-builders and repairers wages jumped from 50¢ to 64¢. The oft-criticized McAdoo then mandated an eight-hour day for all rail employees, with overtime to begin after ten hours and rail companies to pony up eight months of back pay at the new wages!

1919 RR men entering service

Local SP men assembled beside the city courthouse prior to ther induction into military service after the United States entered World War I on April 6, 1917. (Richard Stapp Sr. Collection)

Tucson mayor and career SP engineer E.T. "Happy" Houston ran trains as part of the United States Transportation Corps in France during World War I. (Bettie Houston Crawford Collection)

The war saw Americans contribute money to fuel the nation's mobilization in four Liberty Loan campaigns. SP workers proved slow to come on board, however, as company subscriptions barely topped the million-dollar mark during the first and second drives. Donation figures more than doubled during the third Liberty Loan effort, and reached $6.89 million in subscriptions from SP employees and officials during the fourth campaign. In Arizona, large irrigation projects enabled farmers to

A plaque on the Pershing Memorial Fountain west of University of Arizona's Old Main commemorates Louis Kengla (above), and the eleven other "sons of the University" who gave their lives in World War I. It reads, "The Right is more Precious than Peace." (Dorothy Fitzpatrick Collection)

SP engineer R.J. Blythe (right) joined his cousin Lorene Blythe McAllister and Louis McAllister (left) in front their Original Mexican Restaurant at 271 N. Stone. One of Tucson's early bowling alleys lay across Stone Avenue and the McAllisters hired a chef named Caruso who served an Italian and Mexican fare. Later, Caruso opened his famous namesake dining establishment on North Fourth Avenue. Lorene's brother, T. Herman Blythe, worked for twenty-five cents an hour in the spacious restaurant while attending Tucson High School during 1939. "It was in an old house that had pomegranate trees and a Bermuda grass lawn out back," Herman remembered. "There was a dance floor in back and Jimmy Swittle's Orchestra played on the weekends. Louis McAllister had this policy that if he couldn't make change for you, he'd give you free drinks." Famous "Death Valley Scottie" lived in the Pioneer Hotel at certain times, Blythe said. "Well, Scottie'd always take a taxi to the restaurant and come in with a $100 bill to wrangle a free cocktail. Louis made it a point to run to the bank and get enough change to break Scottie's hundred." (T. Herman Blythe Collection)

produce the mineral and agricultural products needed for the war effort.

Former division engineer and state senator Tom Collins remembered hauling 10,000 troops to the Mexican border during World War I: "You could hardly get through town during those days, there were so many soldiers," said the burly Irishman. "They camped out in all the hills near Nogales." As he reached Nogales with a trainload of troops one day, said Collins, "I heard shooting. When we arrived, we heard that the Villa troops had crossed the border and attacked, but were driven off by American soldiers." Collins's story may be apocryphal, but the world's "first" war cut deeply into Tucson's close-knit rail family with the death of Louis E. Kengla, brother of Arizona Eastern Railroad accountant Herman Kengla; SP employee Alexander Tindolph Berger; and Hugh D. Campbell, son of SP brakeman Horace G. Campbell.

At the time, rails filled Tucson neighborhoods around the local SP operations, rendering each a unique flavor. The Southern Pacific's insistence that rails live within one mile of the local reserve allowed them to hear the whistle code and let the callboy reach them quickly. Rail families settled into downtown, Millville and San Antonio barrios, and Armory Park neigh-

borhoods south of the tracks, and the Fourth Avenue and Iron Horse districts to their north. None of the areas bore those names at the time.

South of the railroad tracks, below Thirteenth Street along the east side of Third Avenue, well-kept yards surrounded the houses of the division master mechanic, superintendent, his assistant, master car repairer, division engineer, chief dispatcher, and shop foreman. Those who lived there referred to the enclave as "Intelligence Row"; those who did not coined much less flattering names. At Sixteenth Street and Second Avenue, the SP provided company housing for shop workers and engineers in company "barracks." Further east, ten portable bunk houses provided

Former division chief timekeeper Elgin Ball (right) and Esther Sheffield ca. 1930. The two grew up at Sixteenth Street and Fremont in Millville with many rail neighbors. (Elgin Ball Collection)

Several boys on Miles School's 1928 soccer team went to work for the local SP. (Elgin Ball Collection)

single rails housing and on the northwest corner of Sixteenth Street and Park Avenue sixteen boxcars comprised the SP's Mexican Quarters.

West of Third Avenue, an attractive neighborhood later dubbed Armory Park teemed with mid-level rail managers, both "American" and Mexican businessmen, and white-collar workers. Skilled blue-collar workers lived at the area's north and southeast ends, while unskilled rail laborers resided to its west.

East of Armory Park, the multi-ethnic rail neighborhoods of Barrio Millville and Barrio San Antonio grew. In the living room of his comfortable midtown home during June 2002, Francisco "Frank" Mendez described his old neighborhood: "I lived on Star Avenue and Fourteenth Street two blocks east of the ice plant. It was on the north side of the tracks." Guzman's Grocery stood at 747. S. Fremont, on the northeast corner of Eighteenth Street. "They sold everything, canned stuff, fresh meat, like all those little stores. They carried fresh vegetables, too. They'd be open 'til 8 or 9 at night," Mendez continued. "There was a corner light at Star Avenue and Fifteenth Street, so we played many games of 'kick the can' at night. All the roads were dirt and when the rainy season came around it was muddy. When it dried out, dust so thick you couldn't see a block ahead of you!" Mendez remembered that railroad families filled the barrio: "Mr. Ball, the engineer, lived on

Fremont. The Bowers lived there, too, and the J.B. Sheffields. It was an altogether different Tucson then, really."

North of the railroad, the Iron Horse neighborhood lay between Euclid and Park avenues, and Sixth and Tenth streets. The area traces its roots to the first building in 1874. At the time, *nativos* built adobe bricks by filling sand molds shaped like egg crates with clay, water, and straw or manure as a binding agent. When trains arrived in 1880, Tucsonans began importing hard-fired El Paso pressed brick for use in construction. Good railroad wages, combined with plentiful open lands north of the tracks, attracted speculators and investors into the Iron Horse.

SP engineer Peter B. Ziegler ran the second passenger train into Tucson in March 1880 and piloted division locomotives for the next twenty years. He also began developing the city's "wild" section in 1881, when he invested in Iron Horse real estate. Peter and his dynamic wife, Mary A. Ziegler, dug a well and constructed an expansive adobe home with broad sleeping porches for their two sons and six adopted orphan children at 126 North First Avenue. The couple built "Ziegler's Row" on the east side of First Avenue between Ninth and Tenth streets in 1885, providing timid townsfolk with vivid proof of the area's development.

Prior to 1893, construction of a large wagon bridge over the "big arroyo," now called Arroyo Chico, just east of the intersection of Third Avenue and Ninth Street, boosted the Zieglers' fortunes and increased trade north of the tracks. In addition, the area's shallow water table allowed residents to develop glorious gardens at little expense. Rails comprised the majority of the Iron Horse neighborhood's 52 residents by 1898. Over the next three years, population expanded to 140 people in Iron Horse, with 57 percent working for the railroad. Ziegler retired from the SP in 1901 and devoted full attention to his properties, a confectionery shop downtown which once included ice cream home delivery, a bottling works, and the Union Park racetrack south of the city.

By 1908, 117 rails lived in the Iron Horse neighborhood, and Ninth Street functioned as a major road for wagons traveling to the city's "northeast side." North Fourth Avenue's expanding business district also augmented the growing area. The Zeiglers built eleven houses for rent or sale by 1911 and replaced their original dwelling with an elegant, two-story Queen Anne-style house at 126 North First Avenue. Rail employees comprised 60 percent of the neighborhood's residents by 1911, and 85 percent of them held blue-collar jobs, while only two foremen lived in the neighborhood. Most men worked high-prestige "wheelie" jobs like conductor, engineer, and brakeman, while several wives of railroad workers held office jobs.

The Zieglers had good company in the Iron Horse District. Stationary engineer J.A. Flood's family lived at First Avenue and Tenth Street. SP pumper Jack Peggs and his family rented one of the Ziegler houses around the corner at 722 East Ninth Street, and city councilman Fred Adams, official watch inspector for the *SP de Mexico*, lived across the street. Elias Hedricks, local SP yard foreman, Arizona senator, and city councilman, owned a huge

Peter B. and Mary A. Ziegler built this distinctive home at 126 N. First Avenue to replace their original rambling adobe structure. The pair might have cringed upon learning that their spire-shaped, upstairs room provided a convenient place for the house madam to hang her red light and for prostitutes to spot incoming trains when the old home functioned as a brothel later in the century. The design continues today as one of Tucson's more unique architectural features. (Kalt Collection)

Pretty Iron Horse resident Mayche Peggs Bryant worked in the offices at the depot in 1928. (Kalt Collection)

Colonial home north of Ninth Street on First Avenue, which still stands almost a century later.

Just forty-five feet southwest of the intersection of Hoff Avenue and Stevens Avenue in the Iron Horse District, the initial SP reading room and clubhouse provided employee fun in the company's well-appointed facility. The brotherhood melded by unity of purpose, similarity of lifestyle, work demands, and close contact bred family-like ties among rails. "There's something about a railroader; they're a breed amongst themselves," explained Frank Hutcheson, former division electrician. "Seems like guys were a little rowdier in the olden days." The Iron Horse neighborhood expanded east, constituting an eastern Tucson commercial suburb by 1936. By the mid-1950s the neighborhood had begun a steep decline that would last more than a decade.

A symbiotic relationship between SP workers and the Chinese grocery store kept the city's economy afloat during the steam era. Tucson rails frequented these corner groceries for their day-to-day staples, along with *carnicerias* (butcher shops) and *tiendas* (general merchandise stores) run by Mexican and American families. Nevertheless, most rails knew little about their grocer and his family. Long-time local pharmacist Raymond Lee and his lovely wife, Louise Wong Lee, shared stories of their southern Arizona roots in their attractive eastside home during July 2005. "Chinese people, to this day, call the United States 'Gum san,' meaning 'Gold Mountain,'" Raymond explained. "My grandfather, Lee Aht, opened a grocery store at 51 and 71 South Meyer Street, on the southwest corner of Congress Street in about 1898." In 1922, Raymond's parents opened the John Lee Market at 474 South Meyer Street. "Each family member contributed to the maintenance of the family market," said Ray-

Lee Aht worked at the Pacific Grocery, 566 Kearny Street in San Francisco, prior to coming to Tucson. (Raymond and Louise Lee Collection)

Lee Aht brought his family to "Gum san", or Gold Mountain, and opened a store in Tucson at 182 W. Congress ca. 1898. (Raymond and Louise Lee Collection)

mond. "We all worked at the store. I raised the awning on the front of the store with a long pole each morning. I also ground hamburger, cleaned, and did things like that."

In 1908, the city directory listed

ninety-two general merchandise stores, sixty-seven of them Chinese-owned. By 1912, Chinese merchants ran seventy-five of the city's one hundred grocery stores. Chinese Tucsonans enjoyed warm collegiality despite a wide diversity among traditional clans in the city. In Phoenix, the Ong or Wang clans predominated, but in Tucson the Kim, Lee, Wah, and several other families populated the Chinese community. "The whole feeling of our community back then was one of brotherhood," explained Raymond Lee. "If you saw someone from Asia on the streets of Tucson, you were sure that they were Chinese. When someone new came to town, say their name

Local pharmacist Raymond Lee's father, Lee Fong (John Lee), and mother, Tom Yuk Gin (Louisa), stand behind their mothers on their wedding day. The Lees opened a family market on South Meyer Street. (Raymond and Louise Lee Collection)

was Lee, then all the Lee families in Tucson would give 25-40 bucks, whatever they could afford, to help them get started," Raymond said, glowing with pride. "The beautiful part was, if the family could pay it back, then they did, but if they couldn't get their business going, then they didn't have to pay it back. No strings attached. It was not a loan."

Peace did not always reign in the local Chinese community, however. Tong warfare surfaced in the Chinese quarter of Tucson during May 1922. When Chinese grocer Louis Eng found a lard can full of kerosene in flames by the rear door of his south Sixth Avenue grocery store, he believed his enemies had set a trap to draw him into the alley and kill him. Prepared for such an assault, Eng blasted several shots through the store's back door with his re-

volver. Two men raced down the alley unhurt, and the grocer hurried to pull a nearby fire alarm. Tucson police chief Dallas Ford promised an "energetic investigation" and pursuit of the two "incendiaries." Chinese leaders called a community meeting to raise reward funds.

Railroad paydays fell on the 6th and the 21st of each month by the 1930s. "Everybody worked for the SP back then," Raymond Lee remembered. "They all charged their groceries and other purchases on credit. When the SP paid its workers, they'd come in to pay their bill. If they paid $40 on their bill, they'd turn right around and charge $40 more for the next two weeks' supplies. We saw very little cash."

Pilones played a key role in the routine at the Chinese family market. "When the people from the railroad paid their bill, they always wanted a *pilon* for their kids," Lee recalled. "It means gratuity in Spanish, something free as a little 'thank you' for doing business at our store. My mother always kept some little candies for *pilones*. Mom and Dad, ha, ha, always hated it when those large railroad families, eight or nine kids, came into the store."

Raymond explained the rationale behind the fervent industry displayed by Chinese merchants. "My parents' store was open from eight in the morning until ten at night every day of the week," he said. "I asked my mother one Fourth of July why we never closed. She told me it was because if someone wanted something and we were

Prominent Chinese entrepreneur Wong Wing Seen first arrived in Tucson about 1900 and posed for this photograph ca. 1911. Seen opened two R&R Fancy Foods stores in Tucson and watched five of his six children graduate from college. (Raymond and Louise Lee Collection)

Well into the 1930s, Tohono O'odham (Papago) woodcutters drove their wagons through town singing "Leña, Leña" selling firewood. Many brought ollas, *earthen water jars, to trade at their favorite Chinese market. Former sheriff of the Tucson Corral of Westerners and local historian Dick Hughes remembered, "It was the custom to drink half the water from your ladle and pour the other half on the burlap to keep the olla cool." In George Webb's* A Piman Remembers, *one Tohono O'odham man explained, "The Chinese merchants in these towns speak our language a lot better than the white people." Once, the man told a clerk in a Chinese market near his reservation he was looking for dessert: "He picked up a strawberry preserve and, to our surprise, said in plain Pima, "Go'ep sitoli we.nags'i.da'," meaning "This is pretty good. It has syrup." (AHS #92870)*

closed they might find it somewhere else and keep going to that store."

Most Chinese youngsters grew up in Tucson understanding the dictum, "Chinese is spoken at home; Spanish is spoken with playmates and in business; and English is spoken at school," said Lee. Astute Chinese grocers also learned the Piman language of the Tohono O'odham (Papago)

people. *Ollas* made by the native people proved highly profitable for neighborhood Chinese grocers. Sold early on in three sizes for 10¢, 15¢, and 20¢, by the mid-1950s the earthen vessels went for $1 and $2 apiece. "All the Mexican families filled their olla with water, covered it in burlap, and hung it on their porch in the shade," Raymond recalled. "Then, they'd wet the burlap and let the breeze keep the water cool. The whole family ladled water from the olla when they wanted a drink. Very ingenious! They always broke, though, so we had a constant flow of ollas through our store."

Still wearing his long, braided "queue" of hair, Louise Wong Lee's father, Wong Wing Seen, arrived in Tucson from China around the turn of the century and farmed land along the Rillito Creek northeast of the city. Soon, the industrious pioneer returned to China to marry and brought his bride to Nogales, Arizona. Seen opened a restaurant in the fledgling Mexican border town but later moved back to Tucson in search of a better education for his several children. He opened the Santa Fe Restaurant at 369 Toole Avenue across from the SP depot. "My father catered to the people that came through town on the train and, of course, to the people that worked for the railroad," said Louise. "Later he opened grocery stores, including two R & R Fancy Foods markets. My mother used to make the railroad customers write their own purchases in the ledger so there wouldn't be any problems." By 1936, just fifty-five Chinese markets served Tucson, 20 percent of city grocery stores. As the steam era faded, Chinese ownership of neighborhood markets fell to forty stores, only 14 percent, in 1950.

Tucson's stifling summer heat helped created the city's "summer bachelor's club," a phenomenon that endured until the advent of air conditioning and beyond. In no way formalized, this coalition consisted of men who sent their wives and families to California during the depths of Tucson's "hot period." Local newspapers published regular items noting that "Mrs. So-and-so" had "gone to the coast for the summer." Rarely, however, did the "Mr." accompany her.

Near the end of June 1903, a poll taken at Vic Griffith's Cigar Shop revealed that 70 percent of the men present had put

One of Gustav Schneider's subjects, "Annie," controls her pooch behind a Gay Alley establishment ca.1915. (AHS #99893)

The female form captured the interest of men at SP's subsidiary Arizona Eastern Railroad, who occasionally demonstrated that their drawing ability was not limited to engineering subjects. (AHS, Schneider Papers)

their wives on a Pullman coach to California for the summer. Too smart to leave, a summer bachelor feigned misery at his wife's departure. "No one seemed to much miss their spouses," noted the *Star*. "That is one of the funny things about Tucson." Then, "feeling ten years younger and looking the part," the summer bachelor went "off by himself to crack his heels together twice and subsequently tell all of the boys that Mary had gone to the coast," said the newspaper. "She need not be surprised if he mumbled Mabel in his sleep when Mary returned. If the wives of the community appreciated how much gratification a coast vacation would afford their husbands, there ought not to be a single married female left in Tucson."

Rail draftsman and historian Gustav Schneider appreciated John T. McCutcheon's depiction of society's fickle ways in his Pendulum of Morals. *(AHS, Schneider Papers)*

In July 1917, city ordinance No. 466 ordered the name Gay Alley changed to Sabino Street. (AHS #ms1080f35_fu)

Local rail historian Gustav H. Schneider recalled that rails enjoyed Tucson's amenities at the "Up-town" club room, on the northeast corner of Stone Avenue and Congress Street. The spot provided "free reading material and good chairs," said Schneider. The former civil engineer for the SP's Tucson-based Arizona Eastern Railroad recalled, "A piano player named Darling helped with quartettes." Schneider remembered Darling as a pale fellow from Chicago who could "handle a little Bach and Chopin too." When not offering his musical fare, Darling reigned as the "professor" at Tucson's best-known brothel.

The allure of the *femme fatale* found completion in Tucson's Gay Alley. A source of dishonor for Tucson's righteous and cultured, this "red-light district" thrived through much of the steam era. The Boyd and Thresher Saloon stood at the corner of Gay Alley and McCormick Street, while the Favorite Saloon and La Violeta Saloon served drinks on the alley. Schneider compiled a list of sixty-nine tainted tarts who inhabited the ramshackle adobes between 1915 and 1917. Asian, French, Belgian, Japanese, and Mexican *puta*s plied nature's longest-running carnival, along with thirty-one "Americans" and one "Texan." Schneider's collection of photographs reveal an attractive group of women who dis-

play none of the brazen and hardened features consistent with the image of prostitutes in rough and dusty frontier towns. With names like Big French Jennie, Toughluck from Phoenix, and Cross-eyed Alice, alias Drunk Alice, their stories, however, might surely have been grist for a good dime novel.

Former conductor Harold "Stonewall" Jackson recalled one early brothel: "South Toole ended at Third Avenue and there was a whorehouse in a two-story building there. The Rialto Theater was a delivery stable, back then." Veteran division engineer Connie Weinzapfel knew of one hovel that housed the popular male diversion on Stevens Avenue during the 1920s. "I was sixteen or seventeen years old when I delivered ice to the houses of ill repute," Weinzapfel said. "I first knew the

Identified as Carmen by Gustav Schneider, this prostitute posed inside her "crib" ca. 1915. Crib No. 12, and its proprietor, Edith Gray, earned the area's most notorious reputation. (AHS#99892)

madam, Mary, when she was across from the depot [206 Stevens Avenue]. You could look right out the superintendent's window and see her little shack." Weinzapfel delivered ice twice a day after Mary Branson and her charges moved operations south to Simpson Street. "I'd put a ten-pound block on the floor, chip it all up, and put it into her five-gallon water container. She had the patronage of all the businessmen, and she had a doctor come down every Wednesday morning while I was chipping ice and examine the girls."

While many shunned or ran from the local madam, Weinzapfel won Branson's favor. "Mary was very fond of me simply because I would speak to her," he declared. "I didn't think she had leprosy on the street. I'd see her cross the street and I'd yell at her, 'Hi, Mary!'" In return, said Weinzapfel, "some of the girls and I would go to Sabino Canyon and go skinny-dipping, or up to 'A' Mountain. Mary lent me her Buick and had her colored cook fix us a lunch." Branson left the business when gangster Lucky Luciano took over Tucson's sex industry after New York governor Thomas Dewey pardoned the "master pimp" on his prostitution and racketeering conviction in February 1946.

Tucsonans' long-held fears that Phoenix would earn a place on the SP main line found fruition in 1926. When SP ran its original line through Tucson in 1880, fewer than three thousand people inhabited Phoenix. SP's main line ran thirty-five miles from the small farming community, and freighters hauled

supplies to the town in wagons. Floodwaters and quicksand in the Gila River made crossings perilous and caused occasional food shortages in the Salt River Valley. In 1886, N.K. Masten organized the Maricopa & Phoenix Railroad Company, which linked Phoenix to the SP main line at Maricopa.

When the SP acquired the EP&SW in 1924, the contract stipulated that the SP would build into Phoenix to accommodate its trains from the West Coast. Early conjecture projected a line from Tucson to Florence, which connected to the Arizona capital. In fact, construction on the Phoenix main line, called the "Picacho Cut-Off," began from Picacho in early January 1925. The crowd cheered lustily as a 4300 class locomotive rolled down the main line with construction supplies. A four-mule team pulled a large scoop to dig the first dirt on the new line. C.W. Clapp, representative for SP president William Sproule, noted: "Epes Randolph, long time head of the system…dreamed of the day of this construction. But it was not for his time. Now…a $15 million project is underway embodying that which Randolph wished to attain."

Opening the SP main line through Phoenix filled the city's residents with great hope for the future. With pomp and circumstance befitting royalty, a seven-car "Goodwill Special" arrived at Phoenix's Union Station from El Paso, where it met an eight-car train of the same name from Los Angeles. The "Lady of the Rails," nineteen-year-old queen Lovenia Hegelund, and her soot-dusted

The Arizona Corporation Commission ordered construction of Union Station to consolidate separate station facilities located several blocks apart in downtown Phoenix. The Arizona Eastern Railroad Company and the California, Arizona, and Santa Fe Railroad commissioned the Robert E. McKee Construction Company to build the Mission Revival style station at a cost of $556,000. Dedicated September 30, 1923, Phoenix Union Station handled up to eighteen trains a day when rail travel reached its peak during World War II. (UASC)

court reigned as the two great locomotives broke a rope of roses in symbolic testimony to Arizona's new rail connection. SP officials stated that it would route its Californian through Phoenix as the line's first passenger train on November 14, 1926.

The SP's completion of a second southern Arizona main line fueled intense acrimony between the railroad and Phoenix merchants, however. Despite charging $30 per car more to ice loads out of Phoenix than for those from Tucson, the railroad stood ready to "fight every move made to lower the present freight tariffs or refrigeration charges," avowed the company's San Francisco attorneys. Arguments played out before Interstate Commerce Commissioner H.C. Barron near the end of November 1926. Captain F.W. Lattimer testified that every organization in Phoenix and 6,500 farmers had supported the SP fight to obtain rights-of-way and privileges only after the company agreed to extend main line benefits to Salt River Valley shippers.

When it issued new rate tariffs, however, the rail company included a "rider," explaining, "Stated refrigeration charges shown in this table will not apply to traffic routed... via Wellton Junction, Hassayampa, Maricopa or Picacho, Arizona," the entire new main line through Phoenix! Infuriated locals formed the Main Line Association and went on the attack. Along with the Maricopa Farm Bureau, Phoenix Main Line Association members claimed the SP's promise of "full main line service" on the new road included reduced refrigeration charges for fruits and vegetables. "I now ask, if the Southern Pacific is going to abide by its agreement?" Lattimer demanded. "If the railroad refuses to abide by its agreement, it will force the people of this valley to...fight for the halting of every wheel on the new railroad until rail officials comply."

SP attorneys argued that company representatives never used the word "reduction." The railroad contended that the high cost of ice in the Salt River Valley justified $10 to $30 more per car than it charged for refrigeration in Southern California. The Interstate Commerce Commission ruled in favor of the railroad, and anger mounted in the state capital.

In mid-December 1926, the SP announced rate cuts between Phoenix and western points along the new main line that saved passengers 95¢ on a one-way ticket. The move reduced fares from the capital city to Los Angeles to $15.33. Phoenix district freight and passenger agent Russell P. Kyle predicted an annual savings of $12,000 to $15,000 for local travelers. The rate reduction did little to appease Phoenix commissioners, however, and their chance for revenge arrived early the following month. Judge Frank H. Lyman's passionate oratory condemned the SP's application to construct spur tracks along west Jackson Street between Fourth and Ninth Avenues in that city's industrial section. Lyman explained that Phoenix "threw open the gates to the city and told the corporation 'come and take what you want.'"

Despite granting valuable franchises to the railroad, including eighteen grade crossings within the city limits, said Lyman: "Phoenix and the valley are still on a branch line in the matter of freight rates. With hilarious alacrity this great corporation comes to Phoenix requesting further favors, further gratuities. Until the Southern Pacific shows some inclination to put Phoenix on the main line, in fact, the city commission should look with extreme disfavor upon the railroad's requests for these gratuitous franchises." City commissioners voted three to two to deny the SP's application, but rumors continued to force SP officials to issue periodic denials that they planned to move division headquarters from Tucson to Phoenix.

Chapter 8

Little but desert surrounded the local SP shops in 1890. (AHS #B200280)

The Shops: Throbbing Heart of a Mighty Railroad

Crash! Bang! Hiss! Belch! The local shops throbbed to the rhythm of the rails. Steam locomotives thundering; drive wheels slamming against "drop rails"; shouted instructions rising above the din. Fire, smoke, smells, toxins, the Tucson railroad shops had it all. Here, strong men did everything needed to keep Southern Pacific Railroad (SP) trains on the road. Most jobs in the shops required heavy handwork. Swinging large sledgehammers, hefting metal, pushing bulky carts, all part of a loud and dirty day's work in the shops.

Throughout the steam era, the railroad held a special fascination for Tucsonans. The bustling shop area provided many with their most enthralling look at rail functions. Two distinct shop operations ran three shifts per day during periods of high local rail traffic. Along south Third Avenue between Fourteenth and Sixteenth streets, workmen serviced the company's locomotives in the roundhouse and backshop. To the west, workers refurbished

and repainted the company's wide variety of rail cars in the car shop.

Maintaining trains in good mechanical condition required the synchronized labor of many different crafts. The specialized work completed by each trade made mechanization impossible on many jobs. Through the years, however, shopmen streamlined and systematized numerous tasks.

Rumors that the SP would move its entire Tucson shop operation to El Paso plagued city businessmen for decades. The local shop force grew from fifty men under Charles E. Donnatin's charge in 1886, to three hundred-fifty when fears of a shop transfer peaked in 1901. El Paso and Phoenix newspapers each reported with virtual certainty that the shops would soon move to their city. Many predicted the loss of shop workers and their families would obliterate Tucson's economy.

Some locals took faith when the SP enlarged its Tucson reservation with the purchase of 40 acres in Reicker's Addition during January 1900. Then, as 1901 ended, division superintendent C.C. Sroufe announced that local monthly railroad busi-

The shop bred tough men who did the railroad's dirty work during the 1890's. (AHS #9228)

Arizona Eastern shop workers tackled this locomotive in Globe during the 1920s. (Stanley M. Houston Collection)

ness had grown more than 300 percent over the last five years. Yet, said Sroufe, the company had not enlarged Tucson shops to match this increased demand. "It will always be necessary to maintain large division shops in Tucson," vowed the superintendent. "In a very short time," predicted Sroufe, the railroad would "make great improvements" in the Tucson shops, including "brick buildings, large cranes, and late machinery."

Anxiety lingered in the business community, however, until SP head Edward H. Harriman arrived in Tucson during 1902. The illustrious rail chief had begun committing millions to upgrade his entire system, and many wondered about his plans for local improvements. When Harriman arrived, five of Tucson's leading citizens approached his private car, the Arden, in the small park west of the depot. Greeting each individually, the exacting rail mogul spent two hours assuring all that his company's shops would remain in the

Well-respected Major Heins assisted Epes Randolph on the Tucson division and implemented the Heins system of job classification on the Arizona Eastern and Maricopa & Phoenix railroads in 1909. The plan changed the title of trainmaster, master mechanic, and roadmaster positions to assistant superintendent. In 1909, the SP had the following in place on the Tucson Division:

Track scales—Yuma 80 ton capacity; Tucson 60 ton; Maricopa 60 ton; Benson 80 ton; and Bowie 80 ton

Mail cranes—Aztec, Casa Grande, Cochise, Dome, Gage, Mohawk, Pantano, Red Rock, Rillito, Separ, San Simon, Vail, Wellton, and Willcox.

Standard clocks—Benson, Bowie, Gila Bend, Lordsburg, San Simon, Tucson, and Yuma.

Icing stations—Tucson and Yuma, with emergency icing facilities at Gila Bend and Lordsburg.

Turntables—Benson, Bowie, Dragoon, Gila Bend, Lordsburg, Maricopa, Mescal, Nogales, San Simon, Steins, Strauss, Tucson, and Yuma.

The railroad also maintained telegraph offices at Tucson, Mescal, Benson, Dragoon, Cochise, Willcox, Bowie, San Simon, and Steins and Lordsburg, New Mexico on the Stormy to the east. On the west end, Stockham, Rillito, Red Rock, Picacho, Eloy, Casa Grande, Maricopa, Estrella, Gila, Sentinel, Mohawk, Wellton, Dome, East Yard, and Yuma housed telegraph operators.

city. Eased for the moment, fears of a wholesale railroad shop departure would continue to haunt Tucson.

The SP initiated a pension system for its workers January 1, 1903. The plan called for all officials and employees to retire at seventy years of age, with pensions for those with twenty years of service. Workers incapacitated between sixty-one and seventy also began receiving pensions. The men in the local SP shops enjoyed an exceptional camaraderie. Hometown boys often described the Tucson operation as being "like family." Local boilermakers stretched kindred connections when they proposed a "sympathetic strike" in support of their Union Pacific brethren during May 1903.

Strike! Strike! The icy word held terror for the railroad's working class. Individuals felt torn between fighting for what they believed right with their fellow workers, and the specter of impending expenses without a payday. Citizens in Arizona's smaller desert towns such as Mobile and San Simon suffered the most during railroad strikes. Many depended upon the train to bring their water by tank car. A long strike could also imperil hundreds of cars of livestock and perishables, threatening food supplies along the division. "It can

easily be seen that the very life of many communities is absolutely dependent upon the Southern Pacific railroad," William W. Wilson, division superintendent, once explained. "In the event of a tie-up of the roads, many towns in Arizona will suffer a food shortage."

A strike at the local shops shot ripples of worry through Tucson. The unsettling labor events engendered strong feelings and harsh actions. Tensions rose across the city as the 1903 strike loomed. Boilermakers should not wage a "causeless strike," cautioned the *Tucson Daily Citizen*. "The public at large has rights that must be respected and interests that can not be jeopardized by rash and wrathful proceedings over a mere matter of sympathy." The local Chamber of Commerce warned that strikers would "be forced to seek labor in other fields and there-by Tucson would lose a goodly number of first-class citizens." To the fine fortune of all, labor representatives settled with the Union Pacific Railroad before union leaders ordered their men to walk out.

SP completed a thirty-stall roundhouse southeast of its existing twenty-five-stall frame structure in May 1905. Expending $15,000 on labor and almost $40,000 on materials, the company used the new facility to work on "live" engines, those needing immediate service to remain on the road. The SP also repaired its old roundhouse for doing long-term repairs and built switching tracks between the two roundhouses. In a $35,000 powerhouse west of the new roundhouse, one twenty-horsepower and two thirty-horsepower, oil-burning steam engines drove the machine, blacksmith, boilermaker, carpenter, and coppersmith shops.

Early on, an SP paymaster rode the Pacific System, paying employees in gold and later cash. Because the railroad considered its compensation ritual "a risky business," it began issuing paychecks in July 1903. The SP paid $100,000 a month in wages across the division by 1907, half of it to 430 Tucson shopmen.

Nothing brought work to a standstill like the monthly shriek of the whistle at the roundhouse on payday. Men came "flocking from all corners of the reserve," observed the *Star* railroad reporter in 1909. "Each individual attired in jeans or old clothes heading for the office of master mechanic Thomas O'Leary." At the roundhouse, a "megaphone man" called names alphabetically, and chief clerk J.B. Ritter handed out paychecks from behind an open window.

In the spring of 1910, SP surveyors laid out a site for brand new Tucson shop facilities, but fire in the blacksmith shop on September 30, 1910, halted plans before building could commence. Blacksmiths figured the small fire for one of the twenty-five to thirty that burst to life each year in the shops. But, fanned by a stiff west wind, flames gained headway into the company machine shop, where oily rags excited a vigorous blaze. Fright flashed through the rail yard as workers realized that a large number of oil cars sat vulnerable to the flames near the shops. A hostler jumped to moving the exposed tankers away from the fire

with a yard switch engine. Other engineers hurried to move locomotives after four ballast cars caught fire.

One engineer blasted his whistle in the yard repeatedly, as rails raced to the shops from throughout the city to lend aid. Each man turned hard to the task, aware of his own loss, the loss to fellow workers, and to Tucson. At its outset, the fast-moving fire destroyed electrical wires running to SP water pumps and thwarted shop fire-brigade efforts. When city volunteers joined rails with their water supply, firemen concentrated on saving the division's car repair barn.

Common reasoning held that if the car barn went, flames would ignite all the freight cars in the yard and thrust themselves upon the 55,000-gallon oil tanks

As shopmen did in earlier times, Henry Sabala (left) and his co-workers halted their work and stepped briskly to the pay window, first at the roundhouse and later at the yard office. (Annie Sabala Collection)

The shop fire devastated company property and the Tucson community at the end of September 1910. (AHS #PC180f187 #138)

north of t he depot. Fire would then send oil running down the nearby "big arroyo" and torch all the buildings along its banks. While firemen battled at the car barn, flames devoured the company's backshop, a frame shell that did little more than protect workers and machinery from rain. The insatiable fire devoured the pipefitting department, the boilermaker's shop, and the division's original wooden roundhouse in succession.

Amid the fierce firefighting efforts and booming steam engines, gawking men, women, and children flooded the rail yard. Dodging locomotives and rail personnel, curious crowds clambered upon the fire scene by the hundreds. Several climbed atop freight cars to sit just beneath the eaves of the division's huge oil tanks and cast blank stares into the inferno. Firemen secured the car barn and turned their attention to saving the storekeeper department's huge supply of rail materials and

provisions east of the shops.

Gritty rails and daring city firemen fought to protect tens of thousands of dollars in company property. Arriving heroes found thick sheets of sparks propelled by the night's remorseless zephyr. More than once, onlookers reported abandoning hope of saving the buildings, but nature's smile brought a shift in the evening's gale, sending the shower of biting, burning debris away from stores department buildings. As embers faded, news reached Tucson that radicals had dynamited the *Los Angeles Times* plant on the same night, and that twenty newspaper workers might be dead. Stories of a possible connection between the Los Angeles and Tucson incidents spiked local fears.

Bitter certainty spiced railroad shopmen's coffee the following morning. "The effect of the fire on the men who depend upon their work there for their daily bread was pathetic," reported the *Star*.

"Fighting valiantly as long as there was any use of fighting, the men finally abandoned the struggle [to save the shops] and watched their means of livelihood go down with wet eyes." Many shopmen lost valuable tools and work clothes in the fire. Most men without savings began searching for work in town, while others who declared themselves "penniless" vowed they would "hit the road" within the next two days. Those with money made plans to leave Tucson and find another job.

Pessimism dripped from the plump fruit of despair in Tucson's business community. Businessmen knew that the enforced idleness of so many workers meant harder times and the possibility that the shops might not be rebuilt in Tucson heightened their alarm. The *Star* reminded readers: "There was great gloom in business circles Saturday morning. Between 200 and 300 men are thrown out of employment on the edge of winter, many of whom are but ill prepared. The outlook now is much bleaker."

Spirits sagged even further over the next week. Now that the company shops no longer stood in Arizona's metropolis, the cities of Phoenix, Tempe, and Mesa, Arizona, and Lordsburg, New Mexico contacted Colonel Epes Randolph, requesting that the company relocate its shops in their community. Randolph eased local minds when he responded: "It [Tucson] is the place geographically, if not morally, for the shops." Local business hopes also rose when the company disclosed that its huge, expensive lathes and ten locomotives emerged almost unscathed from the fire.

SP officials investigated the possibility of a planned sabotage at the local shops. H.V. Platt, general superintendent for SP's southern district, announced plans to visit Tucson and examine the railroad's loss. A stricken *Citizen* admonished, "The community should take immediate steps to insure Southern Pacific officials that it stands ready to do everything in its power to prevent a repetition of this crime."

The night before Platt's arrival, exactly one week after the cataclysmic conflagration, another fire attacked the Tucson shops. This time, railroad police discovered a two-foot length of unburned fuse in the fire's debris that pointed to a malevolent, incendiary cause. Damage totaled only

Buildings and equipment were destroyed or heavily damaged by the fire. (AHS #PC180f187 #138)

Aftermath of shop fire lingered long after workmen removed the debris. (AHS #B89434b)

$1,000, but implications of the little blaze echoed through the city. Rail officials said the fuse confirmed that arsonists had ignited the first shop fire. The discovery also made the connection between the *Los Angeles Times* bombing and the local blaze look all the more probable.

Timing of the second fire could not have been worse. Superintendent Platt caught wind of the previous night's blaze when he arrived early the next morning, in his private car the "Los Angeles." Platt "came in with blood in his eye and talked Saturday like there might be a change in location of the shops unless Tucson affords his property and his representatives better protection," reported the *Star*.

That morning, Mayor P.N. Jacobus and City Councilman Mose Drachman met with Colonel Epes Randolph, Superintendent Platt, and Tucson Division superintendent W.H. Whalen in the latter's office. Jacobus and Drachman expressed citizens' strong desire to retain the division shops. Platt explained that when he arrived in the city, he "felt that the community was indifferent and in some ways countenanced the attacks." His discussions with city representatives had convinced him, said the rail honcho, that Tucsonans held a sincere interest in protecting SP property. When asked where his company would construct its new shops, however, Platt balked.

This photograph captured the roundhouse and shop facilities between 1910 and 1912, after their rebuilding. (AHS #PC180f187_4904)

To head off transfer of the railroad shops, Jacobus and Drachman rallied the city's business community for a 1:30 p.m. meeting that afternoon. The group organized as the Good Government League to support the SP in rebuilding its shops in Tucson.

Authorities failed to apprehend perpetrators of the great shop fire, but local spirits brightened as 1910 wound down. The Good Government League's efforts to mollify the railroad persuaded SP to rebuild its shop facilities in Tucson. In addition, the division took first place in the company's annual system-wide inspection. Twenty-six miles of graded streets criss-crossed Tucson in 1910, with several miles macadamized (paved). Some suggested the city style itself "The Queen City of the Southwest."

Layoffs wracked the company's shop force in 1914, but work picked up the following year. Railroad freight volume declined as United States participation in World War I began in 1917, but rebounded when military shipments of equipment and troops surged. The United States Railroad

Administration took control of the nation's railroads on March 21, 1918 with the Railway Control Act, signaling more tough times ahead for rail corporations. Many railroads suffered huge financial losses and major equipment deterioration during the period of federal control.

Congress returned the railroads to private enterprise on March 1, 1920 and established the Railroad Labor Board (RLB) to review wage and other rail concerns. During summer 1922, SP ran its "Prosperity Special" across the nation to foster a sense of post-war well-being and stimulate business. The railroad ordered twenty $60,000 locomotives to demonstrate its corporate good faith that affluence would yet return to the nation.

Under clouds of billowing steam, twenty "monarchs of time and distance" pulled out of the Baldwin plant in Eddystone, Pennsylvania on May 26, 1922. The largest train of locomotives assembled to date, at nearly one-half mile long, the impressive string of oil-burning behemoths chugged into Tucson at midnight June 27, 1922. A curious throng numbered in the

The changing of the Tucson turntable ca.1918. (Ray Hanson Collection)

gine drowned out most of the oratory. Conductors called the "all aboard" at 10:00 a.m. and, "with flying colors and every engineer in his place in the cab," SP's parade of workhorse locomotives headed west for Los Angeles.

Enveloped in growing labor unrest, the nation paid little heed to SP's symbolic "Prosperity" pageant. An ongoing strike in the coal industry had erupted in repeated violence and other labor unions had called strikes. When legal changes threatened to create an "open" or anti-union shop in 1921, the railroad's "Big Four" union brotherhoods had launched political action in response. Local labor leaders held two mass meetings to kick off their political organization at the city's Labor Temple at 29 South Stone Avenue. Encouraged by a strong turnout, local secretary J.M. Morgan predicted the fledgling labor movement would

thousands and mingled around the engines, enjoying the rhythms of the SP band. SP's classic show of American ingenuity and capital investment stretched east from Sixth Avenue to well beyond the car shops when it "tied up" at the passenger depot.

Superintendent William W. Wilson and City Councilman John E. White mounted the running board of Locomotive No. 2277 to address the crowd. Rail work continued nearby, however, and the banging of rail cars and chugging of the yard en-

The Tucson arrival of SP's Prosperity Special delighted curious crowds in late June 1922. (Richard Stapp Sr. Collection)

"no doubt be wielding a country-wide influence within a few months."

The RLB had raised average railroad wages by 22 percent in July 1920, but reversed field, ordering a $60 million cut in shopmen's pay to take effect on July 1, 1922. National union leader B.M. Jewell proclaimed that board-mandated wages would not provide "the minimum amount found to maintain a worker and his family in a condition of decent living." In addition, new RLB rules portended the dreaded "open shop" in the near future. Union heads prepared a strike for that same July 1.

Brotherhood of Railroad Trainmen president W.G. Lee had earlier predicted dire results from any strike because so many men sat idle, or on "short time" with only a few work hours. "I had hoped I would never see the day that the membership I represented would demand the right to commit suicide," Lee asserted. "The railroad companies most certainly want the strike to go on because it will likely mean the end of our organization." Trainmen refrained from striking, but the men of the nation's rail shops prepared to walk out.

Angst resonated through Tucson streets as the July 1 deadline for the shop strike loomed. At 7:30 p.m. the night before the strike, stationary-boiler fireman Francisco Hughes stepped to the doorway of the SP powerhouse. In that instant, previously unremarkable compressed-air tank No. 109 cut loose a riotous explosion just fifteen feet away. The concussion slammed Hughes to the ground, bombarding him with wood and glass shards. Rattled but not seriously injured, Hughes refused medical treatment and rode home with his wife in a taxicab.

The detonation blew the front off the company power building and shattered windows at the east end of the roundhouse. The *Star* later reported that the "ominous roar and crackling blast" startled those who lived within two miles of the shops, bringing hundreds of people to the rail yard. Subsequent tests showed that the tank's safety valve, which would have prevented any detonation due to excessive pressure buildup, still functioned. "With malicious intent," snarled a railroad board of inquiry, "some unknown person [put] some high-grade oil other than lubricating... into the air intake of the operation's compressor while it was running. Due to the heat generated by the compressor, this oil ignited, causing a terrific explosion." Local union officials declared that none of their members had perpetrated "malicious activity."

The next morning, a sizeable crowd gathered outside the shop's main gate at Sixteenth Street and Third Avenue long before the scheduled hour to strike. Pima County's sheriff issued special commissions deputizing seventeen local SP guards. Each took a ready-for-business stance around the company reserve, aware that their neighbor might soon be their enemy.

At 10:00 a.m., three hundred men, about 95 percent of day shift machinists, blacksmiths, sheet metal workers, electricians, car repairers, and helpers, laid down their tools and walked off the job in the Tucson shops. Thirty minutes later, the shops stood "practically deserted, the roundhouse showed but few men remaining and work was practically at a standstill," reported the *Star*. Many of the striking men attended a mass meeting called by union leaders. Local union spokesman Sam Mills expressed pleasure that non-union men had joined their unionized brothers in the walkout.

On July 2, 1922, rail industry executives launched a dynamic campaign to hire 400,000 Negro men from the South and men from Mexico. The Railroad Labor Board hammered strikers, outlawing six striking shop craft unions and mandating that each organize a new body to represent workers in the future.

On the strike's third day local officials announced that more men than they needed had applied for jobs. SP general manager and former Tucson Division su-

Deputized railroad policemen spread out over the SP reserve in preparation for the July 1, 1922 strike. This aerial view shows the Tucson roundhouse and railroad shops ca. 1920. Note the turntable in center of roundhouse. (Ray Hanson Collection)

perintendent Joseph H. Dyer said workers who did not report for their scheduled shift on July 6, 1922 would lose their positions and benefits. The company would restore all seniority, pension, and pass privileges to anyone who returned by that time, Dyer explained. SP President William Sproule reminded shop employees that the RLB, not the railroad, had reduced their wages. Earlier, Sproule had admonished workers, "When you took up for your livelihood the public service of transportation, you assumed a responsibility to the people of the United States."

The Tucson division reported seventy-three men returned to work on the first shift at local shops by the railroad's July 6 deadline. Trusted master mechanic Otto B. Schoenky noted SP stock had risen one-half point since the walk-out and avowed, "The strike is over, as far as the Tucson Division of the Southern Pacific is concerned."

Violence scarred the nation as tempers raged. In Clinton, Illinois, protesters taunted railroad company guards until one shot a striking worker in the neck and killed his twelve-year-old son. Three hundred National Guard troops took over law enforcement in Parsons, Kansas, and placed a ban on public meetings. With anger stifling reason, U.S. District Attorney Charles E. Cline ordered federal authorities and troops to protect anyone working in place of striking railroad shopmen.

The strain of the strike at the railroad shops spilled into Tucson streets, although it lacked the mean vengeance that characterized other cities. A "miniature riot" erupted at one west Congress Street eatery when four strikebreakers seated themselves across from five strikers. "Scab, scab," screamed a former shop worker, "I won't sit opposite a scab!" An errant sugar bowl proved the battle's sole weapon, as the restaurant's proprietor restored order.

Early on the morning of July 10, a large group of strikers blocked the streets leading to the shops using their automobiles. When news spread among striking workmen that SP had started untrained men as boilermakers and machinists rather than apprentices, anger turned to fury. As pickets worked the immediate area, striking boilermaker E.M. Donnelly allegedly hit W.O. Fortson, a Negro man from Mississippi, in the head with a brick. The SP pressed charges on behalf of its injured employee and berated the pattern of official indifference toward abuse of their new hires. Local superintendent William W. Wilson issued a public statement charging that the Pima County Sheriff's Department failed to act on a warrant for

Donnelly's arrest until forty-eight hours after the court signed it.

The erstwhile boilermaker finally turned himself in and pled guilty to hitting Fortson with his fist. Judge Oscar L. Pease, who earned his law degree through after-hours study while toiling as an SP dispatcher, fined the striking shopman just $20. Pease explained that Donnelly's surrender and guilty plea, along with a "frank relation of the circumstances," left him "disinclined to believe that a severe penalty was justified."

Strikers also beat two Mexican men their way to work that day. Livid, Mexican consul Gustavo Couret shot off a letter to Tucson mayor Rudolph Rasmessen. City police officers clearly stood "in sympathy with the practices" of the striking men, wrote Couret. "There has been a failure to act when action has been needed." All of the workers from Mexico had "financial need and for the most part have families to support," affirmed the enraged consul.

That night, company guards Robert Crowder and Charles Andrews patrolled near the shop's main gate at South Third Avenue and Sixteenth Street. As an automobile crept along Sixteenth Street, six shots rang out in their vicinity. Superintendent Wilson later stated that the shots had mixed with the sound of a car backfiring, concealing their point of origin. Union leaders disavowed all connection with the incident.

Two million workers sat idle in various industries across the United States and positions hardened on both sides of the railroad strike. One rail union leader told President W.G. Harding, "We'll stick it out 'til hell freezes over!" With trepidation building, the U.S. Postal Service notified Harding that it stood ready to mobilize 50,000 motor vehicles within twenty-four hours, should the railroad strike interfere with mail delivery.

Near the end of July 1922, shop foremen Phil Garigan and Mike Robles staged a light-hearted affair behind the local roundhouse to brighten rail employees' spirits. The SP band played afternoon and evening concerts, while the "Sand Stormer's Alcoholic Jazzy Five" offered up the country's new rage, jazz music. The fun-filled night included a snake dance by *Madame Shimmie de la Bivoraiskie* and scholarly lectures. To the delight of eight hundred fans, boxing provided the evening's featured diversion. Garigan, Robles, and "Shorty" Pellon refereed a card that included preliminary fights featuring local youngsters. In what the morning paper termed "One of the fastest and cleanest bouts ever witnessed in this city," 148-

Dynamic car inspector foreman Phil Garigan (standing fourth from left) provided entertainment for rails and Tucsonans over three decades. (Mary Annabelle Garigan Collection)

pound "Happy" Woods beat Harry Simmons of St. Louis in the main event.

Inimitable division conductor Harold "Stonewall" Jackson fought on the under-card that steamy summer night in 1922. "My dad was a conductor, and he and some other fellows set up a ring behind the roundhouse," Jackson recalled eighty-two years later. "I boxed a guy who lived across the street from me. He'd been botherin' my younger brother so I had it in for him, anyway. I pounded him good. They had us fight to help the men relieve some of the pressure they were feeling from the strike." A large number of Tucson men remained out on strike as July ended, and the SP held firm to its policy of not taking them back. Though local and nationwide rancor continued, the strike had effectively ended with the railroad's July 6 deadline to return to work.

The ill-fated strike turned lives upside down. Albert Hammonds met "exile" by the railroad in El Paso. During the summer of 2002, his daughter, Geraldine "Maudie" Hammonds Mackaben, pulled up long-ago memories in her stylish northeast-side home: "My father was a labor ac-

Athletic roundhouse foreman Al Hammonds readies for a golf match in this ca. 1928 photo. Hammonds moved his family from El Paso following the divisive shop strike. (Al and Maude Hammonds Collection)

tivist. He was a leader of his strikers when they rioted at the gates of the shops in El Paso. The railroad had my father arrested, so he hired a young attorney to fight the charges named Ralph Yarborough, who later became a very distinguished senator from Texas. The company finally gave my father the option of going to Tucson or to Roseville, California. He chose Tucson, and loved it. He later became Tucson roundhouse foreman."

Railroad to the core, Caleb Houston ran his first steam locomotive on the day he turned twenty, the initial coal rather than wood-burning locomotive south of the Ohio River, the "Suwanee." Caleb came west in the 1880s and started on an SP construction crew in California. He took work in the railroad shops at Raton, New Mexico in 1885, later founding that town's Odd Fellows Lodge.

Houston began in the Tucson shops in 1890 but left during the 1922 shopmen's strike to work for the Arizona Eastern Railroad at Hayden. The father of SP engineer and Tucson mayor E.T. "Happy" Houston and System Superintendent of SP's mechanical department Stanley M. Houston, Caleb worked in Benson and Globe for the next twenty years before returning to the SP shops in Tucson. Known affectionately in the local roundhouse as "Dad," Houston earned fame as the scorekeeper at local baseball games and for the stunning roses that he grew and sold from his home at 1224 East Sixth Street. Caleb worked for four separate railroads during his fifty-eight year career and offered sage advice when he retired from the SP in January 1939: "It does a fellow good to work for different railroads. It makes a mechanic of you, you see a lot of different country, and you meet a lot of people."

The 1922 strike stimulated the westward migration of many experienced craftsmen. Faced with financial ruin or the personal disgrace of crossing the picket line in their own community, workers opted to relocate to cities where they could enjoy an-

In 1917, while running a trainload of Mexican miners to work during that country's revolution, Caleb Houston came upon a bridge trestle burned by insurgents. After a three-day wait for workers to construct a temporary bridge, Caleb's engine built tremendous steam for taking his seventeen-car train over the makeshift crossing and up a forty-five-degree grade. "I knew the only way we'd make it across was to open up the throttle and hope the momentum carried us up the other side. While we were going down as fast as we could I was afraid that at any minute, the rails would give way and it would be the end of all of us. While I would never try it again, we made it across alright." (Stanley M. Houston Collection)

onymity. Tucson Division superintendent William W. Wilson reported, "I have it on reliable authority that first-class mechanics in the east are asking for transportation to Los Angeles and other western points." Negro men and workers from Mexico also found new homes and lives in Arizona's desert during the strike of 1922.

Some shopmen who lost their jobs in the 1922 strike returned to Tucson after a year. Born at 301 South Park Avenue just three months before the strike, former roundhouse foreman T. Herman Blythe shared his family's story. "My father, Homer Blythe, arrived in Tucson in a Model T Ford and went to work as a boilermaker's helper in 1916," said Herman. "He and a couple of other rails bought land near the corner of Country Club Road and Grant Road. We had two acres and my mother lowered him into our well as he hand dug it. He hit water at about thirty feet."

A strong union man, Homer Blythe refused to cross the picket line during the 1922 shop strike. Instead, he whisked his family out of Tucson and went to work as the fireman on a small engine hauling cars of rock ballast from the crusher at Steins, New Mexico, to the SP main line. "Carl Ball Sr. was the engineer there at Steins," said Herman. "We came back to Tucson in 1923, and my father hired out as a fireman. Men worked fifteen to twenty years before the company promoted them to engineer in those days."

Herman began his own career on the Tucson Division February 10, 1941, as a machinist's apprentice earning 35¢ an hour. The railroad promised the handsome Tucson High School graduate a four-year apprenticeship and a two-and-one-half-cent-an-hour raise every six months. With United States involvement in World War II ramping up rail traffic, the SP upgraded

Hamblin McNeil (rear, second from left) took a job as a blacksmith's helper when he arrived from Mississippi in February 1922, before that year's shop strike. Eighty-three years later, his nephew, James A. Barnes, reminisced. "My father and uncle came to Tucson knowing very little about it," he said. "My uncle Hamblin had been shoeing horses in Mississippi, and he rose to 'lead man,' second to the foreman, in the blacksmith's shop." (James A. Barnes Collection)

Blythe to machinist after just two years. "At that time, if they thought you could do enough work to earn a journeyman's pay they upgraded you," he recalled.

West of the roundhouse, and large enough to hold a good-sized airplane, the local backshop housed boilermakers, machinists, blacksmiths, and other craftsmen. The backshop crew completed light engine repairs on all division locomotives each year, more extensive work every three years, and a general overhaul at five-year intervals.

During the war, as many as twenty locomotives might be in the thirty-stall Tucson roundhouse at any one time. Hostlers readied locomotives for main line service, and moved engines around in the roundhouse and backshop, with a small steam engine called the "Dinky." Mounted with a saddle to hold water for producing its steam, the Dinky remained fired-up twenty-four hours a day. "Trains came from the east in the morning and from the west in the afternoon," Herman explained. "We'd sometimes get backed up, so we'd have to keep an engine ready in case there were any problems out on the line. If the trainmaster called for an engine, the hostler ran it onto the turntable, turned it the correct direction, and had it ready to take out right away."

When mechanics tore the locomotive down, every component went to its own area. Machinists checked tolerances on steel parts, boilermakers repaired the boiler, and pipe fitters tested steam fittings. "The air brake equipment went to the air room," Blythe said. "The feed water pumps went to one place and the injectors to another. The rod bench worked on the link motion. Everything was a specialty."

Tracks extended through two roundhouse stalls, into the backshop, and over a "drop table," Blythe said. "As the Dinky pushed a locomotive over the gap in the rail on the drop table, its huge driving wheels smashed onto the 'drop rail' below with a loud crash. This allowed mechanics

T. Herman Blythe grew up in a rail family and began at the Tucson shops in February 1941. (T. Herman Blythe collection)

Shopmen trained as apprentices or in company schools. The company built a dozen such facilities and trained almost 1,000 men by 1925. (Manuel Gallardo Collection)

This McKeen Motor Car arrived in the Tucson yard ca. 1920. Such a gas-burner worked the Arizona Eastern's line between Bowie and Globe for years. "They were gutless wonders that generally couldn't pull anything except sometimes a specially-built lightweight trailer," explained one ex-rail. The SP gutted a similar motor car to serve as the roundhouse foreman's office during the mid-1950s. (Ray Hanson Collection)

to remove the locomotive's cast-iron wheels and to access its leaf springs."

High-tensile steel tires encircled each wheel of a steam locomotive and needed regular service. Over time, a flange on the edge of the tire wore off, or the tracks carved a concave groove in the tire's tread. "Heat expanded the steel tires so workers could remove and replace them," Herman continued. "We'd bring in heaters, heat 'em up, take the tires off. If the wheels needed it, we'd build them up with steel shims and turn them in the wheel lathe, two wheels at a time. If a tire got too thin to turn and use again, we'd heat up a new tire and put it on the wheel. When it cooled, it would shrink and fit on tightly." When the locomotive pulled steep up-hill grades, however, its wheels slipped on the rails, generating in-

credible heat and loosening the tires. To prevent slippage, shopmen welded seven clips to secure each tire to the wheel.

Charles Stoddard came to Tucson for his sister's health in 1924. One sizzling June day in 2002, the former president of the International Association of Machinists and the Supervisors Union looked back on a successful railroad career in his cool and spacious Oro Valley home. "I started out as machinist helper, greasing side rods and doing 'sod packing'", said Stoddard. "All mechanical moving parts needed greasing, so we put grease cakes in cast iron boxes called "journals" at each end of all the axles on the railcars and engine tenders." The approximately twelve-inch-long metal containers held bearings in need of constant greasing. "The journal box had a screen in it," Charles explained. "We put in a pre-formed grease cake that was contoured to fit the shape of the journal. It was heavy grease. The block of grease slid back and forth through the screen to keep the journal lubricated. We also put grease into the locomotive's main drivers and lubricated its running gear."

After his apprenticeship and a couple of years as a machinist, Stoddard earned promotion to backshop foreman and began supervising almost two hundred people. "We did heavy, classified repairs," said the burly eighty-five-year-old. "You, generally, had four locomotives at a time in the backshop. After a locomotive came in, we'd set it on the Whiting Hoist and lift the whole engine up. Then, we'd drop the wheels out and put temporary wheels under it."

Boilermakers completed a hydrostatic test for cracks in the boiler. "The rules said the boiler had to be washed every three or four trips," explained Blythe. "But, we had a guy that would open the 'blow-down-cock' on the boiler, test the water, and tell us if we had to wash it. We'd blast it with fresh water and blow the scale caused by alkali out of it." Other men made necessary patches inside the firebox or tested and renewed the stay bolts. "They also replaced the locomotive's crank pins and axles, depending on their wear," Stoddard continued. "Sometimes the crown sheet inside the firebox might need replacement." Workers also removed the flues in the engine's super-heater unit and tossed them into the "rattler," a twenty-five-foot-long cylinder. "The flues rolled through the entire cylinder to clean soot out of them and made it real noisy," said Stoddard.

Lurking beneath an engine's jacket, asbestos presented an unrecognized and potentially fatal danger to men in the Tucson shops. Prior to replacing this exterior metal cover, men wrapped four-inch-thick sheets of the toxic material around the locomotive's boiler. To fill gaps between these

sheets, a man ground asbestos into pulp at a "pug mill" behind the backshop. "The asbestos dust was so thick you couldn't even see the guy that was running the grinding machine," said Blythe. "I saw him years later and he was sweepin' in the courthouse and he didn't have cancer." Adding water to the fine asbestos particles created a fire-resistant, treacherous mud. "We used to have fights at lunch time with that mud, like you

Proud Charles Stoddard stands before Tucson's Historic Locomotive #1673 during its dedication in September 2002. Stoddard served as trainmaster on the local division. "The trainmaster used to be just in charge of the road operating department," the avid University of Arizona Wildcat fan recalled. "Then they decided it would be more efficient if the trainmaster controlled a combination of the mechanical and operating departments. This included derailments or accidents, so I kept two suitcases, one for meetings and one for train wrecks. In covering the division, I probably drove my car forty to sixty thousand miles a year." (Kalt Collection)

Schooled at the University of California Berkeley, local shop instructor Ray Hanson poses beside his car near the University of Arizona ca. 1935. During World War II, Ethel Crawford ran a small lunch stand between the roundhouse and the back shops. Crawford and her family made sandwiches using government meats and other inexpensive foods. When men proved slow to pay, Hanson played enforcer. (Ray Hanson Collection)

some two-feet long, to reach into the engine."

Blythe got his start as a roundhouse foreman in a most unorthodox way following his return from the Navy. "I was workin' days, but they called me at eleven o'clock at night to drop a pair of wheels out of the engine on the burro run to Nogales," he remembered. "This locomotive had only two drivers, but they were enormous, over eighty inches. The wheels didn't fit onto the lathe with their tires on, so we placed 'em up on some sawhorses, got the heaters out, heated the tires up, and knocked them off," Blythe recalled. "Well, my helper W. T. Terry and I did real good. We dropped them wheels out and rolled 'em over to the backshop. We'd really worked hard and everything went along pretty good, so about five o'clock in the morning, we took a break."

The pair sat down to rest. "Along comes the general foreman, Johnny DeSpain," laughed Herman. "He says, 'What the hell you doin' sittin' down?' Now, I figured we'd done two days work already that day, and I took offense. I told him 'Go to Hell,' and got up and went home."

When he returned to the roundhouse in couple of days, Blythe received a message to come to master mechanic H.E. Carter's office. "I went into the meeting thinking I might get fired and stopped by the shop tool room and got my local chairman, Kenny Mac," he said. "Carter told me, 'DeSpain says you got a lot of spunk. Says you done a good job out there and didn't take any guff off anybody. How'd you like to go to Yuma as a roundhouse foreman?'"

would snowballs," remembered Blythe, a throat cancer survivor at eighty-four years of age.

Amid blazing fires needed to forge steel, company blacksmiths cut and created all the parts, tools, bolts, and nuts needed to complete the railroad's every task. "If a job needed to be done, a man got the right tool to do the job," said Blythe. "If the tool did not exist, the blacksmiths made it for him and then he completed his job."

Blacksmiths also shaped the "knuckle pins" used to secure an engine's drive rods in tandem. "He'd cut blanks of the correct length from the hand-forged high-tensile steel of old railcar axles," Blythe explained. "Then he hammered out a rough, hex-shaped head that allowed a mechanic to tighten it with a wrench. We always had a pile of old axles nearby for that purpose. We used 'boiler plate' (thick sheet metal from the boiler) to make wrenches to fit all the different hex shapes. We made

Northwest of the roundhouse and backshop, men repaired and refurbished railcars and cabooses in the company car shop. Using a small turntable, car repairmen stripped and replaced everything from heaters to windows, wallpaper, and the "knuckles" used to couple railcars.

Following the start of the Great Depression, the SP transferred one hundred jobs out of Tucson during mid-summer 1930. Twelve to sixteen positions went to El Paso from the "air room," where workers serviced booster pumps, water pumps, and air pumps. The SP next laid off seventy-nine men in the car shops and rumors swirled that the Tucson facility would repair no more cars. Some avowed the company would abolish the Tucson Division and extend El Paso's Rio Grande Division westward to Yuma. At the same time, the Phoenix Chamber of Commerce pressed the SP for more jobs in the capital city. This rekindled fears from three decades earlier that Phoenix would supplant Tucson as the company's Arizona hub. As workers from the blacksmith and electrical shops began to depart the city, the Great Depression deepened.

Former car shop foreman Eddie A. Caballero stood as one of few men hired during the nation's economic doldrums. Eddie started in the car shop in April 1931. "Lookin' like a million bucks" as usual, the gentle ninety-one-year-old settled onto his living room sofa beside his beautiful wife, Aurelia Vasquez Caballero, to tell his tale in the fall of 2002. "My father and mother journeyed to Tucson from Mexico in covered wagons in 1911," Eddie beamed. "I was ready to come to life by the time they reached the San Xavier Mission, so they stopped there to have me. I grew up in Tucson, started working at the SP as an apprentice, and stayed forty-seven years."

The well-liked car foreman explained: "We'd tear down a car and rebuild it, to fix or upgrade it. We might replace the car's wheel trucks or its siding, fix an electrical problem, or replace its seats. We also removed flat wheels for repair in our 'wheel room.' We'd press the tires and axles off the cast-iron car wheels and 'mic,' or measure, them to exact micrometer tolerance. If the wheel needed replacing, I'd bore a hole in a new wheel and press an axle through it. We did it all."

During his years in the car shop, two men earned Eddie's enduring admiration. Master car repairman Donald McIntyre treated his men with respect while heading a productive car department. Division superintendent Ralph Coltrin gave him an opportunity Caballero came to treasure. "Mr. Coltrin was really nice to me at the railroad," Eddie acknowledged. "He invited me to Saguaro Toastmasters meeting and I thought about public speaking for the first time. I became very successful in the Toastmasters. I gained a lot of confidence and won an award for my public speaking."

Eddie Caballero (right) enjoys a cigar during an inspection of the Tucson operation by SP officials. Caballero began with the SP in 1928 and in the car shops in 1931. (Eddie Caballero Collection)

Master Mechanic Donald McIntyre in his office at the local yard ca. 1954. (Donald McIntyre Collection)

The demanding physical work in the railroad shops rolled along day in and day out. The job proved far from a somber affair, however. "There was stuff at the roundhouse that was real comical," said Blythe. "The company used an oily mass of multi-colored cotton strings, called 'waste,' to help lubricate its journals and things," Herman explained. "Big bins of it sat all around the shop and you could get as much as you wanted. Well, back then, men used waste for everything and everybody wore overalls. If he could catch someone walkin' along with a little bit of waste hanging out of their pocket, a guy might light it up with a match for a laugh." The Tucson roundhouse toilets provoked even more hilarity. "Water always ran through a pipe underneath this row of ten toilets," Blythe mused. "If you could catch a guy sittin' at the other end of the toilets, you'd take this oily waste, light it on fire, and put it in the water. It'd float right down the pipe and singe him where he didn't want to be singed, ha, ha, ha."

Over the years, experiences at the shops grew into fond memories for many Tucsonans. Inspirational Korean War veteran, author, and Tucson *nativo* Ruben Moreno found more than he bargained for

when he and a friend snuck into the roundhouse to use the toilets during the 1930s. As the duo settled onto their respective thrones, engulfed by roaring locomotives and pounding in the shops, Moreno's friend yelled, "Ruben, what would you do if one of those big engines just came crashing through that wall?"

"I'd jump out that window there," Moreno replied, just as imagination dissolved to cold steel and a steam locomotive erupted through the roundhouse's brick wall. Turning his words to action, Moreno grabbed his *amigo* by the arm and dove out of harm's way. None the worse for wear and armed with an cherished image, Ruben later went to work as a laborer for the railroad while attending Tucson High School.

Long-time musician and Tucson educator Geraldine "Maudie" Hammonds Mackaben grew up in railroad housing at Second Avenue and Sixteenth Street, three-quarters of a block from the roundhouse. "My father worked the midnight shift, between 11:00 p.m. and 7:00 a.m., so it was very, very handy for him," she said. "He started taking a friend and me to the shops beginning when I was about eight or nine. My dad let us climb on the steam engines and we had a ball sitting on the turntable when they turned an engine. Since they didn't have a storeroom of parts all ready to go, the machinists made parts for the engines. In the process, they created endless spiral metal shavings that were a lot of fun to play with, too."

A tradition of keeping a cat at the Tucson backshop continued for decades. As the twentieth century began, shopmen nurtured a "Civit cat" in the bustling facility, until the 1910 fire forced it to reside in the Owl Drug Store. During the 1930s, Mackaben remembered a cat named Kit that lived in the backshop. "Kit was always having kittens," she said. "My Dad took food to her when he went to work. Kit soon discovered that my Dad lived across the street and she started coming over to meet him every night at our house. That cat was just filthy from living in the backshop. You'd pet Kit and your hand would be all black. My Dad always wet a paper towel and wiped her off."

Pretty "tomboy" Emily Rinkleib Bradley grew up around the bang and clatter of the local railroad. Emily and her father, engineer Bernard "Wrinkle Belly" Rinkleib, often walked to the SP yard office to check his status on the engineer's extra board or pick up his paycheck. "We'd go on Third Avenue to Sixteenth Street and cut through all the railroad housing," she recalled in her luxurious home in the foothills of the Catalina Mountains during November 2002. "There were big trees back then, so you didn't drive through there," she explained. "You'd come out of the Broadway subway onto Second Avenue and up over a hill, because the railroad was built up, and walk over to the roundhouse. There was a gate into the yard that was always open. That was a different era in Tucson." Bradley went to the roundhouse with her father on the weekends and during the summer. "He always stopped by the roundhouse and talked to his friend Al Hammonds," she said. "He'd hold my hand because it was pretty noisy in there. I loved it! I was a tomboy!"

The operation's heart throughout the steam era, Tucson's railroad shops faced a brisk decline in personnel when diesel engines replaced labor-intensive steam locomotives during the 1950s. The new engines required fewer men to maintain, and the SP initiated large-scale cutbacks that

Bright and lovely Safford School eighth-grade railroad girls posed in the southeast corner of the SP barracks lawn at 449-501 E. Sixteenth Street in the spring of 1941. (l-r) Maudie Hammonds Mackaben, Bernice Rinkleib George, Emily Rinkleib Bradley, Frankie Gefeller, and Mary Louise Dubois. Sixty-five years later, children of local rails treasure memories of visits to the loud and dirty shop operation. (Al and Maude Hammonds Collection)

changed the nature of Tucson operations. Blythe recalled vibrant days in the Tucson shops. "Back when I was roundhouse foreman, I signed 102 time cards on the afternoon shift alone," said the good-hearted Blythe. "Now, the Tucson shops employ less than 10 percent of what we did during the steam locomotive's heyday."

Today, people look for a "diaper" to protect them from injury, violation, having to work too hard, and almost every other modern problem. Tucson shopmen valued a different ethic during the steam age. Now, we meet problems with a call to a specialist or a Web search. Back then, shopmen pulled on their heavy gloves to face obstacles with ingenuity, determination, and certain knowledge that they could solve "damn near anything." Now, only a few good men and stories remain from those well-worn shop days during this unique period in Tucson's history.

Tucson shop force 1940. A year earlier, division seniority lists included 88 machinists, 36 boilermakers, and 63 carmen in the car shop. (Ray Hanson Collection)

Henry Sabala (bottom right) and fellow pipefitters paused for this ca. 1945 photograph at the Tucson shops. (Annie Sabala Collection)

Chapter 9

The railroad's large employee base could sway elections, especially under pressure from manipulative local officials. This group (a detail portion of the group picture shown on page 2) gathered August 1, 1959 to honor the career of roundhouse foreman Al Hammonds (center with baby). (Al and Maude Hammonds Collection)

Southern Pacific Political Punch: Power Across the Decades

"When the railroad boys open the throttle there will be a sizz; then things will move, switches will be thrown, and there will be no 'down brakes' until the end of the line is reached. Watch the vote and keep your eye on the railroaders."

*Arizona Daily Star,
June 19, 1898.*

"Robert H. Paul, one of the really brave, courageous men of the Southwest," began city councilman Mose Drachman, "a terror to the stage robber and murderer, was sheriff of Pima County." In 1884, "Paul ran in the primary for the Republican nomination against E.B. Gifford, "one of Tuc-

son's leading gamblers and also a brave man," Drachman explained. "Paul was the choice of the Southern Pacific Railroad (SP), and in those days, the SP was practically the whole thing in Arizona, as well as in California politics."

John A. Muir, Tucson Division superintendent, loved to brandish his political muscle. "He helped Paul all he could," explained Drachman. "In order to control the rail vote, Muir bought up all the paper in town that was green on one side and white on the other and had Paul's tickets printed on it." In fear for their livelihoods, no SP man dared vote against the "Old Man's" candidate. "If Muir found it out, he (the "errant" rail) would certainly lose his job," Drachman remembered. Paul won the primary, but lost to E.O. Shaw in the general election. Muir demanded a recount!

Presiding Judge J.T Fitzgerald's strong bias against the railroad power machine further aggravated Muir. One day came "shocking" news that the entire lot of election ballots had gone missing from Katz's warehouse at Congress and Meyer Streets. When authorities found the voting tickets, a recount produced a sufficient number marked with Paul's name to earn him victory. The following March, "when the perpetrators found that they could no longer bleed him for money, Paul told all, exposing the scandal," said Drachman.

The SP framed the realities of Arizona's political landscape just as it determined the location and growth of communities throughout the West. An age-

The pioneer Kengla family settled near Rillito Creek when they arrived in 1883. (Dorothy Kengla Fitzpatrick Collection)

less triumvirate of position, power, and money drove both company and personal decisions. Five cornerstones formed the railroad's political foundation. A large body of voters with an interest in furthering railroad business often held sway in elections. "Direct influence" and "private counsel" encouraged government officials to cast votes consistent with rail interests. Sitting on legislative committees, rail advocates employed "obstruction" to control policy decisions on railroad affairs. This process held "hostile" bills in legislative committee until they died through lack of interest. Teams of SP lawyers waged protracted court battles to delay anti-railroad forces, while a relentless advertising campaign, meant to counter its villainous public image and promote the company's benefits, completed SP's political array.

The railroad's approach to politics manifest a sharply refined image of self-interest and exquisite understanding of the day's partisan realities. Leading by inspiration and example, Collis P. Huntington directed the SP from its inception. The dynamic rail kingpin played rough in the politics of every state and territory through which his railroad passed, including Arizona. The *New York Free Press* explained: "Mr. Huntington believed in himself first, then in the institutions he directed. Any means to an end was the rule of his life. He didn't see the slightest harm in buying whole legislatures and courts. He was the most daring lobbyist that ever haunted the halls of Congress. At congressional investigating committees, he laughed."

Arizona governor A.P.K. Safford endured accusations of accepting a $20,000 bribe from Huntington to hold a special legislative session and pass a law allowing the

C.P. Huntington
(Kalt Collection)

SP to build through Arizona. Safford refuted the charge in a January 1881 letter to C.R. Drake, Tucson city councilman. "I could not call it [a special session] without someone would pay for it," he explained. "What they [SP] wanted was a general railroad law, perfectly legitimate and of vast importance to the territory. Finally, they concluded to go on without the law and no extra session was called. I was never in the employ of the SPRR directly or indirectly until after my term expired." Safford's name suffers the disparagement of his alleged corruption more than a century later, despite his being "so scrupulous" that he would not accept a single free pass on any Arizona railroad.

C.R. Drake played a crucial role in the SP's venture into southern Arizona. The Civil War veteran journeyed to Tucson, working as a hospital steward at Camp Lowell, in 1872. Drake won election to the city council in February 1878. That year the Walnut Prairie, Illinois native built a lavish home at 204 South Scott Avenue. Hand-carved woodwork and a large skylight over the living room highlighted the gorgeous house, while ancient fig trees and pomegranate bushes lent the landscape a "regal air." The mansion became the center "of the most colorful social and political gatherings," recalled the *Tucson Daily Citizen*. "Drake was one of the most prominent political leaders of the day and a strong supporter of the advent of the Southern Pacific Railroad." Known about town as "Charley," the powerful Republican served as Tucson's assistant postmaster and ran the U.S depository, handling large sums of money to pay all government troops until 1881. Pima County voters elected Drake to multiple terms as county recorder and to the Territo-

[Reproduced from the San Francisco Examiner Wednesday morning, 12th February, 1896.]

The New Washington "Post" March.   Played in Railroad Time.

This 1896 San Francisco Examiner cartoon depicts Huntington directing an assortment of politicians and the Washington Post newspaper.

rial Legislative Council, later called the Senate, in 1886.

Re-elected to the Arizona Council for 1888, Drake also sat as president of Tucson Building & Loan Association. That year, President Benjamin F. Harrison appointed him head of the government's Tucson Land Office, and the territorial governor named him a University of Arizona regent. After several years in the black powder business, Drake and John Norton took the contract to provide men and food supplies to section gangs along the Tucson Division. Norton & Drake Company controlled the SP supply contract in 1893. In June 1900, L.H. Manning took over the lucrative rail supply operation.

After years of political service, Drake moved to Long Beach, California, and managed the Virginia Hotel around 1910. He sold his residence in Tucson to Judge Charles Blenman and his wife, who discovered a wealth of antique treasures in the home's attic. Judge Blenman's dignity and pleasant "English country squire" hospitality lured a "quiet and cultured group" to the home until his 1936 death.

Other local rails joined the territorial legislature. Former division superintendent A.A. Bean entered the Arizona House in 1887; Republican SP engineers Louis Martin and J.S. O'Brien joined Bean as Pima County's legislators in 1889. Two years later, voters chose Republican engineer C.C. Suter to represent Pima County in the Arizona House. Engineer John W. "Jack" Bruce won election to the territorial Assembly in 1893. Bruce helped to organize the Tucson Division's Brotherhood of Locomotive Engineers No. 28 and served five terms as that group's head engineer. Toward the betterment of all rails, he also lent hearty support to the Southern Pacific Library Association. Tragically, the father of five died in the 1903 train wreck near Esmond Station.

The SP had a major problem in the Arizona Territory in 1893. N. Oakes Murphy, brother of long-time SP nemesis Frank M. Murphy, sat as territorial governor. That year, Maricopa & Phoenix Railroad Company's C.S. Masten, wrote Collis Huntington, asking for help in securing a new governor. One who did not act in "every way inimical to the interests of the Southern Pacific Company," said Masten. "I know him well and can say unreservedly that we don't want to keep him as Governor any longer than it takes to get him out. All the influence that Oakes Murphy is able to bring

Pima County legislator and SP master car repairman J.B.Finley stands third from right in the back row in this photograph of the 1898 territorial Counciil. Future Arizona Governor G.W.P. Hunt stands to Finley's left. (AHS# 2444)

to bear on railroad matters as Governor is thrown in with the Santa Fe and against the SP." Masten explained to Huntington that appointment of John S. Armstrong would ensure "no improper meddling with Railroad interests during his incumbency." Despite Masten's efforts, N. Oakes Murphy returned as governor in July 1898, when Myron H. McCord resigned to lead a western regiment in the Spanish-American War.

SP's "obstruction" of legislation harmful to rail interests focused on controlling important legislative committees. California served as SP's base of operations and provided a prime example. The railroad made no effort to control committees in that state's Assembly, allowing the large body of representatives to act as it wished. When a distasteful bill made it to the Senate, however, rail interests helped hold the bill in committee until it died.

In 1893, the *Sacramento Bulletin* noted that an SP attorney chaired California's Senate Committee on Corporations

and several railroad supporters sat on the committee. Calling it "the SP's Game," the newspaper railed: "This game has been played before. It is evidently going to be played again. No anti-railroad bill will ever see the light of day. If Mr. Huntington himself had personally selected the committee he could not have done better." Proud of his influence, the rail tycoon retained the *Bulletin's* account in his personal collection, rescued sixty years after his death from a barn in Westchester County, New York.

Local master car repairman James Buchanan Finley joined the Territorial House of Representatives in 1894. Born in Santa Rosa, California during November 1856, Democrat Finley started with the SP in 1883, as manager of the company's Pullman repair shops at Deming, New Mexico. Two years later, he came to Tucson as a shop foreman. Re-elected to the House in 1896, Finley chaired the assembly's powerful committee on corporations and played an instrumental role in the enactment of Arizona's twenty-five cent poll tax. Pima

County sent the master car repairman to the 1898 Council, where he served as chairman of the enrolling and engrossing committee. Finley's opposition helped to defeat a woman's suffrage a bill that year. Later, the veteran politician took over as superintendent of the *Ferrocarril Sud-Pacífico de México* (Southern Pacific of Mexico) in Empalme, Sonora and rose to vice president and general manager of the Mexico operations.

Charles M. Burkhalter began as local division freight and passenger agent in 1886. He won election to the city council in 1893 and contributed much to the emergence of "New Tucson." When Republican SP machinist Otis R. Hale joined the legislative assembly in 1898, the local master car repairman's shop enjoyed a reputation as "the 'refuge' for embryo statesmen." Chairman of the library committee and member of the judiciary committee, Hale advanced an important bill that appropriated money to fund the University of Arizona. Following his stint in the capital, Hale left the railroad to open Tucson's Myrick & Hale, a locomotive sales and well-drilling company.

Several other departments sent men to leadership positions. Frank E. Russell worked the SP's local telegraph service during the 1880s and served on the city council from 1895 through 1902. Citizens elected railroad machinists George Angus and Thomas O. Clark to the city council in 1899 and 1900.

E.M. Dickerman, Republican master car repairer, lost by one vote to N.W. Bernard in his bid for joint councilman of Pima and Santa Cruz counties in November 1901. Respected for his railroading skills and political acumen, Dickerman edged Bernard five years later and served one term in Phoenix. Pima County voters sent Joseph B. Corbett, Republican division "traveling engineer," or road foreman of engines, to the territory's Twenty-Second Legislative Council in 1902. Labor's voice in Phoenix, Corbett successfully negotiated concessions from SP management for the Brotherhood of Railway Engineers.

Railroad individuals with political and financial aspirations also advanced their personal interests. SP legal kingpin William F. Herrin exemplified men who used inside knowledge and power to build personal fortunes. For many years, Herrin headed a powerful squadron of lawyers that shared in the railroad's wealth and built fierce enemies. The *San Francisco Chronicle* once noted, "It is notorious that the SP's political bureau maintained at Sacramento by the Southern Pacific ... de-

Tucsonans trusted many rails to handle their political business through the steam era. (Dorothy Kengla Fitzpatrick Collection)

Local master car repairman and Republican Edward M. Dickerman won election to the Territorial Council in 1907. In June 1909, Mayor Ben Heney appointed the dynamic rail to finish councilman E.E. Partridge's term.

(AHS #60094 Dickerman)

votes more time to evolving schemes to bleed the railroad than it does in the protection of its interests."

During his short tenure following Collis Huntington's death, SP president Charles M. Hays made an unsuccessful effort to close the company's political bureau. E.H. Harriman took control of the railroad and announced that the SP would no longer "meddle in political affairs but would adhere strictly to the legitimate business of carrying freight and passengers." Harriman "abolished" the railroad's political bureau, vowing to "expend no money for fixing conventions and handling legislatures." In the face of Harriman's heady proclamation, lawyer Herrin initiated "demonstrations of corporate hostility" and "threats to 'cinch' and harass the company," the *Citizen* explained. Despite Harriman's efforts to terminate Herrin's reign, the po-

tent bureau chief continued to profit from his association with the SP.

In Tucson, former Pima County surveyor George J. Roskruge and county engineer Charles Von Erxleben issued a public statement at the start of January 1902: "The Southern Pacific company, we presume from lack of knowledge of the first survey, have extended their line easterly thirty feet and closed up all the streets in the Manlove Addition, and there is no public crossing from Corbett's lumber easterly."

During mid-May 1902, SP superintendent Epes Randolph told the *Globe Record*: "There will be no more railroad building in Arizona while the present obstructive laws remain in force and the attitude of state government and the people continues to be hostile towards transportation companies. None whatever." Randolph pointed to Arizona's recent mandate requiring a Pyle brand headlight on all locomotives. The regulation caused Tucson Division expenses to rise $5,575 in a single month, said Randolph. He criticized the Arizona legislature for hampering railroad operations and pointed out that better headlamps existed. Worse, parties outside Arizona made the Pyle light. Randolph also blasted Arizona's "full crew" law requiring three brakemen on every train. The Colonel called the law "an outgrowth of a grudge against the Arizona Eastern by a former employee who was discharged for incompetency."

The parade of political rails marched forward. Republican train dispatcher Benton Dick served as Pima County Attorney in 1903 and 1905. Democrat Martin Duffy, a former rail, defeated businessman and rancher George Pusch by four votes to win a Ward 1 city council seat in 1904.

The "66 to 44" movement swept across Arizona under the cry of "just and equal taxation" during the fall of 1906. Movement leaders believed that the 66 legislators representing the territory's farmers, sheepmen, and other small taxpayers would compel "the tax dodgers, the copper looters of Arizona, and railroads" represented by 44 legislators, to pay their fair share of taxes.

Railroads, indeed, ran roughshod over Arizona politics. Both the SP and Santa Fe Railroad opposed the Arizona/New Mexico Joint Statehood Bill, fearing it would bring more equable taxation and hurt their interests. "It can not be denied that these great corporations controlled both the Democratic and Republican territorial conventions at Bisbee," said the *Star* during 1906.

Characterizing both parties' conventions as marriage ceremonies between the state's railroads and southern Arizona's candidates for Congressional representative, the paper mocked both nominating festivities in stinging satire: "The stalwart bridegroom, Marcus Aurelius Smith, was attired in a Southern Pacific coat and Santa Fe tails. He had on copper colored pantaloons, turned up at the bottom over senatorial sto-gas (laughter). The slender bride, William Cooper (Smith's Republican counterpart), was radiant in a robe of mosquito netting trimmed with jimson weed. Her raiment was thin, and she shook with apprehension for fear that her bridegroom would leave her at the altar. Both bride and bridegroom were decorated with '66 to 44 NOT' buttons."

Throughout the early twentieth century, Tucson businessmen believed that the SP charged them the cost of carrying their goods from the east to the California coast and back. Said to be well versed in freight rates, Steinfeld & Co. traffic department manager W.F. Ellsworth explained that "many commodities" arrived in Tucson for less than the cost of such a circuitous route. "They crush the industries that do not profit them and foster those that pay tribute to them," wailed the *Star*. "They charge freight rates that allow the grower of perishable fruits barely enough for his products to prevent him from digging up his

trees and vines. They bribe legislators and assessors and seem to have only two objects in view—grand and petit larceny." In late December 1906, SP assistant general passenger agent J.C. Stubbs addressed Tucson merchants in the Santa Rita Hotel's Blue Parlor. Announcing the company's retreat from its practice of charging double rates to ship commodities like cement between Benson and Tucson, Stubbs said the SP would comply with recent federal law.

SP freight and passenger agent Robert Lowrie won a chair on the city council in 1905 and 1906. Lowrie, former Tucson Division superintendent C.C. Sroufe, and locomotive engineer, school board trustee, and former city councilman Leonidas "Lon" Holliday helped build Pima County's Democratic "new machine" in 1907. Local SP historian Gustav H. Schneider recalled that Democrats fell from grace that year and nearly "everyone" belonged to the city's Republican Club for the next decade. "The Republicans had lots of money and paid

Tucson's "Big Four," (l-r) Southern Pacific cashier, Robert Lowrie, dispatcher Gustav Bonorden, Mr. Winters, and Ralph Knigs formed a powerful quartet in 1895. (AHS #24401)

well for brass bands, torches, etc., for their processions," Schneider said.

Railroads had violated laws against favoritism in Arizona for many years, and then "destroyed the vouchers to hide the payment of unlawful rebates to a few favored packinghouses," the *Star* once charged. That railroads should conduct business in such "open disregard of law, must be surprising and offensive to all right-minded citizens."

Price gouging by the SP and its Globe-Bowie line, the Arizona Eastern Railroad, came under investigation in the summer of 1909. Arizona Railway Commission secretary M.O. Bicknell charged Colonel Epes Randolph: "Your Bowie to Globe rate is...thirty times greater on sugar and thirty-three times greater on rice" than the per-mile rate between Chicago and San Francisco." Lubricating oil rates stood thirty times greater; wines, dried fruits, and pickles twenty times; dried fruits in sacks eighteen times; and potatoes twelve times greater.

The Arizona commission held no power to set rates, but formally requested that the Arizona Eastern lower their charges. Railroad officials ignored the territory's fledgling railway commission, so the group moved to file complaints with the Interstate Commerce Commission. Before papers could be filed, the Arizona Eastern offered a schedule that reduced freight rates by 25 percent. The agreement also called for a 32 percent rate reduction on the SP. The new tariffs lifted a tremendous burden off southern Arizona shippers and receivers when they took effect November 26, 1909.

Democrats "packed" the railroad committee at Arizona's constitutional convention in 1910. Saying such a committee would be "nothing more or less than a creature of the railroads," the *Citizen* screamed, "A more amazing piece of bossism... would be difficult to find even in the files of [New York's] Tammany Hall." Approved by territorial voters, Arizona's new constitution

permitted recall elections for judges and met President W. H. Taft's disdain. Arizona conceded and finally gained statehood on February 14, 1912. Legislators quickly

Carl Ball Sr. worked at Willcox in 1914, before starting with the SP as a fireman at Tucson in 1916. Elected to two terms on Tucson's city council, beginning in 1936, Ball lost his bid for the Democratic nomination in 1940 by a coin flip, after a tie at the ballot box with fellow rail Fred D. Lee. (Elgin Ball Collection)

placed a constitutional amendment before the new state's voters, adding recall of judges to the state constitution. Another amendment extended the right to vote in local, state, and national elections to women.

Voters elected "Randolph lines" accountant J.W. "Buch" Buchanan to Arizona's first state legislature in 1912. Born December 7, 1869 in Branden, Mississippi, the well-liked "Dixiecrat" came to Tucson during 1907 and worked in the SP accounting office. Friends described Buchanan as "primarily a railroad man," who stayed in continuous contact with his Mississippi kin and displayed an impressive southern drawl.

Buch Buchanan served two additional terms in the Arizona legislature. He worked for the Arizona Eastern and the *SP de Mexico* in Tucson but when the latter moved its headquarters to Guadalajara,

Conductor Henry T. Stapp and engineer Happy Houston stroll through Tucson ca. 1918. (Richard Stapp Sr. Collection)

Buchanan stayed in town. During an illustrious railroad and political career, he served as Pima County treasurer twice, Tucson city treasurer, and state tax appraiser. An accomplished woodcarver, Buch maintained a complete factory in his garage at 318 East Speedway Boulevard.

Arizona railroads had few critics more prominent or loquacious than seven-term governor G.W.P. Hunt. The first elected governor of the nation's forty-eighth state had the needle out for all big corporations, and railroads presented Arizona's biggest target. "Gigantic combinations, which, by force of unlimited wealth and the heartlessness for which they are proverbial, squeeze the life out of their weaker competitors and, by criminal might, run the business of the nation," Hunt once declared. Buchanan remembered: "Those were fighting days when the state was still a baby. G.W.P. Hunt was governor, and there was constant battle between him and the legislature." Before Buchanan died from injuries suffered in a car crash at El Paso in July 1941, he boasted that he owned "the largest personal acquaintance, among the greatest variety of people of any man in Pima County."

Fred O. Goodell, Colonel Epes Randolph's personal secretary, joined J. W. Buchanan as Pima County's representative in the 1917 Arizona legislature. Born in Hillsdale, Kansas, Goodell came to Arizona in 1902 and lived for many years with his family at 1036 East Sixth Street. Known as the "lid sitter" of the legislature, Goodell protected the state treasury as chairman of the Senate Finance and Appropriations Committee. The trustworthy Democrat served in the fourth and fifth state legislatures before returning to his work as auditor at the Arizona Eastern. A member of Tucson's 1918 city council with Mayor O.C. Parker, Goodell left twenty-eight years of seniority with the railroad to accept an appointment from President Calvin Coolidge as Arizona's Federal Internal Revenue Col-

The Arizona Senate posed for this shot in 1933. Local rails controlled seats in both Arizona legislative houses that year. (Bettie Houston Crawford Collection)

lector in 1927. Sadly, the dedicated public official lost his sons, Ormal, 17, and Howard, 11, in a single-car crash one mile west of Sentinel in July 1928. Goodell worked for sixteen years as Pima County comptroller, until just before his death in early September 1961.

During the World War I period of federal railroad control, General Railroad Administrator William G. McAdoo issued an order prohibiting railroad employees from running for office. "It was a matter of common report that railroads under private control were frequently used for partisan purposes; that railroad corporations were frequently adjuncts of political machines; and that even sovereign States had been at times dominated by them," said McAdoo. "Contributions to campaign funds and the skillful coercion of employees were some of the means by which...many railroads exerted their power and influence in politics. Scandals resulted from such practices, the public interest was prejudiced, and hostility to railroad managements was engendered."

Attacks on the SP came from other fronts. "The railroads of Arizona are escap-

ing taxation on millions of dollars worth of valuations, thanks to a Democratic tax commission," screamed the *Citizen's* Phoenix News Bureau in February 1922. Valued at $48 million, the SP paid taxes on only $20 million. The corporation commission valued the Arizona Eastern Railroad at $11 million, but allowed the company to earn its federally mandated 6 percent profits on $24.8 million. The move meant a more than one-half million dollar loss in state revenue. "The burden of the average tax payer is increased just that much," bellowed the news bureau.

SP conductor John W. Finn and engineer John M. Morgan joined Pima County's House delegation in 1925, the latter serving a second term. That year, voters also elected Democratic SP conductor Thomas W. Donnelly to the first of four consecutive terms in the state senate. President of the board of directors of the Arizona School for the Deaf and Blind, the hardworking conductor/legislator presented and brought into law more bills than any other lawmaker during the 1927 session, including a $60,000 appropriation for his special school.

Senator Donnelly declined his party's nomination for governor and presented rails' views against an SP plan to reduce salaries and wages by 15 percent, in 1931. The Great Depression forced nearly every railroad in the nation to take drastic measures, argued Donnelly, but "all trainmen, enginemen, and switchmen, are piece-workers. They work only when there is a demand for their services from their employer. It will be easily understood that there is a material difference between these piece workers and workers paid by the month."

Donnelly's introduction of Senate Bill No. 28 in the state's Seventh Legislature represented one of the his finest hours. The bill reorganized the University of Arizona into five distinct colleges and funded completion of the school's library. This boosted the university's status as the real institution of higher learning in the state.

Tom Collins came to Arizona in 1903, following his schooling on the Emerald Isle. The "big Irishman, veteran railroader, and veteran in the political life of Arizona" worked in a steam locomotive cab for forty-seven years, many on the Sunset Limited run from Yuma to Tucson. Tom also ran the first streamlined diesel into the Old Pueblo near the end of his career. Collins married teacher Mary Duffy from a long-time Tucson family. The couple lived for many years at 1057 East Eighth Street.

In the fall of 1922, Collins squared off against Republican SP conductor and University of Arizona regent J.G. Compton for a seat on the Pima County Board of Supervisors. To the surprise of many, the SP issued orders prohibiting company employees from holding public office. After G.V. McLennan, local chairman of the Order of Railway Conductors, approached top railroad officials, however, the company rescinded its edict and Collins won election over Compton.

Tom took pride in attending every session of the Pima County board during his term. Once, when he learned of an un-

scheduled board meeting, Tucson's tough engineer called for a "sub" to finish his run to Gila Bend, jumped off his train, and raced by car into Tucson to make roll call. On Collins's watch, the county used the state gasoline tax and labor from the Works Progress Administration (WPA) to pave thirty miles of road. Pima County also reduced its bonded indebtedness from a million dollars to $206,000; saved two million dollars by having the state take over the construction of the Ajo Highway; built a jail kitchen, saving taxpayers several thousands of dollars; and cooperated in paving five miles of the Catalina Highway.

Collins lost his Pima County Board of Supervisors re-election bid by just one vote in 1924 and unleashed a sulphurous attack on his opponent, Homer Boyd, and county assessor Charles W. Taylor. The stinging tirade targeted Taylor's county assessor's office for mailing Boyd's campaign cards. "Taylor violated all ethics," said Collins. "He also keeps a 'Keep Out' sign on his office door. I don't see how any public official can put up such a sign."

Arizona's larger-than-life steam steward next won a chair in the Ninth State Senate and leapt to work on the larger political field. In May 1931, Collins pushed Governor Hunt's administration to include a bill taxing large trucks running on state highways. He wrote State Highway Commission Chairman C.E. Addams: "These trucks are causing much damage to the highways, and I might say paying no tax and running in competition with the railroads which are taxed at the rate of sixty-nine thousand dollars a mile." Tom's effort paid dividends when the state began taxing the gross proceeds of trucks, producing $105,000 in annual revenue. Collins's bill preventing the "bootlegging" of gas by trucks raised another $90,000. While taxing the trucking industry, Collins saved Arizona taxpayers another $350,000, when he initiated a bill that eliminated the "mil tax" assessment for building and maintaining state highways.

Tom Collins pressed for Pima County's purchase of Colossal Cave. Completion of interior stairs and railings al-
lowed tourists to enter the cave in 1936. (Colossal Cave Mountain Park Research Library & Archives)

Strong-willed and opinionated, Tom never missed a Senate roll call over three regular and nine special sessions. He served on the Senate committee for highways and bridges for six years and as chairman of the finance committee for two. During his tenure, he led successful drives to enact a minimum wage law for municipal and state employees and an old-age pension law for all Arizonans. Collins helped pass a bill to fund the oiling of Highway No. 84 from Casa Grande to Gila Bend. He also pushed funding of the Willcox-Steins Pass Road. A member of the committee on codification of state laws and chairman of the Senate committee on state institutions, Tom served as a Senate member of the motor vehicle conference of eleven states. "Tom Collins was a very personable man," recalled former Brotherhood of Railway Trainmen International vice-president, eighty-nine-year-old George R. Perkins.

"Collins was very knowledgeable on state laws."

Of the twelve Senate seats contested in Pima County between 1925 and 1937, SP men filled ten. Conductor and Spanish-American War veteran William C. Joyner had joined T.W. Donnelly in the Senate in 1928. Joyner came to Tucson in 1920 and developed strong political backing among rails. Appointed to the University of Arizona Board of Regents in 1929, Joyner resigned his legislative seat in mid-February 1932 to accept the state game warden's job.

The Pima County Board of Supervisors appointed Democratic brakeman J.S. Hardwicke to fill the fourth legislative district House seat when veteran SP politico Thomas Maloney died in a car wreck during the fall of 1931. Hardwicke won appointment over two well-respected local rails, signalman John M. Nugent and engineer

Cecil Richardson. Hardwicke led brakemen in their fight against Arizona's law that limited trains to seventy cars and reduced the number of workers needed. Nugent won election to the state's 11th Legislature in 1932. That same year, Mohave County voters elected former Tucson SP accountant Joseph M. Peggs. Local rail L.B Wilson won a Pima County seat in the House four years later.

Legislative boards of the various trade unions played a key role in state politics at all levels. Rails formed the Arizona Legislative Board of Railway Brotherhoods in 1918, with Tucsonan Elbert T. "Happy" Houston as chairman. The board worked in tandem with elected officials to ensure that legislation that threatened railroad interests fell to defeat. Tom Collins served as chairman of the Senate labor committee and for twenty-one years as treasurer of the local engineer's union. He also sat on the Joint Legislative Board of Railroad Brotherhoods for many years. In the spring of 1933, legislation proposed in the U.S. Congress sparked action by the national legislative board of the engineers' union. The dreadful bills called for a maximum six hour work day, 42 hours a week, and just 180 hours for an entire month. Board executives calculated such action would reduce a passenger engineer's wages by 29 percent, a road freight engineer's pay by 39 percent, and a yard engineer's by 26 percent. The national organization asked all local unions to use "every honorable means to prevent...the proposed legislation."

"Do everything in your power to oppose" the restrictive measures, Tom Collins implored senators

Carl Hayden and Henry F. Ashurst in May 1933. Secretary-treasurer of the Arizona legislative board of the Brotherhood of Locomotive Engineers, Collins explained, "We are willing to cut our hours during the term of the depression but a bill such as proposed, if passed, will be hard to repeal."

Collins sat on the Senate labor committee when Arizona Attorney General John L. Sullivan upheld state law limiting trucks to thirty-five miles an hour and trucks with metal tires to six miles per hour on state highways in 1936. Defeated in his bid for a fourth legislative term, Collins proclaimed, "I am sorry to leave, but the people did not want me any more. I must abide by the majority, and I am glad that this is so."

Collins continued to enjoy a strong reputation in Pima County and returned to serve on the Board of Supervisors from 1939 to 1944. Tom also belonged group of investors that opened the Rialto block on east Congress Street. He served on the state's public welfare board and pushed fellow supervisors to purchase Colossal Cave.

As UTU general chairman, George Perkins (second from right) represented all trainmen on SP's system, from Portland to New Orleans. He paused during the union's national meeting at the local Ramada Inn ca. 1963 (George Perkins Collection)

Investors recouped 110 percent of their money when Judge Fred W. Fickett named Tom chairman of the collapsed Union Bank bondholders' committee. One ex-rail summed up the feelings of many Arizonans: "In you, Mr. Collins, I feel we have a man who is a square shooter and one not afraid to buck the powers what am."

The appointment of former cattle inspector Charles E. Blaine to the Regional Conference of the American Legislative Association stirred fierce opposition from railroad labor.

Happy Houston (right front) took his seat on the Arizona Board of Regents in March 1937. (Bettie Houston Crawford Collection)

In a June 25, 1934 resolution, unions blasted Blaine as "inimical to the interests of railroad employees." Years later, engineer Constant "Connie" Wienzapfel served on the union's joint legislative board. "That was the greatest thing that I ever did," Connie recalled. "I didn't only help the men; I helped the railroads. Anything that's good for the railroads is good for the men"

The Arizona board held its annual meeting with management in Phoenix each February. Both the SP and the Santa Fe sent several representatives. "I got the thrill of my life," Wienzapfel remembered, "when one of the SP general managers said, 'Imagine having management, having legislators, and having labor under the same roof.' They'd never done it anyplace in the United States, get [those] three sets of people together."

Elbert T. "Happy" Houston succeeded Tom Donnelly to the Arizona Senate during 1933 and won re-election two years later. A division engineman since 1910, Houston took great inspiration from fellow engineer Ben Cheek, who headed the police pension board and administered the Tucson civil service system. Houston chaired the powerful Senate appropriations committee during his second term and also sat on the labor committee. Happy took pride in being one of the original sponsors of the state's Workmen's Compensation Act. He also garnered appropriations for the University of Arizona of $750,000 and $50,000 to repair Herring Hall and the University Theater.

The upbeat engineer declined to run for a third legislative term, choosing instead to return to his regular job, running engines over the Stormy to Lordsburg. Tucson's KVOA radio dramatized Houston's next adventure in a special 1937 broadcast. As he pulled his train into Dragoon Station east of Tucson, a rail yelled: "Hey, Happy! The governor's been tryin' to reach you for the last two hours. I got a wire here saying for you to leave the engine with the fireman while you find out what the governor wants." Plucked off his engine, Houston answered Governor Rawghlie C. Stanford's 1937 call to sit on the University of Arizona Board of Regents and served until 1940. Governor R.T. Jones called Houston off another engine to sit on the state's industrial commission that same year.

Tucson Mayor (center) and Council 1950. (Bettie Houston Crawford Collection)

Happy Houston during SP engineers' Circle Diamond Four Hunting Club's 1927 trip into the Rincon Mountains. He and his rail companions assumed pioneer identities on their annual excursions. Houston took on the persona of Madagascar. (Jim Pfersdorf Collection)

When Tucsonans elected him mayor in 1947, Happy told his brother, noted New Orleans surgeon A.N. Houston: "I don't have to look up to anybody now. I am mayor of Tucson." Houston's administration built a jail farm, which saved the city thousands of dollars in food costs, installed parking meters, and established the non-profit Tucson Airport Authority to take over operations of the municipal airport from the federal government. He also made the city's first call using a dial telephone system on February 27, 1949. Houston's most impressive accomplishment brought an $850,000 "limited-access highway" to Tucson that later became Interstate 10.

The *Citizen* exposed a bit of Houston's drive: "He took to city hall a dynamic character and quickly gained a reputation for getting things done. Just what he did for sleep during his three years as mayor, nobody ever really found out. Night after night he would pilot a locomotive, return to his home for a bath and breakfast, and then appear at city hall as fresh as if he had enjoyed a full night of sleep." Betty Houston Crawford, Happy's daughter, confirmed the assessment: "My father was always on the go. He loved Tucson and loved being its leader."

"Houston was probably the first 'full-time' mayor Tucson ever had," explained the *Star*. "To say his job as mayor was full-time is probably putting it mildly, because he was available any time, day or night, for any civic purpose." Alas, his frantic pace took its toll on the city's dedicated mayor. The man everyone called "Happy"

Mayor Houston (second from right) examines a new piece of city equipment. Star *columnist Bonnie Henry recalled, "I remember Happy Houston when he ran the little train for kids at Kiddieland, on the northeast corner of Alvernon and Speedway." (Bettie Houston Crawford Collection)*

Locomotive engineer and Tucson mayor Happy Houston warmed Tusconans' hearts and worked tirelessly on their behalf. (Bettie Houston Crawford Collection)

remained true to his moniker until he died of a heart attack at fifty-eight, while attending a joint meeting of the Tucson and Phoenix chambers of commerce June 12, 1950. Houston's wife, Ethel Houston, explained, "He tried to do too much. It was a terrible shock. You can't keep going without rest."

Happy's friend, *Citizen* reporter Bob Campbell, remembered: "I decided that any city with such a mayor must be one of the world's best places to live. Everywhere the mayor went, people hailed him by that nickname. He got real pleasure from planning something he thought the people of his city needed, then going out and making it a reality. His reputation for getting action from city departments and governmental agencies was well founded. Time after time he moved into a situation he believed needed remedy and came out with a solution which benefitted the city." The Pima County Board of Supervisors voted to name the new limited-access highway in Happy's honor in June 1950, but road signs saying "Houston Highway" confused travelers, who believed themselves more than 900 miles west of the east-Texas city. The road's name fell into disuse and not even Happy's family realized it still held his name. In 2001, the Arizona legislature designated the length of Interstate 10 through Arizona the Pearl Harbor Memorial. The memory of Happy Houston, however, waits for well-deserved commemoration.

After years of owning Pima County's seats in the state Senate, not a single railroader succeeded for fourteen years. Then, Tom Collins retired from the SP in April 1951 and won election to the

Strong pioneer women Claudia Ball (left) and Etta Mae Hutchinson (right), future state legislator, posed in pretty dresses for this ca. 1920 photograph. Twelve-term Pima County State Senator Richard C. Pacheco remembered sitting behind the brusque Ma Hutch in his very first legislative session. "She told me to sit down, shut up, and listen," said Pacheco. (Elgin Ball Collection)

Senate that November. Behind pledges to work for the University of Arizona and to reduce the number of state legislators, he won re-election in 1953. That year, county Democratic leaders appointed Etta Mae "Ma" Hutcheson, wife of SP conductor Oril O. Hutcheson, to replace resigning Larry Woods. Voters elected Ma to the fill seat in 1955 and she remained in the legislature for a total of twelve years. The strong-willed Tucsonan waged legendary battles in support of society's poor. "Everybody in town knew Ma Hutch," affirmed locomotive engineer James "Nuge" Nugent. "She was a tough old gal but she got a hell of a lot done for the people she represented." Division chief timekeeper Elgin Ball knew the renowned human-rights champion over decades and remembered, "Ma was a real fighter!"

Pima County's final SP legislator of the steam era, Vicente "Vic" Alfaro, entered the United States with his family in a group of eight to ten covered wagons during February 1900. After trying business conditions in Nogales, Arizona, five-year-old Vicente's father, Leandor Alfaro, traveled to Tucson and opened a wholesale grocery

at 144 South Meyer Street. Vicente's *padres* (parents) enrolled him in Catholic school. There, he learned the reading and writing skills that would propel his future at the railroad and in Arizona politics. Astute and motivated, Vicente developed a knack for conversation and successful bargaining while watching his father ply the wholesale grocery trade. He also acquainted himself with such local icons as Tucson Opera House proprietor Emanuel Drachman, and merchants John Ivancovich and W.I. Perry.

Vicente took work at Corbett's Stationery Store, but the store burned down in 1910. Manager Hiram Stevens secured an apprentice's job at the Tucson railroad shops for the bright and industrious Alfaro. Vic earned 17¢ an hour for eleven-hour days and studied locomotive mechanical and boilermaking operations through a correspondence course. Working under the exacting tutelage of boilermaker foreman W.W. McAlister, he mastered the trade.

A member of the Selective Service Board during World War II, Vic won election to Arizona's Twenty-Second Legislature in 1955. He engineered the passage of bills to increase aid to dependent children, guarantee equal opportunity, and hold parents responsible for the wrongful acts of juveniles.

Throughout the steam era, Arizona's gigantic railroad enterprise served up unparalleled political brew. The SP and its employees played politics with vigor, some to their own ends; many for the good of the community they represented. The SP treated Alfaro very well after his election, yet the veteran politician maintained that the company made no effort to influence his decisions. Perhaps the political steam had died on the state's once-dominant railroad "machine."

Chapter 10

*Stallions of Steel:
Firemen and Oil
Burners on the
Tucson Division*

*An oil derrick in the desert after a rain storm graces this early colorized postcard.
(Michael Hyatt Collection)*

Feverish heat shimmies in shapeless illusion above the train track ahead. Lungs fight for oxygen. Fingers burn beneath an unrelenting solar storm. Such heat grinds nature to its lowest and slowest form. Personal experience provides the only serviceable frame of reference. On the Tucson Division's western end, the Gila stretches across blistering deserts north and west of the city, providing one of Arizona's nastiest summertime diversions.

Until the early 1890s, southern Arizonans held a common belief that humans had no business working in such heat. As summer temperatures mounted, projects shut down, including the building of the nation's second transcontinental railroad. Yet, commerce demanded that trains run, so firemen raised infernos in their locomotives' fireboxes to generate steam and power. Enhancing the region's dry desert air and the cab's oppressive temperature, the blaze provided enginemen an almost unbearable companion. Former backshop foreman Charles Stoddard expressed the sentiments of all who witnessed the rage: "To this day I don't know how those engineers and firemen were able to work on a steam engine going to Yuma on those 110-degree days." Tucson native Big Jim "Nuge" Nugent joked: "That didn't bother us any. We'd just get off on some sidetrack, find a shady spot under the water tank, and look out for snakes."

Constant "Connie" Weinzapfel's father, Michael Weinzapfel, made his "fireman's date" on the Tucson Division in 1911. Seventy-three years later, his son remembered: "In the early days it was real hard here. The men were real pioneers, and they had lots of obstacles to overcome. When my dad hired out, I'd go down to Yuma [with him] and we'd sleep in what they called 'cages.'"

Southern Pacific Railroad (SP) built the cages directly behind the Yuma roundhouse. Resembling rabbit hutches, each individual sleeping area measured three to four feet wide and "just long enough for most men." Wire sides allowed rails to raise mesh curtains in hopes of catching a breeze, or lower them in defiance of the Colorado River's ubiquitous mosquitoes. "They also had what they called clubhouses, square buildings with a toilet and shower facilities in the middle," remembered Weinzapfel. "There must have been fifty or sixty of those square buildings."

The SP also built a virtual cold-storage locker, called "the submarine," in Yuma. "It was a tin igloo kind of thing and it looked like a Quonset hut," Weinzapfel re-

Citizens enjoyed "Arizona air-conditioning" in Yuma ca. 1898, "open the window and wait for a breeze." (AHS #25399)

called. "They'd put burlap over the tin, and it had vents to let air flow through. They'd run water over the burlap to cool it down. It was so damn cold in there that you'd nearly freeze to death. You could not stay out in 110 degrees, and you could not stay in the submarine in the summertime." Several single railroad men constructed a porch on the front of the submarine. Complete with chairs and an icebox, the veranda provided a welcome escape from the icy regions.

The Tucson Division operated under "home rule," meaning that men who lived in Tucson, with enough seniority, also worked there. SP paid a penalty if the company did not relieve a man working away from his home within seven days. The railroad made every effort to send a man home within the allotted time. Through the years, efforts to improve railroaders' accommodations in Yuma led to the building of "the modules," rooms similar to those in a motel.

The SP adorned its first steam engines in brilliant reds, blues, golds, and greens. Each locomotive employed an engineer to run the controls and a fireman to make steam for its power. A man began SP engine service as a fireman and worked for promotion to engineer. Early firemen fueled their locomotives with wood loaded from cords stacked along the line. Later, firemen shoveled up to twenty tons of coal over a fifteen-hour period to feed their ravenous combustion engines. Spreading an even bed of coals over metal grates inside the engine's firebox, the "ashcat," or fireman, used his engine's draft to draw an even flow of air over the coal-bed. Executed artfully, the process produced the maximum fire for building steam in its boiler. Both wood and coal produced cinders that stung passengers and ignited fires along the track's right-of-way.

This veteran switch engine worked the Tucson yard for many years. (AHS #28178)

The SP initially used coal on the Tucson division. After three years of fruitless exploration, the SP gave up plans to mine coal at its camp nine miles north of Solomonville, Arizona in 1898. The company shipped its drilling equipment to Tucson and turned to oil to fuel its metal monsters. In place of the coal shovel, firemen took control of an "atomizer" or oil sprayer. Using a blast of steam or air, firemen sprayed a shower of oil into the engine's firebox where it ignited with oxygen. The proper mixture of fuel and air produced a prolonged and uniform flow of heat. This maximized heat to water inside the boiler and ensured dense steam pressure, robust power, and decreased fuel usage. A poor fire retarded air induction, created a smoking engine that leaked, and could cause the locomotive's steam to fail.

Using an engine from a boat in the San Francisco Bay, the SP ran its first oil-burning locomotive in 1879. That year, the company also began using refined oil in a 4-4-0-type engine.

SP put its first oil-burning locomotive into regular service during May 1895. The company completed modification of the local division's first engine in Yuma, during the fall of 1897. The change required mounting a fourteen-hundred-gallon oil reservoir directly inside the former coal bin on the tender, a car pulled behind the engine to carry fuel and water. Because oil burned at a much higher temperature than coal, workers added a concave wall of firebrick within the firebox, to throw the heat back to a point where the draft of the engine pulled it through the flues and out the smokestack. Only two instructors worked the Tucson Division, so it took an engineman as long to master an oil-burning engine as it did to convert a locomotive to the new fuel. By the time engineer Wilbur F. Schoonmaker pulled the "burro," or International Train, onto the Benson-Nogales line in mid-January 1902, twenty-eight locomotives burned oil. Schoonmaker's 4-4-0 American locomotive No. 1326 ran as the second oil-burning engine on the International run.

SP contracted Penwer Steel and Iron Works to build seventy-two steel oil-storage tanks across its rail system during 1902. Five SP work trains and more than two hundred expert workmen began building thirty-eight tanks in Texas, twenty-one from Los Angeles up the coast to Ashland, Oregon, and thirteen on branch lines. In Tucson, Yuma, and Lordsburg, oil tanks served as the division's main supply depots. The railroad shipped oil from Los Angeles to fill the massive reservoirs and men in the local shops soon began using oil whenever possible. By the end of 1904, 108 engines burned almost 69,000 barrels of oil on the local division.

Fuel conservation meant reduced expenses for every mile traveled and more profitable railroading. In early 1921, the company developed a two-part oil conservation motion picture. The movie's first half explained SP's crude oil and by-product industry, while its second section focused on in-cab "leaks" and places where forethought might prevent fuel waste.

The company also introduced its Engine Cab Economists program to achieve greater efficiency in the use of fuel oil. Winners of the system-wide contest

Local workers paused for this June 1900 image at the Tucson SP offices. (AHS #62922)

represented the company at the International Railway Fuel Association's convention in Chicago, "all expenses to be borne by the Company, including time lost." The June 1921 edition of the *Southern Pacific Bulletin* carried the fuel-saving program's early results. Each month, the division with the best overall monthly record won a congratulatory banner for display. The company recognized Tucson firemen M.E. Delahanty, R.A. Dixon, E.L. Marable, G.N. Ashley, and F.W. Hoffman and engineers E.R. Layman, C.E. McMeans, G.A. LaRocque, C.H. Lee, and W. Armstrong for outstanding oil conservation efforts. The SP did not retire its last coal-burning road engine until 1925, and the company used coal-burning helper engines at Steins Pass until after WWII.

SP required a prospective fireman to learn the job during unpaid "student trips" over the division's various roads. One route ran from Tucson to Lordsburg and another from there to El Paso. One traveled west from Tucson to Gila Bend and another from there to Yuma. One went south to Nogales, another north to Phoenix, and the last run from there to Yuma. Following each trip, the engineer completed a report on the student's performance. Collecting thirty signed reports proved the trainee ready to join the company as a fireman. "They didn't even give you lunch money on those trips," chuckled Nuge Nugent.

George "Boots" Lundquist fired his first steam engine to Gila Bend in June 1937. Sixty-five years later, Lundquist reminisced at his smart eastside Tucson home. "The fireman was responsible for keepin' steam in that boiler to make that engine work," he explained. "He tended a fire in the firebox and watched the gauges to keep the right amount of water in the boiler. You had one hell of a hot fire in there! You had to stay on the ball and be pretty darn careful."

Large enough to crawl through, a door opened to the engine's firebox. "That door had a little peephole," Lundquist continued. "You kept the peephole cracked a little bit so you could tell what kind of fire you had. You pulled a valve up by your right hand when you needed more oil on your fire. If you had got a good clean fire, and it was heatin' the water in the boiler, you could tell. Your fire should be clear. If it started getting smoky, you were givin' it too much oil, that's all. The good clean stacks are the ones where you have a good fire."

Steel tires slipping on steel rails fostered perpetual concern for enginemen. Getting a train started and climbing steep grades presented the greatest difficulty. To combat the problem, the locomotive fireman filled his engine's sand dome to feed a "sander," which threw the gritty material on the tracks ahead of his engine. The steel flues of the locomotive's "super-heater unit" ran above the firebox's crown sheet and through the boiler to double-heat its steam. Soot build-up in these pipes reduced the draft of air on the fire, dropped steam pressure, and retarded heat and steam by insulating the flues. To combat the dirty dilemma, a fireman used a good-sized metal scoop to feed sand into his firebox through its peephole and "ream-out" the flues.

In Tucson, "car cleaners" kept a four-foot long by eighteen-inch wide by two-foot deep box filled with sand in front of each engine's firebox door. "You'd be goin' along with a 'clear stack,' no black smoke coming of the smokestack, and suddenly your engine would stop steamin'," remembered Lundquist. "We'd go a long ways to keep that from happening. Shoot, you'd go over there and put a couple scoops of sand in. Out'd come all this crap, and you'd get a perfectly clear stack." Sand flying from the smokestack presented enginemen with constant danger. "You had better look out for it," Boots warned. "Sand might come down on your side of the engine and hit you in the face. One time I got blasted by sand real bad. I had to go to the doctor in Lordsburg and have him scrape my eyes. Oh, man, that was painful!"

(l-r) Wallace, George "Boots," Emmett "Binx", and Harry Esmond Lundquist made time for fun while their father manned the pump in Willcox ca.1919. George began his own engineman's career in 1937. (George Lundquist Collection)

Following the stock market disaster of 1929, a single-switch engine could handle all the trains coming and going through the Tucson yard on many days. Cut off from their rail jobs, SP firemen and engineers found auto bodywork, dug ditches, and worked in service stations to keep their families eating. Former division conductor Harold "Stonewall" Jackson toiled as a meat cutter's apprentice in a local grocery store where many engineers traded during the Depression. "All the engineers hired from 1919 on, 100 percent, were cut off and on starvation row," remembered the savvy ninety-two-year-old. "Finally, during 1931-1932, men on the division began getting a few days' work in the summer melon rush on the west end of the division. They didn't start recalling those 1919 men, really putting them back to work, until 1934-1935. By 1936 they were practically all back."

Gregarious Nuge Nugent started as a fireman in 1936. Nugent's record reflected the uncertainty of regular "head-end" or enginemen's work at the time. The SP called Jim just five days during January of 1938, but he found regular work between February 5 and March 17, when his paychecks ended. SP did not call the husky Tucsonan to fire another locomotive until June 11, for the division's regular melon run. "Cut off" at the end of the "green fruit" rush on July 16, Nugent found no work at the railroad for the rest of 1938!

A locomotive fireman's responsibilities included replenishing the train's supply of water and oil. Steam engines traveled only about thirty miles before they needed water. Oil lasted much longer. The railroad built at least fifteen storage tanks along the division to replenish water on its trains. At each point across the division, a pumper filled his station's tank from the company well to ensure water for passing locomotives. When an engine "spotted," or stopped, by a water tank, the fireman walked back along a metal apron on his locomotive's tender. There, two large tanks, with man-hole-like doors, held water and oil. Swinging a long, metal waterspout from the bottom of the station's tank, he filled his train's water tank. "The hardest thing was taking the big spigot from the water tank and putting it in the tank on the tender," Connie Weinzapfel said. Nugent concurred: "You needed to be careful. You had to pull down on a rope to open the water valve and if you pulled too hard it would raise up and spray water all over."

Firemen filled the tank on their engine's tender using a large water spout. (Jason Burke in T. Herman Blythe Collection)

Gregarious Jim Nugent got the surprise of his life when he walked into a roomful of family and friends at his 1977 retirement party. (Jim Nugent Collection)

Building steam on the west end of the Tucson Division created constant problems. "They could not make water in Gila Bend," T. Herman Blythe, former roundhouse foreman, explained. "It would make the boiler foam. The foaming reduced steam and forced the water up off the bottom of the boiler." In the fall of 1910, the SP completed a 1,180-foot well at Gila Bend, which promised alkali-free water for steam engines. Division superintendent W.H. Whalen enthusiastically proclaimed the water hole "the greatest find of all times on the Tucson Division." Thirty years later, SP adopted a new method for getting water. "They filled up tank cars in Maricopa, where the water was good, and a train took them west," Blythe explained. "When they

Traffic runs through Lordsburg ca. 1890s. During 1902, engine No. 2284's boiler explosion shook the small southwestern New Mexico community. (AHS #PC107,B2,f28)

got to Gila Bend, a shopman hooked up a canvas tube between the tender and the tank car and gravity allowed water to flow into the tender. Then, they'd take the tank cars west to Sentinel, which had good water. An eastbound train'd bring 'em back to Gila Bend and on to Maricopa for a refill of water; back and forth."

The level of steam pressure in the locomotive's boiler concerned all enginemen. Steam locomotives had three safety valves, one for high pressure, one for medium, and one for the lowest, "walking pressure." A shop mechanic started with the high-pressure valve and adjusted a spring in each safety device using two long wrenches. Charles Stoddard remembered the trouble, "It was not really dangerous but, boy, when that thing was hot that wrench got really hard to hold."

T. Herman Blythe ran the steam locomotive at Old Tucson theme park following his retirement from the SP. (Eddie Pecktol Collection)

Safety features failed on at least two dramatic occasions. During December 1902, passenger engine No. 2284 blew up in Lordsburg. An eyewitness said Hostler Woods heard the engine piping off steam and climbed into the cab to check the water level. Just as Woods touched the cocks on the boiler's water gauge, the engine exploded. The blast tore one entire end off the Lordsburg roundhouse. "The engine reared up just like a bucking horse and then fell with its nose dug in the ground," said one observer. The explosion caused considerable damage to adjacent buildings and knocked out every light in Lordsburg. Miraculously, Woods lived to suffer severe scalding.

Tears streamed down the face of many a sun-bronzed, desert-hardened rail when boiler problems caused the Gila's tragic explosion, November 11, 1946. Running in front of a diesel switch engine, locomotive No. 5037 climbed east into the Mohawk Mountains, as the fourth section of "hot-shot" train No. 854. The ill-fated locomotive chugged up the hill past Southern Pacific engine No. 5008 and its extra train, sitting "in the clear" at Bosque siding. Just after both train crews exchanged "highball" signals, the huge, three-cylinder No. 5037's eighty-ton boiler loosed a thunderous blast!

Super-heated steam, sand, and burned carbon flashed through the engine's flues, blowing the door off its firebox. The eruption sent No. 5037's cab soaring four hundred feet ahead of the train. Under a shower of dazzling sparks, her drive wheels spun against one rail in furious misery until a hostler arrived from Gila Bend to shut it down. Heat from the powerful explosion melted the engine's super-heater units, laying them down like a mass of limp spaghetti.

The explosion killed engineer Harry Hall and his fireman, Walter B. Glisson, in an instant. The force flooded the diesel

No. 5037's super-heater units lay in a heap following the brutal eruption. (Jason Burke in T. Herman Blythe Collection)

helper's cab and blew it forward nine inches, knocking engineer Johnny Rhoades to the ground and viciously blistering fireman Frank Bogulas. Brakeman Ted B. Holaway stood looking out a window in the diesel's cab when the boiler exploded. Merciless steam seared Holaway, who survived badly scalded. At least one rail reported wearing soot "tattoos" beneath his skin.

Tucsonans of all races mourned the loss of beloved engineer Harry Hall. A scholarship football star at St. Johns Academy in Wisconsin, the upbeat, travel-loving Hall endeared himself to coworkers and neighborhood children alike during his too-short life. (Elgin Ball Collection)

Investigators determined that the alkali-laden water on the Tucson Division's west end measured 125 grains above the level allowed by the SP when the No. 5037 had arrived in Gila Bend. Crews did not, however, "blow down" (flush) the boiler to reduce its mineral content. In addition, the reflective surface of the engineer's water glass, which allowed him to check the level in his boiler, had worn dark three and one-half inches above the bottom, making it difficult to read. Fireman Bogulas's water glass lay shattered and unreadable among the carnage.

Fear and heartbreak rang across the SP ranks. One shaken engineman vowed, "When you get rid of steam engines, I'll come back." Veteran engineer C.D. Murtaugh remembered, "For many years after the locomotive blew up, everywhere you went over the whole system, you saw

A concerned engineman peers into the wreckage of No. 5037. The incident rattled even the most seasoned rails. The division's alkali-laden water that foamed when used to make steam took the blame. Local engineers agreed that the well at far-away Florence Depot produced the division's best water. (Jason Burke in T. Herman Blythe Collection)

The cab of engine No. 5037 flew 400 feet ahead when its boiler loosed a horrific blast. (Jason Burke in T. Herman Blythe Collection)

Engineer Boots Lundquist (left) battles to wake up in Lordsburg. (James W. Nugent Collection)

posters with a picture of the Engine No. 5037 wreck and the slogan 'Watch Your Water!'"

When Harlan "Hard Rock" Payne began as an SP fireman in June 1941, Tucson's Whitehouse Café and the French Café on west Congress Street filled with enginemen before and after their runs. Martin's Drug and T. Ed Litt's Drugstore also provided convenient coffee break and lunch venues. Finding food out on the line required ingenuity during World War II. "They'd have to send another crew out if yours 'died on hours,' by working sixteen straight hours," said Payne in his handsome foothills home during September 2002. "You'd just sit and wait for your relief. They knew what time a man's shift was over, but they were usually late getting any relief out there for you. During your time waiting, enginemen were entitled to eat.

Every siding had a round telephone holder at each end. You'd just get on the phone and tell the dispatcher, 'We're gonna eat,' and go find some place that served food."

Payne remembered firing a helper engine to Lordsburg for one veteran engineer. "On a helper at the rear-end of a train, all you can do is fire it wide open and sit back and go to sleep," said Harlan. "This old guy slept the whole way into the station." When their train reached Lordsburg, Harlan and the elder engineer shared a room at the old Ownby House Hotel. "He spent sixteen hours on the bed there," Payne recalled. "Then, we had a helper coming back to Tucson and he slept again. He must have slept thirty-six hours in those two days."

Operating a steam engine demanded that an engineer and his fireman work as a team. When the engineer shut down the throttle, steam "popped off" the boiler and shot a huge cloud of black smoke out the locomotive's smokestack. When the engineer shut down the throttle on his engine, a fireman needed to shut down his fire at the same time, or he ate smoke. "It was because you weren't burning hot oil anymore," explained Lundquist. "You see,

Always a frisky lot, engineers continued to gather for fun and frolic after the steam era ended. (Howard Smith Collection)

Tom Davenport (right) and a friend were "Snapped-on-the-Street," ca. 1938. (Maude and Al Hammonds Collection)

keep it there," he said. "One day, I'm firin' between here and Yuma for this ol' goat, who always kept his hand up on the throttle and 'one-notched.' That is, he'd open the throttle one notch and then close it one notch. Back and forth, back and forth. Every time he does that you've gotta change your fire." In time, Lundquist tired of the maneuver. "I didn't shut down my fire because I knew the wind was on his side of the engine," he laughed. "The old guy got himself a big blast of smoke! He knew right now I was disgusted with the way he was running the engine and he quit doin' it. The old guy done it on purpose, not only to me, but to every fireman. He was somebody nobody liked."

Post-World War II firemen worked with many tough men who'd grown old on the railroad. They recognized good engineers among these "old-heads" on the division corps. "Grant Tevis was one of the best engineers you could find," said Payne. "He'd get his train started going west, pick up speed, open it up, and get it goin' a little bit more, and just let her go like that. He'd be on time to every station, just perfect. It was so easy to fire for him. He considered the fireman." Floyd Roberts held the same high regard for engineer Tevis. "He was hell in an automobile, though," said Floyd. "Carl Ball Sr. used to hunt with him and told me he'd never get into his car for fear a dyin'."

Another of Tucson's "good men," Tom Davenport fired his first train on the division in 1890. Geraldine "Maudie" Hammonds Mackaben recalled: "Tom was a very handsome and very polite man. My

some of them hogheads thought they were God Almighty just because they were engineers, and tried to abuse the fireman."

A feisty young rail, Lundquist put the brakes on one veteran engineer. "You see, a good engineer will set the throttle and

A doubleheader steam engine leads freight train No. 244 through the desert four miles west of Steins Pass in January 1913. Smoke, fire, and hot steam formed a dangerous combination for a fireman. Jennie Morales Benitez worked as a locomotive "wiper" during World War II and remembered "firing-up" Locomotive No. 2200. "I lit a piece of dope (grease) and let it go," Benitez told Star *columnist Bonnie Henry during February 1990. "I threw it with all my strength. It made a terrible noise like a bomb exploding. But, I wasn't afraid. My* tío *(uncle) was with me." (AHS #PC180f187_2781)*

Principled road foreman Rhu A. Miller (left) and his twin, Steven O. Miller, provide large bookends for engineers (l-r) W.B. Smith, B.F. Rinkleib, Carl Ball Sr., C.W. Stevenson, R.W.Beene, and Roy Manning, who celebrated Ball's retirement at the local yard office August 30, 1961. (Elgin Ball Collection)

father and he were drinking buddies and played golf together."

Davenport married Arizona pioneer Captain J.H. Tevis's daughter Minnie. "The family roots went way back in Arizona. Their family was never happy about them changing the name of the town from Teviston to Bowie," said Mackaben. "Mrs. Davenport was Temperance and Mr. Davenport wasn't, so she always called him a 'toper' because he drank."

"Tom Binns was another really good engineer," said Harlan Payne. "He always kept a whiskey bottle warm on the boiler of the engine. He said it had coffee in it, but we all suspected it had whiskey too." Payne continued, "B.F. 'Doc' Eaker was a good engineer and Grover Graden was another. He started here in 1912 and was road foreman before I got here. Moorman D. and John B. Gandy were fine engineers. Ben Euler was another real good man. So were C. R. 'Chuck' McGowan Jr. and Byron 'Barney' Nash."

Payne recalled that engineer Samuel 'One-Punch' Bagley earned an imposing

reputation around Tucson. "Sam Bagley was a wild kind of guy, always ready for a fight," he said. "When he was young he considered himself quite a man. If you said anything he didn't like, he'd give you a quick knockout punch." Payne worked many locomotives with the pugilist engineer.

During May of 1946, a nationwide strike of trainmen and engineers sparked tensions across the Tucson division. Rail traffic, except for troop trains, which strikers deemed vital to national security, ground to a halt. One thousand loaded freight cars, including 250 refrigerated cars, and three passenger trains stood idle in the Tucson yard. SP officials ordered three long-time local rails,

Engineer Sam Bagley held a reputation among local rails as a man who took no guff. (AHS #PC198f1)

road foremen of engines Carl Ball Sr. and Rhu A. Miller, and locomotive instructor Jim Pfersdorf, to work in place of striking enginemen. Each man had worked with the Tucson men for many years and held first loyalty to their local union. All three refused to cross the picket line. Ball's son, former division chief timekeeper Elgin Ball, remembered: "The 'Old Man,' Superintendent George A. Bays, called these officers in 'on the carpet' and asked them to handle trains during the strike."

Claudia Ball (left) and Carl Ball Sr., posed beside their new 1937 Chevrolet on Fremont Street. Claudia stood strong beside her husband in the 1946 rail strike. As national anxiety grew that year, the Air Transport Command named Tucson a control center in the event they took over mail and high priority cargo delivery. When strike leaders capitulated the drastic plan proved unnecessary. (Elgin Ball Collection)

"My father lost out in 1946 with the strike," Carl Ball Jr. recounted tearfully, in his beautiful central Tucson living room near the end of April 2002. "He didn't work when they told him to, so they made the job pretty tough for him. Let's just say, they made him ride trains that really didn't need riding. They kept him so damn busy with the job that he couldn't physically do all the things that they wanted him to do." The elder Ball finally told superintendent Bays he'd had enough. "My father just 'packed his suitcase' and moved from road foreman of engines back to locomotive engineer,

based on his seniority," said his eighty-seven-year-old son.

Carl Jr. recalled that when he went for his own promotion, twenty years later, Bays's son told him that his father's actions would not prejudice San Francisco officials against him. Floyd Roberts recalled: "Carl Ball Jr. was a really good guy. He got along well with SP President A.T. Mercier, and it got him to Frisco." One night Roberts worked firing for [Hudson C.] "Pop" Sarrels out of Yuma. "Carl was riding along as road foreman of engines and asked me if I'd change seats with him so he could do some writing in the fireman's seat, which had a light above it." Ball used the back of an SP work report to write a letter to Mercier accepting a job in San Francisco as vice president of labor relations. "Carl said, 'Here, read this.' I read it and said, 'Well hot damn, Carl! Congratulations!'"

Some locomotive stewards stayed past the days when they could safely run an engine. Payne fired for one such engineer on the No. 6 and No. 1 passenger trains. "They ran those yellow No. 4400 engines back then," Payne began. "They were not easy to fire, but we loved 'em. Well, one time we're going across the flat Animas Playa into Lordsburg, and we come to a yellow signal. This old boy's flyin' along at sixty-five miles an hour, and he doesn't slow down at all. He didn't 'set the air' to apply the brakes until after we passed the west switch into the siding, and we were still movin'!"

Payne could stand no more. "I finally yelled, 'Set some goddamned air!'" laughed the distinguished former rail. "Well, he sets a little air, but the opposing train is stopped only partially in its siding with his rear end sticking out onto the main line. I screamed, 'Big hole!' and he big-holes it, which throws it into emergency-brake mode. I was already over there getting down the steps and ready to jump off the damn thing!" When the train pulled into Lordsburg, Payne took action. "I told somebody there, 'He's not thinking. It's like he's dreamin' out there,'" he said. "They made the fellow retire, right then."

Proud of his pioneer heritage, Floyd Roberts started as a division fireman in 1941. During the spring of 2003, the jovial rancher/locomotive engineer relaxed on the porch of his attractive ranch-style, east Tucson home and remembered: "Federal law dictated that a man could work a maximum of sixteen hours in a single twenty-four hour period," said Roberts. "The rule required crews to pull their train off the main line at the nearest siding the moment their sixteen hours expired." Engineers could work just 3,800 miles per month in the early 1940s. "If you got them miles in during the first twenty days, then you got the balance of the month off," Floyd explained.

An exception to the mileage restriction allowed SP to call men who had met their monthly limit back to work in times of serious need. "In July 1952, I was 'off on miles,' as we called it, and the crew dis-

Tucson superintendent George Bays inspects the wreckage after engine No. 4317, on the westbound Imperial passenger train, hit a gasoline truck near Santan, fourteen miles southeast of Chandler, Arizona on July 17, 1952. (Elgin Ball Collection)

Floyd Roberts displays his "Fitz" caricature, the genius of Star *cartoonist David Fitzsimmons. Roberts grew up on his family's ranch in Mule Creek, New Mexico. As a young boy, Floyd's father, Joe Roberts, survived Geronimo's attack on his family at Alma, New Mexico to write a fascinating column for the* Tucson Citizen *in the early 1950s. (Robert "Mac" McCelland Collection)*

Engineer Connie Weinzapfel followed his father, Michael, to the railroad. "I said from the first day I could remember that I wanted to be a locomotive man. That was the second most sought-after job in the United States. President was first." (Union Pacific Museum)

patcher asked if I wanted to take a passenger train to Phoenix," said Roberts. "I knew what they'd do. They'd cut our engine out of the train in Phoenix and put us on a damn, slow, 'drag' freight train back to Tucson. I didn't want to work any more miles, so I said, 'No thank you.'" SP ran a 4400 class passenger engine on the front end of its Phoenix train. "We called them Yellow Jackets," sighed Roberts. "Well, near Santan, Arizona, about ten miles this side of Mesa, it hit a truck and turned the engine over. Dale Embry was the fireman, and Carl Ball Sr. was the engineer. That was one of the lucky deals I passed up." Ninety-year-old Elgin Ball recalled: "The gasoline truck they hit exploded and steam scalded my father very badly around his ankles. He'd been an engineer for a long time, but he never really felt the same after that accident."

When a fireman proved capable, he sought an engineer's chair. Except in periods of great urgency, the company demanded candidates fire a steam engine for a minimum of three years and be at least eighteen, and later twenty-one, years old. A prospective hoghead began classes on the company *Book of Rules* with five or six other men. The exhaustive test covered every aspect of locomotive and train operation including the rules of train movement; traffic signals; all engine parts and repairing minor breakdowns; problem solving in the air brake system; and a mountain of safety regulations. Extending over several stress-filled days, the exam provided an excellent measure of an engineer's readiness for road service.

Hiring patterns on the Tucson Division mirrored the economic conditions of the day. World War I brought a spike in local hiring and the SP promoted 66 Tucson Division men to engineer during

University of Arizona football star Charles R. McGowan Jr. fired steam engines on the Gila in 1942, following his wartime service. (Betty Nowell Collection)

1916-1918. Another burst of rail prosperity occurred between 1924 and 1928, vaulting 38 men into the engineer's chair. The Great Depression rippled through households in Tucson and across the nation, crushing firemen's dreams, many of whom had worked for twenty years without promotion. Work remained spotty through the much of the 1930s, until 1937-1939, when hiring again blossomed. Before these men lay miles and miles of desert railroad, increased prestige, and more money. An earthly Arizona pleasure awaited—to be sure.

Chapter 11

Oh, for the Life of an Engineer:
Hoghead Heaven in the Arizona
Desert

Future Tucson mayor E.T. "Happy" Houston wore leather sleeves while he fired this locomotive ca. 1918. Leather protection gave way to cloth and engineer's sleeves disappeared from the division by the late 1930s. (Bettie Houston Crawford Collection)

Thunder rolling, she sweeps over southern Arizona in a fury, hurling herself against the desert in a whistling blaze of energy. She is the great steam locomotive, she is the turbulent *chubasco*, storm of our desert lands. Both bring such force, one of man's making, the other so much of nature. That they should run the same track seems fitting, and thus the name "Stormy" for the Tucson Division's eastern end.

Only white males took control of steam locomotives on the Tucson Division's main line during its first sixty years. Though racial and gender bias shrank Tucson's labor pool, the Southern Pacific Railroad (SP) selected the best available men as engineers. The chosen entered a dimension atop the great steel monsters, which most only entertained as fantasy. Early rails labeled engineers "hogheads." Though conductors thought the name derisive, most enginemen warmed to the moniker.

After he successfully "wrote the book," by completing a test on the company's *Book of Rules*, a man "made his date" as an engineer when he took his first locomotive out of the yard. The job demanded a steady hand, a calm nerve, good instincts, and keen intuition. Split-second judgment, resolute decision-making, and courage helped, too. Good engineers developed the ability to "sense" what a locomotive needed in order to maximize its power or control its speed. The skill blossomed into instinct and rose to perfection in performance.

Confident, self-assured, maybe cocky, railroad engineers strode Tucson streets with a certain flair during the steam age. A well-trained man with good seniority could earn himself a handsome living. Along with money came a special prestige. An "attitude" or aura swirled around the men who ran the immense steam engines.

Former local railroad electrician Frank Hutcheson remembered: "Particularly in the late thirties, an engineer or a conductor was really looked up to. Not quite like a lawyer or a doctor, but much higher than a plumber, or carpenter, or electrician. They had quite a bit of status." The lifestyle of these uniquely skilled men bespoke of hard work, independence, and genuine affection for their fellow engineers.

Hogheads earned 4¢ per mile on the Tucson Division in 1909, traveling five thousand miles to earn $200 a month. Pima County Supervisor and local school board

Edgar L.Hudnall (third from left) and fellow rails manned the Brotherhood Railway Trainmen float, Southern Pacific Car No. 1776, for a local parade ca. 1920. While running a yard switch engine in 1936, Hudnall and his fireman, John Cordes, barely escaped death, jumping from their switcher in time to avoid a collision with an incoming freight train. (Barbara Salyer Collection)

member Charles F. Richardson, Judson Estabrook, and Wood Walker alternated on the Tucson Division's best run that year, the Nos. 7 and 8 passenger trains between Tucson and Yuma. Each of the long-time rails averaged ten daylight trips to the Colorado River town each month, on an "extremely accommodating" schedule.

South of the tracks, the Armory Park neighborhood housed most engineers and their families early on. After hogheads Peter B. Ziegler and G.T. Riggs built residences north of the rail tracks around the turn of the twentieth century, several locomotive pilots followed them to the city's northeast side. Each morning, the smells of brewing coffee and cooking breakfast drifted across the city, while a grand procession of engineers and other rails walked to and from their jobs at the SP to fuel Tucson's economy. In good times, three shifts a day flavored the local landscape; in bad, the human flow dissolved into a trickle.

Former roundhouse foreman T. Herman Blythe's father started on the division as a machinist's apprentice 1916. "My dad became an engineer in the mid-1920s, and his standard work attire was a blue

denim work shirt, pants, and engineer's cap," Blythe recalled. "On the front of his cap, a one-by-four inch badge read 'Locomotive Engineer,' in recognition of his running the locomotive at its utmost efficiency and saving oil."

Herman continued: "He wore long cloth 'sleeves' that covered his arms up to his elbows. They were black and had rubberized elastic at both ends, so they held tight. He always wore them, but by the time I started working at the railroad in 1941, nobody wore `em."

Born in Tucson during November 1913, venerable Jim "Nuge" Nugent grew up "about three feet from the main line" in the signal maintainer's house at Willcox. The crusty, warm-hearted Tucson native built his home "way out in the sticks," at Harrison Road and Broadway Boulevard, in 1947. One shiny spring day fifty-eight years later, Nugent sat with his lovely wife, Charlotte, at their dining room table and made the steam hoghead's job sound easy. "Most of the things you didn't think about, you just done 'em," chuckled Nugent.

"When the signal went yellow, you'd make your move and slow your train down," he said. "You never stopped to think, 'How much to do here or how much of that?' You just reached over and grabbed your air valve for the brakes, set 'em up, and stopped your train. When the block signal turned green, you'd turn 'em loose, and away you'd go."

In fact, taking charge of a steam engine demanded a great deal more. Safety stood first order in locomotive operation. Enormous thrust and traction, applied over

Jim Nugent and his pipe were mainstays on division steam locomotives. Here, Nugent finishes his career in a diesel engine. (James Nugent Collection)

slick steel rails, produced transportation of previously unheard of efficiency and speed. On the Stormy, its control proved challenging to one and all.

Heading east from Tucson along the SP's Stormy line to Lordsburg, New Mexico, forests of towering saguaros, spiny cholla, and fragrant creosote give way to grasslands and agave cactus. Here, range after range of jagged indigo peaks break broad, hundred-mile vistas. Over hills, through mountain passes, and across ancient seabeds, the railroad runs up and down around its curves.

Ninety-year-old George "Boots" Lundquist grew up on the Stormy. George's father worked as station pumper and his mother served as postmistress at Pantano, Arizona 1930-1950. More than sixty years after his promotion to engineer in 1941, Boots explained, "They always said that if you worked the Stormy you had to be a good engineer because of the grades and the dif-

ficulty in handling the train. Heading east from Tucson you'd top over Mescal, and, boy, it was downhill into Benson. You had to know to handle the air brakes. Anybody could work the west end, toward Gila Bend and Yuma, because it's nothin' but go."

Controlling the train's "slack," or ever-changing distance between cars as they moved over the rails, proved central to good train handling. Depending upon the train's motion, the "play" or "give" between the "knuckles" that coupled the cars created from eighteen to twenty-four inches of slack. Nugent clarified: "The slack on a train would either run in until the cars were knuckle to knuckle, or stretch out to its maximum. If it came in too far, cars would bunch up and slam into each other, knocking some off the rails, what we called 'on the ground.' If the train's slack ran out too far, it exerted a tremendous force on the knuckles and the train broke in half."

The winding trip through the San Pedro River basin held the Stormy's stiffest test. Traveling west from Sybil over the river into Benson, "You'd get a train with the first bunch of cars going uphill, the next group on flat ground, and the last going downhill," said Nugent. "They're all doing different things. That's where you can make mistakes and really tear things up. You've got to work your engine under power and keep that slack as even as you can. You really had to watch it, or you'd break in two.

The engineer's whistle played a key role in safe train operation. The SP conducted extensive testing to determine "with scientific exactness" the "proper length of blast for each signal and a definite interval that should be allowed between blasts." The company placed "whistling posts" at a

Diesel power heads east from Mescal summit, downhill into the San Pedro River Valley during 2004. (Kalt Collection)

standard 1,320 feet before every rail crossing. Long whistle blasts required two-and-one-half seconds and short blasts one second each. "Engineers should take care to not slur blasts and cut them off sharply," explained one *Southern Pacific Bulletin*, so that whistles were not "jumbled into one continuous blast." While adhering to SP regulations, some engineers used their whistles for personal fun. Many developed unique variations in their tone by inserting a piece of wood into their whistles to keep family and friends apprised of their arrival in the city.

Because a heavy train could take up to a mile to stop, hitting obstacles on the track proved unavoidable. Wagons, automobiles, cattle, and humans all stood fair game on the slippery steel. This precipitated the "suicide by train" phenomenon, described by more than one division engineer. Tucson native Constant "Connie"

A quiet sunrise at the San Pedro River Bridge belies the heavy rail traffic that rumbles over the steel structure each day. (Kalt Collection)

Wienzapfel remembered killing six people during his career. "Sometimes you'd see them, look right into their faces, sometimes not," Wienzapfel said. "I couldn't stop in time. But you always stopped afterwards."

In 1921, one hundred miles constituted a day's work for SP engineers. Men running passenger trains earned $6.56 per day. When Nuge Nugent started in 1936, division engineers earned $7.77 a day on a switch engine; men on road engines earned a bit more. In contrast, explained Dennis Simmerman, presidential assistant for the Brotherhood of Locomotive Engineers and Trainmen, "In 2006, the basic day is 130 miles, and an engineer makes about $425 for the run between Tucson and Yuma." Over the last seventy years, railroad engineers' pay increased fifty-four times, while transportation industry wages rose only fifteen times.

Most men saw the engineer's life as a little bit of hoghead heaven. "I liked working outside," Nugent recalled. "I liked that kind of work and the people. Even the officials here were beautiful. It wasn't a job where you were being stepped on all the time. You talk about low pressure, low problems, all that. I had lots of leniency." Nugent continued: "The officials here came from the ranks. They had all worked these same jobs, and they knew what could happen. I fought with 'em, but I liked 'em. If you done somethin' wrong, they'd take a chunk out of you. You'd just sit there and take it because ninety-nine times out of a hundred it was yours, meaning you deserved it. A rule's a rule but sometimes there's a reason, ha, ha,

*Engineer Floyd Roberts's children, Dennis (right)
and Toni Roberts, enjoyed a Rodeo Days ride in the
cab of B.F. Eaker's locomotive No. 3002 during
February 1948. (Floyd Roberts Collection)*

*O'Rielly Chevrolet donated this truck to the Diamond 4 Hunting
Club for their locally renowned hunting trip in 1931. (l-r) Future
city councilman and road foreman of engines Carl A. Ball Sr.; two
Rincon Mountain turkeys; star THS athlete and engineman's in-
structor Jim Pfersdorf; O'Reilly representative; division engi-
neer, future Arizona senator, and Tucson mayor Elbert T.
"Happy" Houston; and engineer Carl Padgett. (Bettie Houston
Crawford Collection)*

to be a little bit flexible. The people had to
have the flexibility because there was no
flexibility in the Book."

Nugent remembered a dreaded
"main-line meet," two trains running on the
same track in opposite directions. "We did-
n't have a wreck, but it was still what they
called a main-line meet," he recalled.
"That's a no-no, a dismissible offense." That
day, the Tucson native headed to Phoenix
as a train ran east toward him with "right,"
or priority, over his train. "It meant I had to
stay in Mesa until the other train passed,"
he explained. "As I ran past this siding, I
saw this train sittin' over there with its engine working. It had the number I was looking for, except for one number."

The ninety-year-old shuddered at
the memory: "I identified him as the guy I
was going to meet, so I ran right on by the
meeting point. As I went by, here come the
real train I was supposed to wait for! We
both got stopped before we hit each other."
Nugent backed up to allow the oncoming
train to pass and then pulled his train into
Phoenix. "When I got there, the
trainmaster asked me, 'Do you have anything you want to talk about?' I answered, 'If you're talking about
that main-line meet, yeah I do.' He
told me he knew about it before I
did. The conductor on the train I
passed had turned me in."

The railroad held its re-
quired investigation into Nugent's
mistake while he pondered his inevitable dismissal. "George A.
Bays was superintendent, and I
knew I was going to get fired. Had
to be fired. Couldn't do anything
else! Sometimes those investiga-
tions could take four to six hours
but mine lasted only twenty
minutes."

Nugent continued, "I told
them exactly what happened and
they wrote it down. Trouble was,
Mr. Bays forgot to send the transcript of the investigation to head-

quarters in San Francisco within the mandatory thirty days. So, he just gave me thirty 'brownies,' or demerits. The boss in Frisco come back and told Mr. Bays he had to fire me.

"He told them, 'Can't fire him because I sent the transcript in too late. We can't do anything after that.'

"Well, Mr. Bays took a lot of guff for that, but that's the kind of people we worked with in Tucson."

Nugent's scare in Mesa was the only one he would acknowledge. "During the war, main-line meets happened all the time," he said. "Because of the immense weight of the trains with all their machinery, weapons and such, you would sometimes roll past the block signal. That's technically a main-line meet, but no one ever did anything about it."

The SP had added a new engine to its passenger service between Tucson and Yuma early in the twentieth century. Designed by France's Anatole Mallet, one boiler powered two separate engine units and provided improved steam pressure and motive efficiency. "Articulated," the Mallet locomotive employed a pair of wheels on a "truck," at the engine's forward end, which allowed the boiler to slide on a pivot. The novel advance made negotiating curves easier for engineers.

In 1908, SP superintendent of motive power Taylor W. Heintzelman pioneered a Mallet-patterned engine to limit the toxic fumes engineers faced going through tunnels in California's Sierra Nevada range. Heintzelman's 2-8-8-2 locomotive placed the engine crew in front of the smokestack. This design allowed men to see the track ahead more clearly and reduced the amount of smoke they breathed.

Tucson Division engineers liked running "Back-up Mallies," as they called them, for their weight and muscle. SP paid

Tucson Division rails grew to respect and admire George Bays's (left) leadership style and jovial nature. (Arnold Bays Collection)

engineers according to the tonnage over the locomotive's driving wheels. Some engines needed assistance climbing the division's "ruling grade," or steepest climb of 1.48 percent from San Simon to Steins Pass, New Mexico. Other "helper districts" ran east out of Tucson to Mescal and up to Dragoon Station.

If a hefty train required three helping engines to climb through a pass, the engineer collected his pay based on the total weight of all three helpers and his own locomotive. Running the Stormy meant a robust paycheck, and certain engineers claimed it as their own. "The Stormy was the best damned little railroad in the world," Nuge Nugent affirmed. "You had to know what you were doing. It was a real challenge with all of its up and down grades. We loved the money, though."

Using helper engines to run what rails called "up-the-hill" to Mescal required the SP to pay for the brakeman, fireman, and engineer to ride back into Tucson "light engine," with only the locomotive and tender. The introduction of the 4100 and 4200 class Mallet engines meant the SP no longer needed helper engines heading east out of Tucson, except on heavier trains. This saved the company money.

"Mallies were built for heavy freight," T. Herman Blythe recalled. "But we used them between here and Lordsburg for long passenger trains, fourteen to sixteen cars of people, baggage, and mail. I remember they ran them on the No. 6 Argonaut over to Lordsburg. When it got there, they'd turn it around and it'd bring the No. 43 passenger train back to Tucson."

Harlan "Hard Rock" Payne remembered that firemen struggled to keep the correct water level in the Back-up Mallet's boiler. "You read the water glass backwards from the way you read it on other locomotives. Too little water meant 'dry steam' and no power," Payne said. Harlan made his first trip as an engineer over the Gila's Tucson to Yuma run in 1942. He recalled that his fireman had little experience on the thunderous half-million-ton Back-up Mallet. "He was running the water level too high in the boiler. Well, we were goin' along when all of a sudden the brakes began to lock up throughout the train. It just ground slowly to a stop right there in the desert. Damnedest thing!"

Hurrying to one of the dome-shaped concrete telephone stands along the line, Payne called division headquarters. "I learned that excess water in the boiler could wash enough lubricating oil off the pumps for the air brakes to lock them up completely. They told me to climb up onto the 'apron' and hand-rotate two ratchets to relube the air brake pumps. I gave them a few turns and we were back under way."

The performance of steam locomotives varied, as did the skill of division engineers. An efficient power cycle depended upon maximizing the temperature and pressure under which the engine's steam expanded. The challenge for locomotive designers lay in developing greater steam while remaining under the maximum al-

Between 1941 and 1944, SP purchased 89 huge cab-forward, AC class, articulated locomotives. John B. Hungerford remembered the Mallet locomotive's sweet music, in his Cab-in-Front: the Half-Century Story of an Unconventional Locomotive, *"This whistle-like sound, followed by a wheeze made a friendly chorus...a harmonic much missed on the SP nowadays." (AHS #pc180f188_b)*

lowable weight as defined by the load capacities of the countless trestle viaducts that stretched across the deep canyons and ravines of the West.

"You could get a good steamer," remembered Carl A. Ball Jr. "You'd make steam easily with some locomotives and with others you couldn't make steam at all. The 5000s were peculiar because they had three cylinders as opposed to the 4300 Mallie two-cylinder passenger engines we had. I remember that the 5042, 5043 were good engines." The 5000 class engine used two high-pressure cylinders, each twenty-six inches in diameter, to drive coupled rear-drive wheels. Beside the firebox, another forty-inch, low-pressure cylinder powered a forward pair of drive wheels. Blythe remembered the behemoth locomotives. "The 5000 class had a 'three-bang' driver," he said. "They needed a booster engine to help the train get started. It was its own little steam engine with a wheel that

ran on each rail. After it got the locomotive started, the booster would shut off."

Payne recalled the frustration of getting the big 5000s moving. "They were very powerful," he said. "But, to get a heavy train started you had to shove the 'reverse gear' all the way forward and get all the slack stretched out between the cars. Then, you'd get the throttle all the way open and hope she started rollin'. If it didn't get movin', you'd kick the little booster engine on, and that just might give it enough power to get you goin.'" As the train began moving, the engineer applied more throttle. "We called it 'hooked up,'" said Payne. "The more you hooked it up, the faster you got going and the more you heard a 'chunk, chunk, chunk' sound from the center piston of the three-bang engine."

Engineers "checked the extra board" at the yard office, west of the roundhouse to determine when they might next run a locomotive. "It was hard to tell when

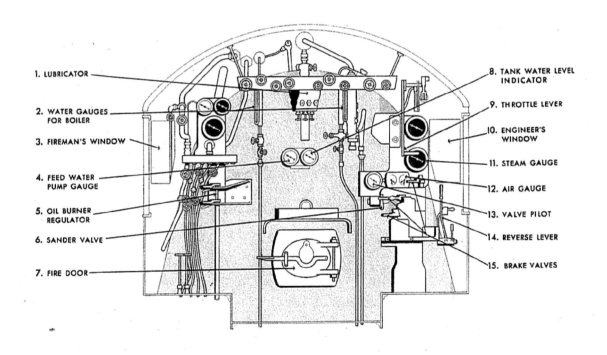

1. LUBRICATOR
2. WATER GAUGES FOR BOILER
3. FIREMAN'S WINDOW
4. FEED WATER PUMP GAUGE
5. OIL BURNER REGULATOR
6. SANDER VALVE
7. FIRE DOOR

8. TANK WATER LEVEL INDICATOR
9. THROTTLE LEVER
10. ENGINEER'S WINDOW
11. STEAM GAUGE
12. AIR GAUGE
13. VALVE PILOT
14. REVERSE LEVER
15. BRAKE VALVES

The SP initiated a Junior Engineers program to train young boys with an interest in locomotive careers. An accompanying booklet described each SP engine and included this diagram of steam locomotive controls. (Undated SP brochure)

Engineman Bill Codd's broad grin brightens the cab of Locomotive No 1673 during the 1955 celebration of SP's arrival seventy-five years earlier. (Sid Showalter Collection)

you were gonna get out on the extra board," Carl Ball Jr. explained. "Unless a man was on a regular job, such as between Tucson and Lordsburg, it was hard to guess when he might get called. I guess everybody felt the same way. You either got out without any sleep or you got too much."

When his name reached the top of the board, a man could chose to take out the next available locomotive or "lay off" and wait for a better job. Personal priorities dictated the decision—Connie Wienzapfel chose to work. "They'd set you up as an engineer on the extra board, and you had to go wherever your seniority would take you," he recalled. "I spent 272 days working out of town during my first year, away from my family. The second year it was 243, until I could get enough seniority to hold a regular job running from Bowie to Globe."

Boots Lundquist remembered a conversation with Wienzapfel early in their careers. "One day I went to the bank with Connie," Lundquist recalled. "Now, he never did let up and worked every hour they ever called him. He would put money in savings accounts for each of his three kids, his wife, and himself. The rest they'd live on.

"I asked him, 'What'd you make this payday?' He says, 'I cleared $310.'

"Well, I had made $115 because I'd been layin' off," Lundquist shrugged.

"I said, 'Connie, I don't know how you do it.' "He said, 'You're layin' off all the time, George. You gotta work if you wanna make money like this. You gotta take every call.'

"Another thing,' he says, 'You enjoy your family and I never do see mine.'

"I was getting further and further in debt, though, and there came a time when I had to work more," said Boots.

Bernard "Wrinkle-Belly" Rinkleib arrived from Germany in 1911. He hired out in SP engine service at Tucson in September 1917. Eighty-nine years later, Bernard's daughter, Emily Rinkleib Bradley, shared memories of growing up in a steam-era railroad family. "My father was a little guy," she said. "He was about five-foot-five and couldn't have weighed

Bernard F. "Wrinkle Belly" Rinkleib treasured his career on the local division. (Emily Rinkleib Bradley Collection)

During the mid-1930s, Tucson's Whitehouse Café and the French Café on West Congress Street filled up with enginemen before and after their runs. Martin's Drug and T. Ed Litt's Drugstore also provided comfortable lunch counters. (Elgin Ball Collection)

over 110 pounds. They used to call road foreman of engines Rhu Miller, who was a very big man, and my father 'Mutt and Jeff.'"

The erstwhile German loved the SP. "My father was very proud of his job," Bradley continued. "During World War I, he had to report his status to Earl Boyd at the railroad because he was not a citizen yet. He didn't take off time from work; we always needed the money."

For more than thirty years, if Emily's father "laid off" for a special occasion he received no pay. "He missed many a family Christmas and birthday," said Bradley. "The SP had no paid holidays until after World War II. Sometime in the 1950s, they started to get a paid vacation. Dad made it to the Sunset Limited the last couple of

years before he retired. Then he knew he was going to go out at an exact time. It was exciting when he got on the Sunset Limited. You knew when he'd be home."

A company "crew dispatcher" set work assignments and put together train crews on the railroad. With the flip of a whim, he could turn heaven to hell in a hoghead's instant. In early November 2002, veteran engineer Floyd Roberts recalled one crew dispatcher who played favorites with work assignments.

"This guy worked regular, but he was a real good drinkin' man," Roberts laughed. "He sure liked to 'move his arm,' if you know what I mean. You could promote things through him a little bit dishonestly."

For a little cash, the large fellow saved a shift's best runs for his most gener-

Playfully thumbing his nose at company regulations, Nuge Nugent jumped forward off his last engine rather than backing down the ladder as the Book of Rules stipulated. Because the SP paid engineers by the weight of the engines, the Tucson crew dispatcher loaded Nugent's train with ten diesels, as a going-away present when he retired in 1977. (Jim Nugent Collection)

A favorite among his fellow engineers, Hudson C. "Pop" Sarrels (center) is congratulated on his sterling career by Gilbert L. Salsbury (second from left) and superintendent Ralph Coltrin (right) among others. (Glibert L. Salsbury Collection)

ous friends. "If you 'got along with him,' he'd either lay you off or 'shove the board,' meaning shove some guy around you to deadhead (ride without working and without pay) to El Paso or Yuma, instead of you," Roberts explained. "Then you'd go out on the better run."

When inequities grew too abusive, local enginemen took the matter up with the Brotherhood of Locomotive Engineers. "We made it so that the only way that the roundhouse could accept a call for men to Yuma was from the west-end dispatcher at the depot, and not from the crew dispatcher," remembered Roberts. "We took calling crews out of that guy's hands."

Staying awake proved the hardest aspect of the engineer's job for many. Nuge Nugent remembered: "When you work sixteen hours straight, that's a damn long time. You're off duty eight hours but you usually only get about three or four hours sleep, then you get another sixteen hours of work. By that time you're really ready to fall asleep."

Some enginemen slept during the locomotive's long uphill climbs. Many used the changing sound of the engine as it crested the hill to wake them for the train's

downhill run. When sleep weighed on Connie Weinzapfel, he rested a large wrench in his lap while his locomotive worked up hill. The wrench slid off his knees and slammed to the floor of the cab when the engine crested the summit, awakening a snoozing Weinzapfel. "Connie took a lot of heat from fellow engineers when he divulged that trick publicly," remembered his friend, Tucson historian and author David Devine.

Jim Nugent never slept in the cab of his locomotive and nobody on his engine slept. "I had a nasty name," the sturdy hoghead said. "Everybody knew there was no sleeping on Nugent's train. I went to work one day, and a young brakeman was asking the crew dispatcher, 'Who'd I got for a hoghead?'"

"The dispatcher says, 'You got Nugent.'

'Oh my God,' the kid says. 'I'm sooo... sleepy.' He complained about that, but he stayed awake."

Long hours away from home taxed marital relations in some rail families. "A woman had to be a good woman to stay with a guy," Lundquist said. "One story we told was about this 'ol engineer, who had been down in Yuma for about thirty days. He called his wife and said, 'I'm gonna lay off. I'm comin' home. I gotta take care of some business.'"

Answered the understanding woman, "You just keep right on aworkin' and I'll bring that business right on down to you."

Boots recalled: "I enjoyed being out there on the road in a certain group of people that you lived and worked with. The thing I didn't like most about the railroad was that I couldn't spend time with my family. You didn't have time to go to church or into the schools. If you did, then you'd have to lay off. Then you wouldn't get paid."

Lundquist's promotion to engineer strained his social relationships. "I had little kids," he said. "My friends were all firemen my age, and we liked to get our families together and have a big party. They all had regular jobs, and they'd go to Lordsburg, come back, and then they got a day off. As a beginning hoghead, I'd be on the extra board and maybe I'd get a switch engine. They'd come in and have a party. I'd have to lay off in order to go to the party.

"I happened to be in a group of people that all got to be good friends," Lundquist continued. "The wives did a lot of things together. They were always arranging a picnic to Sabino Canyon or up on the Pantano. Maybe twenty different families would come. I think that kept the bunch that I belonged with together. We had two or three divorces, but overall it was good." Nuge Nugent recalled: "All of our wives were all pregnant, so we'd cook a big bunch of beans and play Monopoly. We played it so much that I finally wouldn't let any more Monopoly sets in my house.

"Sometimes, we'd go to the show together or go swimming at the Mission swimming pool or go up into the mountains," Nugent continued. "We'd have a fire and cook hotcakes or wieners or steaks. One time, about six of us went up to White House Canyon in the Santa Rita Mountains, and when we turned back to look at Tucson, we saw the Northern Lights!"

Not all enginemen thrived in the freedom of railroad life. "Lots of guys played around and mommies got to playin' around at home," said Lundquist. "It was hard on the families because it was a seniority job. Until a man got enough seniority to hold a regular job, he was on the road a lot."

The company's Rule G prohibited alcohol on the SP, and violators faced stiff penalties. Floyd Roberts declared: "There weren't any angels on the railroad. Five or six men committed suicide from that class of 1936." Sharper than a whip at

A pensive Tucson lass beautifies a large rock in Sabino Canyon, ca. 1910. The canyon, northeast of Tucson, remains a favorite almost a century later, though dramatic floods destroyed millions of dollars in improvements during the summer of 2006. (Dorothy Fitzpatrick Collection)

eighty-five, the former engine-man added, "I also know of several times when the fireman saved an engineer's job. The hoghead would be so drunk that he couldn't do his job and the fireman would have to step in."

The Ownby House stands in the twenty-first century, cracked plaster revealing its adobe core. (Kalt Collection)

"In the early days they couldn't dare get on an engine all pie-eyed because they'd have some real terrific accidents," Connie Wienzapfel recalled. Never a drinker, Wienzapfel earned a nickname from his personal run-in with the railroad's infamous edict. "One time, I hid a six-pack of beer given to us by Golden Eagle Distributors for my brother," Connie explained. "It was from a case of beer that had been damaged in transit, and so the SP had already paid for it." Weinzapfel took the liquid contraband into a nearby company restroom. "Two Department of Public Safety and two SP officers burst in on me," Connie remembered. "The officer told me to read Rule G from my rule book. It said you could be fired for just being in possession of alcoholic beverages. They fired me for thirty-two days, and I got the name 'Six Pack.'"

To make the best of their days and defray living costs, Nugent, Payne, Verne Bingham, and several fellow hogheads pooled monies to rent a house in Lordsburg. Just a block south of the depot and yard office, J.P. Ownby opened his Ownby House Hotel to track-laying crews in 1881. Nugent remembered, "We lived for while in the hotel, but eventually we rented the little house at the south end of the hotel's back yard. It had a big kitchen and a nice fig tree outside."

Beloved Hector Mackenzie mugs for the camera in 1977. (James Nugent Collection)

The home's three bedrooms and sleeping porch accommodated several men in New Mexico's most "wide-open" town. "We'd get into Lordsburg and go right over to that house to eat, or sleep, or whatever," explained Payne. "A really good friend of ours, Hector McKenzie, cooked up the greatest meals you'd ever have. Hector could fix up the best meatloaf. You could cut off a slice, put it in a frying pan, and cook it up. Delicious! It really broke our hearts when Hector died."

Everybody contributed to the Lordsburg operation. "My job was to make chiles," Payne recalled. "They taught me how. I'd take a big can of roasted and peeled green chiles and layer 'em up in a brown crock with oil, vinegar, oregano, garlic salt, and garlic powder, five things. They were

Each man took a chore to insure good maintenance of the engineer's house behind the Ownby Hotel. (James Nugent Collection)

delicious. You could eat 'em with crackers or with meat. You could almost eat 'em with ice cream." Payne best expressed the sentiments of his housemates: "It was a nice way to live because you had a place to stay, your own bed, and you could fix good meals. It was kinda fun to be over there when the other guys were there. Something I will always remember. Great guys."

To this day, Lordsburg remains a crew terminal, where train crews "turn over" and new workers relieve them. The bedraggled, southwestern New Mexico city stands legendary among rails as the wildest stop on the division; a place where, given time, "everything" was bound to happen.

Ralph "Chicken" Smith owned the Hidalgo Hotel and Restaurant across from SP's Lordsburg Station. Smith, who earned his nickname when he sold chickens to "Fat Hoy" (D.S. Pon), did his best to keep the town's reputation alive. Behind his restaurant, Smith opened what he called "the Railroad Club." A bar, card tables, slot machines, and women made the notorious venue a prime place for rails to drink and gamble away the hours during long layovers.

"Lordsburg was a cookin' place," said Payne. "In back of the restaurant Chicken Smith had a dance floor, and he usually had a group playing music. Every turnover, or change of crews, they had gambling games ready for rails back there." Chicken Smith employed a profes- sional gambler to

Madeline O'Dell (seated third from left) and Tommy O'Dell (to Madeline's right) joined Lordsburg revelers in their cocktail lounge, the Copper Inn, ca. 1940. "A doorway connected the bar to the restaurant, so you didn't have to go outside to get a meal," remembered barber Leon Speer. "Real nice place." (Leon Speer Collection)

keep his poker game going round-the-clock. "I'd stand behind the dealer and watch 'em play poker," laughed Payne. "I didn't trust him as far as I could throw him. Those guys would gamble some big stakes. They had card games at most railroad terminals, like Tucson, Yuma, and Gila Bend."

One old-time railroad card game, "panguingue," reigned as a favorite among division rails. A form of rummy that called for payouts throughout the game, panguingue often made quick work of a rail's paycheck. "I'll tell you what, that panguingue was a disease more than a game," Nugent recalled. "I never learned to play, but some guys would come off their trick (shift) and head straight to Chicken Smith's. They'd play all the way through their rest, then go right back to work without sleeping. Sometimes they'd take a break and walk back to the Ownby House. That short walk could be a freezing one, in Lordsburg, during the winter."

Many hogheads held a clear image of a "good engineer." When he first went to work for the SP, Lundquist lived with Fred Mayes. "He got me to go to work at the railroad," the old hoghead remembered. "Mr. Mayes told me, 'George, you'll have a good job as long as you keep your nose clean. Just stay out of trouble and don't be blowin' your mouth off all the time. You'll get along fine on the railroad.' I took that to heart. I didn't go to Lordsburg and get drunk and start raisin' hell."

Connie Weinzapfel followed his father, Michael, into the cab of an SP steam locomotive and grew to love his work. "Harry Huddleston was the one who first made me understand," Connie said. "He told me, 'It's a man who will take what [train] they give him and get over the road without disturbing the dispatcher, because very seldom will you get a perfect train to handle. Something's going to go wrong and you have to overcome that.'"

Most of the men who ran steam engines on the Tucson Division appreciated working for the SP. Not so veteran hoghead E.C. "Moonbeam" Webster. One early October morning in 2002, at his comfortable home in Bowie, Arizona, Moonbeam leaned back in his chair and let loose a stentorian guffaw. "You'll hear a lot of guys say how much they love the SP, but not me," swore Webster. "The railroad had a job and I done it, that's all."

Born in Solomonville, Arizona, Webster hired on with the company in 1942. He worked the engineer's job serving four

History surrounds Leon Speer in the barbershop his father, Claude Speer, first equipped in Lordsburg during May 1935. "He soon saw he could make a go of it and upgraded equipment in 1937-38," said Leon. "These are the same sinks and chairs. Most of the railroaders were nice but some could get ornery if they'd stayed up all night and lost all their money in a poker game." (Leon Speer Collection)

Pistol at the ready, Moonbeam Webster refused to divulge the origin of his rail nickname and did as he pleased on the railroad. (Sid Showalter Collection)

bined velocity of their rock and my train means that if that rock hits me in the head, I'm gone!

"I'd see those little kids come out from under the bridge with a rock in their hand," Webster explained. "I'd shoot about three feet from 'em and hit the sand right there. They knew to do it no more! That was great fun! Those kids just loved that! Havin' a good time!"

Boots Lundquist concluded, "It was an interesting life. It was different from most people's lives. You just had, more or less, a railroad family." Nuge Nugent also spoke of his love of the engineer's life: "It was a good job. I got to wave at the kids and I'd give lots of 'em a ride when I got a chance.

"Besides," smiled Nugent, "we hogheads were responsible for the baby boom. You see, the train whistle caused all these people to have all these kids. Wake everybody up at four o'clock in the morning, and who wants to go back to sleep?"

mines south of Tucson on the Calabasas line. He also ran the "Bowie local" to Globe, Arizona, for several years. Respected by his peers, Moonbeam executed a career-long war against SP rules. "We used to stop at a bar called Blake's Place, east of Fort Thomas," recalled the talented hoghead fiddler. "We'd have a beer and kill some time. The old boy that owned the place come up with this idea that drinks would be half price as long as the train was goin' by."

One time Webster brought his train to a complete stop in front of Blake's Place. "We all got off and went into the bar," the old charmer smiled. "We were still 'goin' by' in a way, and the guy says, 'Damn, move that train! You're breakin' me!' One day, he bought me a bottle of Scotch and was standin' out there in front holdin' it up. We had a lot of fun on the railroad."

Webster recalled another favorite trampling of the company rulebook. "On the Bowie-Globe run, Indians used to throw stones and shoot arrows at the caboose," Moonbeam remembered. "They usually didn't bother the engine, but if they did, they'd get shot at! You see, if they hit me with a rock they could kill me. The com-

Friendships endured for decades after engineers retired. (Jim Nugent Collection)

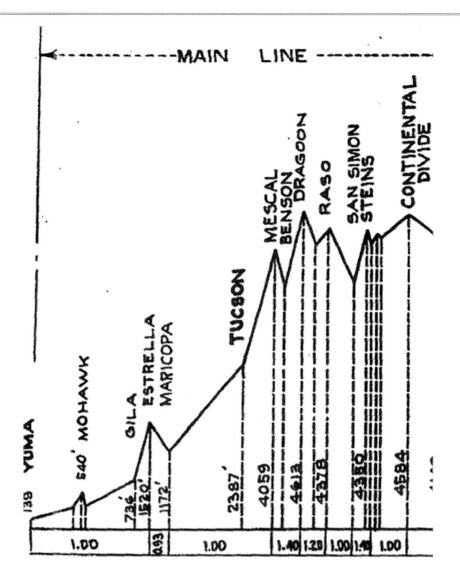

Riding aboard a Southern Pacific steam locomotive pulling a train into Arizona at Yuma we head to Adonde Wells (Wellton), then up a one percent grade over Mohawk Summit at 540 feet elevation (Mohawk) to Gila Bend (Gila); from there we chug eighteen miles up the hill to Estrella at 1,520 feet. Down to Heaton we run, formerly a major shipping point into the Salt River Valley. Then, we sail around the longest curve in the world during the days of steam, a ten-degree curve five miles long! From there we travel along the SP's longest piece of straight track, forty-seven miles, to Maricopa (formerly Maricopa Wells), where originally the only water for hundreds of miles could be found. Chugging past Casa Grande and its native ruins, our locomotive moves uphill through Picacho, Red Rock, Rillito, and Stockham into Tucson.

We head east onto the Stormy out of Tucson, up past Chamizo and into the San Pedro River Valley, through "Pay Car Curve," and into Benson. Our engine next climbs 2,000 feet in elevation in just twenty miles to Dragoon at 4,613 feet, before descending into the Sulphur Springs Valley, past ancient Lake Cochise and Willcox. Up we rumble to Raso (Railroad Pass) at 4,378 feet on a 1.2-percent grade, then, down into the San Simon Valley past Luzena to Bowie. We soon leave Arizona and thunder through the Peloncillo Mountains to Steins Pass at 4,350 feet. From there we fall upon the alkali-laden soil of the Playas Valley, and into Lordsburg, New Mexico. Though changes often altered it, most considered this the main line of the Tucson Division.

(Southern Pacific Bulletin, February 1, 1921)

In 1900, F.M.Whyte's system of Locomotive Classification listed the engine's leading wheels, its large driving wheels, and its trailing wheels. "Back-up Mallies" or "articulated-consolidation" locomotives had a 4-8-8-2 configuration, meaning four leading truck wheels, two independent sets of eight driving wheels, and two trailing truck wheels.

Other differences in locomotives included length; boiler pressure; weight; horsepower or power a locomotive develops when it is moving; tractive power or "pull"; cylinder diameter; and length of piston travel (stroke). Some of these characteristics were clearly marked on the side of the cab of each locomotive as seen in this detail of the top picture on page 178:

3002 Locomotive number

A-6 Locomotive class

A-81 Atlantic (4-4-0 type) 81 inch drivers (driving wheels)

22/28 cylinder bore and stroke

127 weight on drivers (127,000 pounds)

B-64 "B" indicates the presence of a small steam "booster" engine on the trailing truck to facilitate smoother starts and 64 is the weight resting on the booster (64,000 pounds)

SF this locomotive is equipped with superheater and feedwater heater.

(Floyd Roberts Collection)

Silhouetted against one of the region's powerful thunderstorms, the Mescal coal temple symbolized a bygone steam era. Built by the EP&SW early in the century, the tower stood until the Union Pacific tore it down in the spring of 1998. (Elgin Ball Collection)

Automobiles hurry along the dusty road (right) as the No. 11 train steams westbound near Picacho ca. 1912 (AHS # 4913b)

Chapter 12

The Black Cavalry of Commerce:
U.S. Mail, Ores, and Cattle

> *"The railways of the United States are the arteries of the nation's life, and upon their employees rests the immense responsibility of moving the products of the nation promptly and properly."*
>
> *President Woodrow Wilson*
> *1917*

American Railway Express messenger Harry S. Stewart turned off the lights in his car when the Golden State Limited left Tucson in the early morning hours of May 15, 1922. The well-liked resident of El Paso settled onto his bed and slipped into sleep. Down the track, two miles west of Jaynes Station, six despicable train bandits concealed their large black automobile in the area's thick brush. One member of the evil coterie ran up the line to place "false lights and signals, red fusees, and torpedoes" on the track. These railroad devices would signal the engineer of the Golden State to stop at a point where three bandits, armed with revolvers, lay in wait.

The plan worked well. As the train came to a halt, robbers ordered a tramp off the blind baggage, located between the locomotive tender and baggage car, to help them uncouple the express and mail cars from the rest of the train. Then, they drew down on engineer George Reid and fireman J.A. Ingram, ordering them to pull the two cars about twelve lengths up the track where four other desperados waited in an auto.

Conductor D.M. Madigan stuck his head out a vestibule door to see the cause of the commotion. "Keep back," a rough voice commanded, just as a bullet shattered the door's glass window. Roused from his slumber, expressman Stewart thought he heard the train crew having trouble with hobos and grabbed his shotgun and a revolver. A voice ordered Stewart to come out of his car. Pistol in hand, the plucky package-man slid open the car door to see masked men. In a flash, Stewart blasted two shots into one of the crooks, who crumpled to the ground. Another thief shouted for his cohorts to retreat and, jumping into their vehicles, the gang raced west along the Casa Grande Highway.

Dead in the dirt, with his homemade black mask slipped halfway down his face, lay local goat rancher Thomas O. Dugat. Pima County under-sheriff Charles Pogue, a twenty-year acquaintance of the dead outlaw, later identified the body. A lonely thermos bottle of nitroglycerin and three sticks of dynamite, for use on the express car's safe, rested beside the failed outlaw.

Because the city airfield had housed no planes for the previous four months, two "aeroplanes" came from a San Diego military base to ferret out the criminals. Authorities soon nabbed Frank W. Jirou. Southern Pacific Railroad (SP) boilermaker George Lockmier told officials that the six-foot-seven-inch bandit, his former roommate, had expressed interest in robbing a train. Jirou confessed to his role in the bungled heist and implicated George Winkler and his two sons, Edward and George Jr., along with goatherder Santiago Valdez.

A habitué of downtown pool halls, Jirou said Dugat held three meetings to plan the hold-up. Jirou led authorities to a spot along Silverbell Road where the gang had stashed a bag of ammunition and clothing. The day following the debacle near Jaynes Station, Sheriff Ben Daniels's posse raided Dugat's goat ranch on the road to Silverbell mine and found a moonshine distillery. Its entrance disguised, a ten-foot tunnel ran under the ranch's stone house to a storeroom where authorities found corn, sugar, and other ingredients for corn whiskey. Officers found only five barrels of liquor but felt sure Dugat's accomplices had removed the distilling apparatus and a great deal of whiskey from the hidden alcohol factory following the failed train robbery.

William H. White Jr. sits atop a huge plow horse at Jaynes Station seven years after the botched robbery. White spent his early childhood in the small rail and farming community eight miles north of Tucson. Born in the Stork's Nest birthing facility at 233 N. Court Avenue during 1924, White recalled: "I heard talk of the robbery while I was growin' up. My sister needed goat's milk and my father bought it from that fellow who was killed trying to rob the train. There weren't many places you could buy goat's milk around here at the time." (William White Collection)

Hijacking the train's express and mail cars proved a favorite industry among the iniquitous. A string of "brazen and gigantic" train robberies during the summer of 1921 had prompted federal authorities to arm all railroad postal clerks and post office employees with revolvers. The U.S. Marines stationed armed guards on trains and a twenty-man squad at each end of the local rail division. Marines guarded mail trucks between the SP depot and Tucson's various post offices, while residing at the YMCA and local hotels.

These efforts failed to deter Tucson's band of thieves, but hard-nosed rail clerk Stewart had thwarted their plan. Authorities exonerated the expressman in self-defense for killing felon Dugat. The American Railway Express Company presented the division's hero with a letter of commendation and a check for $1,000. When Stewart's El Paso buddies heard that their nearly-blind friend had killed one of the bandit gang, their mouths filled with laughter and their hearts with glee.

Because the state produced little else but copper, cattle, wool, and cotton, most consumer goods arrived in Arizona as finished products. Copper mining paid the SP's bills on the Tucson Division and the interplay of two forces defined mining fortunes in Arizona during the twentieth century's first two decades. On one edge, "boosterism" by local newspapers and mining corporations worked hard to sell the advantages of investing in Arizona. Loaded with plaudits, regular reviews of the region's thriving mines filled dailies in Tucson and southern Arizona. Across the territory, scribes screamed, "The richest find yet," or "Bonanza find!" on behalf of countless mines.

Against this background of reverie and soaring expectations, the period's proverbial but elusive "knocker" bid fair to trash the territory's financial and mining prospects at every opportunity. Filled with tales of hoax, swindle, and failure, these amorphous cads spread "rumors of a knocking nature." Often launched to spite a competitor, such lies threw icy water on the legitimate schemes of local merchants and miners.

Preceded by early Spanish conquistadores' mines, discovery of rich copper mines near Clifton heralded southern Arizona's mineral potential prior to the Southern Pacific Railroad's arrival. While many derived mining profits, fraudulent claims and short-lived veins often scared off possible investors in the unregulated territory. Arizona historian F. C. Lockwood stated, "Many ambitious schemes for north and south and other branch lines came to naught in the seventies and eighties but some of them were realized."

Mining enthusiasts came to Arizona's metropolis "in droves" around the turn of the twentieth century. Sam Drachman's cigar store sat at the eastern head of Tucson's infamous Wedge in this ca. 1898 photograph. West Congress Street runs to the left and Maiden Lane to the right.(AHS #24815)

After several years of declining fortunes, mining spirits rose in Pima County during 1898, but some investors worried the territory's remote location and lack of statehood made it ripe for mining swindles. Scurrilous characters practiced "highgrading," by walking off with a prosperous mine's best samples and planting them on claims they attempted to sell. Wily cads provided fuel for the territory's knockers during March 1899, when the Spentazuma Gold Mining and Milling Company enticed investors into a phony gold strike in Graham County. Perpetrators' claims of "a vein one-half mile in width and two miles in length, every foot of it rich in gold, copper and silver," failed to materialize. Officials

Robert Benzie, Tucson Division director of water operations, and his wife, Clara, posed during their August 1891 wedding festivities. Born in 1862, Benzie enjoyed a gift for "witching" wells. His grandson Robert Bushnell recalled: "Grandpa located many of SP's water wells across Texas, New Mexico, and Arizona. I was blessed with the same talent." An inveterate miner, the well-respected Benzie worked an Arizona mining claim until the age of eighty. (Robert and Elizabeth Bushnell Collection)

arrested the company's officers on the streets of New York, accusing them of employing methods "not calculated to inspire confidence in any one familiar with mining." Despite the notoriety, investors and their agents continued the rush to inspect mining properties in southern Arizona.

A thriving fascination with gold pulsed through the veins of both the savvy entrepreneur and the small-time prospector. "Look for gold, prospect for gold," admonished the *Arizona Daily Star* in 1904. "When you have found it develop your claim or get someone else to assist you in developing it." At one end of the mining spectrum worked countless rails and others who hunted the desert for gold. Tougher-than-nails J.D. "Jack" Peggs ran the pumping station at Rillito, north of Tucson, in 1904. After filling his water tank, Jack jumped on an SP train, or packed into the nearby hills, to seek out the glistening metal wonder. Along with SP director of water operations Robert Benzie and resident engineer Irving McAvoy, Peggs filed claims on Ajax No. 1 and No. 2 quartz mines, one-and-one-half miles south of Rillito, in 1907. Miners often found gold veins running through quartz and, while no record exists of Peggs's success as a gold prospector, the trio of rails could sell the ultra-hard mineral to mining companies for use in the copper smelting process. Despite his fifteen years as an SP pumper, when Jack died, the *Tucson Daily Citizen* labeled him "a well known miner here and in Gila City."

At the other end of the mining continuum stood operations such as the Copper Queen Mine in Bisbee, the fifth-leading copper producer in the United States early in the twentieth century. The Arizona & South Eastern Rail Road Company completed a thirty-six mile line to ship their ores over the New Mexico & Arizona Railroad at Fairbank to the SP mainline at Benson on February 1, 1889. By November 1898, the Copper Queen operation employed 1,000 to 1,200 well-paid miners.

This 1911 post card portrays the strong-willed, fiercely independent individuals who mined Arizona's hillsides and gulches. In 1907, prospector Manuel Ceron and his partners worked a promising claim in the Catalina Mountains, north of the city. Adolfo Vasquez brought in 100 pounds of the richest copper ore ever seen in Tucson from a separate stake. Vasquez displayed the find at Russell & Sheldon's carriage shop on Sixth Avenue. Helvetia Mining and Smelter Company led the way during 1907, producing 1.4 million tons of copper. That March, forty teams hauled copper ore into Tucson each day. Others lugged rich sulfide ores to town from the Pontotoc mines, seven miles north of the city. The Tucson, Cornelia & Gila Bend Railroad helped bring one-third of the world's copper through Tucson from Ajo, Arizona by 1921. "The Ajo mine is one of the wonders of the mining world," wrote Tucson rail superintendent William W. Wilson. (Kalt Collection)

Mining intrigued railroad powerhouses (l-r) Epes Randolph, H.J. Simmons, Frank Murphy, and Walter Douglas when they stopped at Douglas, Arizona for this 1905 photograph. (UASC)

Future road foreman of engines and Tucson city councilman Carl Ball Sr. (left) worked at the Mascot Copper mine ca. 1914. (Elgin Ball Collection)

Southern Arizona mining fortunes received a great boost in May 1903, when the Imperial Copper Company paid Albert Steinfeld and partners $515,000 for the "Old Boot" mine and other Silverbell properties. The Arizona Southern Railroad Company (ASRR) incorporated in January 1904 and built a standard gauge line from Silverbell east to the SP main line at Red Rock. The line climbed a 3.4 percent grade through one-and-one-half switchbacks over famed Jesuit Hill. It also required five trestles over a seventy-six foot section of Imperial Creek. The ASRR carried 1.4 million tons of ore a month during 1907. The company also offered tours of Silverbell to Tucson residents. Visitors arrived by train or by Oldsmobile, Cadillac, or Buick automobiles converted to run on rails, or Buda cars.

The size of the mineral strike, price of metals, and an inconsistent national economy combined to dictate the rise and

Engines Nos. 10 and 11 chug up hill near Red Rock in 1927. The Arizona Southern Railroad ran between the Southern Pacific mainline at Red Rock and the Silverbell mines. During 2006, Silverbell Mining, L.L.C. worked four open-pit copper mines, extensions of the area's original El Tiro and Oxide underground mines. Fifty percent of the company's output was "rubbilized" by drilling, blasting, and leeching the earth with water. The company shipped the other half of its production to off-site leeching plants. (AHS #26379)

Steam power hauls ore cars across southern Arizona. (AHS #B93528)

fall of many mining towns in the West. Silverbell faced an additional dilemma. A high mineral content in the town's drinking water forced company officials to haul clean water in by tanker. American Smelting and Refining Company (ASARCO) purchased the Silverbell mines in 1911, and four years later, a copper depression crippled the once-thriving town. By 1920, however, a revitalized Silverbell boasted twelve hundred residents. Decline followed once again, and by 1931, only forty-five people remained in town. Rail service continued sporadically until December 30, 1933, when operations ceased and workmen removed the tracks and dismantled the smelter. The post office in Silverbell remained open, however, until 1984.

W.C. Greene, a man of grand dreams and decisive action, reigned as one of the top players in the region's mining scene. The dynamic entrepreneur built Greene Consolidated Copper Company at Cananea, Sonora and boasted a payroll of 7,000 workers by January 1902. His Cananea, Yaqui River & Pacific Railroad incorporated in June 1902 and began hauling copper ore to the smelter at Naco, Sonora. The SP purchased the road within days, when Colonel Epes Randolph wrote a $1 million check on E.H. Harriman's account and informed him of it after the fact. Greene entertained financiers and legislators from the East with elaborate excursions into the wilderness to entice their investment. The affairs included the finest in food, including wild game, and drink.

Trains ran copper ore concentrate cars from the Anamax, Duval, and Pima mines near Green Valley on one daily SP mining job. Empty trains climbed the steep slope out of the Santa Cruz River basin to rock crushers working above. Then, loaded with ore, they descended a steep hill to the

Founded following the discovery of the McMillen Silver Mine in the 1860s, Globe reflected Gila County's prosperity ca. 1922. (Stanley M. Houston Collection)

SP main line and ran the ores into Tucson for distribution to smelters in El Paso and Hayden, Arizona. George "Boots" Lundquist recalled working the "mine job": "You were carrying up to 150 tons of ore in those cars and comin' down some pretty steep grades. Before I got there they had a runaway and spread cars all over the ground. So they wanted me to watch it very close." Company rules required brakemen to set "pops," or brake retainers, on the precipitous mountainside. This held the train in place, allowing the engineer to recharge his brake line with air before he moved again.

E.C. "Moonbeam" Webster took a relaxed approach toward working the steep Santa Cruz County hillside. "We had a lot of fun on that mine job," Moonbeam smiled. After his brakemen set pops a couple of times, Webster complained. "I told 'em, 'You guys are just wasting your time,'" said the jovial Bowie resident. "You sure as hell don't want the brakes hangin' up when you're tryin' to make some time back to Tucson.'" Webster vowed he would do anything to save time. "Now, the speed limit down the hill was fifteen miles an hour, but who-

ever made it that slow had never worked the job. I could come off that hill at forty miles an hour." When the company warned Webster about speeding on the job he paid little heed. "We could only work sixteen hours before we had to take time off. We could finish our work, drive into Tucson, eat a meal, and still make it back to the mines to tie up by 15:59."

Veteran switchman Sid Showalter worked the northern half of the "Hayden Local." In the fall of 2002, Sid recalled: "They'd bring cars of ore into Tucson from the mines and we'd build the Hayden Local train. They'd leave for Hayden on the midnight shift when they had enough cars." The train traveled west, down the mainline to Picacho and onto the Phoenix line. "When you got to Magma Junction, you ran the engine around on the siding and put it on the other end of the train," Sid explained. "Then, you headed up to Hayden Junction and the Magma Copper Company smelter. You crossed the Gila River a few times but at the Hayden-Ashurst Dam, where they took all the water out of the Gila, you went out of a tunnel and crossed the river right away."

Engineer J.R Kerby stands beside locomotive No. 2587 at Globe in 1927. Joe retired in 1977 after 51 years, his last ten in passenger service. (Tom Kerby Collection)

laid out the town site of Superior in 1900 and established a post office in November 1902. Two years later, many tents, several primitive board homes, a store, blacksmith shop, and a post office filled the town. The Magma Copper Company constructed a huge smelter in 1914 and began working a large body of high-grade ore near Superior. In 1920, the Magma Arizona Railroad ran 30.2 miles of track between Magma and the main line, between Florence and Queen Creek, Arizona.

Several large mining enterprises centered around Globe, Arizona. Underground mining began at one of the nation's richest high-grade copper producers, the Old Dominion Mine, in 1882. Before it closed in 1931, the mine produced almost 765 million pounds of copper, 89,000 ounces of gold, and more than 4.5 million ounces of silver.

Three miles west of Gila County's governmental seat at Globe, the Inspiration Copper Company and Miami Copper Company developed two of the largest low-grade copper mines in the world, producing huge quantities of ore for Miami's up-to-date International Smelter. Twenty miles further west, the Arizona and Lake Superior Mining Company worked a large body of high- grade ore at the old Silver Queen mine near Hastings. George Lobb

The Magma smelter closed in 1981. However, Jake Jacobson's Copper Basin Railway transports 27,400 tons of ASARCO ore to the Hayden concentrator, seventy miles northeast of Tucson, each day. Hayden smelter now refines 720,000 tons of copper a year. Eighteen miles west of Hayden, an open pit mine produces 30,000 tons per day at the Ray concentrator. One hundred three million pounds of solvent is processed through an extraction-electrowinning operation each year. The sulphuric acid produced at its plant is used in leaching operations or sold into the market.

Thirty-eight miles south of Globe, the Arizona Eastern Railroad moved 10,000 tons of copper ore from the open-pit copper mine at Ray to the Hayden smelter

This Porter Air Locomotive used air from lines in a tunnel to haul men, ores, and supplies into the Ray Copper Company mine early in the twentieth century. (Kalt Collection)

each day during 1921. Former roundhouse foreman T. Herman Blythe recalled that by mid-twentieth century: "The railroad worked around the clock to run three twelve-car 'shots' of cars a day. It took a whole shift to push those twelve cars loaded with ore up hill to the smelter."

The SP housed its operational center in Hayden Junction, two miles west of Hayden. Later the company rebuilt its system to run ore trains from Ray directly to Hayden for unloading onto a new conveyor system. "Guys called Hayden Junction 'Alimony Junction,'" said Blythe. "They'd get divorced in Phoenix or Tucson and move up

Former roundhouse foreman T. Herman Blythe remembered men called Hayden Junction "Alimony Junction" because of its many divorced rails. Blythe maintained a metal shop in his eastside garage, complete with micrometers, lathes, and grinders, in 2003. (Kalt Collection)

there. The railroad had beds in a bunkhouse and men played a twenty-four-hour card game there. J.V. Moan Commissary served real good steaks and chicken at 25¢ for a family-style meal in the dining room. So it was pretty good livin' for some of those guys."

> Regular rumors surfaced that SP planned to alter its main line to run through Phoenix and trash Tucson's economic supremacy. Arizona's capital city struggled to earn a place on the company's primary route. The railroad's habit of charging discriminatory freight rates fueled Phoenicians' long-running dispute with the SP. Adhering to the "all the traffic will bear" principle in structuring its tariffs, the company rode roughshod on shippers in the nation's southwestern reaches until legal sanctions demanded otherwise.

The Arizona Eastern extended tracks 6.35 miles from Winkelman, four miles southeast of Hayden, to Christmas, Arizona during 1911. Four decades later, the SP still hauled cars of slag from the Christmas Mine into Hayden Junction once a week. "Redwood rail ties made the roadbed soft, and the cars or the locomotive would often slip off the rails," said Blythe. "Our mechanical crew had to ride on the train's caboose to help out if it had a derail. A section gang walked along in front of the engine with a 'bat-wing.' That was a big metal piece that they'd lay it over one of the rails, and we'd all push the car or locomotive back on the track."

The SP developed "Piper Springs" about five miles east of Winkelman, Arizona for its steam process. The railroad ran eight-inch cast iron pipe into two storage tanks at Hayden Junction. When Kennecott Copper Company built the town of Kearny in the late 1950s, the company dug four wells that produced bad tasting water due to a heavy concentration of manganese. "People came in from Kearny to get their drinking water from the tanks," said

Globe hopped with mining activity ca. 1922. (Stanley M. Houston Collection)

Blythe.

Two rules governed train movement on the SP: "Safety First" and "Keep Trains Moving and the Line Open." Within the context of the former, the railroad did everything as fast as possible to achieve the latter. Time equaled money on the steam railroad. Each delivery of freight and satisfied passenger augmented SP revenues.

"Get that car to market 'fore the fruit spoils," went the company cry. "Get that train to the mine 'fore the next ore run. Get the Roving family to Grandma's for the holiday. Do it all, safely, on time, with a smile," on the "Friendly Railroad"—as SP advertising proclaimed.

The SP required every man in train service to carry an approved railroad watch. The company established its standard time after a head-on collision of two trains in Cleveland, Ohio, during the 1880s. The crash killed both engineers and nine clerks, terrifying the nation. Investigators discovered that one engineer's watch ran a full four minutes slow and the conductor had failed to look at his watch at all. General time inspector of the SP Time Service Webb C. Ball designed a system of watch and clock inspection, adopted by most of the country's large railroads. Each day at noon, Ball personally received the correct time over the wire from the Naval Observatory in Washington, D.C. and set his clock. He placed "standard clocks" across the SP system and inspectors made

O.H. Weigle captured this 1912 image looking west from the Tucson SP Reserve. (AHS #63558c)

twice-a-month time checks. Ball decreed that each standard clock vary by no more than ten seconds from naval time.

By 1920, rails on SP's Pacific Sys-

Jeweler Herbert L. Tucker and his wife Rozella relax on their couch at 525 S. Fourth Avenue ca. 1940. Tucker earned local rails' admiration, while inspecting SP watches for decades. (James W. Nugent Collection)

tem set their watches according to 150 standard clocks. The company certified jewelers as "competent to be entrusted with the work of inspecting and repairing railroad watches" in Tucson and at other principal points along the division. "Railroad watches needed to be checked every two weeks," Floyd Roberts explained. "The railroad permitted employee watches to vary up to thirty seconds between inspections. When I started in 1941 and prior to that, the front and back of railroad watches could only be unscrewed and removed. Pop-open watches were not legal on the railroad, they had to have screws." Rails pulled a lever in the front of the watch to set the time. "When the jeweler took the back off, he would write in the date of his inspection on the inside of the watch," said Roberts. "He also wrote it on a report he turned in to the company each month. When I gave my watch to my great-grandson, it was covered with dates in the back."

SP's operating department adopted the motto "A Careful Man and An Accurate Watch" and reviewed 24,000 inspection reports a month during 1920. Local rails visited J.A. Black's jewelry store for their inspections during the 1880s. Roberts remembered that by the 1940s: "Men took their watches to Gruenwald & Adams, Daniel's Jewelers, or the Time Shop on Congress. I always went to Tucker's across from the yard office on Toole."

Watches became less important after Centralized Traffic Control (CTC) arrived in the mid-1950s. "They still needed them on the Phoenix line, from Picacho to Phoenix and over to Wellton," Roberts said. "They still used only train orders and block signals there. That's also true of the line from Clifton to Lordsburg. Between Globe and Bowie, they only have the track, not even block signals. You need a railroad watch to run your train there."

Beginning in 1906, the nation's railroads agreed to pay a daily "per diem" charge of 50¢ for each of its cars on another company's tracks at midnight. By August of 1953, a freight car cost $2.40 a day. "You had to keep those trains movin'," said retired Tucson Division dispatcher James W. Elwood. Customers also paid a demurrage charge for delays caused during loading and unloading of shipments. A "free time" provision allowed for forty-eight hours before charges began. "When you have a car on a siding and you're going to load it with grain you have two days of 'grace' when you aren't charged. After that, if that car ain't rollin' you start payin' a demurrage charge to the railroad."

The constant influx and outflow of shipments required that specific types of cars be on the ground in the Tucson yard at the correct time. Some lines moved freight much faster than others, creating dramatic imbalances as commerce concentrated all cars of a particular type in one area of the rail system and caused shipping delays. The problem often resulted in congestion in the great consuming centers of the nation like Chicago and Denver.

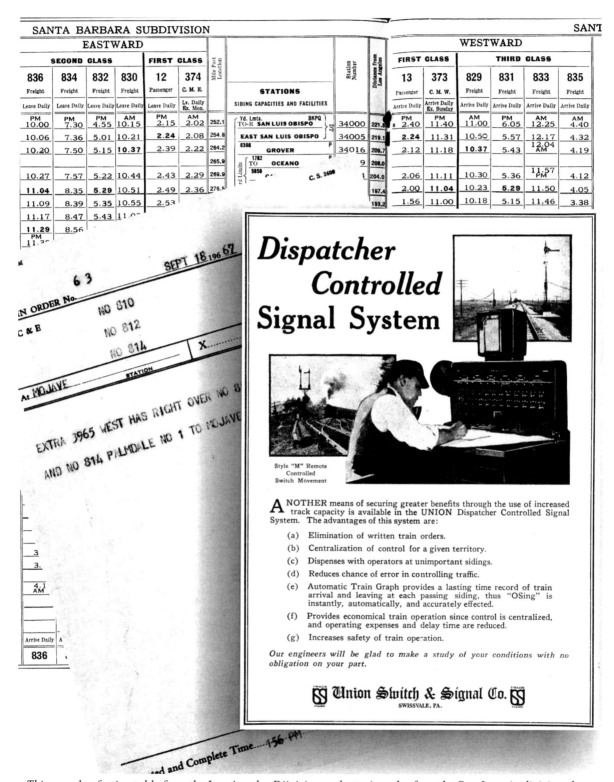

SANTA BARBARA SUBDIVISION

SECOND CLASS				FIRST CLASS		Mile Post Location	STATIONS SIDING CAPACITIES AND FACILITIES	Station Number	Distance from Los Angeles	FIRST CLASS		THIRD CLASS			
836	834	832	830	12	374					13	373	829	831	833	835
Freight	Freight	Freight	Freight	Passenger	C. M. E.					Passenger	C. M. W.	Freight	Freight	Freight	Freight
Leave Daily	Leave Daily	Leave Daily	Leave Daily	Leave Daily	Lv. Daily Ex. Mon.					Arrive Daily	Arrive Daily Ex. Sunday	Arrive Daily	Arrive Daily	Arrive Daily	Arrive Daily
PM 10.00	PM 7.30	PM 4.55	AM 10.15	PM 2.15	AM 2.02	252.1	Yd. Lmts. TO-R SAN LUIS OBISPO BKPQ	34000	221.8	PM 2.40	PM 11.40	AM 11.00	PM 6.05	AM 12.25	AM 4.40
10.06	7.36	5.01	10.21	2.24	2.08	254.8	EAST SAN LUIS OBISPO	34005	219.1	2.24	11.31	10.50	5.57	12.17	4.32
10.20	7.50	5.15	10.37	2.39	2.22	264.2	6308 GROVER	34016	209.7	2.12	11.18	10.37	5.43	12.04 AM	4.19
						265.9	1782 TO OCEANO	9	208.0						
10.27	7.57	5.22	10.44	2.43	2.29	269.9	5850 rd Limits C. S. 2600	1	204.0	2.06	11.11	10.30	5.36	11.57 PM	4.12
11.04	8.35	5.29	10.51	2.49	2.36	276.5			197.4	2.00	11.04	10.23	5.29	11.50	4.05
11.09	8.39	5.35	10.55	2.53					193.2	1.56	11.00	10.18	5.15	11.46	3.38
11.17	8.47	5.43	11.0												
11.29	8.56														
PM 11.3															

SEPT 18 196 67

6 3

N ORDER No.

C & B

NO 810

NO 812

NO 814

X

At MOJAVE   STATION

EXTRA 3965 WEST HAS RIGHT OVER NO 8

AND NO 814 PALMDALE NO 1 TO MOJAVE

3

3.

4.1 AM

Arrive Daily A

836

...d and Complete Time....1.56 PM

This sample of a timetable from the Los Angeles Division and a train order from the San Joaquin division show the dependence upon time associated with that system of operation. CTC replaced the watch with signals along the line as the means of traffic control and collision prevention. (Thomas White Collection)

West-bound SP freight trains, called "identified" or "notified" trains, had superiority over eastbound trains of the same class. "They used the company timetable to move from sidetrack to sidetrack, avoiding the eastbound trains' movements as they were specified on the timetable," said Floyd Roberts. "A west-bound train could never be late." Former division superintendent

Wild as the range they rode, men in a typical cowboy outfit relied on the chuckwagon cook (pouring coffee at the right) for their sustenance. This group may be the Diamond-A crew that ranged across Cochise County from Animas, New Mexico early in the twentieth century. (AHS #43839)

Ralph Coltrin described a constant problem during his tenure: "Because the preponderance of business went west over east, you always had more trains going to Yuma than you did to Lordsburg. To balance crews, you'd have to make the westbound trains proportionally longer so you'd have an equal number of crews going both ways. Otherwise your crew expenses go out the roof."

The railroad also faced a constant struggle to avoid "time away from home terminal" and "deadheading" costs, when employees rode as passengers to or from their work assignments. "Sometimes you'd find yourself deadheading the same crew both ways," Coltrin said. "A crew would be deadheaded to provide relief, and by the time they arrived they were close to going on 'away from home terminal time.' We'd need to deadhead them right back to save the railroad money. I'm sure it looked pretty foolish to the men involved. But there wasn't any other way."

Cattle provided mining's economic complement on the SP in southern Arizona. Just as the ore industry ebbed and flowed with the national economy, so the fortunes of the area's cattlemen fluctuated with the region's rains. Sparse rainfall often brought tragedy, but thick, well-watered grasslands meant fatter cattle and a better price for each head. Twice each year, buyers arrived from the north and purchased one, two, and three-year-old cattle for fattening on the lush grasslands of Colorado, Kansas, and Montana. Every fall and spring, local American cowboys and Mexican *vaqueros* scoured the hillsides and arroyos to bring cattle to shipping points along the main line including Red Rock, Pantano, and Esmond.

Dry horror descended upon area ranchers in 1891 and 1892, killing 40 to 60 percent of southern Arizona cattle. The drought ruined more than three-fourths of the region's cattlemen when only a couple of outside buyers ventured to Tucson to purchase cattle. Hopes rose at last in 1895,

Dust from the SP stockyards obscures much of the Santa Catalina Mountains north of Tucson in 1899. (AHS #13416)

when rancher and real estate developer R.G. Brady opened the first cattle broker's office in Tucson with Harry Levin. Brady ran cattle on two excellent ranches, one in the Santa Catalina Mountains north of Tucson and the other outside of Cottonwood, Arizona. He soon began to lure several large northern buyers into town for a look at Pima County herds.

Thirty-seven-thousand cattle shipped out of holding lots across the Tucson Division during the spring and fall seasons of 1897, buoying the morale of Pima County stockmen. Born along the Gila River at Bryce, Arizona, in September 1898, Alma "Jack" Bryce remembered ranching in his father's day. "They made long rides on horseback and had to pack everything on mules and horses," he said. "They camped out in all kinds of weather, and the only shelter they had were tents. Much of the time a bed on the ground with a tarp over them to keep out the rain, wind, and cold was all they had."

By spring 1898, a lack of eastern beef drove cattle prices higher than normal in southern Arizona. One eager Midwestern buyer bought cattle at $2-$2.50 higher

than usual. Yearlings went for $18, two-year-olds $22, and three-years-olds $25. Almost all northern buyers lost money that year because they paid too much for their cattle, but in the spring of 1899 local ranchers pressed for high prices once again.

Brady attended February 1899's National Livestock Growers Association convention in Denver, Colorado, intent upon enticing northern buyers into purchasing cattle at Tucson. So cold that "his moustache was frozen off and people [took] him for a Philadelphia lawyer," the aggressive livestock broker reported that agents of big packing houses would "come to Arizona for cattle...provided prices [were] low enough for them to come out even" in their transactions.

Prospects shone as 1899's spring cattle sale began. The Erie Cattle Company announced that it expected to ship almost 26,000 head of cattle locally, with total shipments for the year projected at 37,000 head. The *Citizen* reported, "Cattlemen be-

> *The SP maintained three 80-ton and two 60-ton track scales on the division to ensure charging shipper's the proper rate in 1909. State inspectors tested SP's forty-thousand-pound test cars two to three times a year. Seals attached to the cars' locks verified its accuracy. During 1919, the SP tested 449 track scales and 218 freight scales, and targeted twenty-one for rebuilding. Each could vary one pound per thousand, according to company standards.*

77		C—Both hips. H. C. Hooker and Florence G. Moore, 4731 Willcox, Arizona			C—Left neck to hip. F. W. Mead, 6464 Ft. Huachuca, Arizona
77		C—Left ribs. C. E. Goddard, 2976 Canon, Arizona			C—Left ribs. Roberts & Sneed, 6343 Bisbee, Arizona
-7-		H—Right thigh. Mrs. Sarah Trainor, 8171 Nutrioso, Arizona			C—Right shoulder. H—Right shoulder. J. B. Wallace, 7967 Mesa, Arizona
8B		C—Left ribs. Rosario Brena, 6332 Tucson, Arizona			C—Left ribs or left hip. Bar Diamond Land & Cattle Co., 9689 Prescott, Arizona
8I		H—Left hip. G. E. Goodfellow, 4865 Tucson, Arizona			C—Left hip. H—Left thigh. Mrs. N. Hocker, 1268 Livingstone, Arizona
9		H—Left shoulder. J. C. Epley, 2367 Solomonsville, Arizona			H—Right thigh. Wm. Garland and Stephen Ross, 854 Ash Fork, Arizona
9A		C—Left hip. Antonio Lopez, 6625 Nogales, Arizona			C—Right shoulder, wattle on nose. Bar Diamond Land & Cattle Co., 853 Prescott, Arizona

Arizona cattlemen fought rustlers, who stole cattle in bold forays. Early rustlers often succeeded in raiding herds because few cattle owners dared follow them. By the mid-1860s, most stockmen began branding their horses and cattle. Brands read from top to bottom and left to right. Small wings denoted "flying"; a horizontal letter, "lazy"; an oblique letter, "tumbling"; a half-circle under a letter, "rocking"; a horizontal line, "rail," and a diagonal line, "slash." (Arizona Live Stock Board Brand Book, UASC)

lieve that the present high price for cattle will not depreciate for at least a year and probably two."

Eastern brokers offered $16-$16.50 for Pima County yearlings, but local ranchers held firm to their high dollar demands. Rather than capitulate to such low offers, Tucson ranchers John Brown, N.W. Bernard, and George Pusch decided to fatten their own herds. The trio sent four trainloads of cattle north to pastures for a five-to six-month season of feeding and fattening at $1.00 per head. Pusch then boarded a train for Kansas City to arrange a fall sale of the group's plumpened herd.

That spring, the intransigence of local cattlemen frustrated city mayor C.F. Schumacher. Calling Tucson prices the highest in his sixteen-year experience, the well-respected butcher journeyed to Salt River Valley to buy beef for his Tucson Meats market. The previous year's prices created a "financial disaster" and "ruined a great many buyers," said hometown cattle broker R.G. Brady. Disgusted, Brady purchased 8,000 head of cattle from the Sonoran ranches of Ramon Soto and

Rosario Brena at the end of March. "I am very sorry that I have to go into Mexico to buy cattle this year," he declared. "I would rather buy Arizona cattle but have no call for them from purchasers at the prices asked. Human nature has its ridiculous side." The *Citizen* expressed hope that more cattle sales would "be made now, since the suspense has been broken so effectually by Mr. Brady."

Plentiful water, larger grazing areas, and good *vaqueros*, who worked for much less than American cowboys, made it cheaper for many cattle ranchers to raise their herds in Mexico. During the 1897-1898 seasons, well-known cattle owner Colin Cameron spread the word that buyers had imported a lot of "crub" or inferior cattle from Mexico. "Nothing can faster deteriorate and [more quickly] give a bad name to our cattle," Cameron declared. In addition, Dr. James Collier Norton, territorial veterinarian, battled Texas Fever ticks in Mexican herds that spring. Though few cattle shipped out of Arizona, Mexican cattlemen sent five to six thousand head a month out of Chihuahua and Sonora in

The SP moved its Tucson cattle pens south in spring 1902. Beginning at Park Avenue between Fourteenth and Fifteenth streets, the stockyards (above) lay north of the local ice track almost to Broadway Boulevard. South of tracks a five-foot high pile of "klinkers," discards from locomotive fireboxes, ran almost 100 yards in the same area during the 1920s. (AHS #B89447)

1899. To avoid depleting their breeding stock, Mexican ranchers ceased the frantic beef flow as the summer ended that year.

A major player in the region's cattle industry, "Copper King" W.C Greene held title to ranches totaling two million acres in 1901. Almost 90 percent of Greene's expansive holdings lay in Sonora, where he purchased some of Mexico's oldest existing land grants. He ran 60,000 head of cattle over five separate ranches including the historic, four-hundred-thousand acre Gird Ranch. Greene's diverse property allowed his cattle to graze throughout the year over a wide variety of elevations. Soon, he began fencing the three-hundred-thousand acre Arizona portion of his land with five-strand barbed wire affixed to posts at one-rod intervals. In addition, the imposing inter-

national entrepreneur developed plans to irrigate five thousand acres and grow alfalfa to sell during severe winters and summer heat shortages.

Other ranches prospered. The vast Aguirre Ranch southwest of Tucson; the Fiegre Summit spread in the Dragoons, owned by a Connecticut millionaire; and SP master mechanic's secretary W.S. Sturgis's ranch near the Mexican border all thrived during the steam age. Rollin R. Richardson also maintained a fine outfit on his Monkey Springs Ranch near Patagonia.

Wagon builder Fred Ronstadt sold forty acres in Riecker's Addition, east of the railroad reserve, to the SP in January 1900. To relieve congestion at the head or east end of Tenth Street, the company built new stockyards across from Fifteenth Street near Barrio Millville during the spring of 1902. The company transplanted the area's trees to locations around the railroad reading room and bunkhouse north of the tracks.

Crippling drought again pummeled southern Arizona in 1904. That summer, the San Simon Cattle Company skinned at least forty victims of drought and lack of feed every day. The following January, the United States imposed a quarantine that allowed no cattle to enter the country from Sonora because of rampant Texas Fever. Over the next few years, the cattle industry struggled to recover.

"Loco weed," astralligis, began plaguing local stockmen when ranchers first started running livestock on southern Arizona ranges. Opening large holes in the animal's brain, locoweed caused horses, in particular, to crave the plant and seek it out. Staggering animals, with an appearance of "unthriftiness" or lack of "heartiness," characterized an affliction for which no cure has been found. In July 1907, the insidious weed slaughtered two hundred horses on the Stevens Ranch in the Sierrita Mountains, thirty-five miles south of Tucson, in just three months. One hundred years later ranchers' problems with the infamous devil weed persist across the west, forcing stockmen to manage grazing around the heartless predator.

John Tyrell ran the local stockyards for many years before his death in 1907. May 1, 1909, the local division ordered 551 cattle cars, with 325 cut out at Tucson. By the middle of June, the last of 8,000 head shipped out of Tucson cattle yards, after R.G. Brady, Tom Wills, and Andrew Cronly drove their 2,080-head herd into the city from Steam Pump Ranch.

In the spring of 1909, Miller and Lux of Southern California purchased the 1,000-head beef lot of Sabino Otero, 800 head from the Arivaca Land and Cattle Company, and 900 from cattleman Bernabe Robles. Around 1887, Robles had used his mule team to start a mail route to

Ajo. Later, the Arizona pioneer located a short-cut to Quijotoa, creating Robles Junction, about 25 miles west of Tucson, near Three Points. Through the years, his extensive Robles Ranch grew into one of the largest spreads in the region. Bernabe grazed eight to ten thousand head of cattle at a time in the vast deserts west of Tucson, until the federal government's designation of the immense Papago Reservation divided the Robles Ranch in half during 1917.

Willcox cowboys on the range ca. 1915. (Elgin Ball Collection).

Local cattle inspector Willard Wright received 5¢ for each head he checked for disease. In October 1910, Wright reported that the SP shipped 32,144 head during the previous eleven months, at an average price of $20 per head. Nearby butchers also slaughtered twenty head each day for home consumption, at $35-$40 per head. Tucson's cattle business totaled more than $300,000. In addition, the transport of horses yielded $660,130. In all, the railroad earned almost $1 million revenue through the livestock industry, and Wright netted more than $1,600 from cattle inspections.

Too old to continue cattle ranching, Robles sold his ranch. Then, at the end of March 1917, West Coast Cattle Company bought the Robles herd for $250,000. The *Citizen* reported that the sale "depopulated the country" west of Tucson and almost wiped out the cattle industry in the area. Señor Robles moved his family into a two-story, wood-frame house at 157 West Franklin Street. There, he capitalized on the long-standing troubles Mexican people encountered securing mortgage and other loans in Tucson. Decades of prejudicial treatment created a lucrative opportunity for the bright and industrious Robles.

Bernabe used the proceeds from the sale of Robles Ranch to establish a lending operation similar to a bank inside his home. Many landowners in the city's Mexican community arranged their first loan through the former rancher. Through the years, Robles acquired large property holdings as people defaulted on their mortgages, eventually owning a good portion of the West Congress business district.

Lovely 1940 Tucson High School graduate Dorothy Kengla Fitzpatrick remembered visiting her robust grandfather Bernabe. "Papa had his office on the porch at the back of the house. Whenever we went to his house we always had to go to the back and give Papa a kiss," Dorothy said. "If you had a pocket, he would put a quarter in it. If you ever lay that quarter down, he'd pick it up, and he wouldn't give it back. He taught us all to hang on to our money."

Local newspapers covered the demolition of the old Robles home on West Franklin December 28,1977, but Bernabe Robles's legacy continued. Today, much of Ajo Road runs over Bernabe's original mule track, while portions retain the name Robles Road. The community of Robles Junction now sits on the site of the old Robles Ranch. Bernabe's greatest contribution endures, however, in local Mexican families who first established credit through his enterprise.

Hignio B. Aguirre ran the Tucson Meat Market in 1903. By 1906, Aguirre had moved to the SP Meat Market at 215 N. Sixth Avenue. Through the next twenty-seven years, the master butcher became a favorite among Tucsonans of Mexican descent for his low-priced beef. "His nickname was 'Pelavivos,' meaning skinned alive," Francisco "Frank" Mendez

recalled. "He worked for the SP at the stockyards, and got all the injured cattle that couldn't make it out of here. They'd been trampled, fallen, or gotten hurt somehow. They were ready for the slaughter." Pelavivos gained local fame. "He did the butchering at his home," Frank continued. "His meat was much less expensive than in the market. He also had some cattle that he kept alive at his home. Whenever you wanted fresh meat, Pelavivos would have it. He was a true *carnicero*, a butcher."

The bellowing and unmistakable aroma of cattle emanated from the heart of Tucson for decades. Early agricultural laws allowed the SP to confine cattle without food, rest, or water for no more than twenty-eight consecutive hours. Despite the stricture, the company battled thirty-three $500 lawsuits claiming livestock abuse during 1907. Later revisions mandated livestock stand on the ground for at least eight of every twenty-four-hours.

The railroad's "cow law" meant a constantly rotating flow of cattle through local pens. "When I was firin' we'd take forty empty cars to pick up cattle in San Carlos," said Moonbeam Webster. "The Indians would round 'em up and bring their cattle down there. They'd load the cattle cars, and we'd bring 'em towards Tucson. We'd get 'em cattle into Bowie and then we'd caught on the 'hog law.' It said, after sixteen hours of work, we had to 'rest' for eight hours before returning to the job. The railroad called relief for us, and we'd deadhead back to Bowie, while they took 'em cattle on into Tucson."

Beginning at Park Avenue between Fourteenth and Fifteenth streets, the Tucson feedlots stretched almost to Broadway on the north side of the tracks. Former division timekeeper Elgin Ball remembered: "When we were growing up in the 1920s and 1930s, that place always hopped with activity as they loaded and unloaded cattle." Former commercial printer Mendez recalled: "In the old days we had a lot of fun goin' to the stockyards whenever they unloaded the cattle for rest. They'd bring horses in on the trains with the cattle all the time. As kids, we'd try to get on those horses and ride 'em. You could smell the stockyards all around Tucson. Manure was real plentiful here, ha, ha."

During the early twentieth century, most of southern Arizona cattle herds contained upgraded Mexican cattle. In February 1921, U.S Forest Service representative Robert H. Hill explained that Southwestern deserts offered minimal coarse grass, water, and shelter while the rugged terrain demanded great durability. Suitable stock also needed the ability to put on flesh and mature quickly, and be a prolific breeder. A cow "should be a first-class rustler," and if ranchers imported purebred cattle from the east, they "could expect fifty percent to die of starvation in the first year," said Hill.

The Great Depression hit Arizona ranches hard, and Amos A. Betts, Arizona Corporation Commission chairman, led cattlemen in their fight to keep the SP from closing its line from Douglas through Courtland to Willcox during the fall of 1932. Three years later, business increased as the nation rebounded from its doldrums, and Salt River valley stockmen shipped almost 70,000 head out of the out of the valley in the fall of 1935. SP relocated local cattle pens to Twenty-Second Street and Campbell Avenue in 1943. Sid Showalter recalled: "They built stock pens out of railroad ties placed on end. As the steam era ended, they started tearin' everything down and they got rid of the SP stockyards. Ranchers drove up in their pick-up trucks and took ties for their fence posts. I collected some date nails before they got rid of all that." With the tumbling of the stockyards fell yet another pillar of Tucson's steam age.

Painted by nature, this idyllic scene captures Locomotive No. 3095 as it pulls the local train into Willcox durng 1934. (Richard Stapp Sr. Collection)

Chapter 13

The Human Cargo and "Grape Trains": A Dangerous Job, that Railroading

"The railroad was phenomenally dangerous, as hazardous an invention of everyday use as any in American history. Railroad work crippled thousands. Shop or yard foremen in the nineteenth century were said to be able to judge a job applicant's experience by the number of fingers he was missing."

William Deverell, Railroad Crossings, *1994.*

(California State Railroad Museum)

Marching across Europe and the nation's East and Midwest they went, using attractive brochures to portray California as an idyllic Shangri-La. Wise counsel told orators to hold off advertising the Southern Pacific Railroad (SP) directly, selling, instead, the fabulous American West.

The story of SP passenger service begins with the company's astonishing effort to populate the West. Mountainous profits, derived from filling the needs of cities, industries, and people on the growing frontier, proved strong motivation for ambitious and insightful SP executives. Grounded in the principle that the railroad could profit only by creating more business in the regions it served, the SP transported thousands upon thousands of settlers over the continental divide.

Following a rate war with the Santa Fe Railroad in the 1880s, the SP ran countless colonists westward with "Zulu" cars. These cars let one member of a family ride with their livestock and other possessions, while the rest rode at discounted rates in passenger cars. Seventy percent of all west-

ward colonists rode the SP, and one hundred emigrant cars arrived in California each day at the peak. Sixty new townsites sprang up within a three-year period as Southern California gained 137,000 new residents. By 1889, colonist business had fallen off and the SP discontinued the reduced fares for several years.

The SP car department published the first issue of *Sunset Magazine* in May of 1898 under the creed: "Publicity for the attractions and advantages of the Western Empire." The company reintroduced colonist rates in 1901 to encourage immigration of skilled and unskilled labor to California cities. By mid-February 1903, these second-class tickets to Los Angeles cost $33 from Chicago and points along the Missouri River between Sioux City and Kansas City; $30 from St. Louis, Memphis and New Orleans; and $25 from Houston.

SP advertised its train ride to the west coast in colorful advertising. Because passenger locomotives ran oil rather than coal on its southern transcontinental line, the SP trumpeted an "Open Air Route" after 1900. After Sunset Magazine debuted in May 1898, the company continued to use colorful and informative literature to lure travelers onto its westbound trains. SP's Wayside Notes detailed the exciting trip west. (UASC)

SP ran its featured passenger train over the 3,600-mile Sunset Route from the west coast to Washington D.C. at the start of December 1898. The eastbound train stopped in Tucson on Wednesday and Saturday at 12:55 a.m. and the westbound stopped at 1:35 a.m. on Tuesday and Friday. This meant arrivals and departures in the "wee sma' hours." The latenight timetable prevented businessmen from selling to travelers. The SP provided passengers with home remedies free of charge and assured all that "In order that our parties may be congenial, every possible effort is made to prevent the sale of space to objectionable persons." The SP furnished both Tourist and Regular Standard sleepers with similar towels, bedding and linens. Standard sleepers used rattan upholstery, "for the sake of cleanliness," and tickets from Tucson to New Orleans cost $4.25. Passengers paid double for the Tourist car's plush appointments and could rent a special Pullman car or a dining car for $45 per day, or a private car for $75 a day.

Set to terminate in six weeks, the sale generated 1,523 of the colonist fares during its first week.

The railroad distributed eighty million pieces of literature during its wholesale recruitment to the West. The Pacific System spent $5.5 million advertising the states they served. *Sunset Magazine* reached a peak circulation in 1913 with 135,000 copies distributed by the railroad, chambers of commerce, boards of trade, and county supervisors.

Early rail transport of people and goods faced challenges throughout the west. This wood-burning locomotive pulled a narrow gauge train into Grass Valley, California during 1905. (Ray Hanson Collection)

Settlers flocked to the Imperial Valley, when Colorado River water rendered it livable. (Imperial Valley Irrigation District)

And pilgrims came! More than 625,000 on one-way tickets in the twentieth century's first decade. Between 1912 and 1922, the company carried 4.5 million travelers west and the population of the region that included Oregon, New Mexico, California, Nevada, Utah, and Arizona increased more than 60 percent. The railroad also purchased millions of dollars in acreage to "protect land which is ideal for industry, from being gobbled up by housing tracts." An SP Public Relations Department memorandum trumpeted the significance of the grand colonist migration, declaring, "The boom ...wiped out forever the last traces of the Spanish-American pastoral (agricultural) economy which had characterized California since 1769."

After 1907, SP and Pacific Fruit Express (PFE) contributed joint monies toward the development of disease-resistant seed types for various crops. *Sunset Magazine* established

its Homeseekers Bureau during 1909, initiating another intensive campaign by the SP car department to sell the West. The massive effort shattered long-standing sensibilities. "To break the monotony of life is to live longer and better," sang one brochure. "The desire for new scenes and varied experience, which possesses all intelligent persons, is a natural and healthful impulse. The journey upon which we invite you involves more of the elements of delightful change...than any other on the continent."

Early SP passenger service demanded much of its patrons, even more in Arizona. Small, drafty, wood-framed coaches with board seats, and only wood-stove heating and oil lamps, ensured a rough ride. When the SP opened its Sunset Route along the 32nd parallel, the company's wayside stations barely generated enough income to pay their own way. "Recall what Arizona was before their [limited trains] advent," swore company literature. "Its deserts were...'the land that God forgot' and its hundreds of thousands of acres seemed to be a barren, desolate waste."

First schedules called for travelers to ride a stagecoach from Phoenix to Maricopa in order to board the SP's

This early freight wagon stands at the Gila Bend, Arizona stage station. (AHS #9847)

main-line trains. The company could never envision earning a profit on a train to Phoenix. The Maricopa & Phoenix Company connected the Salt River Valley with SP's main line in 1886. Later, the SP allowed travelers to remain on a single coach throughout their trip and pay a single fare. SP canceled this "combination rate" agreement with the Maricopa & Phoenix on April 22, 1902. Two "local" rates now applied on trips into Phoenix, forcing passengers to deboard the SP train at Maricopa and board

Dr. Clarence Gunter (center) and fellow travelers wait for an Arizona Eastern train at Kelton, Arizona during December 1908. (Lovell Gunter Welsh Collection)

a new train into the capital city.

Waiting for the train proved a common pastime during the steam age. Travel from Tucson through Arizona's Gila River Valley required a lengthy stop at Bowie. Passengers from Nogales also spent a tedious spell in Benson before the next train to Tucson arrived. SP added a daily "mixed" train from Nogales in June 1900. Annexing a passenger car to a freight train, the railroad made travel easier for people who only

took the trip when "compelled to do so," explained the *Star*. Train No. 35 left Benson at 9:10 in the morning and arrived in Tucson at 11:40 a.m. Its eastbound counterpart, No. 36, departed the Old Pueblo at 1:00 a.m., reaching Benson at 4:15 that afternoon.

A large lighted sign above company headquarters in San Francisco proclaimed SP the nation's "Friendly Railroad." The company set out to provide each traveler with the most commodious train ride available. One company bulletin noted, "The American public is a luxury loving people. The traveling American is particularly exacting in his demands." To satisfy the American thirst for opulence, the SP inaugurated its fabulous Sunset Limited between San Francisco and New Orleans on November 1, 1894. Each year, the luxury "flyer" ran through the winter season until early May, when the railroad removed it from the timetable for summer.

"Vestibuled" and outfitted with gas lamps throughout, SP's "palace on wheels" ran a "smoker" as the first car after the baggage and mail coach. Inside this "composite" car lay "an apartment of ample proportions, given over to the gentlemen for smoking," explained the company. Large plate-glass windows, a library and writing desk, "restful lounges, and great comfortable armchairs" fashioned a cozy cabin for the day's cultured male. Complete with buffet table, barbershop, and bathroom with toilet apartments, the smoker also had a forward compartment that kept men's bags readily available.

The ladies' compartment car followed the smoker. This car's seven drawing rooms each contained a lounging area,

The Star *made sure its paper went to press in time to catch the east and westbound trains. This allowed "telegraphic news" to reach eastern points along the Stormy 24 hours before other territorial papers, and 15 hours earlier across the Gila. Beck & Barkley Transfer Company posted arrival times of SP passenger trains on a bulletin board in front of its store at 12 W. Congress. Updated hourly reports kept travelers in the know during 1903. Local baggagemen collected ten cents per bag for each twenty-four hour period. Those who used Beck & Barkley's transfer services to and from the depot did not pay for their first day.*

The open end platforms of nineteenth century passenger cars were dirty and dangerous. (Thomas White Collection)

Wide vestibules provided clean, safe passage between cars, augmenting the Sunset Limited's wide array of amenities. (California State Railroad Museum)

sleeping quarters, and a private toilet. In addition, an interior door opened to make the drawing room into a suite. A maid stood ready to serve all the car's occupants, while an "expansive parlor" filled with books, and a desk equipped with "elegant stationery," occupied the front end of the car. Drawing-room sleepers ran behind the women's compartment car. Comfortable drawing rooms with individual lavatories, ladies' dressing room and a men's lounge, featured "variegated polished woods, rich upholstery, beautiful [wall] hangings" and genuine English Wilton carpet.

The Sunset Limited's last coach, the dining car, provided "the crowning feature that makes travel the pleasure that it is today," said SP advertising. Potted plants hung in fashionable alcoves around mahogany tables surrounded by individual chairs, instead of the customary pew-like seats. Fine china, glass, and silverware set off what the company deemed "As toothsome and savory a meal as was ever served up at Delmonico's or Marchand's. In elegant comfort and without haste the inner man is satisfied and refreshed. In every respect [the experience] compares to most palatial hotels, while it has all the conveniences and comforts of a luxurious home."

George M. Pullman's experiences riding in a jerking, primitive sleeping car with hard wooden "bunks" and coarse blankets, during the 1850s, convinced him to build his "Pioneer" in 1864. The car gained fame when it transported President Lincoln's body for burial on its maiden voyage. Pullman first utilized the raised car roof and overhead ventilation, and continued to make improvements to his sleeper. In 1901, the SP purchased ten overland passenger trains for $1 million from the Pullman Company for use on its Sunset route. Tri-weekly service from San Francisco began on December 6, 1901.

Pullman's new coaches ran with the latest advance, a generator in the train's baggage car that powered four hundred incandescent lamps and electric fans in its

Old No. 9, the First Pullman Sleeping Car, was rebuilt from a
wooden day coach in 1859. Wood-burning stoves heated the car.

Lavatories and retiring rooms graced turn-of-the-twentieth century excursion sleepers, a great improvement over earlier passenger amenities. (Kalt Collection)

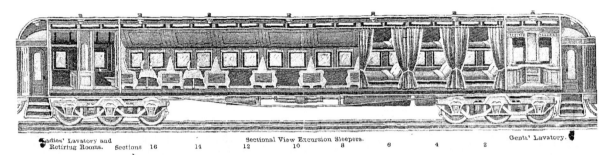

Ladies' Lavatory and   Sectional View Excursion Sleepers.   Genta' Lavatory.
Retiring Rooms.   Sections   16   14   12   10   8   6   4   2

sleeping, dining, and observation cars. A Philadelphia Book Lover's Library branch facility in the smoker kept passengers enlightened. Inside, a decorative arch separated the rest of the car from the library, and a telephone connected occupants to telephones in cities where the train stopped. Pullman furnished its sleeping cars in sage green carpet with bright green and gold decorations, Cuban mahogany, and marquetry work. A large plate glass window filled the rear of the observation car for tourists' viewing enjoyment.

"Personally conducted" tours offered the services of a company porter to meet a single traveler or family's needs. The presence of these well-trained African-American men also allowed ladies and children to travel unaccompanied, "as safe from molestation and intrusion as when they are within the confines of their own homes," stated the SP.

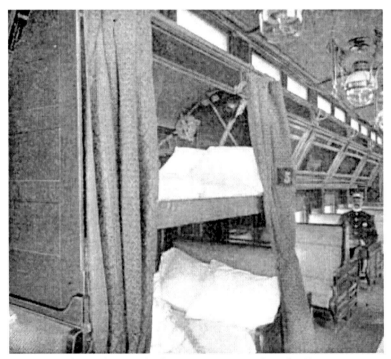

Porters made up the train's sleeper sections each night. Discretion concerning their occupancy proved the best course for most. (Kalt Collection)

Legend said company founder George Pullman paid his daughter Florence $25,000 each year to name the company's cars. In truth, an executive committee chose each car's name. The *Tucson Daily Citizen* remembered, "Pullman service, as natively American as baseball, made rail travel a sleeper's delight, with

SP's Sunset Route through Tucson promised "all the color of a foreign tour," including "motor side trips" over the "marvelous" Apache Trail and across California's Carrizo Gorge.

Women enjoyed the services of attendants on cross-country trips.

SP dining service delighted travelers during the heyday of passenger trains.

Porters did the bidding of demanding passengers. Many former slaves joined the Pullman Company and earned tips meant to insure promptness. "Fish" like Humphrey Bogart and "Diamond" Jim Brady left the best gratuities. Cheapskates Babe Ruth and Jackie Robinson tipped so little they earned the epithet "snakes." (All images: Kalt Collection)

such euphonious names as 'Woodhue Hills,' 'Walalah Bay,' and 'Juniper Meadows.'" Officials named one sleeper the "Tucson," which ran on the Golden State Limited Nos. 3 and 4 between Chicago and Santa Barbara, California in 1909.

The SP offered barbershops, valets, stenographers, maids, and a manicure on its cross-country trains by 1912. In the spring of 1917, the company introduced "wagonette" service, a light, two-wheel, three-shelf cart loaded with pies, fruits, sandwiches, and thermoses of hot chocolate and coffee. Through the next decade, SP

(Kalt Collection)

provided lunchboxes, sandwiches, and other items in its coaches, and added "cabinet" service with coffee, hot-water urns, and a small refrigerator. Though never earning the acclaim of the Santa Fe Railroad's Harvey House Program, the SP dining service grew with pride under Allan Pollock.

A smooth ride formed the company's other service tenet. Each locomotive engineer held responsibility for his passengers' fluid, jerk-free trip. Trains with nine cars or more presented the most handling problems. To avoid disturbing passengers, a 1917 *Southern Pacific Bulletin* recommended a "two-application" stop on all such trains. The maneuver involved applying the airbrakes in time to allow the train to "float" for some distance before the engineer set his air a second time and brought the train to a smooth halt at the station or depot. On an incorrectly stopped train, the brakes remained set in all the cars behind about the third car back. When the train started again, its front end slammed against the "stone wall" anchor created by these stationary cars.

Long before the days of air-conditioning, former Kansas Senator John J. Ingalls observed that Tucson was "said to

The SP dining service ordered 265,031 pounds of fish in 1926; 3 million pounds of vegetables, including one million pounds of potatoes; 183,381 gallons of milk; 70,870 gallons of cream; 3,890 boxes of grapefruit; and 7,205 boxes of oranges. Passengers consumed 307,000 gallons of coffee annually, 23,783 gallons of ice cream, and 5,451 cases of soft drinks. Ham and eggs proved the most popular breakfast, necessitating 226,922 pounds of ham, and 3.4 million eggs, 203,940 pounds of rolls and 811,960 pounds of bread. Each dining car required 837 pieces of silverware, 2,400 napkins, 670 tablecloths, and 506 pieces of china. These items, along with furniture and food preparation equipment, brought the total cost for equipping each car to almost $11,000.

be hotter than a crematory." In March of 1898, the U.S. Department of Agriculture Weather Bureau released official data demonstrating the difference between the region's "actual" and "sensible" temperatures. An early substantiation of Arizona's claim, "but, it's a dry heat," the chart showed that Yuma's actual July temperature averaged 89 degrees, while the sensible temperature (what it felt like) stood at a cool 65 degrees.

North of the Tucson depot, "car cleaners" used large hooks to drag three-hundred-pound ice blocks into the bunkers below incoming passenger cars. George Clark took over direction of the Pullman Company's Tucson operation in the fall of 1908. Each day, Clark's crews

hurried to refresh arriving sleepers on six trains that came through the city.

By June 1909, work kept ten men and four clerks hopping on yardmaster James Griffen's yard crew. Local "car cleaners" loaded five tons of ice into bunkers beneath Pullman and private cars each day. Conductor Harold "Stonewall" Jackson remembered little benefit from railroad's bright idea. Despite SP efforts to make its coach rides enjoyable for the traveling public, a ride in the chair car or day coach proved hot and uncomfortable. "There was no air-conditioning, so we kept windows open in most cases," he said. "The only time we'd close the windows, when it was hot, was to keep the cinders from blowing back on us from the engine. If you were in the rear chair cars, it was tolerable. But when they'd sand out the engine to clean the flues, that hot sand would fly back and hit you in those cars right behind the baggage cars at the front of the train. Other than that it was just sweated out." The SP began installing air-conditioning in dining cars in 1932 and by 1936 the company had the largest fleet of air-conditioned cars in the West.

Former Tucson chief dispatcher A.D. Butler described a puzzling railroad phenomenon during the days when trains provided the nation's main transportation. "Prior to the late 1930s and early 1940s, people lacked the mobility that would become commonplace in later decades," remembered Butler's son, University of Arizona Campus Life Ombudsman David Butler. "Because they traveled little, some passengers became disoriented as they came west, especially over the Continental Divide in New Mexico.

"People never left the town they'd been born in, and

Armando Pain (left) and his co-workers lugged 300-pound ice blocks to the bunkers of waiting passenger cars at the Tucson depot during 1942. (Armando Pain Collection)

The Tucson car cleaner crew paused from the wartime rush, ice hooks in hand, for this 1942 photograph. (Armando Pain Collection)

when they'd come out west they'd somehow get confused," David continued. "Dad said many times he would get a telegram from a conductor saying, 'Please have an ambulance meet the train as it comes in because we've got this guy who's gone goofy on us.' It seemed that the altitude somehow affected them."

Three days after Christmas 1918, the No. 10 passenger train sliced through the desert just past Rillito Station headed for Tucson. When a stream of harsh words like "you can't" and "just try it" and "never" spilled forth from one of his passengers, alert conductor John L. Seamands ambled toward the front of his car. Suddenly, the crazed traveler began shouting "don't crowd me" and, drawing a pistol, plugged Seamands in the thigh.

Wounded, Seamands turned and ran for the rear of the car, only to have the miscreant drill him in the back with another bullet. John Bolton, of Courtland, and another gentleman lunged for the assailant. Each grabbed a side of the armed man

and fought to wrest the gun from his hand. While the pair held the wild man, passenger Fred Hastings fired three accurate shots. The last pierced the man's heart, dropping him in a heap. Passengers scrambled over each other seeking safety, later wearing their bruises as symbols of their role in the melee. Taken to St. Mary's Hospital in serious condition, conductor Seamands recovered and again took his regular run on the division's west end.

David Butler observed his own calamity one cold night at Red Rock. "Besides typing and hanging train orders, I watched trains as they went by to see if I could detect hot boxes, shifted loads, anything like that," he explained. "As this freight train came through Red Rock, I saw this fellow, disoriented and freezing in the cold night, just standing up on top of a box car with his shorts on! Ha, ha."

Butler notified the dispatcher, who stopped the train at Rillito Station. "The deputy sheriff searched and found blood on top of the car but no evidence of the guy," he continued. "The train left Rillito, and just a minute later the operator got on the phone and said, 'Send the sheriff back. This guy just showed up at my door.'" The operator let the poor soul into the Rillito station, wrapped him in a blanket, and gave him hot coffee. "The sheriff came and picked him up," said Butler. "We never knew what happened to him after that."

Coincident with its passenger trains, SP freight trains clogged rail lines. Shortages of particular types of cars plagued the railroad during peak periods. Huge shipments of materials and supplies caused severe car shortages during World War I. The railroad identified underused car capacity as the main culprit. A 1916-1917 company study showed average capacity at 39.7 tons, but the average load only 15.5 tons, just 39 percent of available space. The report projected that loading each car with just two more tons would free 200,000 additional cars.

The rail car shortfall reached the largest in the nation's history on May 1, 1917, at 145,449 cars. Although it represented just over one-half of 1 percent of the approximately 2.5 million cars in service, the shortage gave the nation's railroads fits. SP encouraged employees to hurry cars down the line and asked shippers to help in the nation's World War I mobilization by loading their cars 10 percent above full capacity. The company admonished shippers to work closely with their local freight agent to avoid duplicating orders with other lines, and causing unnecessary switching delays. SP encouraged receivers of goods and materials to order by the carload, not in less-than-carload (LCL) amounts. "Be specific about the derail track wanted for unloading, and unload promptly," said the railroad.

The U.S. Department of Commerce offered its suggestions for relieving the car shortage in 1917. The department said carriers should use trucks and wagons rather than the rails to transfer items to their final destinations. In addition, small buyers could "club" together and pool their orders, to attain full carloads. These ef-

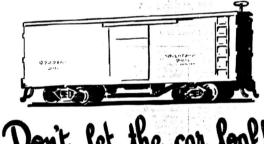

Don't let the car loaf!

Load quickly.
Unload promptly.
And load to capacity.

Two tons more per loaded car will at once add 200,000 freight cars to those available for public use.

Good Railway Service Association of California

SP continued its program to reduce car shortages after World War I, publishing this reminder. (Southern Pacfic Bulletin, June 1920)

forts bore fruit, and by spring of 1918, the average carload had risen by 11 tons on the Southern Pacific System.

In September 1918, seventy-three white-flagged "special" SP trains flew across the division, carrying 26,766 soldiers without accident. That year SP also provided a continuous stream of fuel-oil cars for loading at Midwestern oil fields to meet the military's fuel requirements. Its central role in the war effort became a source of pride among SP rails.

The company instituted a "Sailing Day" plan during fall 1918, to improve handling of LCLs that clogged packing houses and ran up fuel costs. The campaign helped the SP release an average of 3,249 more cars a week within the first month. The railroad also saved almost one-half- million car miles by rerouting freight shipments from circuitous routes to more direct lines.

During October 1918, 126 fruit specials ran from California to Chicago and the Missouri River valley. Regional Director Hale Holden reported to federal railroad administrator William G. McAdoo that "better car loading, consolidation of terminals and more direct routing of freight" had improved traffic flow significantly.

The SP had suffered almost $5 million in passenger revenue losses during 1916, with $1 million "de-

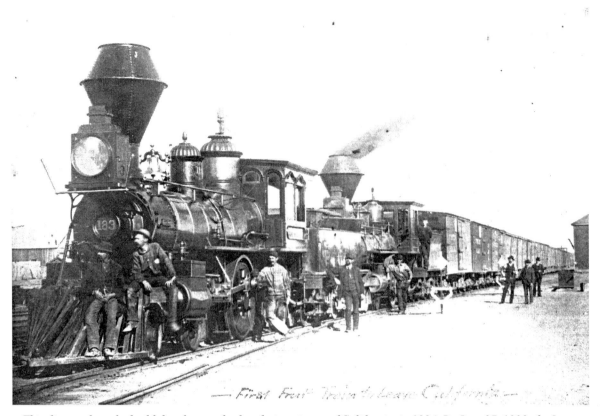

This diamond stack, doubleheader ran the first fruit train out of California, in 1884. By June 27, 1922, the Imperial Valley cantaloupe harvest had reached a record 647 carloads. (AHS#28752)

prived" by automobile competition. SP executive vice president Paul Shoup later explained that the rail industry's problems stemmed from World War I. "Low freight rates did not cause the depression in the railroad business," Shoup said. Rather, the day's high prices forced merchants to buy "from factory to shelf" and "hold very small inventories of goods, thus reducing rail shipping." In addition, he said, "the public in general has spent its surplus of ready money and ceased to travel about the country."

Rail business rebounded, reaching its peak during 1920, but harbingers of increased motor-vehicle competition rang across the Arizona landscape. Mule and horse-drawn freight wagons first gave way to motor transport in May 1909, when a large, gasoline-powered truck began running freight in and out of the Cababi mine, seventy miles west of Tucson. Grooved,

Automobiles provided Westerners with their own "horse" and freedom to roam the hills and valleys. Claudia and Carl Ball posed beside their Buick, near Tanque Verde Falls east of Tucson, ca. 1926. (Elgin Ball Collection)

solid rubber tires aided in negotiating the region's sandy roads. The auto-truck's ninety-six horsepower engine powered it up to fifteen miles per hour. The new vehicle reduced the time needed to cover 100 miles from several days to only one.

In January 1921, the city's Builders Exchange began construction of Tucson's first auto park north of Sixth Street between the EP&SW tracks and Contzen Avenue in Barrio Anita. Several businesses contributed to the innovative project. Local lumber dealers, Pima Brick & Tile, and A.C. Smith Plumbing sold materials to builders at cost. Tucson High School vocational students volunteered to do the woodwork.

Other forces fought the rubber-tire brigade. Spurred by Hiram "Hi" Corbett, the Tucson Chamber of Commerce announced opposition to a "motor truck" franchise between Tucson and Nogales in October 1921. "Heavy trucks would render the roads unfit for travel by automobiles," maintained Corbett. The SP had "arranged" to provide improved service on its Nogales line, said the peerless local baseball supporter. Reduced rail traffic helped SP run a record 96 percent of its trains on time during the first half of 1922. Revenue problems mounted and SP registered only $413 in freight receipts, and less than $129 in express mail, between Benson and Tucson during April of 1922. That July, the SP challenged Felix Miller's right to provide freight service on a motor trucking company that paralleled its existing railroads. Pointing to the potential loss of many rail jobs if the state corporation commission granted motor trucking franchises, railroad labor brotherhoods joined management in a forceful display at hearings in Phoenix.

The commission denied Miller's application to run his auto-freight line between Benson and Tucson, signaling SP's first victory over motor transport. Some felt the ruling would set a precedent for quashing projects that competed with the railroad. Others predicted a "forced abandonment" of the motor freight stage line between Nogales and Tucson. The *Citizen* wailed, "Now the battle cry of 'no more motor freight lines paralleling railroads' will be heard more insistent than ever." Such visions soon withered.

Along with mining, livestock, and passenger service, the region's seasonal crop harvests fueled SP business in southern Arizona. In effort to indemnify the success of hopeful, nascent communities, the SP dispatched crop management and animal husbandry experts across its system. "At the behest of the railway, the lecturer takes the field with stereopticon and by entertaining, educates," the *Star* once noted. SP also helped western growers remain competitive with eastern markets, especially Florida. The company applied "hold downs" to agricultural rates despite increases in general freight charges.

Developing an agricultural livelihood upon which to construct viable communities demanded the collaborative efforts of the SP and the federal government. On the Tucson Division's west end, the Arizona-California Yuma Reclamation Project's Laguna Dam utilized an "immense" inverted siphon, fourteen feet in diameter, to provide silt-enriched water from the Colorado River to lands along the border between the two states beginning June 29, 1912.

U.S. Reclamation Service officials sold the six-thousand-acre Yuma Mesa Auxiliary Project, on the highland mesa east of the Colorado in December 1919. Eager settlers bought five thousand acres during the first twelve hours, yielding $100,000 per hour. Tucson superintendent William W. Wilson remembered, "It was the most remarkable sale of public lands ever held in the United States." Said Wilson, "Citrus fruits grown on the Yuma Mesa are out of the market [sold] long before citrus fruits in other sections of the United States are ripe enough for shipment. There are many orange, grapefruit, and lemon trees that have produced upwards of twenty-five boxes of fruit per year."

Other Arizona agricultural projects flourished. The Gillespie Dam Project irrigated ninety thousand acres around Gila Bend. Sixty-three miles east of that river city, four thousand acres of irrigated lands stretched across the Casa Grande valley. The Ashurst-Hayden and Sacaton Valley diversion dams created the 62,000 acre Florence-Casa Grande Project to provide water to *Tohono Akmiel* (Pima) people and area farmers. The Coolidge Dam formed a thirty- one-square-mile lake on the San Carlos Apache Reservation. Near Tucson, the Post Project encompassed the towns of Rillito, Marana, and Cortaro. Between 1918 and 1921, irrigation watered 5,500 of the project's 22,000 acres.

Green and ripening produce from these projects, California's Imperial Valley, and Phoenix's Salt River Valley provided a needed burst of

Illinois strawberry grower Parker Earle developed the first modern refrigerated car in 1872. Earle suspended 3,000 pounds of ice in a V-shaped bunker from the car's roof. (Betty Stein Collection)

work for local rails. "You could go by the seasons and the business to tell if you'd be working," explained former backshop foreman Charles Stoddard. "The melon season began about the first of June in Yuma and Phoenix. It'd run 'til about the Fourth of July. I'd usually keep workin' until about the first of August. Then, I'd get cut off and not get back on until October or November."

Shipping perishable foods on the railroad demanded cooling. Without chilling, fruits and vegetables might develop bacteria or mold before reaching their destination. Refrigeration using ice triggered the birth of the fruit industry in California.

By the beginning of the twentieth century, Tucson Ice & Cold Storage made fifteen tons of ice three days a week for loading into passing SP reefers (refrigerator cars). The railroad contracted with private companies for refrigerated cars, including 2,000 from the Armour Company during 1901.

In October 1907, SP entered into joint ownership of the Pacific Fruit Express (PFE) with the Union Pacific Railroad. Led by C.M. Secrist, the fledgling operation ran a fleet of 6,600 forty-foot reefers. Bunkers at each end of the car held ten thousand pounds of ice, while two-and-one-half-inch-thick flax panels insulated the roof, walls, and floor. The car's natural airflow worked with the ice to cool the cargo. Throwing salt into the bunkers lowered temperatures to 10-12 degrees Fahrenheit.

The PFE built tracks, warehouses, storage yards, and icing and car-repair facilities in Tucson and maintained icehouses in Yuma, Nogales, and Mesa. The company hauled "green" fruit and vegetables in groups of thirty-thousand-pound carloads called "fruit blocs." The rush of "green fruit season" required PFE to keep ventilated cars "on line" and ready for shipping unripened fruit to the nation's canneries. "They had what they called the 'grape trains' that ran out of Indio on a passenger schedule," Stoddard continued. "These were high-speed refrigerated specials headed east carrying all kinds of produce. They ran lettuce in the wintertime, and you'd have plenty of work."

Work they did! The Tucson operation stood as one of eighteen plants that made artificial ice, along with seven employing natural ice production. The PFE carried more than one billion oranges eastward from California in 1916, along with apples, asparagus, lettuce, and other crops.

Lettuce provided a "vertebrae" for the nation's perishable industry. Arizona's production centered around the Eloy and Toltec stations. In 1919, irrigation systems began feeding water to 1,500 once-barren acres. Tucson rail superintendent Wilson reported: "In the 1919-1920 season, eighty-nine cars of lettuce were shipped east, produced on 105 acres of land. The local (lettuce) crop commanded the highest prices paid in the New York markets. One car alone brought over $23,000."

PFE expanded its Tucson ice storage capacity from seven thousand tons to thirteen thousand tons during 1922. The company installed 18,000 feet of two-inch pipe and a stand-by transformer for electrical emergencies. Five inches of cork insulation lined the new addition's eight-inch walls. Bay Engineering Company of Los Angeles mounted a $20,000 compressed ammonia gas chiller to freeze its water.

Each winter, crews worked to build a backlog of ice for a late spring rush when desert heat began to climb. As temperatures warmed, between 125 and 175 men joined the plant's permanent staff of 30 to handle the increased demand. Tucson fire chief Joe Roberts agreed to cooperate in providing fire protection to the PFE plant during 1922. In the past, the city fire department did not respond to fires at the ice facility because no city water mains existed in the area. Now, the company arranged to fill a large storage tank from its two, two-thousand-gallon-a-minute wells to fight fires.

In 1926, PFE introduced a forty-foot car that more than doubled reefer carrying capacity to seventy thousand pounds. On a steel under-carriage, four to six inches of hair-felt insulation lay behind tongue-and-groove siding in the new car. Trap doors at both ends created a "ventilated refrigerator" for products that required a flow of air over them to insure freshness. PFE installed a ninety-ton compressor for ice production at the Tucson plant in 1928.

At the time, workers loaded one-and-a-half tons of ice into each reefer and completed a seventy-car train in about forty-five minutes. Men hung blue flags on a refrigerated train, indicating "hands off, don't move" when it pulled alongside the company's ice deck. Icing required six distinct steps. One crew raced along the train opening each car's ice bunkers, while another removed or smoothed the existing ice in each car using crowbars.

By 1966, the PFE plant stood boarded-up, a hollow husk of the vibrant operation it once housed. Fire destroyed the building in 1970. (Sid Showalter Collection)

"Estimators" followed behind, calculating the amount of ice needed. Another gang broke three-hundred-pound ice cakes into two to three pieces and filled each bunker. A "salting" crew came next, followed by workers that closed the hatch doors on each car.

The local plant stood just east of the subway about two hundred yards south of Broadway Boulevard. Workmen iced a record 776 cars at the local plant during the summer of 1928. Big Jim "Nuge" Nugent began pulling old ice out of incoming reefers for the PFE in 1930. "We'd get up into the hoppers on top of the car and get the old ice out of them so they could be filled again," said Nugent. "We used a big old stick with two prongs on it to break up the ice and throw it out. You'd hang this thing that looked like a sled with the runners on the top, up on the edge of the car inside the hopper hole, put the ice on there, and push it out. They paid 35¢ an hour." Former division superintendent J.J. Tierney recalled the local operation: "The train came in and they'd cut the engines off and 'blue flag' the train, which meant it couldn't be moved. Then, the ice deck people went to work. They'd scurry around just like a bunch of ants up there getting the cars re-iced."

The Great Depression forced the layoff of almost 50 percent of SP's employees and many company shops had closed by 1932. Within three years, SP's ton-miles fell to one-half of those in 1929. Net income tumbled from $29.8 million in 1930, to $3.9 million in 1931. During late May 1931, the SP auditing

bureau snuck out of Tucson under cover of darkness, on the No. 104 train bound for El Paso. Long a fixture in a small building at the western end of the local yard, the bookkeepers' evacuation prompted the *Citizen* to lament, "Now the building is a hollow echo of the halcyon days…when an army of employees would sally forth to enliven East Congress Street and add life to the town."

Motor trucking and automobiles proved more relentless than the Great Depression. SP revenues peaked during 1928-1929, but truck registrations tripled nationwide that same year. The SP opened Pacific Motor Transport (PMT) freight delivery service operation in most large towns in the West during 1930. The PMT synchronized truck schedules with company trains, allowing the railroad to handle "less-than-carload" freight on a much more flexible schedule. Former system vice-president of labor relations Carl Ball Jr. worked for PMT in Tucson, prior to starting at the railroad. "It was called Tucson Motor Service and located on South Sixth Avenue near the old fire station," Ball recalled.

Tucson PFE shopmen repaired refrigerator car (wheel) trucks. (California State Railroad Museum)

SP remodeled the former EP&SW freight station in 1931. Physicians C.A.Thomas and S.C. Davis headed the new facility's medical staff. Former local assistant chief dispatcher Robert DeHart recalled, "My father, chief dispatcher A.F. DeHart, said it was a pretty rough place with separate waiting rooms for men and women." Dr. Thomas directed medical operations at the SP hospital until 1963, when Clyde E. Flood, son of SP engineer Maynard Flood, headed the medical team. Late that year, with the SP cutting jobs due to dieselization and the population of rail workers dwindling, the hospital began admitting patients from the general public. Renamed the Carl Hayden Community Hospital in 1967, the railroad facility closed in mid-October 1974, and fell to the wrecking crew in 1979. Dynamic doctors Thomas and Davis had opened their first health clinic in 1920. Later, they established Thomas-Davis Clinic at 130 S. Scott. This clinic moved and endured as a Tucson fixture until its closure on August 31,1998. The old building is now home to the Morris K. Udall Center for Studies in Public Policy. (AHS #BN205055)

heat waves of the sun" and enhance cooling, explained the *Star*. Huge food-conveyor belts ran to each room for meal service, while a sward of green grass and a five-foot hurricane-style fence surrounded the property. The railroad hospital accepted forty patients from other institutions soon after its early September opening.

The federal government cut railroad wages by 10 percent on February 1, 1932. Nevertheless, SP suffered a $9 million loss, the first year in its history that the company did not pay stockholders a dividend. That March, Tucson's Chamber of Commerce and Eloy and Casa Grande

Despite depressed economic times, SP opened its hospital on the southwest corner of Congress Street and Granada Avenue, during 1931. Using company director and New Yorker Edward F. Harkness's large donation, the railroad remodeled the EP&SW freight station into a tubercular "sanitorium." Physicians Charles A. Thomas and Stirley C. Davis took charge of medical care at the 27,000-square-foot facility. Screened porches enhanced the hospital's twelve four-bed wards for white patients, four wards for black patients, and eighteen private rooms. Walnut-finished wood and light green walls complemented its marbleized-linoleum floor. Celotex in the roof and ceiling promised to "cast off

farmers waged vigorous protests, demanding Arizona's Corporation Commission deny SP's application to stop running its Nos. 107 and 108 local trains. Each train cost $20,500 to run between Tucson and Phoenix every month, while earning the railroad just over $5,000 a month. When the commission denied its petition, the SP withdrew its famed Sunset Limited and Argonaut passenger trains from both east and westbound service in April 1932. In addition, the railroad filed application to close the stations at Rillito, Winkelman, Cochise, and Dragoon due to lack of business. That July, the SP shut its downtown Tucson ticket office in the southwest corner of the Pioneer Hotel, where it had operated since the hotel opened December 12, 1929.

Cutbacks crippled the once-vibrant local workforce as SP revenues crashed. Passenger rates fell 40 percent over a six-year period during the Depression and promoting rail business became everyone's job. The company founded "Get the Business Clubs" and local SP employees joined in the cooperative push to keep Tucson's economy afloat. Club literature reasoned that merchants who shipped by rail created demand for more railroad employees. These workers would spend their money in city stores and live in town as property holders and good citizens. "As a natural consequence, property values are bound to rise," declared the club.

In time, Tucson and the nation loosed the Depression's economic strangle-hold and commerce returned to the rails. To rebuild business during the summer of 1935, the railroad touted its new "air-conditioned and air-cooled" Sunset Limited. The elegant train ran from New Orleans through Tucson to Los Angeles in forty-two hours. With a true air-conditioning system, passengers at last closed their windows and shut out the dirt, dust, and noise of the railroad.

Tucson superintendent Wilson announced that the local division ran its largest freight volume in ten years during the initial two months of 1935. For the first time in four years, the railroad finished out of the red for a single month. The SP soon recalled men who had seen no work for five years. Two-hundred-nineteen men soon joined PFE's local workforce, boosting its Tucson payroll to almost $122,000. The company purchased its first "steel-sheathed" cars in 1936, doing away with wooden siding. The metal units used three inches of Kapok insulation and had an 80,000 pound capacity. SP's Tucson Division payroll stood at $448,396 by June 1937, a $75,000 jump over the previous June, and higher than before the crash in 1929.

Fifty thousand carloads of lettuce ran SP lines in 1937. More railroad troubles lurked, however. One in every thirty-five citizens owned a truck large enough to haul freight by 1937. That July, the company cut prices on their dining-car meals to stimulate sales. A diner might henceforth enjoy a filet mignon for $1.10, down 12 percent.

Patience and "fill-in work" won the day for Tucson rails but the Depression lingered and privation ruled in many families. "It was hard," conductor Gordon Manning recalled: "I got cut off the railroad and went to the Mammoth-St. Anthony Mine and Mohawk Extension at Tiger, Arizona. When my oldest son was a baby, we lived in a tent. The company provided the materials and we built it ourselves, including the floor. Many people didn't have floors. Lots of families that worked for the railroad had to do something and we were one of them. As soon as I could hold a job they called me back to Tucson. That was 1939."

The SP initiated a "speedy overnight freight train" on February 1, 1939. It boosted the company's tonnage hauled by 200 percent. In conjunction with its motor trucking subsidiary, the railroad adapted to changing buying patterns. Buyers that previously ordered carload lots of canned goods or sugar now purchased only 10,000 to 20,000 pounds of an item. The change spread the railroad's business over the year rather than in seasonal bursts and caused "less-than-carload" volume to skyrocket above its 1929 peak.

At 10:00 a.m. each morning the overnight special tied up at Tucson's SP freight depot. Thirty-five minutes before the first scheduled passenger train, a flurry of industry met the swift rail caravan. Ninety minutes later, workers had loaded all the merchandise into PMT vehicles for distribution to Globe, Casa Grande, Miami, and other southern Arizona towns.

A shipper of perishables on the SP came to know his local freight agent well. The railroad agent arranged for a refrigerator car to be "spotted," or parked at the

PFE's Tucson operations grew to cover 608,000 square feet and handle 1,000 cars a day. By comparison, the company's largest facility handled 1,300 cars daily at Roseville, California. The PFE hauled almost one-half million refrigerated carloads at its acme in 1946. By 1955, the company ran a fleet of 39,000 refrigerator cars. PFE built its last new reefer in 1971, but still employed 35,000 cars in 1996. The Tucson operation closed in late 1997. (Betty Stein Collection)

nearest packing shed for loading on shipment day. In even the most remote locations, a shipper could expect on-time service because each little bit of business helped fill railroad coffers. PFE iced the loaded cars then coupled them to the next passing train for transport to a "concentration point" in the area. The SP shipped by three o'clock the following morning, with guaranteed delivery to points around Chicago by early on the seventh morning. A sixteen-hour slack in the railroad's schedule allowed for delays caused by the "diversion" process.

Diversion allowed a farmer to use the telegraph, and later the telephone, to reroute his cars as often as he wished to reach the highest-paying market. If he chose, and many did, a producer could ship his crop without knowing the load's final destination, altering it as market conditions fluctuated. A 1935 study showed that shippers diverted 64 percent of all refrigerator cars, some as many as nine times.

The SP also provided "passing" services that notified receivers as cars passed specific points along the line. This allowed time for entrepreneurs to arrange for the transfer of perishables upon arrival. Former assistant chief dispatcher Robert DeHart played a crucial role in the harvest season: "I worked at Tolleson sealing lettuce cars during the perishable season. After the lettuce cars were filled, they had to be sealed, so no one could open the door. They were tin seals with a lead clamp that left an imprint on the seal of the station where it was loaded."

The volume of commercial processed frozen foods grew during the 1930s. PFE increased insulation in its reefers to six inches and filled ice bunkers with 30 percent salt to transport the new products.

PFE installed its first mechanical floor fans to provide a more even distribution of air through the car in 1941. A rubber wheel, turned by contact with one of the car's steel wheels, powered the fans. The first electric fans that ran on power from a generator or alternator attached to the car's wheels appeared in 1951.

Sid Showalter began as switchman in the Tucson rail yard November 11, 1951. In the comfort of his midtown home, Sid explained the PFE job during October 2002: "They could put a one-hundred-car train on every one of their five receiving tracks at the PFE yard over by Pueblo Gardens. They'd get a 'bloc' of reefers in and wash 'em out and refurbish them as needed during the day shift. Then, the afternoon shift would switch 'em out to go back to work. If a car needed heavy repair, they put it in the PFE back shops. If it needed repainting, they had an assembly line for that, too."

Showalter remembered a short ice deck near Country Club Road and Aviation Highway: "It held about five cars," Showalter said. "They kept ice in an insulated building and used it mostly on banana cars. These cars ran at the back of freight trains, right next to the caboose. A shipper's agent, called a 'Zulu,' had his own car so he could watch out for the bananas. The PFE pulled the refrigerator cars, the Zulu's car, and the caboose off the train and put 'em in this little ice deck. We'd open the doors and use a thermometer to check on 'em bananas. Show stock, both horses and cattle, had Zulus, too." Almost all loaded PFE cars went eastward from the breadbaskets of the West, requiring continuous relocation of cars for future shipments. Despite company efforts to find "dry loads" for return trips, a high percentage of reefers returned empty because ice remained inside them after unloading. PFE purchased its first mechanically cooled cars in 1953. A small diesel engine on each car powered an electric motor that drove a refrigeration compressor to cool the fins of an evaporator coil. "Envelope" construction on initial mechanically-cooled cars allowed the cooled air to circulate in air space between each car's exterior and interior walls.

Showalter "cut the crossing" in the Tucson PFE yard, as part of his regular workday. "We cut four crossings, so they

The SP used a short ice deck near Aviation Highway and Country Club Road for icing carloads of bananas. To ensure market freshness, PFE workers "top-iced" lettuce and banana cars by blowing crushed ice over the entire load. The introduction of mechanical cooling began eliminating the practice of top-icing in 1953. (Sid Showalter Collection)

could get through there with all their equipment," said Sid. "Workers cut the train apart about every twenty-five cars to allow pedestrians and vehicles to cross through the train." As a train pulled into the PFE yard, "You'd get 'hold of the rear end and signal the engineer to back off the steam and stop," Showalter explained. "Then you'd reach in and turn the angle-cock, pull the pin, and back the engineer up. When you stopped him, you'd have your crossing clear. The guy up at the next crossing did the same thing twenty-five cars ahead."

Tracks No. 14 and No. 15 ran farthest east of the depot. "They ran on either side of the ice deck and held seventy-five cars," Showalter said. "If you had a long train that hung out on the main line, you'd have to cut off the rear end and move it to the other ice track. Then, when the train was ready to go east, you'd put it back together." Though Showalter made the switchman's job sound simple, all work around the trains swelled with danger. Massive machines and railcars sailing over slick steel portended no less.

Conductor Harlin Marlar "accidentally" hired out at the SP yard office in Tucson during June 1941. "I took my neighbor down there to apply for a job and was sitting outside the trainmaster's office," he said. "Well, the trainmaster came out and looked at me, and said, 'Stand up, kid.'

"I stood up and said to him, 'I don't need a job. I just brought my friend down here.'

"The trainmaster told me, 'We need long-legged boys that can catch a caboose at twenty miles an hour or more. We'll hire you, if you fill out this application.'"

Inimitable division engineer Jim Nugent fired brakeman Marlar's first steam engine to Lordsburg. "I sat beside Jim the whole trip, and he pointed out what my job was going to be," Marlar recalled. "He explained how I had to watch both sides of the train and 'call' all the signals for the engineer to make sure he saw 'em all. We worked sixteen hours into Lordsburg." Harold Jackson recalled his surprise at seeing Marlar working on the railroad several weeks later. "Here he was comin' over the top of the train at Park Avenue, knockin' the brakes off," he laughed.

A brash and impatient young brakeman, Harlin regretted one mistake he made. "In those days, the conductor could paint and decorate his caboose like he wanted it," the bright eighty-six-year-old explained. "The brakemen lived in the caboose, too. We each had a bed in there. We'd take our caboose off the train at Gila Bend and stay with it 'til they called us back to work."

One night a group of rails played poker in the caboose next to Harlin's. "My

Sunlight framed twenty-six-year-old brakeman Harold "Stonewall" Jackson as he headed downtown to the local yard office December 20, 1940. (Jackson Family Collection)

railroad buddies were getting pretty loud," he continued. "My conductor was in there, too. Well, I was tryin' to sleep, and they were makin' so much noise playin' cards and laughin' that I got tired of it." With little thought of consequences, Marlar grabbed a handful of explosive "torpedoes" used to signal problems on the rail line. "I climbed up over the top of our caboose onto theirs and dropped 'em torpedoes down the smokestack where they had a fire burning," he gulped. "Now, a torpedo was much more powerful than a shotgun blast. It blew the top off the stove and some windows out of the caboose. They all run in opposite directions hollerin' and cussin' and I was back in my bunk, innocent. I've been sorry for doin' that ever since."

The SP promoted men in rapid succession as World War II strained the com-

pany's labor pool. Marlar "made his conductor's date" with his promotion in 1943, after only two years as a brakeman. Five years later, he earned $6.71 for a sixteen-hour workday. Modeling himself after men like Earl Strasser, who made his date in 1925, Earl's brother, Frank Strasser, Gordon Manning, and Bob Wakefield, the proud rail worked the local division for forty years

Marlar remembered other outstanding conductors. "Jim Guyton hired out in 1929," he said. "Jim was a big jolly guy that treated everybody all right. I came to love the guys I worked with out there on the road. We depended on each other to stay out of trouble on the railroad. You worked sixteen hours and often had to wait another three or four 'til they got some relief out to you." More than once, freight conductor Marlar walked to a ranch house and begged food for his brakemen. "You couldn't figure out much until the SP finally got radios on its trains," he said.

Harlin defied a scalding death to save his rail comrades, when steam locomotive No. 904 tumbled off a bridge into a flooded arroyo at Tempe in August 1943. "I was on the caboose, and we only had eight or ten cars," he said. "We hadn't gone but a few miles when we came to a sudden stop that knocked us all flat on our backs. We run up to the head end, and found that floods had washed the bridge out. The steam engine was bottom-side-up in about ten foot of rushing water, with its ol' wheels a-chuggin' for more than an hour."

Eyes darting across the water's surface, Marlar saw legs with shoes protruding from beneath a boxcar. "I thought it was one of my buddies, but it turned out to be a hobo," he sighed. "I could not find any sign of the three men who worked on the engine. Water rushed through where they sat and a carload of kerosene had flipped over on top of the engine." In addition, a six-inch stream of oil ran off the cab, perilously close to its firebox. "I dived down under the water and felt around and searched for them without any luck."

When the trainmaster arrived at the scene three hours later, Marlar stood on the bank of the arroyo, drenched in black engine oil. "The men are down there," he told the boss. "I've done my best, but I can't find 'em."

"No, they were swept down the river and we've got all three of them in the hospital in town," replied the trainmaster.

His ears scalded by the engine's boiler water, courageous conductor Marlar went to the hospital to have oil cleaned from his body. "The nurses thought I'd been burned to a crisp," Marlar chuckled. "They called in doctors who realized it was just oil. I still wake up at night rememberin' that locomotive layin' there chuggin' away, getting slower and slower 'til it run out of steam." Harlin Marlar earned a commemorative plaque from division superintendent H.R. "Hard Rock" Hughes for his sterling efforts on behalf of the rails he'd grown to love. Dangerous job, that railroading.

Conductor Harlin Marlar directed engineer Tom Kerby's "officer's special" train in 1979. Harlin lent a hand to many less fortunate souls during his years on the division. His daughter, Jeannie (right), served as fireman on her father's train that day. Today, she enjoys a more than twenty-five year career on the local division. (Harlin Marlar Collection)

A charging Golden State Limited passenger locomotive smashed into a gasoline truck at the Main Avenue cross-
ing October 25, 1940. Tossing the fuel tank 130 feet from its chassis, the wreck spilled more than 3,400 gallons of
gasoline. This ignited a blaze that destroyed five small businesses, eight homes, four baggage cars, and express
cars containing fifty U.S. mailbags. There is no record of injuries or fatalities as a result of this collision but the
picture serves as a reminder that, yes, railroading is a dangerous job. (AHS #14-8402)

Chapter 14

The Eviscerous Octopus: Everybody's Workin' on the Railroad

> *"The railroad forced individuals to make room for it in their lives. It was more visible and accessible than other technological advancements of the age; it exuded a certain permanency, demanding that individuals accept the consequences of its fixed existence."*
>
> *William Deverell,* Railroad Crossings: Californians and the Railroad, *1994*

SP officials met at San Francisco to discuss important issues ca. 1945. Extending the practice of founder C.P. Huntington's crowd, company bigwigs sent cypher or coded telegrams for certain eyes only. Tucsonan Ray Hanson (seated fourth from left near the table) earned his engineering degree, paving his way for early advancement on the railroad. (Ray Hanson Collection)

Southern Pacific Railroad (SP) tentacles reached into virtually every dimension of life in Arizona during the age of steam, justifying its "Octopus" moniker. The SP's pervasive presence produced benefits beyond calculation. Many people viewed the railroad and its purveyors as the ultimate blessing. Chas. A. Dinsmore captured the essence in a May 1909 letter to the *Arizona Daily Star,* "With the coming of the 'Octopus' comes energetic, far-seeing people, eager to take a hand in the up-building of an empire." The *Tucson Daily Citizen* added: "Railroads and their great trains, are the compulsory school masters of the people in every region they traverse. Savage and civilized, are both enlightened and made stronger by the sight of these moving trains."

Not everyone appreciated the massive rail matrix, however. That the railroad should control all comings and goings of everyone and everything, both in and out of town, grated on some. That it engaged in power brokering, cheated the government of legal tax revenues, imposed rate favorit-

Early twentieth century travelers and locals discussed the railroad beast's pros and cons over a drink at John Heidel's (right) Cactus Saloon across Toole Avenue from the SP depot. (John Heidel Collection)

ism and gave rebates to treasured customers, and applied financial coercion and levied unjustified surcharges on those in disfavor, enraged many Tucsonans.

Dramatic events hardened public opinion against the railroad. In May of 1880, SP agents arrived to evict a family along a railroad right-of-way near Mussel Shoals, California, north of Ventura. Eight farmers died in a bloody confrontation and SP removed two hundred families from their farms. During the mid-1890s, the company's ongoing feud with Oakland, California ferry operator John Davie further tarnished SP's image. When the railroad refused to open a drawbridge for him, the prickly East Bay businessman tied onto a support beam and pulled the bridge into the bay. A grand jury refused to indict Davie, mirroring the public's hostility toward SP's vast enterprise. During late January 1901, an Interstate Commerce Commission (ICC) investigation found: "Defiance and open violation of the law is the general rule with many of the great railroad corporations. This was especially true when it came to giving rebates to favored shippers. Not all anarchists in this country reside in the slums."

Frank Norris fueled public enmity toward the rail company with his 1901 novel, *The Octopus: a Story of California.* Spinning a rich fictional account of a thinly disguised SP, Norris reinforced the anti-railroad beliefs of many citizens. Nevertheless, an air of impunity and supremacy enveloped the nation's rail rulers.

With operational headquarters in San Francisco, much of SP's political drama played out in California. *Fortune Magazine* explained, "The state government came under the spell of the most gigantic industrial organism in the West. It is on record that the railroad not only dictated the legislation but the actual membership of committees and commissions."

Southern Arizona anti-SP sentiment cried, "Railroads are too wealthy, grossly arrogant, and have forced their wishes upon whole sections of the territory through heavy-handed use of their political might." During early October 1906, the *Star* roared: "Railroad corporations are the most rapacious and most insolent of all the trusts. They discriminate on freight rates."

Pima County Assessor John W. Bogan's discovery that the SP failed to declare more than $120,000 taxable property exacerbated the company's image problems during 1907. Bogan exposed omissions in "stocks of goods and materials," as well as the land for the new freight depot at Franklin Street and Stone Avenue. Rail officials claimed that they "forgot" to record the items in their annual report.

In 1909, a representative of the Interstate Commerce Commission explained to reporters that the nation's railroads viewed the commission with "scarcely concealed suspicion [and] obedience to its ruling(s) was of a reluctant, begrudging kind." Railroads had adhered to legal tariff rates better than at any time in the past ten years. Yet, said the spokesman, corporations continued to have an "avowed intention of circumventing and thwarting" the commission.

Citizens began to express anti-railroad rabidity with greater vigor and broadened their range of tactics after 1910. Vowing to "drive the Southern Pacific out of politics," Hiram Johnson won election as governor of California that year.

Local officials met at the freight house ca. 1920. (Ray Hanson Collection)

From that time until the Great Depression, "the SP was not the master of the public but its prey" in California, *Fortune Magazine* concluded.

The force and volume of those who sang the SP's praises matched the vigor with which thousands excoriated the company. The *Star* captured the complex railroad beast's perplexing essence in October 1910. "These railroads are 'soulless creatures,' they are the very 'meanest of monopolizers,'" said the paper. "But, it certainly is wonderful when the head of a railway finds there is a considerable area of fertile land, or a mineralized belt, or whatever, he will build up a line to it and open it up. It seems strange, too, that these men who foist upon us 'the menace of the age' are the ones who make possible the improvement, the upbuilding, [and] the prosperity of the country."

SP worked hard to dispel its sinister and heartless image. Company vice president O.E. McCormick espoused an ideology that endured for decades. "The policy of courteous treatment of complaints, of promptly remedying real grievances, of fair dealing with all shippers, big and little, of helpful aid willingly rendered, of liberal efforts to advertise and build up the state, of doing our best to provide manufacturers and farmers with new markets are in my opinion the greatest things we are doing."

John "J.J." Tierney, former Tucson Division superintendent, came face-to-face with the public's attitude toward the SP as assistant vice-president of public relations in Los Angeles. "People wanted to sue the railroad and everybody that walked along the railroad," said Tierney during September 2002. "Anybody who was connected with the railroad was *persona non grata*. The railroad settled the West and was a big factor in the growth of many towns, but people forget about that when it becomes an inconvenience and they're delayed at a crossing."

During his tenure, the Los Angeles County district attorney held neighborhood meetings. "The guy told people how bad the railroad was and how they were going to put us all in jail and shut us down," Tierney said. "It was a terrible situation. My job was to keep peace with the cities and counties. We had miles and miles of track, so we always had some situation where we were blocking crossings and delaying traffic."

One chap owned a house next to the railroad tracks on a branch line and had a problem with trains. "He called me in the dark of night and asked me, 'What the hell is this train doin' goin' down these tracks?'"

A steam locomotive tears across the California landscape. Many appreciated the train's speed and convenience, but others took offense, remembered former Tucson superintendent J.J. Tierney. (J.J. Tierney Collection)

laughed Tierney. "Of course, those tracks had been there since the 1800s. I said, 'Didn't you see them tracks when you bought the house?'

"The fellow tells me, 'Well, yeah, but we never saw any trains on them.' I'd told 'im, 'That's what those tracks are there for, trains! You got a good deal on the house, didn't you? Now, you know why.' That sort of stuff kept people pretty busy at the railroad." Explaining why the railroad could not move a train immediately, due to a derailment or an accident, proved especially difficult. "There was a lack of understanding of what the railroad was about and how it operated," Tierney said. "People thought we sent that train down there to deliberately delay them.

"The police were terrible," he continued. "If you had a crossing accident, they'd want to see the 'that engineer's license to drive that train.'

"I'd say, 'They don't have any license, they're qualified under the company rules to run their locomotives,'" the ebullient Tierney recalled. "Sometimes it was

very comical, sometimes it was very frustrating. Certain policemen thought you were lying to them and would threaten to take the conductor and engineer to jail." Tierney encountered a different attitude when he arrived on the local division. "In towns like Tucson, people got frustrated when a train blocked a crossing, but they were more tolerant and understanding than in other towns," the former division head recalled.

Building and maintaining a money-making steam railroad demanded successful coordination of myriad tasks. A railroad ran from the ground up, with the safety of passengers and products primary. The railroad completed preliminary and location surveys, acquired land for a right-of-way, constructed a stable roadbed, and laid track. Track begat locomotive power and railcars. These spawned terminals, icing facilities, signal systems, a telegraph system, and much, much more. Once established, the railroad needed ton-upon-ton of ties, spikes, lanterns, paper clips, tables, chairs, timesheets, and the like.

Amid the railroad's frantic rush of immense hardware and bureaucratic procedure flowed the lifeblood of the company, its people. Each of their stories depicts one thread of Tucson Division life and times. As late as World War II, rails held strong cachet and "everyone in Tucson" seemed to work for the SP. A "queer lingo" fueled rail culture. The conductor answered to "skipper"; train orders came on a piece of tissue paper called a "flimsy"; torpedoes, small explosive devices used to signal engineers of track obstructions, became "guns"; a water car, a "keeley"; switches, "gates"; a typewriter, a "threshing machine"; a clerk, a

Despite every safety effort, wrecks proved common early in the twentieth century. Henry T. Stapp captured this photograph of fellow brakeman Ed Peel (left), when locomotive No. 2702 wrecked at Soto crossing on the Nogales line in 1916. (Richard Stapp Sr. Collection)

"pencil pusher"; and railroad police, "bulls" or "cinder dicks." If you, or anyone in your family, worked for the railroad you knew the meaning of every term.

The SP *Book of Rules* outlined clear discipline procedures and a framework within which employees could operate. The company instituted the nation's first corrective, rather than punitive, system of employee discipline in August 1896. Devised by George R. Brown, the plan called for adding demerits, called "brownies," to an employee's record for minor misconduct, instead of suspending the worker. Following an investigation, the division superintendent might levy fifteen or twenty brownies for rough handling of trains, going too fast, rough coupling or uncoupling of passenger trains, or failing to observe track signals. By maintaining a clean work record, a man could erase ten to fifteen demerits in about six months. The SP, generally, dismissed men who accumulated sixty demerits or who committed a serious violation.

Most rails swung in step with the company beat. "A railroad man was pretty well wed to his job and most handled authority pretty well," recalled Carl A. Ball Jr., at his handsome midtown home in late April 2002. "I think the men understood what it meant to do a good job for the railroad. They learned the job and knew their work pretty well. Overall, they took pride in their work."

SP officials appreciated the ethic. "The railroad tried to promote people who would carry on the operations of the railroad in a wholesome (way) as far as the equipment was concerned," said Ball. "All in all, the men operated safely and with the attitude of getting the job done, but as company officials, we always carried a rule book with us. Most men were satisfied with the way the Southern Pacific operated and the way they were treated."

Frank Hutcheson began as a laborer at the local yard in 1947. Frank's father, conductor Oril O. Hutcheson, supervised

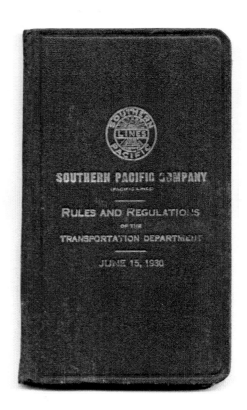

The company's Book of Rules set exact performance and behavior standards. During 1910, SP's local "education board" bulletin listed rule infractions on the division every two weeks. That September, the SP discharged seventeen men from service and suspended twenty-two. Penalties ranged from a ten-day suspension for a brakeman who could not be found when called for a run, to a switchman who received sixty days for failing to handle a cut of cars according to company rules. (Betty Nowell Collection)

trains for almost thirty-five years, mostly on the Stormy, the eastern end of the Tucson Division. "Working for the railroad meant an awful lot to him," Frank said. "It did [to] the whole family. Everybody thought working for the railroad was great. Generally speaking, rails would even go to work sick. If you didn't work, you didn't get paid. I don't remember any sick leave on the railroad, even when I went to work in the 1940s." Most rails held an "us against them" attitude toward rail officials. "Of course, everybody cussed management, but they wouldn't change or go anywhere else.

And, boy, let anybody attack the railroad!"

The path to a better life ran through a railroad job for many young men. Conductor Gordon "Nose" Manning grew up in Deming, New Mexico, and married the town's 1936 rodeo queen, Ruth Bonine. Memories of their more than sixty years of railroad life filled the Manning home on east Tenth Street during late April 2002. Gordon began, "I worked in a garage that stored tour buses for Carlsbad Caverns during 1936-1937, but I was real interested in a job at the railroad. A wonderful engineer named Del 'Ole' Olson came by every day on the Sunset Limited. We always had fun tryin' to shake hands with him as he went by, because the garage was so close to the track. Ole said to me, 'You be a brakeman. You little and light on you feet. You can run on top of de trains.'"

Olson "put in a good word" for Manning with railroad officials. "Ole was right," smiled the erudite ninety- year-old. "They called me to start as a brakeman in Tucson the next week. I just needed somebody to speak up for me to get on with the SP." After completing the required thirty unpaid student trips, Manning jumped aboard his first train as rear brakeman in July 1937. Strenuous and demanding, the job tested a man's body, heart, and mettle. "Every car had a ladder and a hand brake," Gordon recalled. "You ran up and down over the train through storms and all kinds of weather, carrying a brake club. It was shaped like a pick handle and gave you leverage." Using both hands, the brakeman shoved his brake club between the spokes of the brake wheel on top of each car and turned. "When you got the brake tight, you put your foot against the

'dog,' a gear at the base of the brake assembly, that locked it," said Manning. "In those days, you'd seldom see a brakeman without his brake club."

Each of the train's brakeman owned a specific responsibility. Generally, the least senior man served as flagman on the caboose. Whenever a train stopped unexpectedly, its rear brakemen ran back one-fourth mile and secured a small exploding charge, called a "torpedo," by crimping its metal tines around a rail. Then, he raced another half-mile back along the track and set two more torpedoes. Any oncoming train first triggered back-to-back explosions, warning its engineer to slow his train to twelve-and-one-half miles per hour for one mile and prepare to stop. The lone charge one-half mile up the track signaled an engineer to stop for a problem ahead. Torpedoes set, the flagman remained at that position until signaled to return by the engineer, using the locomotive whistle.

A rear brakeman also tended his "markers," a kerosene lamp with four faces that worked to signal following trains. One side held a red lens and each of the others a green. On the main line, the flagman set his red marker to the rear. When the train

Rails like Ray Hanson took pride in their work and encountered few problems with the company's Book of Rules. (Ray Hanson Collection)

went into a siding and cleared the main track, he changed it to green. This signaled the following train that his train's rear end sat clear of the main line.

Next in seniority, the swing brakeman took particular care to check over the entire length of both sides of his train for problems. At the end of every axle a metal box, called a journal box, surrounded wheel bearings. Lack of lubrication created a burning journal or "hot box" that could cause a derailment. Broken "drawbars" between cars and other problems might also cause a car to "go on the ground." At the front of the train, the head brakeman held the most seniority. He called out all track signals for the engineer and also watched the train for problems. After three years as a head brakeman, a competent man might "write the book" to demonstrate his knowledge of company rules and ascend to a conductor's job.

The brains of the outfit, as the engineer provides its eyes and hands, and the shop man its heart; the conductor controlled all train movements and kept his train on time. Tucson Division electrician Frank Hutcheson explained, "A conductor on the passenger train in those [steam engine] days was the first cousin to God." The SP promoted an average of six conductors on the Tucson Division each year during the twentieth century's first decade. That number jumped to 30 in 1917 and 21 in 1918, as World War I broadened. Between March of 1924 and October 1927, 146 men rose to conductor, 58 of those in 1926.

Freight trains ran across the division according to train orders issued by dispatchers in Tucson. Passenger trains moved to the tune of published SP timetables, but when they fell behind schedule, they relied on train orders to direct their movement. Using a precise railroad watch, each conductor determined the exact moment his charge departed a station, cut out cars, delayed for a connecting train, or stopped at a flag station for a passenger.

Respected conductor Henry Stapp imbued his son Richard with a love of Arizona history and the railroad. Former United Transportation Union general chairman and Tucsonan George Perkins remembered, "Henry Stapp was one of the conductors I admired most. Gordon Manning and several others fit that category." (Richard Stapp Sr. Collection)

Prior to World War II, a conductor conveyed his wishes to the engineer using a set of six whistle signals and a cotton whistle cord found in the vestibule of most cars. "One whistle meant stop, two to start, three to back up, and four to call the flagman from the east, five from the west," remembered Manning. "When the engineer whistled several short blasts, it meant he was losing air."

Passenger conductors "called" their trains on station platforms at Yuma, Tucson, and El Paso before the war. Powerful tenors and domineering baritones shouted out the important details of their train above the din of screeching whistles, clattering wheel trucks, chugging locomotives, and chattering passengers. "A lot of trains in the yard made it real loud at the Tucson

These "old-heads" in the San Xavier No. 313 local of the Order of Railway Conductors commanded Tucson Division trains as the twentieth century approached. The master of the rail caravan, a conductor ruled its movement from his castle, the caboose. (AHS #B93491)

Conductor Eddie Pecktol started in Tucson as a brakeman on June 11, 1946. "We had an old boomer brakeman, which is a drifter who bids jobs from one place to another," Eddie reflected. "His name was Fred Campbell and he was a fireman on the Denver & Rio Grande but came here as a brakeman. He taught all of us guys how to fire that stove in the caboose. He'd start his fire by banking the coal in back and giving it air in front. Then, he'd go up in the cupola and watch it like you would a steam engine. He knew what he was doing. If you banked it, you could leave the fire alone. But, us greenhorns would build a fire and poke it over and over. The fire just went back and forth between hot and cold. Boomer told us, 'Bank it, let it breathe. Shake the fire grate from below and leave poker alone.'" Eddie served as local chairman of the SP blood drive committee for thirty-five years and, accompanied by his beloved dog Spuds, enthralled Tucsonans with rail tales following his retirement. Pecktol played an instrumental role in preserving Tucson's historic locomotive No. 1673 and has become a familiar face at local rail functions. (Eddie Pecktol Collection)

depot," explained Manning. "You had to call your train big and loud. The best show in the Southwest was in El Paso. Six different companies ran first class trains into there. Each conductor called his train with his own special style." The ritual provided the only sure way for passengers to find their correct train. "You made sure people matched your train's name and number with the track that you were on, so they headed for the right spot," said Gordon. "Following World War II, stations had loudspeakers and the practice of calling trains quickly died."

A conductor's castle, the caboose earned nicknames like the "crummy," "monkey wagon," and "hack." At the end of his shift, the train's commander made sure the railroad "spotted," his caboose on the "cab-track" until the SP called him to work again. Inside, the caboose's proverbial stove warmed a

Passengers board train No. 39 in Lordsburg during 1954. Six verified trips riding trains beside an experienced conductor qualified a man for his own "Streamliner," complete with a wage increase and enhanced status. (Richard Stapp Sr. Collection)

The Railroad Post Office (RPO) handled mail for the SP when former division conductor Gordon Manning began as a train baggageman (TBM) in 1937. The prosperous real estate investor remembered: "The RPO had space for mail storage in the head car on every train. You pushed out an arm on the car to pick up the first class bags from each station, going about sixty miles an hour. The arm curved so it threw the mailbag right into your car. At the same time, I'd set the mail bag for that station down by my foot and kick it right out the door. The telegraph operator at each station also worked as its postmaster."

pot of stew, soup, Salisbury steak, or other delicacy for the crew. The men's beds swung down on hinged straps from metal boxes built into the ceiling, and strapped back into the box when not in use. "Before the war we had to buy our own beds," remembered Manning. "After that we started getting an allowance for them."

Conductor Henry T. Stapp began as a brakeman on the Tucson Division in September 1915 and directed trains over the Stormy until he retired in 1956. His son, Richard Stapp Sr., treasured the time he spent on division rails with his father. Rumbling back from Esmond Station in an 1985 Jeep Cherokee during the winter of 2003, Richard reminisced: "My usual perch was up in the cupola on top of the caboose. Along the left side was kind of a chaise lounge. You had a big padded mat underneath that sloped up at your waist like a chair," he said. "I could brace my feet against the wall of the cupola to keep from slidin' around."

Richard learned a valuable lesson playing stowaway on SP trains. "Dad always told me, 'Keep your hands full of steel!'" said Stapp. "That meant, 'Hang on whenever this train is mov-

ing!' That really stuck with me. I made sure I held on to the steel poles running from ceilng to floor when I walked down the caboose's aisle way."

Richard found confirmation of his father's aphorism one day in 1956, when the slack between their train's cars "ran in" abruptly. "Now, when that happens," he explained, "there is not a uniform slowing down of the train. The train's caboose slammed into the preceding car and our rear brakeman failed to grab steel. The concussion shot him across the car and into the heavy wire mesh that covered the glass in the front door. He cut his face pretty bad and wrenched his wrist. The man had to lay off for a few days to recover. I kept that in mind whenever I was out on the rails with my dad."

Not withstanding the conductor, SP dispatchers held the most crucial role on the railroad. Maestro in the railroad's grand ballet of train movement, the dispatcher noted each train's vital information on his large "train sheet." He also used it to record the progress of every train, as telegraph operators along the line reported it passing their station. When a train encountered delays, he wrote orders specifying its movement.

The caboose's cupola provided trainmen with an excellent vantage point from which to inspect their moving train for "hot boxes" and other problems. (Sid Showalter Collection)

Dispatchers entered service on the SP as telegraphers. An August 1917 *Southern Pacific Bulletin* explained the nature of the energetic men who did the tension-packed job: "No man of phlegmatic disposition can become a great telegrapher. Only one of fervor, of imagination, and of emotional temperament ever rose to high rank."

SP had opened a school of telegraphy in Los Angeles during October 1907. The company required enrollees "be equipped with a common school education, be physically fit, and be between sixteen- and twenty-six-years-old." Students practiced the duties of station agent and used the company's working wires to learn the telegraph key. Telegraphers' salaries ranged from $65 to $95 per month. Non-rails paid $75 tuition, the sons of SP employees $37.50, and the sons of employees killed in rail service attended without charge.

Straight of spine and vigorous, long-time Tucson dispatcher Robert DeHart has enjoyed a daily stroll down Third Street to the University of Arizona mall for years. One especially brisk December day in 2002, he returned from his walk ready to talk railroad. "My dad, A.F. DeHart, came to Tucson in 1914, as a teleg-

Dispatchers Henry W. Cassidy (right) and A.F. DeHart (rear center), and chief clerk and stenographer M.B. Mudge kept trains moving from the local depot's second floor office ca. 1940. Cassidy worked 36 years on the Tucson division. "We started with 65-pound (to the yard) rails," he remembered in 1953. "Today it's up to 131 pound rails." In 2006, continuous one-quarter-mile rail predominates on the nation's modern railroads. (Robert and Louise DeHart Collection)

rapher for the El Paso & Southwestern," DeHart began. "Dad worked nights from 6:00 p.m. to 6:00 a.m., seven days a week! When the EP&SW pay car came around once a month, he got $90 in gold!" Robert recalled that his father worked on March 9, 1916, the day Pancho Villa invaded Columbus, New Mexico. "An Army officer came in on the telegraph wire and reported that his men had taken casualties in an ongoing firefight there," he said. "My dad always told that story with excitement in his voice."

When Robert DeHart hired out as a telegrapher in 1937, Grover Baker manned the chief dispatcher's chair in Tucson. "It was all single-track when I began and that required you to pay a lot of attention," he explained. "They'd usually fire you for having two trains on the same line at once, a main-line meet." The constraint chal-

A Snapped-on-the-Street photographer captured SP assistant chief dispatcher A.F. DeHart on Congress Street during the 1940s. DeHart began at the EP&SW in Tucson in 1914. "They just worked all the time," remembered his son Robert. "Dad and his friend had a thing going with the lights at the beautiful little park by the EP&SW depot. He'd turn out the lights around the park. Then, one of them would snap the lights back on, while the other silently rode his bicycle through all the necking couples. (Robert and Louise DeHart Collection)

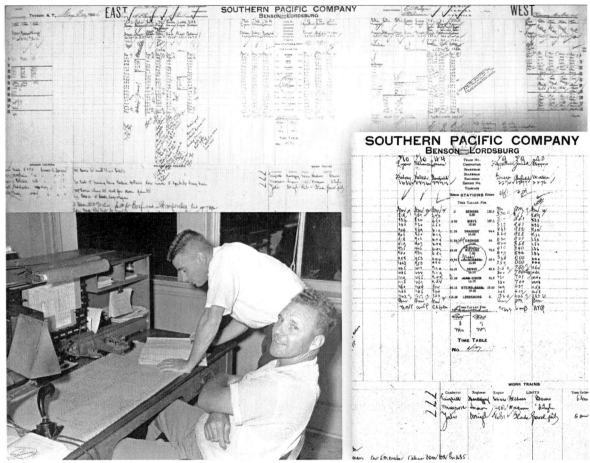

Robert DeHart (right) and C.K. Claytor worked the dispatcher's office on the second floor of the SP depot in 1943. The local office sat above the letters TUCSON at the depot on Toole Avenue. It remained there until the railroad installed Centralized Traffic Control (CTC). Then, machines took over monitoring the location of trains for dispatchers and SP did away with the train sheet. The trainsheet shown here is for the Benson - Lordsburg district, May 31, 1905. (Photo: Robert and Louise DeHart Collection, train sheet: Ralph Coltrin Jr. in Gene Ball Collection)

lenged even the best of dispatchers.

Former division dispatcher James Elwood explained another aspect of the stressful job. "The yardmaster might have a lot of extra cars and say, 'Jim, I want to order up an extra train,'" said Elwood. "So, you'd get the cars that had piled up out in the yard and make up a train.

"When I got the call, I'd tell the crew caller, 'Order me up a crew, I want to go eastbound,'" Elwood explained. "I'd write down the conductor, engineer, how many units (locomotives) he's gonna have, how many cars in the train, the tonnage, the number of feet in length, etc., all on my train sheet."

Each midnight, Tucson's assistant chief dispatcher started a new train sheet in order to record the location of all trains on the division. He copied the names of each crew off the previous train sheet and told every man his assignment. Station operators along the line notified the dispatcher by telegraph each time a train passed. He created a record of every train's progress and noted all transmissions on his train sheet. "I'd figure the new train in with all the trains I already had on the railroad and decide where to fit it in," Elwood continued. "You'd have to keep in mind the length of the train, to make sure that it was not longer than your sidings."

Dispatchers issued written orders to a train that ran behind the timetable. "If a train was late, I might write him an order to run two hours late to Picacho and three hours late on into Phoenix," said DeHart. "On busy days some dispatchers put out one hundred orders during an eight-hour shift."

One set of train orders went to the conductor and another to the engineer. "When the conductor got his 'clearance' it gave him the authority to pass the 'red block,' or stop signal, and keep on highballin,'" said Elwood. When telegraphers received train orders, they wrote, and later typed, the instructions and hung them outside the station. "We had a bamboo pole shaped like a wishbone, with hooks on each end," Elwood said. "It had a string in it, and you'd fold the train order and put it on the string. You stood real close to the track and held up the hook." The engineer and the conductor each grabbed a copy of their orders off the hook. "If they missed it, they'd have to back up and they'd cuss a little bit," laughed the veteran dispatcher. "Sometimes you'd knock the glasses off the engineer with that hook."

"Dragoon Station had a little woman named Maggie Uhls who could stand up real close to the trains as they flew by," remembered Gordon Manning. "Maggie had her spot marked, and she'd stand there while the conductor and engineer hooked their arm through the bamboo loop

High atop one of the unique rock formations near Dragoon Station, this dance floor provided rails and ranchers with enjoyment during the 1920s. (Leon Speer Collection)

and grabbed their train orders." Long-time University of Arizona administrator David Butler remembered, "Maggie listened to the other telegraph transmissions and kept train sheets of her own. She monitored the progress of all trains, and my dad told me that many times she would get on the phone and challenge the dispatcher, 'Are you sure that's what you want to do?' She was really good but unfortunately she could never be a dispatcher because she was a woman."

All odd-numbered SP trains ran west toward San Francisco, and all-even numbered trains went east. Call letters identified each station on the division. To reach a station, operators tapped out its call letters and twisted a ringer that caused a telephone to ring at the selected location. "The telegraph was like a party line because everybody was in on it. It really worked pretty well," explained Bob DeHart.

Trains did not always start on schedule, forcing dispatchers to make rapid-fire decisions about which trains received priority. "A timetable might say they leave at 9:00 every night," DeHart said. "One night they might already be two hours late and still have work to do, spotting or picking up cars along the line."

H. R. "Hard Rock" Hughes held the superintendent's chair when DeHart started on the division. "George A. Bays followed Hughes as the local 'Old Man,'" he said. "Next came D.R. Kirk. He was a real nice guy, tall, and a nice-looking fellow. After Kirk, came A.S. McCann, and Ralph Coltrin, who rose from assistant superintendent.

"George Bays's son Arnold Bays took over next. One Sunday after diesels came in, I thought he was going to fire me," DeHart said. The Tucson native was working the chief dispatcher's job when a diesel engine got away from the engineer at Picacho and headed for Tucson. The thought of a huge engine racing into the Tucson metropolitan area shot chills through all who knew its horrible itinerary.

"It was a runaway," said DeHart. "It had a new type of diesel engine that would go through transitions and pick up speed automatically." DeHart could see it on the CTC (Centralized Traffic Control) board. "So I called Mr. Bays. Boy, did he unload on me! He was scared to death!" Trainmaster Gordon Toncheff and the road foreman of engines drove a truck to a spot near Marana and blocked catastrophe. "They shot the train's air hose out with a shotgun!" said DeHart. "That put the engine into emergency-brake status and stopped the train."

An SP telegraph operator 1953-1957, David Butler remembered that his father, chief dispatcher A.D. Butler, told him: "Son, if you really want to learn to operate the telegraph key you should go out to Red Rock and see ol' Ken Walker. There's no better man to teach you."

"That was the best advice I probably ever got," David said. "I needed a job that allowed me to go to class, work, and still complete my studies. Telegraph operator on the SP was the perfect job because when you're out on the line at night you're not busy all the time. I was able to study while I was on the job." Fifty years later, Butler remembered: "C.R. Smith was in charge of telegraph operators and very accommodating in trying to find work for me while I was going to school. I really owe the railroad for my college degree."

As his father predicted, the aspiring college student learned Morse code and railroad procedure in the hands of master telegrapher Walker. By the time Butler headed for his first job as a relief operator at Mohawk, Arizona, he felt confident that he could do his part to ensure the safe passage of trains. Butler worked at Gila Bend, Picacho, Estrella (pronounced es-trel-a on the railroad), Rillito (ri-lit-o), Steins, New Mexico, and other small stations during his railroad tour.

Butler remembered one exciting incident on his relief telegrapher's job. "The SP line runs downhill to the west," he said. "If a car broke loose in the Tucson yard, it

Arnold Bays served as the younger half of Tucson's only father and son superintendent team. (Arnold Bays Collection)

would roll all the way to Picacho. This one train broke apart and the guys in the caboose didn't realize it. The front end eventually pulled away from the back end." When the train stopped at Picacho, the head brakeman noticed his train had no rear end. "Before he knew it here came the back end with thirteen cars of cement!" said Butler. "The crash showered cement everywhere! The front end had stopped, so they were hit by their own rear end." The accident delighted area farmers who hauled cement away by the truckload.

"Estrella was very isolated," Butler continued. "I didn't have a car, so I rode a lot of engines, coming in and going back. Estrella sat at the top of a hill, so freight trains traveled very slowly as they topped the crest. I'd signal the engineer, palms up, and when he slowed down, I'd jump on the engine as it came by." Butler smiled in reflection: "My dad did the same thing on coal burners growing up back east. He always dressed up to go to town and by the time he got there he was covered with soot!"

Estrella bustled early in the twentieth century. Down the road at Gila Bend, railroaders stayed at the Stout Hotel. (UASC)

David recalled Mohawk Station as the most primitive on the division. "It didn't have any electricity," he explained. "You had to use Aladdin lamps both in the office and in your living quarters. They used kerosene but had a wick like Coleman lanterns do today. It smoked a lot but gave off quite a bit of light. In order to keep the lantern from smoking, you had to close the windows to keep the wind down, which caused the room to heat up like an oven! Sometimes you'd hang wet sheets over the windows and try to catch a breeze or just throw a wet sheet over you."

Division "pumpers" lived a unique rail life. Responsible for keeping one of at least fifteen division water tanks full, the pumper worked when rail traffic demanded. George "Boots" Lundquist's father, Harry Lundquist, began on the division in 1907 and filled the water tank at Pantano from 1930 to 1950. "My father took a pumper's job at Fairbank, Arizona," Boots began. "When my parents were first at Fairbank, they went to a hotel that charged a dollar a day. They couldn't afford that so

Relief telegraph operator David Butler worked jobs across the entire division while he attended the University of Arizona. Here, he waits outside the primitive Mohawk Station in 1954. "One permanent telegrapher bought an electric generator to run a cooler there," he remembered. "We'd all go to his house in the evening to relax. All in all, it was a real good life."(David Butler Collection)

they moved into the SP pump house. My mother was pregnant, and one day the supervisors came by and seen where my mother and dad were living. They sent a boxcar out there that my folks made it into a little house. They moved a wood stove in to cook on and heat with." Later on, the elder Lundquist "bid in" on the pumper's job at Willcox. "We lived there 'til I was in the sixth grade when they electrified the plant and done away with his job. Willcox put in a well and SP started buying their water from the city.

"My Dad took a leave of absence and opened a restaurant in Willcox, which was a bad thing," Lundquist said. "After a couple of years he was broke, so he bid in a job at Cutter, eight miles east of Globe. That was in the mid-1920s." Harry Lundquist filled three water tanks. "There was a pump station at Cutter, one at Rice, and another at San Carlos. He had a little motor car that he rode back and forth. He'd go to one station and spend the day filling the water tank. Then he'd go to another station the next day. All his life he was a pumper."

In 1930, the Lundquist family moved to Pantano. "When he went there it paid $35 more than the job paid at Cutter, $135. We lived about five hundred feet west of the water tank, on the north side of the tracks. We had a pretty comfortable house in the old depot. It was a big place, with three bedrooms, a dining room, and a kitchen. My brother's and my bedroom was the old baggage room."

The now-vanished community bustled when the Lundquists arrived. Boots remembered, "Mr. J.W. Purifoy ran the town store. The post office was in the front of the SP depot, where they sold tickets for the train. The Bejarano family of woodcutters also lived on the north side of the tracks. They were a good family. They worked for their dad and used axes." Lundquist's mother took the job as postmistress in Pantano. "That job paid between fifteen and twenty dollars a month but they closed the post office in the 1940s. A section gang

Harry Lundquist found time to play with his kids while he worked pumper jobs across the division. (Back row, l-r) Wallace, Harry Esmond, Maybelle "Sis", (middle row) Alice, Puff (Alice), Harry, (front row) George "Boots," and Emmet "Binx." (George Lundquist Collection)

Pumper Harry Lundquist paused for this 1920s photograph near the Willcox water tank prior to moving to Pantano in 1930. (George Lundquist Collection)

with about twelve men lived in a house the company provided across the track from the depot. The section foreman had his own house on the north side. The crew was all Mexican, except one year my brother went to work on the section gang."

Division water demanded treatment for use in steam engines. Harry Lundquist serviced the water softening unit at Pantano, Arizona. The town bubbled with activity when Harry began in 1930. (George Lundquist Collection)

Pumper Harry Lundquist's job provided special benefits. "My dad's time was mostly to himself," Boots recalled. " He would start up his pumping engines and fill the tanks with water. After that, he could go home. Dad had a stamp collection. He grew a garden, he raised chickens, and kept rabbits. He had all this time when he was getting paid to work but could do other things. The engineers had good-paying jobs. Well, my dad's job didn't pay much, but they furnished him a house and that meant a whole lot."

When Boots started as a fireman on the division in 1937, one of the older engineers said he'd rather have the pumper's job than one on a locomotive. "I said, 'Danny, you're crazy!'" Boots remembered. "He told me, 'Your dad's home all the time. You're gonna find out before you retire that you're spending a third of your time, maybe more, away from your family.' That meant something to him, and to me too. My dad put his feet under the same table for every meal. He didn't have to eat in grease joints

like I did during my career as an engineer."

Early on, section gangs composed primarily of Mexican men raised and leveled the division roadbed. Wielding hand tools, men also replaced rail ties, spikes, and switches. Born in Hidalgo, Sonora during 1930, Adelberto Langston hired on with a division section gang in 1949. His demanding, physical job took Langston over the Stormy from Bisbee Junction to Marsh Station. When he started, Langston recalled, section foreman Joe Talamantes called him "Boy" because of his youth. "I learned things that made the work easier from watching the older men," he said. "I earned 98¢ an hour for an eight-hour day. By the 1960s very little had changed." Work crews stayed four to five weeks in each location. Men with good seniority lived in section houses along the division with their families and kept weekend homes in nearby towns. Langston lived in an outfit car with other less-senior workers. Equipped with a heater and stove, SP outfit cars held a water tank on the roof that let occupants pump

The pumper's family lived in the old depot at Pantano ca. 1930. (George Lundquist Collection)

their water. "The water was so hot in the summer, we had to wait until midnight to take a shower," said Adelberto. "We kept our drinking water in a wooden keg, and brakemen brought us ice wrapped in burlap. If it was real hot, we'd bury the ice to guard it." When winter's chill settled across the desert, the uninsulated wooden coaches meant tending the stove's fire throughout the night.

SP charged section workers $2.50 a week for room and board. Men provided their own bedding and enjoyed good food. "They had a dining car for the men with long tables and a cook, usually Chinese, with his own kitchen car," Langston said. "Great breads and cakes!" Far from town and without transportation, section men often spent tranquil evenings searching the desert for arrowheads or playing games. "I like quiet places," remarked Langston. Railroad paydays found many section workers at the general store in Fairbank, Arizona. "They had everything the men needed there, even beer," Langston said.

"We'd gather to visit and gamble on their nickel, dime, and quarter-slot machines. They made that illegal sometime in the fifties."

Another of the wealth of exceptional men and women who worked on the local division during the steam age, Sid Showalter's jet-black hair and bright eyes belie his seventy-nine years. During October 2002, Showalter spoke fondly of his thirty-five years on the local division. "Switchman was all a walkin' job, and you really worked hard," he said. "We serviced warehouses up and down the main line in Tucson and South Tucson all night long."

Straight sections of track called "leads" ran off the main line at a switch point into the Pacific Fruit Express and the North yards. "A dozen tracks might take off from one lead," explained Showalter. "You just 'lined the switch' to the track you needed and the cars would roll down the track." One of the division's most fun switching tasks, the "Shotgun" job, ran three shifts each day, at the west end of

Beloved foreman Sebastian Castillo (back row, center) ran section crews across the division. His son, Elias Sr., and grandson, Elias Jr., both followed him to careers on division section gangs. (Carolina Castillo Butler Collection)

Carolina Castillo glowed as she orchestrated this August 1956 birthday cele-
bration, in front of a section workers' house at Rillito, Arizona. Beginning in
1971, the award-winning Mexican-American community activist, successfully
fought construction of the Orme Dam, which would have forced relocation of
the Ft. McDowell Yavapai Nation. Carolina's family lived in the section house at
Peak, Arizona from 1936 to 1943. Her father, Sebastian Castillo, worked as
section foreman at Picacho 1943 to 1951. (Carolina Castillo Butler Collection)

and throwing it forward. "The engine would charge up the lead full-throttle and a 'pin-puller' would yank the pin from between the correct cars as they went by," said Showalter. "The engine foreman would stop the engineer and those cars would sail right up the track where one of two 'field men' would 'catch' or stop them. Then, the engineer waited for another kick signal. We'd kick cars until the whole train was sorted out."

The daily Shotgun job inspired certain engineers. "Jim Nugent was one of the men who really enjoyed puttin' on a show," Showalter laughed. "He'd put a little extra into it." Nugent confessed: "We'd really get to rockin' and rollin' down there some nights, ha, ha, ha. Those steam engines would get to clangin' and bangin' all over the place. It was a wonder anybody got any sleep at that Coronado Hotel across the street!"

Stopping trains proved a hardy challenge for engineers and switchmen on the Tucson rail yard's grades of almost one percent. The steep slope meant engineers often "bled off," or released, almost all their brake system's air to set the train's brakes. This left very little air in the brake reservoir to hold the cars on the local yard's incline. To prevent cars from rolling, switchmen tied hand brakes, fifteen on the west end and ten on the east end of every train.

Railroad "shanties," or shacks, provided switchmen with space to do their paperwork and escape from nature's

Tucson's North yard. "We worked the Shotgun right in front of the passenger depot and we'd attract quite a crowd to watch us 'kick' cars," Sid boasted good-naturedly. "We'd put on a pretty good show for 'em, especially when a passenger train came into town.

"It was fun to kick cars on the Shotgun," Sid smiled. "You might embellish your kick sign a little bit for the crowd. Some guys acted as if they were conducting a symphony. Sometimes the engineer'd kick 'em a little bit too much, and you'd watch 'em slam together real hard!" Many times, two engines worked the Shotgun together. While one crew readied a cut of cars for dispatch down the designated lead, the other worked cutting cars off the train. The performance began when a switchman or engine foreman gave Sid the "kick sign," by waving his hand in a circle above his head

Julia Peters Newman (left, behind typewriter) arrived in 1943, full of vinegar. When one SP supervisor told her that he wouldn't hire her "because she lacked experience," Julia shot back, "Sir, if you learned it, then I sure can!" and walked out of his office. Another official overheard Julia's retort. "He told me to apply at the freight office and I had a thirty-six year career." Conductor Harlin Marlar remembered, "Julia would always stand in the window, when she was working upstairs, and wave to us as we passed the depot." (Julia Peters Newman Collection)

elements. At the shanty across from the local depot, one regular visitor got more than a little close to the men and earned notoriety among switchmen. "She lived on Ninth Street," Showalter explained. "She was married to a brakeman, and she'd come over to the shanty drunk just about every day." The free-living woman provided regular diversion for local rails, complete with occasional romantic liaisons. "She didn't care if it was the middle of the night or the daytime, she'd come by," chuckled Showalter. "That gal was always good for a little entertainment."

The westbound railroad tracks entered Tucson and split at the Park Avenue shanty. One set of rails headed west, behind the shanty to company shops, the roundhouse, and turntable. The other crossed in front of it and ran northwest to

the coal chute and sand house. Switchmen cut cars off trains a half block east of the Park Avenue crossing and watched them roll downhill. "Twenty-four hours a day, guys would be ridin' on top of cars rollin' down the various tracks," said Showalter. "You would have never been able to stop your cars, if an automobile crossed in front. People who drove the route daily knew to watch out for rail cars. I never saw a single automobile hit in all those years. I'd try to keep my rail cars going slow so that if they hit an automobile they wouldn't hit it very hard."

Switchmen employed the natural grade to send cars west from the North Yard's east end and the Pacific Fruit Express (PFE). "We did the same type switching in the west end of the PFE yard at Twenty-Second Street, but we didn't call it the Shotgun," Showalter said. "The other difference was, if a cut of 'loads' or loaded cars got away from you on a clear track at the top end of PFE's yard you had trouble. They could easily be doin' fifty miles an hour by the time they got to Twenty-Second Street! They had to have a derail device at Cherry Avenue to keep them from going out on the main line."

One switchman acted as a rider on the first car in each cut of cars coming from the east. "The rider cranked the car's hand brake with a brake club to control and stop it," Showalter continued. "He'd set the brakes on several cars and wait there, if his work list called for more cars to go down that track. If not, and he'd walk back to the lead and ride a new cut of cars into another track."

Some switchmen worked as "herders" at the west and east end of the local yard, and at the Cherry Avenue derail. "When I started in 1951, all the Cherry Avenue herder had to do was line the derail so westbound trains could get out of the yard," said Showalter. "It was a pretty boring job." One young man, who worked at Cherry Avenue, brought his pajamas to work. "He'd curl up and go to sleep each night," chuckled Showalter. "The railroad paid the herder for one hour less work than the switch crew because he didn't have to couple and uncouple the train's air hoses. They called the coupling a "glad hand" because it worked so smoothly and if you worked that job you'd write "claiming cannonball" on your time sheet to get your extra hour's pay."

Emotion filled conductor Gordon Manning one sultry, end-of-summer day, sixty-two years after he started on the Tucson Division. Proud of his years as a railroad man, delighted in his role as a Tucsonan and Wildcat fan, and honored to re-enact his part during the thriving days of steam engines, Manning reflected. Then, Tucson's handsome, silver-haired rail general "called his train" one final time, following the dedication of Locomotive No. 1673

at the Tucson depot during 2003. Gold star denoting his qualification to run streamlined passenger trains sparkling on his left sleeve, Manning belted forth, "The Sunset Limited with stops at Picacho, Casa Grande, and Phoenix. All aboard! All aboard! Porters pick up your step boxes and close your vestibule doors." Captured on tape by KUAT-TV, for one brilliant moment the glory days of streamline passenger service came swimming back to life in Tucson—a southwestern railroad town. Then, using his antique marker lamp, Gordon gave Tucson's steam days their final "highball," signaling the engineer, and time itself, to proceed.

Gordon Manning (Kalt Collection)

Chapter 15

On the Ground in the Tucson Division: Seniority, Nepotism, and Racist Realities

"Mommy, what happened to Daddy?" young Edith Sayre asked. She'd seen the bruises before and wondered. Now she had to know. "They beat him up," her mother answered softly. "They don't like Mexicans working as firemen at the Southern Pacific Railroad (SP). He was walking to his car by himself, and some union firemen beat him." William Frank Sayre "loved to box" said his daughter, Edith Sayre Auslander, now vice president and senior associate to the president of the University of Arizona. "He was a Golden Gloves contender when he was young, so there must have been several of them."

Sayre's Tucson High School High School classmate Gilbert L. Salsbury had played it smart in June of 1941. Gilbert kept his mother Guadalupe Alvarez's Mexican heritage to himself when he hired on as a division fireman. He knew the score in Tucson and his last name divulged no connection to her roots. He could do his job as well or better than any man and none need know

William and Artemisa Castelan Sayre found a comfortable arbor for this 1937 photograph. As a boy, Guillermo climbed barefoot up Sentinel Peak ("A" Mountain), lunching on mesquite beans and volvena bulbs, or stealing carrots from the truck farmers along El Rio Santa Cruz. Edith Sayre Auslander remembered, "Being a railroad man's daughter, you'd plan a picnic at Sabino Canyon and my dad would call in and check the board before we headed out. They'd say, 'That board's moving.' Trains would come in so we couldn't go on our outing. I remember being disappointed about that with railroading. Mother was a very spiritual woman and would always say, "Don't complain, it's your father's job." (Edith Sayre Auslander Collection)

his background. Salsbury ran his first main line locomotive in 1945 and enjoyed an outstanding 42-year career.

Blond and blue-eyed, with a grin from here to Mexico, Bill Sayre never could hide his *sangre Mexicano* (Mexican blood). He wore it as a badge of honor. His American father and Mexican mother had nurtured him in the Mexican culture, and Guillermo spoke only Spanish until he started school. Throughout his life he identified most closely with his rich Mexican legacy. "Everyone knew Dad was Mexican, though he didn't look it," Edith said. "It didn't take very long for people to know his heritage. My father spoke Spanish and English and was very proud of being Hispanic. If he saw a Hispanic person, he spoke Spanish to them."

William called Tucson his hometown. "He was a very lost child," Edith explained. "Dad was born in Patagonia in 1914, but his mother died when he was five, and my father moved to Tucson. He didn't have a stepmother until his late teens so Dad grew up kinda wild. One of his teachers, Edith Cowan, took an interest in him and helped him get on track. That's why my name is Edith." Spending long summer days climbing barefoot up Sentinel Peak ("A" Mountain) with friends, Sayre grew up "doing what boys did," he recalled in a 1984 *Star* article. *Éste era*

Gilbert L Salsbury sits aboard Locomotive No. 2587 at Globe, Arizona in 1943. The quiet, history-loving engineer provided support to Mexican and African-American workers, as they entered the labor force during the 1970s. (Gilbert L. Salsbury Collection)

su tierra (This was his land), and he resolved to make good. Young Sayre scrambled for money where he could find it, sometimes walking from Barrio Libre to caddy at Randolph Golf Course. Bill's vision of becoming a sportswriter crumbled under a barrage of his own wordiness but he played baseball and football at Tucson High School.

Concluding that a pharmacist's career might serve him well, but lacking money for college, he took a job at Martin's Drug. On the southeast corner of Congress and Church streets, William Sayre's resolute determination met Andrew Martin's principled convictions. The friendship would shatter local "glass ceilings" and establish a precursor to federally mandated equable hiring practices. "Dad found a real happy home at Martin's Drug," said Auslander. "He was a 'soda jerk' and once served Betty Grable and her musical beau, Artie Shaw. Dad loved it there."

Mexican men had worked as hostlers, moving engines around in the yard and roundhouse, as early as 1905. By 1932, six Hispanic surnamed men worked the nine-member local hostling crew. Yet, ten years later, no man had declared his Mexican heritage and run a locomotive on the main line! Spanish-American Democratic Club member Raul Samaniego remembered, "During World War II, the club worked to get something done about getting more Mexicans on the SP payroll as enginemen and switchmen. The SP hired two

'thick-skinned' young men from the Leon family, but co-workers soon harassed them into quitting."

One of Barrio Libre's toughest young men also sought a hoghead's seat on the Tucson Division. "Dad went to the railroad because he thought it would be a good long-term career," Auslander recalled. "They told him they only hired Mexicans to be yardmen, but never to work in the cab as a fireman." William approached his former boss Andrew Martin, seeking help in getting past the long-standing prejudice in railroad engine service. Amiable eighty-year-old A. Martin "Marty" Ronstadt, worked stocking liquor the day Sayre walked into his granduncle's drug store. "I remember that conversation well," Ronstadt said. "Edith's dad came in while I was unloading booze and putting it in this wire cage. He talked to Uncle Andy about getting a job with the Southern Pacific Railroad and the discrimination against Hispanics. Mexicans could only work in the roundhouse or at Pacific Fruit Express, but weren't allowed on the train. That was demeaning."

During World War II, Sayre worked for Baum and Adamson Tire Company, but military needs cut rubber supplies and slowed the tire industry. Local Democratic kingpin Andy Martin's influence eventually held sway and, encouraged by his good friend SP car repairman Eddie A. Caballero, William began firing steam locomotives in March 1942. "My father always said it was Andy Martin who got him his job at the SP," remembered Edith. "Those union guys could really muster the troops."

Pacific System assistant vice-president of labor relations Carl A. Ball Jr. explained. "I grew up in Tucson's Barrio Millville, south of the railroad reserve. It was a big hodgepodge of cultures and many of our neighbors were Mexican," he said. "But, when I started at the railroad in 1937, there were still no Mexican men in engine or train service. Not a single fireman, engineer, brakeman, or conductor. Mexicans did all the ground work." Ball elaborated: "There was this unwritten rule that they didn't hire any Mexicans. It was pretty much local to the seniority group down here in Tucson. Without ever saying a word, the union's seniority group put pressure on the company not to hire Mexicans." The same held true for Chinese and African-American men. "A few Mexican men worked mainline engine service on the Los Angeles Division but that didn't get over into Tucson," he continued. "There were times when there was a feeling or undercurrent of unrest among the local Mexican men, but it never got out into the open and became a hard problem. Finally, we had one young man name Willie Sayre that made it as a fireman." William's son, Federico Castelan Sayre, remembered: "At first, they'd try to catch him individually off work or in darkened parts of the yard. They didn't realize my father was a street fighter and a trained professional boxer." Good men such as T.O. "Oakie" Baker and Constant "Connie" Weinzapfel stepped forward. "They didn't like what was going on, so they and some of their friends started escorting my dad to the parking lot nightly," he said. "The cowards ran from them and my father kept his job."

Willie Sayre came to love the physically demanding and dangerous job of firing steam engines. "Things simmered down over time," Edith explained. "My dad was enormously proud to be a member of the railroad. He made his runs to Lordsburg and always stayed so true to the rules. He was so proud to be a member of the Brotherhood of Locomotive Firemen and Engineers." Her father encountered one nasty problem as a fireman: "He had beautiful eyebrows that my mother just loved. One time, he was working on a steam engine and got blasted by fire. He had a really bad

Carl Ball Jr. (Carl A. Ball Collection)

burn, particularly his on forehead. It singed off all of his eyebrows and my mother always lamented the fact that they came back in all bushy and big. Luckily, the doctor had just prescribed him glasses. My mother, who was a very spiritual person, always said that the grace of God saved my father's eyesight because he wore those glasses. She was sure it was God reaching down."

Sayre earned promotion to engineer in 1954. His vivacious spirit and friendly nature earned him the respect of his colleagues. Former road foreman of engines Harlan "Hard Rock" Payne recalled, "Sayre was a very nice, jolly man, always friendly. He was a good family man and had a good reputation." A strong union supporter, Bill Sayre served the SP, the Mexican people, and himself *con orgullo* (with pride) for thirty-eight years. Following retirement, Sayre achieved notoriety for his volunteer work in local schools and his superb physical conditioning. In 1984, the notable local character could often be seen cruising Tucson streets on his bicycle. During June 2006, local rail Rudy Benitez spoke of the outgoing kid from Barrio Libre: "He opened a door when no one else had been able to. William Sayre's name evokes pride among rails of Mexican descent in this part of the country."

Three powerful forces worked to control SP employment practices on the Tucson Division. Seniority controlled when the next man worked on any given day; nepotism primed the pump as railroad employees cleared a path to employment for relatives; and racism barred the door to minority workers in several rail services. Each SP employee established a seniority date on the day he began work. For the duration of his career, every employee knew the company would call him to work after calling all the names on the list ahead of his and before all those names below his. If a man went into military service during wartime, he usually retained his original seniority date when he returned.

Because the company trusted their fathers, many young men from rail families found apprenticing at the SP simply a matter of applying for work during peak business periods. When the railroad needed workers, they sent notices home with their employees,

Born in 1857, Ed Lundquist (above), began as a watchman on a Colorado railroad in the 1880s and led a lengthy parade of Lundquist railroaders. Ed's son Harry followed him to the railroad, as did his grandson, division engineer George "Boots" Lundquist. (George Lundquist Collection)

saying, "Good jobs available. Send your sons to the local yard office." Former SP electrician Frank Hutcheson recalled, "I had cousins and uncles and nephews; they all worked for the railroad. Railroad was a family business. In fact, you couldn't get a job on the railroad until World War II unless you were a relative. I mean you couldn't get a job as a track layer without relatives." Long-time division hoghead Floyd Roberts added, "The railroads liked nepotism. One reason was, if my dad worked on the railroad then I knew he worked Christmas, New Year's, he worked nights, and he worked days. If I wanted to work on the railroad, I knew what I was gonna get in for. That's why they went from father to son."

Hiring family members proved good business for the railroad. Oril O. Hutcheson made his conductor's date on the Tucson Division in 1915 and lived "railroad all the way." His son Frank recalled, "You know, like a policeman's son wants to be a policeman, the son of a fireman wants

Tom Kerby (left) fired for his father, engineer J.R. Kerby (right), when the proud pair posed before train No. 40's engine, No. 6436, in Phoenix during the early 1960s. (Tom Kerby Collection)

to be a fireman; I was the son of a railroad man and I was fascinated by that." The elder Hutcheson pushed his son toward the University of Arizona, hoping he might choose a different path. Frank discovered the depth of his father's desire when he "bombed out" of school and went to work at the SP full-time. "My dad went to the general foreman," said Frank. "He told him, 'Give the kid the worst damn job around here. I want him to quit and go back to school.'" On his first day as a laborer on the Tucson "rip," or repair track, a supervisor assigned Hutcheson and another fellow to empty fifty tons of slag from a ballast car. Fresh from "running around in a fraternity at the U of A, drinking, chasing girls, and staying up all night," Frank found

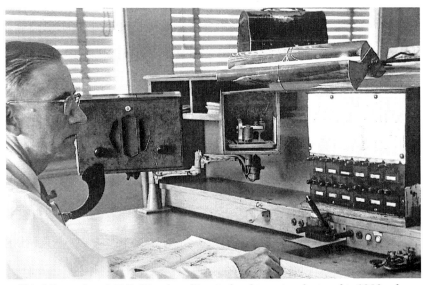

Chief dispatcher A.F. DeHart kept his mind on his trains during this 1950s photograph. DeHart retired in 1963 after 46 years of service and lived 100 years. (Robert and Louise DeHart Collection)

that "within two hours I couldn't bend over or stand up straight. I had blisters all over my hands. Like an idiot I forgot to bring gloves." Ever harassing superiors for advancement, Frank Hutcheson served the SP as an electrician until 1957.

The nepotism practiced by the SP stands illegal in the twenty-first century. "Along came the new generation and said, 'Hey, we're not getting a chance to get on the railroad,'" Roberts explained. "They said there was too much nepotism so they put a stop to it. My dad and my wife's dad were railroaders. We were all railroaders, and I'd like to get my grandson on the railroad, but I don't know anybody who can get him work."

Jim "Nuge" Nugent's father, John Michael Nugent, came to Arizona in 1898, after serving in the Spanish-American War. "His brother, Gleason, was already here working as a locomotive engineer," Jim explained. "Dad took work as a signal maintainer. He was responsible for insuring that the signals worked properly. They were semaphore signals with a paddle on top. Horizontal was 'stop' and vertical was 'go.' It was a very important job for safety."

Bob DeHart joined his father in the Tucson dispatcher's office and they worked together for over twenty years. SP frugality is credited with ending the common practice of beginning letters with, "in receipt of yours of the 12th instant" and other pleasantries. One 1915 company directive dictated: "Effective at once, please instruct that the phrases 'Will you please,' and 'Will you kindly,' be eliminated from Company and Western Union in-house telegrams." (Robert and Louise DeHart Collection)

Jim worked steam locomotives for forty years. "My parents moved around a lot, to Gila Bend, to San Simon. But, they had a real house in Willcox," he said. "Signal maintainer wasn't much of job. One

Jim Nugent's father, signalman John M. Nugent (back row, far left), represented Pima County in Arizona's Eleventh Legislature. Former Tucson SP accountant Joseph M. Peggs (seventh from right in the third row) represented Mohave County. (Kalt Collection)

hundred dollars a month was not real good pay. With five kids, we never had enough money to blow any frivolously." The low-paying rail job meant plenty of money-saving schemes. "My mother made her own bread, cookies, pies," Jim said. "We ate codfishes that came in wooden boxes. It was really just dried mackerel, but we loved it. My mom would soak it to get the salt out of it. Granddad always saved the bones and ate them like candy." The Nugent family returned to Tucson in 1921, when Jim's father left the railroad to open the Palms Café with his brother Gleason's wife Nora.

A railroader's kid could find good times in Tucson during the early 1920s. "We had plenty to do," Nugent recalled. "We'd walk to Colossal Cave from downtown carrying a rifle and some bacon. We'd be gone for six or seven days at a time. On railroad paydays, we'd go down on Congress Street and watch the people. It was part of our lives." Most rails cashed their checks at Penney's and Myerson's Whitehouse department stores. "Papago (Tohono O'odham) Indians walked through town hawking their firewood, yelling, 'Leña! Leña!'" said Nugent. "It was a very

different Tucson back then. Later on, I got my first charge account at Myerson's Whitehouse department store. I knew Joe and Hymie Myerson real well."

When the Palms Café went broke, Jim's father returned to work at the railroad. "My father served in the Eleventh Arizona Legislature in 1932-1933," Nugent continued. "He moved into the signal tower in about 1934-1935. Then he operated switches electrically. Dad didn't like the job. He said he'd rather operate switches by hand." Jim Nugent's long career as an engineer reflected the man's good-hearted nature. "Nugent, why he's a hell of a guy," said fellow engineer Roberts. "You could always count on him for a good story, a warm handshake, and a quick train."

Generation after generation, Tucson's young men followed their relatives into rail service. During November of 1949, the *Star* featured the Donald McIntyre family. Led by the elder Donald McIntyre, who began with the SP at El Paso in 1882, five family members had worked 180 years of combined SP service. One son, conductor Douglas McIntyre, began continuous employment in 1906, and another, Albert,

started in 1908. Three
generations lived in
the "old McIntyre
home" in Yuma, occu-
pied by members of the
family since 1884.
Douglas's brother,
Donald McIntyre, first
came to Tucson in
1909, to work in the
railroad stores depart-
ment. "I've never
drawn a paycheck from
any company but the
Southern Pacific," the
local master car re-
pairman recalled forty
years later. "I was thir-
teen years old as a wa-
ter boy with an extra
gang at Yuma. My next
job was call boy, and
then I became a helper in the
car department." During
March 2006, McIntyre's
granddaughter Lee Goerke
echoed her family's pride in its
Arizona rail heritage, "Tucson
was a railroad town, back then,
and we were very proud of
Papa. All his men loved him
and looked up to him."

Rails developed a cama-
raderie and brotherhood that
transcended their jobs. "There
was a railroad clique in Tucson, I'm sure, in the twenties
and thirties," remembered
Frank Hutcheson. "There was
still strong evidence [of it] even
after World War II. There was
not a big turnover. Second-,
third-generation people were-
n't uncommon at all. Everybody knew everybody else. It was almost a family-type
thing. The job itself was almost a family.
Oh, a sense of belonging is a word I would
use."

Prior to the Gadsden Purchase,

*Tucson master car repairman Donald McIntyre (standing third from right) re-
tired in 1955, with his grandaughter Lee Goerke, at center stage. Car repairer
Eddie Caballero sits at the front left. (Donald McIntyre Collection)*

*Local engineers Carl Ball Sr. (second from left) and R.W. Beene (third
from left) enjoyed a family-like friendship with their rail brethren.
(Elgin Ball Collection)*

when the United States bought the region
south of the Gila River in 1854, this land belonged to Mexico. In his *Del Rancho al Barrio*, Dr. Thomas E. Sheridan declared: "The
railroad brought Tucson's frontier days to
an end. It also destroyed the economic and

political foundations of the town's bi-ethnic, bi-cultural elite."

A large middle class Mexican-American community thrived in Tucson during the 1860s and 1870s. Entrepreneurs and community leaders enjoyed a status parallel to that of "Americans," as local newspapers referred to whites, *norteños*, or Anglos, until well after the railroad's arrival in 1880. Mexican males continued to play prominent roles in Tucson politics during 1903, filling ten of Tucson's Democratic Committee's thirty-three slots and two seats on the central committee. Praise and respect often filled local news stories. "It is an undisputed fact that Mexican people are a music loving people and their artists are as a rule the very best trained," sang the *Citizen* in May 1898. "A thing of beauty," gushed the same paper over one *Dieciséis de Septiembre* Independence Day celebration. "A picturesque display of Mexican citizenship in Tucson."

By the beginning of the twentieth century, however, dual social structures had developed around racial, geographic, and cultural heritage. Interdependence that characterized relations between "Americans" and Mexicans gave way to racial isolation and growing disparity.

A series of incidents likely contributed to the growing rift between cultures. Reports of Spanish sympathizers in Nogales during the Spanish-American War sparked distrust. In October 1898, Mexican police incarcerated *SP de Mexico* conductor H.J. Temple for a railroad accident, aggravating already strained relations. That same month, Mexican guards arrested, shot, and killed James Ryan at Naco, Sonora and left his body "to lie in the boiling sun." Border "cowboys," the rough group of men who rode southern Arizona ranges and never dodged trouble, began "feeling ugly" and threatened the guards. Both the U.S. and Mexican governments used troops to limit violence. Then, in September 1899, a famous Mexican band destroyed its local reputation when three of its members went

on a "fighting jag" at Eve Blanchard's Gay Alley establishment. When Blanchard locked the door, the nasty trio forced their way inside, drank *mucho* mescal, and "held high carnival," the *Star* said. During May 1906, calling it "The Peon Scourge," the *Star* reported that 27,000 Mexican people had entered the United States, further increasing American animosity toward their southern neighbors.

Episodes such as these fueled a growing fracture between Tucson's largest two cultural groups. In addition, stories of outrageous debauchery and violence occasionally flew from Barrio Libre in Tucson's southwest section. One elderly Anglo described the area: "It was the wild part of town. There were Mexicans and Indians, but there were some tough Americans living there too. That district was free; it was completely wide open. Anything could happen down there."

"Most *Tucsonenses* lived sober, industrious lives, building their homes and raising their families in relatively stable and peaceful surroundings," said Sheridan. "To them the term barrio was positive rather than negative, embodying solidarity and ethnic pride. Mexican culture flourished, and bonds of kinship, neighborliness, and *compadrazgo* (god-parent relationship) enabled families to survive economic depressions and the growing economic dualism of Tucson society." Barrios "were places of refuge and vitality," added Sheridan.

"As early as 1860...Tucson's Hispanic work force was clustered in blue-collar occupations—carpenters, blacksmiths, freighters, cooks, laborers, and washer women," Sheridan affirmed. "Most *Tucsonenses* lived and worked in a blue-collar world...with Mexicans, by and large at the bottom, and Anglos on top." He pointed to an unrelenting northward flow of Mexican immigrants, class divisions among the Mexican community, disorganization within the Mexican labor movement, and outright bigotry as the foundation for embedding this imbalanced paradigm.

Discrimination that arose out of language and educational disadvantages became common in Tucson and throughout the Southwest. "This institutionalized subordination of Mexicans in Tucson was not a conscious conspiracy masterminded by the members of the Old Pueblo Club or the officers of the of the Southern Pacific," Sheridan explained. "Rather, it was often a complex, often contradictory historical process involving subtle demographic, economic, political, and psychological variables."

Citizens began emphasizing their differences rather than commonalities. Magnified through each retelling, stereotypes in both camps widened the social gap between the two cultures. The growing American throng accorded Mexican people second-class status and held the power to discriminate in hiring, housing, and recreational opportunities. Mexican citizens first organized a *Mutualista* to combat discrimination in 1894. The *Alianza Hispano Americana* incorporated December 5, 1902, "to unite fraternally" and "give moral and material support" to the Mexican community. The group also promoted education and established a fund for sick members and widows. In 1907, the *Sociedad Mutualista Porfirio Diaz* formed in Tucson to protect and promote Mexican business. H.V. Anaya served as supreme president and F. Portillo as vice president.

Bias found inroads, however. In 1919, several respected Mexican-American families fought Paramount Pictures for showing an anti-Mexican movie at the Tucson Opera House. Protesters declared that the film degraded the "long-suffering Mexican community" by depicting Mexicans as lazy cowards, thieves, and murderers. The issue surfaced again when the short-lived Pima Theater screened *El Automóvil Gris* (The Gray Automobile) in 1922. Filmed by local artists in Mexico, the eagerly awaited movie created profound disgust in Tucson's

Mexican community. Local Spanish-language newspaper, *El Mosquito*, called it, "*una cosa que no nos honra en mucho por cierto*" (a thing that does not honor us much, by the way). The paper dubbed local Chamber of Commerce ex-secretary Orville S. "Speedy" McPherson "*el anti-Mexicano*," because he attacked *El Mosquito* as *nocivo al comercio* (harmful to business). That same week Paramount Pictures promised Mexican president Alvaro Obregón to stop making movies "*que pudieron de algún modo lastimar a México*" (that could hurt Mexico in any manner). The Lyric Theater soon showed the debasing *Un Puerto Mexicano del Pacifico* courtesy of "*la hipocrita y artera Compania de Vistas Paramount*" (the hypocritical and cunning company of Paramount Pictures).

Life had its lighter moments for Eddie Mendoza and Freddy Castillo at the section house in the small rail community of Picacho in 1950. Edith Sayre Auslander, vice president and senior associate to the president of the University of Arizona remembered, "President Peter Likins told me, 'When you move here you realize very quickly if you are going to be part of the culture, you need to join into the Hispanic culture that exists.'" (Carolina Castillo Butler)

Tucson's Sociedad Mutualista Porfirio Diaz organized to protect and promote Mexican businesses in 1907. SP accountant J.W. "Buch" Buchanan hired the first Mexican-American worker in Pima County government after voters elected him county treasurer in the 1930s. General shop foreman Phil Garigan (far left), master car repairman Donald McIntyre (front row, fourth from left), and carman Eddie Caballero (far right) demonstrated their support for the Socieadad in 1955. (Eddie Caballero Collection)

Though stories of prejudice rarely drew ink in the pages of Tucson's *Star* and *Citizen* newspapers during the steam era, two 1936 incidents did. The Spanish-American Democratic Club had formed to counter entrenched racism in the city. Club members discovered that the Tucson employment office kept two separate lists of prospective workers, one for Americans and another for Mexicans. Ed Herreras and others took their outrage to Isabella Greenway, then Democratic National Committeeman, who succeeded in having the responsible Tucson employment office official fired.

Mexican parents accounted for 54 percent of the births in Pima County in 1935. Late the following August, Tucsonan Joe M. Lovio called attention to a racially motivated firing, in the *Star's* Voice of the People. Mr. Moore, new manager at the local Kress store, dismissed "without notice or explanation" nine-year employee Carmen Muñoz, said Lovio. The previous Kress manager had not sacked an employee for a long period. Moore, however, fired Muñoz on the evening she should have received $39 for her annual two-week vacation. Six-year workers Mary Avanzino and Lola Flores soon got the shoe from *el gerente nuevo* (the new manager), followed by Lupe Castano, Hortencia Zepeda, and *el joven* (young man) Raimundo Reina. "For the past five or six years, they had been doing their duty of taking care of the Mexican trade," Lovio explained. Mr. Moore quickly replaced the fired employees with American girls, confirming that "the present agent does not want much of the Mexican trade in his store."

Discrimination ruled the financial world of Mexican families and businessmen. Most faced invisible barriers to loans. When Roy Laos sought to upgrade his Occidental Bus Line equipment, which had been over-worked during World War II, he could not secure a loan. "Roy talked to Emery Johnson who agreed to become his partner and they got the loan," said Edith Sayre Auslander. "It's a fact!" The pair bought ten new buses over the next three years and the line endures today as part of the city-owned Sun Tran bus services.

Bias held forth in Tucson streets, as well. Filled with rail families, the Armory Park neighborhood reflected racial multiplicity, but residents lived along clearly defined lines. Native Tucsonan Frank Hutcheson explained: "The white people lived along the main streets, Third, Fourth, and Fifth avenues, and the cross streets, Twelfth, Thirteenth, Fourteenth, and Fifteenth streets. The laborers and lower-paid people who worked for the railroad were usually of Hispanic origin and lived in the alleys behind the other railroad people. The alleys were paved in the late forties. There was definite segregation as far as work and as far as housing were concerned."

Another powerful force in Tucson's cultural mix, the Chinese people, faced callous racial abuse across the United States during the early twentieth century. Enduring bitter epithets, such as "slant-eye celestials of the washee-washee proclivity," Chinese immigrants first visited Tucson during the 1860s. When three members of the Wong family opened the OK Restaurant at the corner of Church Plaza and Mesilla Street in 1870, it signaled the beginning of a more permanent Chinese community. Low Tai You began the first Chinese vegetable garden north of Congress Street in Levin's field, east of the Santa Cruz River, in 1878. Santa Cruz bottomlands owned by Sam Hughes, Leopoldo Carrillo, Solomon Warner, and the Sisters of St. Joseph provided excellent soil for skilled Chinese farmers. Despite frequent disputes with Mexican citizens over water rights, Chinese farmers cultivated more than one hundred acres along the river. "The wagon loads of fine vegetables which the Chinamen [sic] bring in daily are positive evidence of their industry and skill," the *Citizen* noted. "As a nation they are not great fighters but as agriculturalists they are a success, demonstrated in many parts of the world." By the time the SP reached Tucson in 1880, 850 Chinese laborers received half the wage of their American counterparts working for the railroad in Pima County; 50¢ for an eleven-hour day. Some suggested that such willingness to work hard for so little pay contributed to American's growing prejudice against Chinese people.

The United States Exclusion Act of 1882 prohibited Chinese laborers from immigrating to work in mining and other unskilled jobs. The law allowed diplomats, students, and merchants into the country, as well as those related by blood to current U.S. citizens. Chinese-Americans began identifying friends and children of friends as family members, creating countless "Paper Sons and Daughters" who entered the United States. Tales of bribery and deprivation surrounded its enforcement, but the Act served to strengthen local Chinese self-sufficiency and solidarity.

Arizona passed a law criminalizing Chinese competition for American mining and unskilled labor jobs in 1890. Only low-paying jobs such as wiping down locomotives remained open to Chinese railroad workers. Chinese men found themselves at the bottom of a narrow-minded economic and social ladder. Tucson's Ying On Association (called a tong by "Americans") formed during 1890, in a drab, gray building on Main Avenue between Broadway Boulevard and Ochoa Street. The group vowed to protect its members against discriminatory business practices and provide housing and social opportunities for Chinese people. Tucson's original Chinese section, centered about Pearl Street at the west end of Pen-

Chinese emigrants needed documents like Lee Aht's 1920 papers. One early Chinese ritual produced an annual feast of roast pig, rice, and other food. Celebrants carried the delicacies in procession to the graves of loved ones and left them for their enjoyment. Sadly, hobos and "the unregenerate living" had discovered the banquet by the beginning of the twentieth century, forcing Chinese people to alter their ceremony. (Raymond and Louise Lee Collection)

nington Street, lay traditionally quiet before noon. Then, as each day blossomed, the area's joss house (house of worship), few grocery stores, and several laundries bustled with a vibrancy that evoked images of the larger Chinese community in San Francisco.

An enigma to the "American" population, Chinese culture flourished. The 1880 U.S. census showed 158 Chinese men and just two women living in Tucson. Two-thirds described themselves as self-employed. By 1900, 224

Religious faith and strong cultural bonds kept the Chinese community together in Tucson. "The Chinese community was jubilant when the first Chinese boy, Don S. Hoy, graduated from high school," recalled a 1937 Chinese Digest, *two decades later. (Raymond and Louise Lee Collection)*

Chinese people lived in the city and several Chinese women worked as overseers for wealthy Tucsonans such as Leopoldo Carrillo. Then, the United States closed the Mexican border to keep Chinese immigrants out. In 1901, authorities shipped "forbidden" Chinese to Lordsburg, New Mexico. The following May, Tucson's laun-

drymen formed the Chinese Laundry Protection Association. The group established a uniform scale of prices and blacklisted any customers who beat one of their members out of the bill, or complained about poor service.

Chinese rail workers took the hindquarter when paychecks arrived at the SP

Sino-American clubs provided brotherhood, competition, and socializing opportunities for young Chinese men and women. This basketball team ran local courts in 1947-48. (Raymond and Louise Lee Collection)

roundhouse in May of 1909. Chief clerk J.B. Ritter sat at a window distributing checks, while a "megaphone man" called out employees' names in alphabetical order. The caller decided to cut out the "wipers" because he could not pronounce Chinese names. The move forced these men to wait until everyone else had been paid and clerk Ritter could do the honors.

Construction of the Tucson Women's Club, on the northwest corner of Main Avenue and Alameda Street, destroyed much of the city's original Chinese area in 1910. Tucson's Chinese community re-developed around Gin Lung, Gin Gong, and Yee Teung's long-standing OK Restaurant. In the heart of the Mexican business community, the eatery anchored four blocks of Chinese businesses along south Meyer Street and Main Avenue. Dominated by laundries before the Pearl Street demolition, the local Chinese area featured ten restaurants and sixty grocery stores by 1920. Until then, Chinese culture thrived

in colorful festivities that filled the area's Chee Kong Ton (Chinese Free Masons) building, but a gradual shift out of the area by Chinese businessmen brought the heyday to a close.

Equanimity under the law demanded Chinese cash in post-frontier southern Arizona. Housed in a building on south Meyer Street, the Chinese Chamber of Commerce formed to protect Chinese legal and economic interests in 1920. That year, the cold-blooded murder of a local grocer named Lee galvanized the Chinese people. Leaders called a meeting of the entire community and attorney Louis G. Hummel proposed a reward fund to grease the wheels of justice. Chinese citizens raised $2,000 and the perpetrator soon sat behind bars. The incident marked a turning point in local Chinese political strategy. A perpetual reward fund grew, with the stipulation that the money go to the victim's family if authorities did not apprehend a criminal. The Chamber named Louis Hummel permanent legal counsel, and the skilled lawyer defended Chinese Tucsonans for the next twenty years. Hatred roamed Tucson in the 1940s because of Chinese self-sufficiency, said Tucson *Doña* Esther Don Tang. Tang reported that the day after her parents made a down payment on a house in the central-city Belmont neighborhood, a disgruntled neighbor wrote, "No Chinks Wanted" in letter 12 to 14 inches tall on the wall. The family chose not to live where neighbors did not welcome them.

James A. Barnes's father, J.C. Barnes, and his uncle, Hamblin McNeil, came west in 1922. Being part of a railroad family paid off for young James when he began as a laborer at the roundhouse in 1946. Bright eyes dancing, the eighty-six-year-old chuckled: "My dad was pretty well known around the roundhouse and, when I started as a laborer, the foreman set it up so that I started on the Fourth of July. My first shift paid me double-time-and-a-half!" James enjoyed a long career on the local division. (Kalt Collection)

James A. Barnes (left) holds his son James Fredrick, while his wife Freddie Ella cradles daughter Jacqueline ca. 1952. The family remains a proud member of Tucson's African-American community. (James A. Barnes Collection)

Chinese people overcame Tucson's early bigotry, earning respect for their intelligence and industry from the Americans. Vestiges of the 1882 Exclusion Act lingered until 1943, when President Franklin Roosevelt reversed course due to the U.S. alliance with China during World War II.

Racial bias toward African-Americans, called Negroes during the steam age, manifest itself in institutionalized discrimination, supported across the nation by the laws of the day. None of the wicked lynching or cross burning that plagued the South afflicted Tucson, but socio-economic-educational equality remained elusive. The emergence of George M. Pullman's sleeping-car factory gave the Negro community a rallying point around which improved education and political organization grew. The heart of Pullman, Illinois, the plant built its first commercial sleeping car in 1864. Pullman hired ex-slaves to do his customers' bidding, relying on the subservience of the darkest colored Negro men as they broke free from long-conditioned bonds. Ever "smilin' through" request and abuse, porters provided "very particular" passengers with everything from clean linen, to shined shoes, baby-delivery services, and discretion as to who slipped into whose sleeping berth during a long and rambling railroad night. Pullman crews worked non-stop from San Francisco to Washington while "hot-bedding," or sharing the same bed, with fellow workers as they rotated shifts. All in exchange for a small wage and a "tip," meant "To Insure Promptness."

San Francisco's Pullman porters premiered in gold-buttoned white coats during mid-March 1901. The company announced: "Their duties will be to assist passengers in every way possible, directing them to proper trains, boats, entrances, etc., helping ladies and children without escorts on and off trains, and showing attention to the traveling public as will tend to make them a popular feature of the Southern Pacific service." Tips fell off dramatically in 1901, and the following January, Morris Burroughs, John Williams, and Spencer Corbin incorporated the Colored Men's Railway Mercantile in Chicago.

In early June 1909, Gillie Scott, the regular porter on SP's No. 8 tourist car from Los Angeles to El Paso, stopped in Tucson. Eight gold bands on his coat sleeve testified to Scott's forty years of Pullman service. The aged porter declared that he still served George Pullman in heaven, though he had been dead for several years. "I am sure he has joined Abe Lincoln," proclaimed Scott.

Pullman's sound business plan perpetuated social pigeonholing of Negro people and hampered their upward mobility. Indicative of their dehumanized role, passengers called all porters "George," many believed after the company's founder. Yet, the steady work provided tremendous opportunities for Negro males. While most Negro travelers journeyed no farther than nearby towns, porters returned from the railroad with tales of big city pizzazz and far-away adventure. In his *Rising from the Rail*, Larry Tye explained that these men held high status in the Negro community because they worked steady jobs and earned good money relative to other Afro-Americans. Grabbing daily newspapers and current magazines left behind by passengers, porters read and discussed the black man's future and other ideas in "Belly Stove Clubs." Leading their community's push toward literacy, Pullman porters represented a significant percentage of black property owners through the steam age.

A. Philip Randolph battled incredible attacks to form The International Brotherhood of Sleeping Car Porters in August 1925, under the motto "Service Not Servitude." When Randolph's brotherhood canceled a strike during March of 1928, half of its membership quit. Struggling to survive, the porters' union took a new approach in 1934, initiating one hundred legal actions against the railroads. President Harry S. Truman's executive Order No. 9981 integrated the Army in 1948 and initiated a marked change in race relations. The porters' union merged with the AFL-CIO in 1955, and president George Meany named Randolph to the mega-union's executive council. Randolph's perseverance provided the intellectual and political basis for the Negro Civil Rights movement led by Dr. Martin Luther King during the 1950s and 1960s.

Regardless of their heritage, early Tucsonans had to make their own fun in the isolated Old Pueblo. "Whatever you had [for recreation] when this town was small was a tremendous pleasure," sportswriter Abe Chanin recalled. "In Tucson, you learned young to entertain yourself and make do with what you had." Negro Tucsonans faced additional problems. Passengers sat in separate waiting rooms at the Tucson depot. If they stayed in town, Negro men and women found some of the same exclusions in restaurants and accommodations that they encountered in towns across the Pacific system.

James Barnes remembered that no restrictions existed on lunch-counter seating when he arrived in Tucson during 1935. However, at Mission Pool on the corner of Ajo Way and Mission Road, and Wetmore Pool, near where developers opened the Tucson Mall in 1982, common practice relegated blacks to swimming only on the night before workers drained the pool . "They didn't want anybody swimmin' in that 'dirty' water," Barnes said. "Finally they opened the pool at Estevan Park. That was 'our' pool."

Though few "Americans" seemed aware, Barnes recalled: "In all the theaters, the Lyric, the Rialto, the Fox, blacks had to sit in the balcony. There'd be a woman at the base of the steps, and you'd know to go upstairs." Raymond Lee, honored member of Tucson's Chinese community, remembered, "If it hadn't of been for my good friend Leland Brown, I never would have known that such discrimination existed in Tucson. Leland always told me that he just liked sitting upstairs. Well, one day I went upstairs in the movie house. Then, I realized that all the black kids were sitting up there."

People in Tucson's Negro community did not despair. "We didn't think about segregation back then," said Olivia G. Smith in Rudy Casillas's 1999 KUAT-TV production, *Tucson Memories*. "That's just the way it was." A member of Dunbar School's last segregated class in 1950, Smith explained: "We had our role models. The great singer Marian Anderson and poet Langston Hughes came to speak to us at Dunbar. The American League's first black player, Larry Dobie, and the great pitcher Satchel Paige came, too. Years later, I understood that it was an all-black, segregated school."

Tucson avoided the harsh violence of racial hatred but local railroad hiring continued to reflect the SP's preference for the family members of their employees and local unions' long-held racial prejudice. As late as 1969, no Mexican surnames graced the Tucson Division seniority list among the more than 300 engineers. Local hoghead Henry Zappia remembered: "There was one other Mexican engineer hired after William Sayre, but engine service remained closed to minorities. It finally opened up by the 1970s when the SP began hiring women and minorities in engine service because it was the law."

In yesteryear, Tucson's railroad clique held a vise-like grip on SP's best jobs. Today, legal edicts draw lines of fairness and the custom of handing down railroad jobs through selected families lies virtually extinct.

Spiritual faith helped many African-Americans endure indignities. While racial barriers set the framework, most Tucson families found happiness and good lives. (James A. Barnes Collection)

Chapter 16

(James A. Barnes Collection)

World War and Strong Women: A Different Tucson

"Turn that train's headlight out, or we'll shoot it out!" bellowed the strident police officer. "The Japanese have bombed Pearl Harbor! A lot of people are sure California's coast is next, and we have orders to make sure all trains run dark."

December 7, 1941 found local conductor Harlin Marlar atop a U.S. Navy steam locomotive running through California. "That's how World War II began for me," remembered Marlar. "We shut our headlight off and ran in the dark for about fifty miles into Sacramento. The police thought we had already heard about it and were just ignoring the order. Of course, we'd never do that in a national emergency."

Harlin enjoyed a more-than-sixty-year friendship with conductor Harold "Stonewall" Jackson. The two shared memories of the days of steam, in Jackson's attractive central Tucson home during February 2005. "I was in Lordsburg when the Japanese bombed Pearl Harbor," Jackson remembered. "I had just come down to Chicken Smith's restaurant, and they were saying war had been declared. It just seemed like everything broke loose."

The SP's Tucson work force had reached 1,400 employees and local payroll topped $2.8 million in 1940. Work slowed before the war, however, and the SP "cut off" almost all Tucson brakemen. Work grew so scarce on the local division that men began sleeping under the trees near the local yard office. "They'd tell the call-boy, 'Just in case you can't find who you're lookin' for, I'll be right over here,'" explained Marlar. "They just wanted to eat and feed their families."

"The railroad laid you off and gave you a ticket outta town," Jackson added. "A lot of us from Tucson went to Sacramento and Roseville, and we did some real railroading." One brakeman worked every twenty cars when the SP ran "Over the Hill" through Emigrant Gap in the Sierra Nevada. "There were lots of tunnels and the smoke'd damn near kill ya," said Stonewall. "The old heads wised me up. They told me to climb down the ladder in between two cars as close to the ground as possible and get some fresh air."

SP began a projected $68,000 repainting and enlargement of the Tucson depot in the spring of 1941. Lacking an air-cooling system, when many city buildings employed them, the old 1907 depot endured a barrage of criticism. The company constructed a four-thousand-square-foot temporary building east of the existing depot so that business might continue. SP employees completed the plumbing, electrical, structural steel, painting, and foundation work during the remodeling. The new décor's oak-stained wood fixtures complemented its light green walls, while "TUCSON" in gray-brown lettering contrasted nicely against the building's tan stucco exterior. Adding loading ramps and a "breezeway" beneath the tracks that allowed passengers to catch trains on any of a dozen tracks, helped to balloon the year-long job's final cost to $234,000. Sadly, the great self-winding clock in the old depot's passenger waiting room never returned following construction.

Because it classified their roles as essential to the war effort, the federal gov-

Remodeled in 1941, the local rail depot fell into disrepair in the late twentieth century, but has since enjoyed a rebirth with improved Amtrak facilities, and the Southern Arizona Transportation Museum. (AHS #9135)

ernment exempted conductors, engineers, dispatchers, and other key rail workers from armed service. Those workers considered "non-essential" to the nation's war build-up went to battle and returned with their seniority dates intact. With troops training at Ryan Field in Avra Valley and at the University of Arizona's Bear Down Gym, wartime traffic flooded the nation's rail lines. Using one-third fewer locomotives, one-fourth fewer freight cars, and one-fourth fewer workers, railroads moved almost double the amount of freight and more than twice as many passengers as they had in the first World War.

Once a crew reached the federally mandated maximum of sixteen work hours, they "died on the law." Then, the men stopped work and waited for transportation to take them home or to their road quarters. "During World War II, there was more work than the railroad could handle," explained former backshop foreman Charles Stoddard. "They didn't have CTC (up-graded communication system) back then, and everything worked with train orders."

The system did not always work in a timely fashion. "Troop trains started coming, and they had priority over everything," Jackson remembered. "It was a nightmare, I'll tell you. We exceeded the sixteen-hour

law, in many cases by as much as two hours." Harold did not like working the endless lines of troop trains. "Many times trains didn't have heat," he said. "It caused a lot of confusion for a while." The traffic boom meant six or seven sections or separate units of the division's regular trains ran each day. "They'd run on schedules, but they'd be hours late," said Jackson.

As U.S. involvement in World War II deepened, Tucson's young soldiers gave Mom, or their gal, one last kiss and chased a train bound for military service. Men's clothier Herb Bloom recalled: "About 150 juniors and seniors in the ROTC program got on the train for Fort Reilly, Kansas, headed for basic training. At the Southern Pacific depot bands played, and it was quite an event." Conductor Gordon Manning recalled: "Some of those boys would be hugging their loved ones in the station right up to the time that the train started, and then come racing out to jump on. They'd hang on the outside of the train waving good-bye until long past where anyone could see them. They were going to war."

Others rode beneath the cover of secrecy. Tucson *nativo* Francisco "Frank" Mendez remembered, "I completed basic training in the east and they put us on a troop train headed west to California. We stopped at the depot in Tucson and it was a

Its land grant status obligated the University of Arizona to provide male students with two years of R.O.T.C. training. Snow covers the Santa Catalina Mountains behind fabled Old Main, while construction continues to its (right) south in this ca. 1920 photograph. (Mary Anabelle Garigan collection)

beautiful morning. We had to get off the train and rest, so we did some calisthenics and ran around a little before we took off again." Francisco's family lived just two blocks from the depot that day. "My mother didn't even know that I was on that train," he said. "It was just hush, hush; nobody knows where you're going. You can't even tell your folks that you're coming through Tucson. You didn't know where you were going and didn't tell anyone where you were going. Loose lips sink ships, you know."

Rail historian Gustav H. Schneider recalled one mournful Tucson day during the war. "Great billows of black smoke could be seen rising just east of town; from the upper floor of the SP station it was possible to see the flames," remembered Schneider. "A plane had crashed, and the entire crew had perished." Later, the dead pilots' coffins rolled toward the local station platform in silent procession. "No sound except the chocking of truck wheels and the steady groan of the tractor pulling the eight baggage trucks," Schneider recalled. From

Charles Stoddard grew up in Tucson and recalled: "I spent most of my time on the university campus and the football field was just two blocks north of my house. Notre Dame traveled to play USC every year and they would stop here for four or five days and practice. I remember meeting Knute Rockne. The baseball field was also close and we'd watch the game and get the broken bats. The polo field was where the football field is now and we'd get the broken mallets and shorten 'em up and get on our bicycles. I guess we had the first halftime entertainment at the university playing bicycle polo. A pretty rough game, I'll tell ya. I was twelve or thirteen years old. As Boy Scouts, we sold soda pop and candy during the games. I knew a lot of the football players then." (James W. Nugent Collection)

each, men loaded a solitary pine box holding a flag-draped coffin onto the baggage car of passenger train No. 6. "Those were tense moments," Schneider continued. "The oleanders along the approach to the Fourth Avenue subway were in bloom. An old Negro man went over to them and plucked eight clustered blossoms. Slowly, with a tottering walk, he carried them to the line of coffins and placed one on top of each." Known as William, the gracious gentlemen had cooked for Colonel Epes Randolph twenty years earlier. "Some grimy men, many railroad men are that way while on duty, rather self-consciously wiped away tears," said Schneider.

The SP used its south line, the former EP&SW tracks through Douglas, as its westbound road. To relieve wartime congestion, the railroad occasionally stopped all westward traffic to run a group of four or five troop trains east on the south line. At Fort Huachuca, Jackson remembered, black soldiers often disconnected their cars from the rest of the train before it pulled away. "Sometimes it would take four or five tries to get their car on the train and moving. They didn't want to go. They'd just pull the pin and get out and do the Lindy Hop."

Finally, the antics damaged the train's connections for steam heating. "We'd have to go cold," said Jackson. "They finally quit that. We punished them, and after freezing to death for several hours, they got to where they'd wise up and not damage the train."

A new rail passenger rode the Tucson Division as the U.S. Justice Department held more than 8 million German, Italian, and Japanese prisoners of war under Executive Order No. 9066. Between May 1942 and June 1946, passenger coaches hauled the broken soldiers to more than 140 internment camps nationwide, including the Gila River Camp, Camp Papago Park, and Camp Florence in Arizona.

Near Ulmoris rail siding in New Mexico, Camp Lordsburg housed Japanese prisoners about four miles southeast of town. Gordon Manning remembered: "We'd get a message to stop the train beyond the regular Lordsburg station. Military guards armed with machine guns would step out onto the station platform when we arrived. They loaded the prisoners into trucks right from the train and took them to that camp."

Hard drinking Lordsburg camp commandant Colonel Clyde Lundy staged frequent elaborate costume balls and used his prisoners to clean up the clutter. "We heard that a lot of rough stuff went on over there," Manning said. "Sometimes we'd hear the machine guns popping, but we never really knew what was going on. We had nothing to do with any aspect of their transport other than the operation of the train. That was fine with us; we didn't want to know a hell of a lot about

Local rail James A. Barnes took this photo of the sergeants in his 777th Field Artillery Company during a seventeen-month tour of duty in France. (James A. Barnes Collection)

what was going on." The killing of prisoners Kobata and Isomura, during the spring of 1942, marked a low point in Camp Lordsburg's history.

Fear of sabotage led the military to station guards at bridges around the clock, including ones at Pantano, Yuma, and Dome, Arizona. "They were as worthless as a roll of wet toilet paper," Jackson said. "They were usually elderly or middle-aged men, and they did very little patrolling. They was just there, that's all." Saboteurs "could have come up, set their charges, and walked away without a problem," he said. "I never saw one of them carrying a gun."

War-era railroad labor agreements dictated that overtime pay began after thirteen hours, seven minutes going east from Tucson; and ten hours, thirty minutes heading west toward Gila Bend. Men paid for all their own meals and rented rooms for 75¢ to $1.25 a day depending upon accommodations. Everyone's life included gasoline and food rationing in wartime. Sometimes, food shortages forced SP rails to go to work hungry. "I remember when we staged a sit-down outside of Gila Bend," Jackson continued. The brief labor action worked. "They stopped passenger train No. 6 and set the dining car out and fed all the crew. Then, they put it on the back of a freight train and brought it into Tucson."

Wartime demands taxed SP operations and equipment to the maximum. Almost 21,000 company employees served in the armed services. Freight volume rose two-and-one-half times over its 1939 level, passenger traffic rose fivefold. Safety suffered under the pressure to move trains. "Engineers were concerned that repairs be done properly," said Carl Ball Jr. "Like any other piece of machinery, lubrication was important. Running the engine too hard or not working it hard enough also created problems. It was pretty difficult to do all the things that made a locomotive perform right. Federal inspectors still checked all our locomotives, but went easier on inspec-

tion than they normally did, so they could release the locomotive to go to work."

Tucson's economy flourished during the war, and railroad men found it difficult to "lay off" from work. Crew caller William Crowell remembered, "Everybody was working hard. They were working long hours, and it was tough to get guys to come to work. I'd have them sign the call sheet because they'd go back to sleep after we'd called them. They'd say, 'Well, you never did call me.' We'd have to show them that they'd signed the call sheet."

"I had as many as six or seven sixteen-hour shifts back-to-back without laying off, absolutely no laying off," chuckled Jackson. "If you laid off, you had to have a doctor's certificate to get back on." Because rail traffic clogged division tracks, some trains required several days just to travel 125 miles to Phoenix during the war. "The first day I got to Rillito, the second day I got to Wymola, and the third day I got into Chandler. I got into Phoenix the next day," said Jackson. "I'd come to a side track and find a dead train [due to the sixteen-hour law] and have to back up."

Single railroad men had rooms in several big boardinghouses along Tucson's south Third and Fourth avenues. "We didn't have any trouble getting them to work the holidays because they weren't going back home," Crowell said. "But on holidays we had trouble getting the men that lived in Tucson to come to work." Local dispatchers had such a tough time finding workers during December that they referred to the holiday period as "White Christmas."

Armed forces needs added 1,200 troop sleepers and 400 kitchen cars to the nation's rail fleet during World War II. SP prepared more soldiers' meals than any other two railroads combined. It also ran 28,000 troop and mixed special trains for the government, along with 86,000 special military cars on passenger trains. A 1943 brochure admitted that its wartime passenger service had not kept pace with earlier company standards. Military demand for troop trains required constant diversion of passenger equipment, and trains frequently ran late. Overcrowded cars sometimes required passengers to stand, and poorly maintained coaches failed to look "as bright and shiny as they used to be."

SP's dining-service department now served three times the number of meals it did before the war. In addition, the company served uniformed passengers traveling in groups their meals first, before civilians. SP purchased no new dining cars and meals no longer presented "the enjoyable affairs they once were." In addition, the company struggled to train new personnel. Expressing corporate regret, the SP declared, "War has created conditions which are difficult, often impossible to lick." Company literature offered "helpful wartime hints," encouraging passengers to travel only when "really essential"; avoid weekend travel because of heavy traffic; eat before boarding the train when possible; pack light luggage; and, in the dining car, "Don't bolt your meal; but please don't linger over it."

Conductor Oril O. Hutcheson was a product of the rough-and-tumble days when size and might got a man his druthers on the railroad. During World War II, a brakeman on Hutcheson's troop train missed grabbing train orders off the hook at Fairbank Station. As the train backed up to retrieve its orders, Oril jumped to the ground and walked back to talk to his brakeman. When Hutcheson saw a group of four drunken soldiers, he ordered the men to clear the vestibule and return to their car. The chaps mistakenly met the conduc-

The Trains never used to be this way!

The SP acknowledged reduced passenger service during World War II. (Kalt Collection)

tor's edict with a barrage of profanity. "So the old man and the coach porter, a very large black man, tied into those four soldiers," said Hutcheson's son Frank, an eyewitness. "When we left Fairbank, all four of them were laying unconscious on the station platform. I guess they figured that my old man and that black porter couldn't do too well, but they did it with a brake club and a railroad lantern."

Oril Hutcheson repeatedly proved himself one crusty conductor. "He was a very tough man," Frank recalled. "He didn't know what courtesy or consideration of passengers was. He was brought up in the days of the teens and twenties when there were tremendous physical battles on the freight trains between the train crews and hobos. Therefore, his public relations skills were zilch. He was a very large man. He weighed 255 pounds and was backed by a strong union, so he could get away with almost anything."

One day in 1942, dressed in a business suit and carrying his own railroad lantern, six-foot-four, fourteen-year-old Frank scrambled aboard another of his father's passenger trains. Following train orders, the elder Hutcheson's troop caravan took a siding and waited for a passing eastbound train. A portly military officer approached during the stop. "This soldier came up and he had one star on each corner of his collar," recounted Frank. "He was a brigadier general! He asked my dad, 'Are you the conductor?'

"'Yes, I'm the conductor,' Dad answered. 'What the hell do you want?'

Families across the nation welcomed their young men home with serious injuries and illnesses after war's terror. Joseph G. Peggs (back row, right), University of Arizona football star, and son of former SP accountant Joseph M. Peggs, returned from the South Pacific emaciated from malaria. The proud veteran served a long and illustrious career with the Federal Bureau of Investigation. (Kalt Collection)

"The general said, 'Get this train going.'

"Well, my dad could have easily explained to him, 'We're on a side track. If we pull out, we'll hit another train head on. Instead, he said, 'Shut up your goddamned mouth and go sit down in your seat.'"

Profanities and anatomically impossible suggestions flew in furor, before the brass yelled, "I'm a general, an officer in the Army of the United States. This is wartime. I'm ordering you to get this train running."

When the opposing train finally passed Hutcheson's caboose, his head brakeman began to "highball" the engineer, signaling him to proceed, but the hard-nosed conductor stopped him. Gestur-ing toward a concrete telephone booth at the end of the siding, Hutcheson yelled at the general, "You can go down there and get on that telephone and call the chief dispatcher and tell him your problem."

Frank recalled his father's next move, "So my old man waits until the general walks past the last car on the train, then 'highballs' the engineer and off we go. We just left him. Those phone booths were made of five-inch-thick, poured concrete. They had three-inch-thick doors with very large padlocks. So there was no way in the world for him to get in there. I don't know what ever happened to that general."

World War II brought with it all the horror one human race could handle. In Tucson, families grieved for loved ones, who sacrificed beyond the pale for their country. More than a million troops passed through the city during World War II. Industrial expansion helped fuel a post-war gain of three million people in the eight states served by the SP. The unprecedented traffic flow initiated dramatic changes in the lives of women. Working strenuous physical jobs, previously done by men, they entered the American workforce as never before. Not always a smooth road, the work experience in local SP yards paid the bills and broadened women's horizons. It also expanded the perspective of the men who ran the railroad.

These pioneer women and their husbands carved out lives for their families in Tucson's Rillito Valley, ca. 1883. (Dorothy Kengla Fitzpatrick)

Discussion of the female role in male-dominated societies has proliferated across centuries and around the world. Though oratory and legislation supported the principle, equality remained a fleeting fantasy in many realms. Forward thinking surfaced in Tucson during 1898, when the *Star* proclaimed: "One of the auspicious signs of the times is the proper recognition which is being accorded to women and a growing appreciation of their value as factors in our civilization." Calling women "moral and social forces," the newspaper concluded, "The new era of womanhood is dawning and in a few years the dawn will be refulgent and glowing like the noon-day sun of woman's greater power and recognized influence."

Not all Tucsonans shared such warm feelings regarding women's societal ascension. That year, T. Seddon Bruce, Tucson's Board of Trade emissary, urged his male cohorts to deny women voting rights. "In asking her to step down from that sphere where she is surrounded by a halo...to mix in politics, to elbow her way among those of our sex, we ask her to descend to our sphere and...deprive ourselves of the only romance of life," said Bruce. Claiming man had not profited as much as woman from the advance of civilization, Bruce continued, "There shall be a change in the functions and life of women equivalent to a revolution...that practically blots out the glory of her womanhood. She has now a delicacy and beauty of presence; graces and charms of person; and bearing the intuitive affinities of the true, the pure, and the good...She has no right to diminish the glory of one of them by making herself a numerical factor in the political economy."

Arizona's war hero and Prescott mayor William "Buckey" O'Neill took a more egalitarian view. O'Neill pushed the territorial legislature to pass law No. 76 in 1897, guaranteeing all taxpayers the right to vote in municipal elections "without distinction of sex." When Tucson voted on the question of taxing city property to fund water bonds in May 1898, however, the local election board prohibited female taxpayers from voting, because their names did not appear on Pima County's Great Register.

Tucson's water bonds measure passed, but Andrew Cronly challenged the election's outcome on behalf of taxpayers. The territorial Supreme Court ruled law No. 76 "inoperative and void" on a technicality. Tragically, O'Neill died in the Spanish-American War. Suffrage leader and Arizona's first woman senator Frances "Fannie" Munds remembered, "We have always felt that had he lived he would have rectified the mistake. At any rate we would have had a champion because his was a noble mind filled with a sense of right and justice toward all."

In the spring of 1903, a bill granting suffrage to women sailed through the Territorial House on a vote of sixteen to seven. Predicting the measure would die in committee, the *Tucson Daily Citizen* reported, "Many of the members who voted for the bill did so as a joke to put the Council in a hole." The bill passed, but Governor Alexander Brodie vetoed it under pressure from his "avowedly-antagonistic-to-the-principle-of-equal-rights" wife. Bars and gambling halls erupted in spontaneous celebrations at the news. "The saloons in Phoenix were a scene of the wildest joy... and the governor's health was drank a score of times," reported the *Star*. In Tucson, entrepreneurs flew Brodie's name on banners above their business houses. Phil Brannen,

Augusta "Gussie" Cordelia Lovell O'Connell Manning combined intellect, beauty, and grace. Few Tucsonans knew that Gussie drew the plans for her family's famous Manning House. "Gussie designed the house after the governor's palace in Mexico," explained her great-granddaughter Lovell Bonnie. "Banks would never loan money on a home designed by a female architect in her day. She would take her drawings to the local architect to get them reviewed and approved for building. That is how Henry Trost takes credit for her work. He did not design the Manning house but merely reviewed Gussie's plans." Architects who reviewed her plans "seldom had to make any changes, i.e., move walls for bearing purposes, etc.," said Bonnie. "Gussie designed all the Manning homes. These included the one called the Steinfeld house, one that became a men's club (Owls), and an apartment house that was across the street from the Manning House. She also laid out the streets in the Paseo Redondo area and designed houses on the family ranches." (Lovell Gunter Welsh Collection)

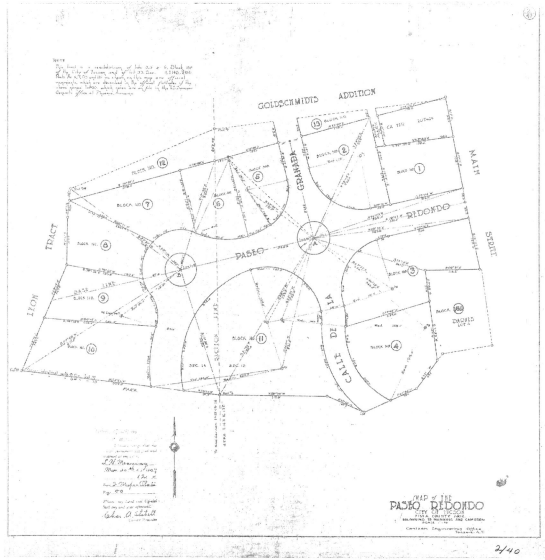

(Maps and Plats, Book 2, p, 40, City of Tucson Transportation Department)

Real estate broker, political activist, and future wife of "Irish" Phil Garigan, Mary Anabelle Gilligan (second from left), and her companions rode through the University of Arizona campus ca. 1919. That year, comedian Douglas Fairbanks attended a performance of Tucsonan Sarah Y. Mason's comedy "When Dreams Come True." The day following her play, the famous funny man created a "perfect whirlwind" around Tucson in his search for Mason. Fairbanks located her at last, singing tunes from her production while hard at work in the offices of Albert Steinfeld's mercantile. Mason left town with Fairbanks that very night for Los Angeles. She began writing for actress Zazu Pitts. Later, she signed with Louis Zelnick to write exclusively for his star, Owen Moore. During her first six months, Mason wrote for Zelnick's "The Poor Simp" and "The Chicken in the Case." (Mary Anabelle Garigan Collection)

of Hanny & Brannen's Clothiers, captured the sentiment of many males when asked the gender of his newborn child. "She's a little lady," answered the clothing manager. "No, I had hoped it would be a voter, but it's alright."

By 1909, more than thirty women worked for the SP and the Arizona Eastern Railroad in Tucson. Two-thirds worked in auditor J.C. Vinson's office as clerks, stenographers, and typists. Following the policy of "higher-ups," rail officials assigned women to clerical jobs wherever possible. Minnie Perry, Emma Smith, and Miss White worked in the "Randolph Lines" offices in Tucson. Sigrid Carlson labored in the SP offices, along with Tinnie E. Haley, conductor Alonzo "Lon" Haley's wife, Millie Mariner, the spouse of conductor Barnett "Barney" M. Mariner, and Mary S.

Holladay, wife of engineer Leonidas "Lon" Holladay.

SP locomotive engineer Tom Collins voted against women serving on Arizona juries in the state senate in 1933 and Superior Court Judge Fred Fickett commended Collins. Fickett cited increased court costs for stenographers to prepare jury lists with the additional names, and the need for special toilet and extra sleeping accommodations for women on sequestered juries, as solid reasons to kill the even-handed bill.

During the Great Depression, local rail union "ladies societies" maintained a constant flow of social activities. Tucson's Flower of Cactus Lodge No. 56 associated with the Brotherhood of Locomotive Firemen and Engineers on April 22, 1899. The San Xavier Auxiliary No. 241 served the wives of Brotherhood of Locomotive Engi-

The Ladies Society of the Brotherhood of Locomotive Firemen & Engineers, Flower of Cactus Lodge No. 56 gathered in 1936. The local chapter of the women's auxiliary began in the spring of 1899, with 14 members. (AHS #BN205057)

neers members. Ruth Manning joined the Saguaro Division No. 313 of the Brotherhood of Railroad Trainmen's auxiliary when her husband, Gordon, gained promotion to conductor in 1940. "Our lodge was founded for any railroad lady," said Ruth. "The Knights of Columbus Hall at Sixth Avenue and Broadway Boulevard had a a piano and we'd meet once a month and sing songs and eat potluck meals. Our goal was the fellowship and friendship of people." The women of the Saguaro Auxiliary used the "Friendship Grows" poem to guide their relations.

> *Friendship is a chain of gold,*
> *shaped in God's own perfect*
> *mold,*
> *Each link a laugh, a smile, a tear.*

> *The grasp of a hand, a word of*
> *cheer, as steadfast as the mighty*
> *oak.*
> *Binding forces soul to soul.*
> *No matter how far or how heavy*
> *the load, sweet is the journey on*
> *Friendship Road.*

Manning remembered the auxiliary's glory days. "Minnie Hudnall was president in 1932, 1933, 1939, 1940, 1943, and she was wonderful," Ruth recalled. "Minnie lived on North First Avenue. The area near Tenth Street, between Euclid and First avenues was all old railroaders then. Anna Swift lived on the north side of Tenth Street at Second Avenue." Women of the Saguaro Auxiliary also performed. "We

Minnie Ash Hudnall led the local ladies auxiliary of the Brotherhood of Railway Trainmen and maintained her membership for fifty years. Established January 23, 1889, the local organization provided its members a $1,000 life insurance policy and many hours of enjoyable social activities. (Barbara Salyer Collection)

Ruth Manning (left) and her husband, Gordon, enjoy a meal at the monthly National Association of Retired and Veteran Railway Employees meeting in 2003. (Robert McCelland Collection)

(l-r) Ethel Houston, Claudia Ball, and Helen Pfersdorf proved strong partners for their engineer husbands. (Jim Pfersdorf Collection)

were a very close-knit group, and by the late 1940s, we had 140 members," Ruth said. "We marched and executed drills to music. It was formal, and we all had dresses alike." Manning served as the group's president in 1954, and the marching corps performed at the auxiliary's national convention in Columbus, Ohio. "That was a tremendous highlight for our members," she said. "We were all so proud."

The Saguaro Auxiliary continued long after the steam era ended, until workforce reductions and societal changes brought it to an end. "We were going strong in 1968, but soon after that it seemed like women just didn't want to be here anymore," remembered Manning. "We got down to about 20 people, and it wasn't worth the time. The young women were working and not interested."

Lacking the usual family ties necessary for an SP job, Juanita Bernal rode in on the wave of increased rail business generated by World War II. Bernal came to work for the SP in 1944 as a dispatcher. The seventeen-year-old Las Cruces, New Mexico, native completed a six-month SP training course in just three months. Bernal tricked her mother into signing a minor's work release, required by the SP, and headed for Tucson where she earned $36 dollars a week. In July 1945, Juanita and her husband, Raymond, made their first home in an "outfit car" that SP furnished for section gang foremen along the line. "An outfit car was just a boxcar that was fixed inside like a little trailer," Bernal explained. "It had a bedroom, a living room, and a kitchen with cabinets on the top and bottom. They had a water tank on top of the cars, and we had water inside, in a faucet if we were lucky." The young couple spent seven years in the outfit car before they moved into the section foreman's house, after Raymond took a job at Montezuma. "The car had a wood heater and a wood stove in the kitchen," Juanita said. "Some of them had a little refrigerator, and others had just an insulated box that you put ice in."

In February 1990, former locomotive "wiper" and roundhouse janitor Jennie Morales Benitez explained to *Star* columnist Bonnie Henry, "I was told, 'If a girl is going to work for the SP, she is going to work like a man.'" Born on a small ranch at Cortaro, Arizona, the single mother joined

SP converted these cattle cars to outfit cars for use as employee living quarters before the days of trailer homes. (Sid Showalter Collection)

thirty-two other women in helping the railroad meet World War II's business surge. Jennie's uncle, who worked as a locomotive "oiler" at the local roundhouse, told her about SP job openings for women in 1942. After the interview, Benitez remembered, "I was shaking when I got out of the office, the questions they asked me! Could I lift heavy equipment? Was I in good health? I was five-foot-three and weighed 118 pounds."

Dressed in shirt, blue overalls, and steel-toed boots, wartime female engine wipers cleaned four engines on most days. "We worked in teams," Benitez recalled. "Two girls cleaned the windows, and two girls cleaned the tenders." Tender work proved most strenuous, requiring the women to dump sand over spilled oil, absorb it, and remove the sand. "There couldn't be a speck of sand left or the engineers would complain because, when the train was going, the wind would blow the sand around," Benitez explained. Next, a hostler moved the locomotive to the steam house where crews cleaned the entire unit with soap, a brush, and a steam hose. With engines "screaming" around the yard, Benitez had to scale the tender carrying a five-gallon can of oil and refill its reservoir. "I was very careful climbing up the ladder because I knew if I fell, it would kill me. After I poured the oil in, I threw the can down and got off the ladder fast."

Benitez's co-worker Lily Liu took a casual approach to sexual overtures by men in the yard. Jennie would have none of it. "I had four men fired. They were making suggestive comments to me. They were supposed to leave the women alone, so they were fired."

Born in Bisbee, Arizona on March 4, 1923, Louise Schulthiess DeHart grew up twenty miles west of Casa Grande at SP's Mobile, Arizona siding. "There were seven of us in my family," said Louise at the kitchen table of her beautiful university-area home in early February 2002. "There were about one hundred people and the Phoenix garbage dump was right there. About fifteen Mexican section workers

"Snapped on the Street" during 1943, SP employees Louise Schulthiess DeHart (left) and Jacqueline Requarth amble downtown on their lunch hour. (Louise and Robert DeHart Collection)

lived there, and several black families raised pigs on their homesteads. We were the only white family. I think it was quite unusual for blacks to have homesteads. That's where I became acquainted with black people and realized they are beautiful just like anybody else."

Louise continued: "My dad worked as a signal maintainer and the railroad provided homes for its employees. He built an above-ground swimming pool. He also made an air-conditioner with wet gunny sacks on the windows so we'd have a little bit of cool air." SP ran a small store, in Mobile during the 1930s, which stocked life's necessities. "We'd sit on our fence to watch the trains go by because we were right by the tracks. We had one of the old-fashioned telephones on the wall that the railroad provided because they had to contact my dad by phone. It was very unusual to have a phone. We used to get a kick out of hearing the phone ring."

Louise lived the railroad life growing up. "My dad rented a house for my oldest sister and she stayed in Gila Bend to attend high school," she explained. "When it was time for me to go to high school, my sister Marge and I rode the train to Casa Grande about seven every morning and returned at seven in the evening. My father found a woman to feed us supper, and we went to her house. I can't imagine people going to that extreme to get an education now days." When her family moved into Tucson, Louise took a job at Woolworth's department store downtown. "After a while, I decided that I didn't want to work at the dime store the rest of my life. My dad got

Women from the SP offices enjoyed each other's company away from work during the 1960s. (Julia Peters Newman Collection)

me started at the Arizona College of Commerce on Congress Street. I took typing, shorthand, and bookkeeping. We had to demonstrate 90 percent accuracy and I learned to type ninety-some words per minute."

Louise built solid skills during the fourteen-month-long course. "I could take dictation real fast, and I really gained a good background in writing," she recalled. "The instructor was a stickler with writing and grammar. He made you feel that you could be independent in an office." With World War II blazing, the SP contacted the college to find a secretary in 1942. "They really reviewed my background before they hired me because my maiden name was Schulthiess. My dad had worked at the SP so that helped them to know that I wasn't a Nazi spy.

"I was the first woman hired in the dispatcher's office," DeHart said. "Up until that time they had only men secretaries. I started out taking dictation from chief dispatcher H.W. Cassidy. I was only nineteen, so the men tried to clean up their vocabularies. I was sort of a conversation piece." In the days prior to CTC, telegraph operators at each station communicated by telephone with the Tucson dispatcher. "I would mark where each train was on my chart," Louise explained. "I had to keep track of four or five trains at a time. If they put cars out at sidings along the line, I would record each car's number." The SP began hiring more women after Louise had worked at the railroad about a year. "There were female telephone operators and some telegraph operators," she said. "We had three shifts of dispatchers, and I was told to interview them and choose. I remember Margie Long, whose family started Long Realty, began on second shift. She and I had a good time together." Just as her friend moved on from

SP workers gathered outside the freight house. (Julia Peters Newman)

the SP, Louise found a rewarding career. She earned a master's degree in education at the University of Arizona and spent her final eight years teaching special education at Peter Howell Elementary School.

Life on the streets of Tucson possessed a special charm before World War II. People walked around town much of the time. They called each other by their first names when they met on the street. KUAT-TV's Rudy Casillas captured the waning steam era in his superb documentary, *Tucson Memories*. Using interviews with successful local citizens, Casillas painted a picture of the fast-fading era in Tucson. "There was the mystique of the old west," Roy P. Drachman, businessman and local icon, recalled. "Many people wore western hats and dressed western all the time." Norma Stevenson Grove, member of the 1940 class at Tucson High School, remembered: "The small town we grew up with ceased to exist once the war affected Tucson. The local economy boomed. There was a lot more action then, a lot more [social] options."

"Tucson grew up with its unique fragrance," remembered Barbara Amos, former member of the Tucson Modeling Club. "Around the Arizona Inn there was a fragrance of jasmine and orange blossoms that was very special. Very romantic. So much of Tucson used to have that fragrance. I miss it." Herb Bloom bemoaned the passing of the face-to-face age: "I miss walking down the street and knowing everybody and saying hello to everybody. If someone came along I didn't know, I'd go up and say, 'You're new in town.' Everybody knew everybody."

World War II dances at the local USO Club sparked new liaisons. Local author Alva Torres recalled, "That was when it started to change. Many soldiers started coming to town and dating the local girls. A lot of girls married soldiers that they met at those dances."

As working women became comfortable wearing pants to rail and factory jobs, many opted for the outfit in social settings. Local fashion exemplar and Tucson *Doña* Cele Peterson described an important aspect of Tucson society during the steam age. "Women did not come downtown unless they were 'dressed,'" Peterson recalled. "I like to call it 'appropriately dressed.' Two pieces, singles, skirts, and blouses." War-time changes surprised her. "I thought that pants would last only one or two [fashion] seasons and then fade," said Peterson. "Just a fad! Boy! Was I ever wrong about that!"

By 1949, the Mountain States Telephone & Telegraph Company's new sixty-five-position switchboard needed two hundred operators to handle its round-the-clock service. Tucsonans made an average of 110,000 long-distance calls each month, and a faster and more accurate "key pulsing" system allowed operators to use keys instead of dials. Yet, the curious enchantment that defined the Old Pueblo lingered during the 1950s. A veteran local television executive, warm-hearted George W. Wallace came in 1952, and recalled, "The town shut down at noon for siestas, literally." Well into the 1960s, most Tucsonans lived with unlocked doors. Long-time realtor and pillar of the local Jewish community Morton Solot recalled, "We'd go to the mountains and leave [our] doors unlocked the whole time."

Along with the advent of air-conditioning, the onset of World War II changed Tucson forever. Population growth and television joined the city's first shopping mall outside of the downtown area in altering the city's flow. Under assault from an ever-encroaching uniformity that characterized late-twentieth-century material, architectural, and social culture, the stewardship of Tucson's special flavor demands concerted design and constant renewal. Local sports columnist Abe Chanin best expressed the sentiments of the city's *nativos*, "I hope all the newcomers appreciate it as much as the old-timers have."

Chapter 17

Diesel power brought great changes to railroading. The nation, too, trembled beneath the weight of change.
(Ralph Coltrin Collection)

The Day the Music Died: From "Ch, ch, ch, Boom!" to "Whrrr" in the Blink of an Eye

> *"It was a whole revolution that was cultural, going on through the nation."*
>
> *J.J. Tierney, April 2002*

Fearsome new energy propelled changes on the railroad after World War II, paralleling dynamic shifts in American culture. Tucson's first diesel motor had arrived for the shops back in April 1903. Diesel freight engines debuted on the Southern Pacific Railroad (SP) main line during 1946 as workhorses for a sleek, post-war railroad.

Technological advancements had brightened outlooks before the war. Air-conditioned and streamlined passenger cars, fast merchandise trains, and enhanced locomotive power signaled a "New Era" for the Southern Pacific Railroad following the Great Depression. The company led the way in using radios to improve communications with dispatchers and trainmen. SP installed two licensed transmitters atop the Sierra Nevada range in California. Radios remained in limited use as late as 1946 because the railroad battled to find a consistent signal. Workmen installed the first four hundred miles of SP Centralized Traffic Control (CTC) in the mid-1950s, giving single-track lines almost

"Covered wagon" No. 6457 pulled train No. 39 into Tucson ca. 1955. (Richard Stapp Sr. Collection)

75 percent capacity of a double-track railroad.

Local changes that began during World War II gained momentum as the 1940s became the 1950s. Haberdasher Herb Bloom remembered that the smart money rested on Tucson "drying up" and becoming a "ghost town" like other cities that had grown because of the military. Despite such grim visions, downtown remained vibrant. "Tucson never missed a step," Bloom recalled. "Servicemen came back, married, and raised their families."

The SP ran two thousand steam locomotives when World War II ended. During the next thirteen years, the company invested more than $300 million on two thousand diesel engines. The new engines needed light, high-cost fuel when idling, so the SP employed a dual-fuel system that allowed them to switch to a cheaper, heavier fuel when running the line. Division chief timekeeper, Elgin Ball, remembered: "The company sent Glen Hewitt down from Omaha. He instructed the road foremen of engines in diesel operation. Then, they'd teach the rest of the engineers. He worked here several weeks." Ball recalled lending his 1941 ruby-maroon Chevrolet Club Coupe to Hewitt during his Tucson stay. "That was one great car," chuckled Ball. "I

used to see him riding around town sometimes."

The increased use of diesel engines met with mixed reviews on the local division. Rail historian Gustav H. Schneider wrote to his friend Joseph Reed of Phoenix: "I, too, care little for the modern type of railroad train. Such trains are entirely devoid of character when compared with those of fifty years ago." Schneider added in a follow-up letter: "You deplore Dieselizing of our motive power. Well, so do I, from a sentimental standpoint. Steam locomotives are more picturesque. With their cadenced puffing, they take on a sort of consciousness, even a personality. These are qualities that diesels will never possess." Schneider often visited the Tucson rail yard and enjoyed watching a steam locomotive pull its load by the station: "It seems to say, 'Look at me! Here I am doing my work, pulling with might and main! But no one wants me any more...'"

A sharp dresser, Glenn Hewitt trained the engine crew as diesel engines came on the local scene. (Elgin Ball Collection)

Elgin Ball stands beside the ruby-maroon 1941 Chevrolet Club Coupe he lent to Glenn Hewitt during his Tucson stay.(Elgin Ball Collection)

"By 1948, diesels were numerous," recalled former conductor Harold "Stonewall" Jackson. "Enginemen liked the diesels because they were inside, out of the weather. We didn't need near as much doubling (adding extra) engines for the hills." The diesel's dynamic brake utilized the engine itself to slow the train, creating an effect similar to that found when down-shifting a standard transmission automobile. "It made stops a lot better," he said. "It reduced injuries and slack action between the cars on the train." Diesels brought other advantages. "Before, we'd have three or four attempts to get the train started," said Jackson. "We'd have to get a switch engine to help get us out of the yard. Diesels reduced the hours and made it an all-around better job. The wear on the rail with a diesel is only about 30 percent of a steam engine, and you don't kink any rail with a diesel."

The diesel's insinuation into the company's locomotive power mix proved inexorable. Assistant Superintendent Ralph Coltrin came to Tucson during the SP's conversion to diesel. "We were still running several steam engines when I arrived," said Coltrin in the dining room of his comfortable midtown home in late June 2005. "During the steam engine days, the Back-up Mallies

worked real good on trains No. 5 and No. 6, the old Argonaut. As the diesels became available, we brought them in. It was much easier, much nicer. The only trouble was some of the older engineers didn't like the smell of them, but they soon got over that when they compared the trip on each."

Connie Wienzapfel exalted the steam locomotive, once proclaiming: "It

was a LIVE thing! It was something terrific! I used to love to run a steam engine when we were kicking or segregating cars in the yard. You'd put up heavy steam and 'ch, ch, ch, boom,' and away the cars would go. Where, with a diesel there's no noise. I used to fight over getting my steam engine, and those others would fight over getting the diesels." However, Wienzapfel also delighted in the diesel engine's power. "The speed of the train tripled itself," he said. "You can go 78 miles an hour on those diesels, and you don't even feel like you're going 30. On the Hogs [2-8-0 wheel configuration] and Mallet engines, they'd throw you out of the cab if you went over 45 miles per hour. The track was not built for that. Now the track is safe to run over, at 120 miles an hour or more." Jim "Nuge" Nugent also saw both sides. "It was a lot easier with the diesels, real smooth power," Nuge said. "It took the fun out of it for me, though. It was like the difference between driving a motorcycle and driving a truck."

Former crew dispatcher William Crowell explained: "The steam engines were pretty unbearable in the summer-

time, and in the wintertime because they were so cold. Even though the old steam engine was glamorous, there was nothing like sitting in a big old diesel engine where it was warm and comfortable. They had the road foreman of engines riding along with them to instruct them on these things. It was a new and exciting way."

"When the diesel came, everything changed," Jackson concurred. "Safer, more efficient, and not so many injuries in the caboose because of the dynamic brake. We got over the road better, and we didn't have water stops. It was absolutely a disaster for the roundhouse and boilermakers and all those employees. It just wiped them out. But it was the greatest thing."

SP's steam-to-diesel transition vexed some older division engineers. Emily Rinkleib Bradley remembered her father, engineer Bernard "Wrinkle Belly" Rinkleib, struggled to make the change from steam power. "The stress from studying for the diesel engine test caused my father to contract shingles," she said. "He was so anxious because it meant his family's livelihood, but he passed the test."

The new engines did not prove trouble-free. "When diesels first came out, their transitions caused problems," recalled Charles Stoddard, former backshop foreman. "They had four different series of transitions depending on the voltage and the speed of the engine. You had to ride in them under load to check the engine speed and the governor. Boy, that was hard work. I did that the first year, and then the company came up with a way to test the transitions in

Sid Showalter captured snow fall in the Tucson yard, where SP stored up to twenty-seven diesel engines. (Sid Showalter Collection)

Long demolished, the hotel at Sentinel, Arizona served travelers early in the twentieth century. The company closed section workers housing on the division's west end at Sentinel, Mohawk, Mobile, and Wellton during the 1960s. (UASC)

the shop." With diesel power, longer trains challenged long-held notions of rail procedure. "I remember the day we put 125 cars west out of Lordsburg for the first time," said superintendent Coltrin. "I sweated that out because I was afraid that it just wouldn't work, that we were going to have those cars all over the side of the hill out there and the railroad would be tied up. I shouldn't do that."

Concerns wracked the local workforce as advances in technology fueled SP's march toward progress and eliminated jobs. Company literature heralded an exciting new era: "Today's railroad scene is one of powerful diesels, radar-controlled classification yards, revolutionary new freight cars, and centralized traffic control for a new speed and efficiency to better serve the West." Crowell remembered, "When the modern equipment came in it was different. You saw men going, jobs being abolished and lost. Many of the men that worked on the old steam engines lost their jobs because you didn't have a boilermaker working on a diesel engine!"

When Stanley M. Houston learned that the SP planned conversion to diesel, he

arranged a transfer for boilermaker Vicente "Vic" Alfaro to the company's mechanical department. Alfaro attended diesel motor school for almost six months and passed the test over the railroad's new engines. The former state legislator, who served the SP for fifty-four years, remembered that some fellow employees expressed jealousy because he was not originally in the mechanical department.

"Lubrication was no longer needed," engineer Wienzapfel recalled. "It cut the roundhouse work to nothing." Roundhouse foreman T. Herman Blythe added: "When I started at the railroad, I went from the third shift, to the second, and then to the first shift. When the diesels came in, I went back down the same way. They started cutting men off about 1947, and my seniority wouldn't let me hold the roundhouse foreman's job in Tucson. The diesel wheels were a lot smaller than a steam locomotive's driving wheels and that cut out a job. They also didn't use tires like steam engines did."

The SP removed its passenger train from the line between Tucson and Ambos Nogales (both cities on the international border) during the fall of 1950. Dubbed "El

Future division chief timekeeper Elgin Ball and Pacific System vice-president of labor relations Carl Ball Jr., grew up at Fremont Avenue and 16th Street and ran the dusty streets of Barrio Millville. "We'd get ice that they threw out when they re-iced the reefer cars and sell it," said Carl. "We'd pull around a wagon and get a nickel for a good-sized chunk. This was about 1920. I stayed in Millville until my parents moved in 1940." Sixty-six years later, former neighborhood residents still speak with pride of their neighborhood's diverse heritage and harmonious relations. (Elgin Ball Collection)

Rapido," the train had rambled over the bumpy swaying 55-mile road for forty years in two hours and five minutes on the good days. Engineer Tom Collins recalled: "Frank Dietz was on the Nogales run because he had only one good eye. Since one-eyed men weren't allowed on regular runs, a series of men blind in one eye pulled the Nogales run. Besides Dietz, there was Sam Falvey and M.D. Huddleston."

Divsion superintentdent Ralph Coltrin (left) watches work from the observation lounge aboard the Tucson during Centralized Traffic Control (CTC) line changes. Led by Berkley-educated civil engineer Tom Lewis, a crew that included instrument man William Lynch and rodmen William Peterschmidt and Jim Conners began laying out the project for a line change and siding extension at Sybil east of Benson. Division extra gangs completed the track construction. (Tom Lewis Collection)

As workers left the company, the SP purchased their seniority rights. "They bought seniority from a lot of the younger firemen," Crowell said. "Some of them still hung in there though and kept their seniority. They didn't work for a few years but eventually the company called them back. It seemed like, if they had ten engineers, they only had to have three or four firemen, so the SP could 'blank' [eliminate] four [sic] jobs." Crowell recalled, "We did lose the callboys, and when the shops closed, back shop and roundhouse jobs were lost, but they found other work for them."

SP vice-president of labor relations Carl A. Ball Jr. remembered, "Firemen didn't leave the railroad right away. Men who had seniority worked out their time until retirement. Eventually, we eliminated firemen on everything except passenger trains. So there was some remaining work for firemen."

Ralph Coltrin waves adios to the steam era from his private business car, the Tucson. (Ralph Coltrin Collection)

In short order, the SP restructured its southern Arizona operations. Soon after Coltrin took over the division, the SP abandoned its line from Charleston to Tombstone. "There was nothing to ship out of there," he said. "The same with the Fairbank to Patagonia line. The only thing that came out of there for the last couple of years was an occasional car of stock. I used to haul my family up there when we wanted to make a little Saturday trip."

During Coltrin's tenure, the company also abandoned the old EP&SW road to Douglas or south line. "They didn't need it either," said Coltrin. "They had the main line via Willcox, which was straighter and shorter. It was upgraded and had CTC. It just didn't make sense to maintain this entire additional railroad over there for a local train, which was all that was running at the time." The job of the "gandy dancer," repairing the track, also changed as "continuous rail" allowed the company to close section-workers housing on the Gila at Sentinel, Mohawk, Mobile, and Wellton.

Another casualty of the times, SP's high-class passenger service tumbled into oblivion. Because it averaged only 4.5 passengers per 125-mile trip, SP's Gila Tomahawk made its final passenger run between Bowie and Globe on New Year's Eve 1953. By 1955, the Old Pueblo's population had increased ten-fold since the trains arrived in 1880. Powerful engines now pulled long trains through the city, and freight-handling delays, traffic delays, and crossing accidents created economic problems that demanded resolution.

In 1880, the city's business community endured a revolution engendered by the railroad's low prices and speed of transport. Two decades later, the city's central business district had moved eastward, up Congress Street from Main Avenue toward the SP reserve. The post-World War II trucking boom effected changes that paralleled those precipitated when the SP first arrived in Tucson. Freed by large, efficient trucks, firms began to abandon once desirable warehouses near the railroad. Reduced traffic congestion, better access to their service area, and cheaper land prices lured several concerns away from downtown.

In the mid-1950s, proximity to the railroad became a liability. Most warehouse operations moved toward outlying areas. Community planners explained that "northward spurts" of business development followed completion of the Fourth Avenue tunnel in 1916, Sixth Avenue subway in 1930, the Broadway subway in 1931, and the Stone Avenue subway in 1935. But, these "tended strongly to fringe types of business," because their "frontage contact and continuity" remained severed from the main business district by the SP tracks, and warehouses and plants that bordered

Proximity to the railroad paid dividends for local businesses early on, but motor trucks and congestion changed the Tucson commercial landscape by the mid-1950s. (AHS #B24005)

them. "A subway, itself, further accentuates this separation," claimed planners. Railroad "operations at street grade through the growing congestion of Tucson's central business district have become burdensome and costly to all."

In early February 1955, city planners presented the O'Dowd Plan to railroad officals. It called for lowering the SP main line and constructing a "by-pass" through downtown Tucson. A twelve-thousand-foot track alteration would veer from the existing line at Park Avenue, run west along Fifteenth Street, and emerge to surface grade

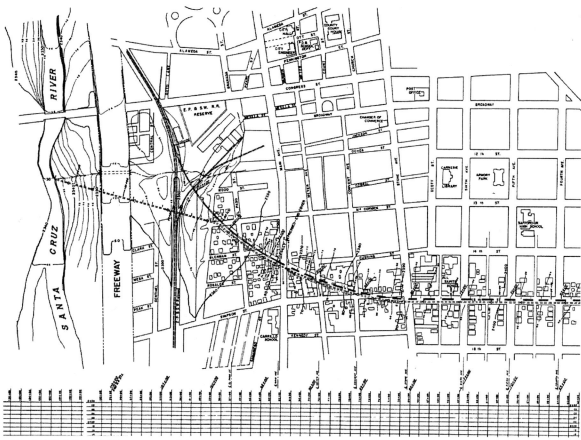

The 1955 O'Dowd Plan proposal (above). During a single year, 1959, the city doubled in size, from 107,300 to 213,000 people. (City of Tucson Planning Department)

in the EP&SW station near Congress Street and Interstate 10. The design added one-half mile to travel distance through the city, running around the SP passenger and freight stations; the roundhouse and company shops; the ice plant and platform; fifty-one warehouses and their spurs; and almost twenty-seven miles of track.

Because the diesel engine rendered several repair shops and other facilities unnecessary, the O'Dowd Plan recommended the city purchase those unused portions of the local SP reserve. Tenants occupied all but 13 percent of industrial property in the city. The railroad property "could further supply" a need "for close-in industrial loca-

tions," declared planners. The purchase "could create a profitable industrial neighborhood out of the nearly vacant SP reserve and render the area quite compatible with neighboring uses." Planners pushed hard on SP corporate officials to accept the O'Dowd Plan: "The former advantages of centrally located railroad facilities have disappeared with the growth of Tucson and the changed character of transportation generally. The design of existing facilities does not maximize diesel operation and the new methods of rail-motor-truck freight handling. They occupy land more valuable for other purposes and are a hindrance to the sound growth and development of the central business district."

The railroad rejected the O'Dowd Plan as too costly. Today, Rio Nuevo funds might best be applied to revitalize Tucson's heart through purchase or development of the former SP right-of-way. Piercing the railroad track barrier, such efforts would meld the city's two halves with people-friendly linkages such as shopping, housing, and parks.

Charles R. McGowan Sr. ran locomotive No. 1629 on the last steam engine from Phoenix to Yuma, December 5, 1955. McGowan earned $31.68 for his seven-hour-twenty-five minute run. Locomotive No. 1673 ran as the last steam in

Hard-nosed A.T. Ash, former El Paso night yardmaster, slugged a conductor in the jaw after a dispute in 1907. When his fellow rails banded together to support him, the railroad fired Ash and 55 fellow workers. He hired out in Tucson as a conductor during 1912, and posed for this photograph on his last run in May 1953. (Barbara Salyer Collection)

C.R. McGowan Sr. boards his engine at the Hayden Smelter in this 1951 photograph. McGowan ran the last steam engine between Phoenix and Gila Bend. (Betty Nowell Collection)

Tucson on March 20, 1955, to celebrate the railroad's arrival seventy-five years earlier. The small engine also saw regular duty as the "Dinky," moving engines around the local roundhouse. Prior to that, Connie Weinzapfel remembered running the historic engine on the local run out of Benson, three days a week to Fort Huachuca, and three days to Patagonia.

Old heads reminisced about the days of steam when they gathered in Tucson during May of 1956. "Every trip was an adventure fifty years ago," said retired rail,

Henry F. Gaul of El Paso: "We had to clean our own engines. Even had to scour the brass all the next day, after a late run at night." A.T. Ash, EP&SW's local night yardmaster ca. 1912, remembered using "man brakes," when he turned brakes by hand on top of each car, before trains had air brakes. "Several times I twisted a brake staff off with a pick handle," said Ash. 'Once in Naco, I tumbled backward off the top of the car. I landed on my shoulders and the other boys said they heard me grunt. Then I got up and caught the train. Today, I suppose you'd have to go to the hospital. And they'd have to get permission to repair the damages and start an investigation."

With passenger traffic dwindling and unprofitable, the SP appealed to the Arizona Corporation Commission for permission to discontinue its fast Argonaut train from New Orleans in September 1957. Eliminating service between Wellton and Picacho, the new train would not stop at Casa Grande, Eloy, or Gila Bend. Arizonans felt discriminated against because the railroad planned to continue its long-distance service between El Paso and New Orleans. Commissioners denied the railroad's petition, rejecting SP's assertions that eliminating the Argonaut would cut the company's Arizona operating losses by $2.7 million. Despite the ruling, the SP discontinued the Argonaut at the start of October and replaced it with an intra-state train, the Imperial. Arizona's Corporation Commission found an "epidemic of unsafe equipment" in October 1957.

That year, company president D.J. Russell predicted, "The jet plane will spell the end of the transcontinental passenger train. The Pullman [sleeping] car will be extinct within 20 years." Ninety-year-old

Under superintendent Ralph Coltrin (far right), SP employees benefited from a Toastmasters speaking program. (Eddie Caballero Collection)

Bright and energetic George Perkins appears far younger than his ninety years. "I made a lot of enemies," he explained. "According to the brakemen, I either put on too many crews or not enough crews. I couldn't ever do it right. Nevertheless, I got ninety-eight percent of the votes out of my home lodge, when I was elected general chairman. (Kalt Collection)

George R. Perkins explained: "During the time I was local union chairman, SP was trying to do away with passenger service. When the company petitioned the government to let them do away with certain passenger trains, there was always an Interstate Commerce Commission mediation hearing." Perkins attended one negotiation session that lasted two weeks in Phoenix and another in Deming, New Mexico. "We were given an opportunity to present the union's side. The hearing in Deming was the last one we ran." SP contended there weren't enough riders to justify continuing their passenger trains. "The union felt there was a need for passenger service," said Perkins. "We felt that the bus would not replace it and that the airplanes would never replace train service.

I think they're gonna find out in the end that there's still a need for railroad passenger service."

Coincident with the diesel engine, a $17,000-per-mile CTC system revolutionized communication on the SP. Actuated by electric circuits, lights on a track diagram produced continuous reports on the progress of each train. Atop the dispatcher's desk, electric pens, with clockwork synchronized to railroad time, recorded a train's every movement on a chart. The system allowed dispatchers to route two trains with such precision that neither had to stop as they passed. "CTC changed railroading like night and day," remembered Weinzapfel. "It was similar to your 'stop' and 'go' signs. You've got four directions, red, green, yellow and flashing yellow. If you get a red signal you stop. You don't have train orders anymore."

"During the mid-1950s, they first put the CTC machines upstairs at the de-

Vance E. Shirley studies his Centralized Traffic Control board while controlling trains over the Gila or Tucson Division's western end during 1977. (Union Pacific Museum)

Happy Houston (center) welcomed American Airlines to Tucson in 1950. (Bettie Houston Crawford Collection)

pot," explained former assistant chief dispatcher Robert DeHart. "But, on an inspection tour, the president of the railroad saw what problems could occur. He didn't want the machines up there in case of fire or disaster. The company built a separate house for the CTC next to the Fourth Avenue subway. They used a very big fork-lift and took the CTC machines out through the windows of the depot's second floor." DeHart explained, "We had four dispatchers that sat in front of a board that had lights running around on it. If the dispatcher wanted you to stop your train, or head into a siding, he pressed a certain number. The signal went to a control room and threw a switch that might be three hundred miles from here, going into El Paso. With CTC, all you do is go according to the lights."

Conductor Jackson commanded the first "all-CTC" train from Tucson to Lordsburg in 1959. "When they put in CTC, why, it just become like a picnic," he said. "You just raced over the road. You could go to Lordsburg in five or six hours where before eight, nine, ten hours was a fast trip. They got so good with it, the SP took out twenty-five sidetracks between Yuma and Tucson." Rail work also grew less physical. "The job today, if you wanted to base it on actual effort expended, both enginemen and trainmen don't put out 30 percent of the

effort they did during the steam era," claimed Jackson. "Now, you go all the way to Yuma without stopping. You stay inside an air-conditioned cab. You've got 'yo-yo-cushioned' drawbars, and you've got detectors [for sensing track and equipment problems]. Compared to the old days, it's a pension!"

President D.J. Russell had ordered SP agents to begin selling United Airlines tickets at the start of October 1958. Fittingly, SP's final "Salute to Steam" took place in Sacramento, California on the 19th of that month. Here, the railroad first burst to life west of the Rocky Mountains ninety years earlier. The SP band played lustily as 4-8-4 General Service locomotive No. 4460 completed that last steam run, a round trip from Oakland, California to Reno, Nevada.

Equally appropriate, at the podium that morning stood the ceremony's keynote

(1855 - 1958)

SALUTE TO THE STEAM AGE
on Southern Pacific
DEDICATION PROGRAM
Sacramento, California   October 19, 1958

(Ray Hanson Collection)

speaker, Stanley M. Houston. The highly successful son of Tucson roundhouse foreman Caleb "Dad" Houston, Stanley now headed the company's mechanical department in San Francisco. Houston, surely, took pause that fall morning to reflect upon his early days with the Arizona Eastern Railroad as a fourteen-year-old shop apprentice at Globe in 1913.

"Bob the Cat (Caterpillar front-end loader) man" readies to push up old rail as changes begin at Sybil, Arizona to accomodate CTC in 1958. (A.T. Lewis Collection)

SP donated about sixty steam behemoths to various communities around the nation as the age came to an end. A thrilling new era graced railroading and the nation. For many, however, the music died on that sad California day.

By mid-December 1959, Steve Reibel's Acme House Moving & Wrecking Company crews had begun lassoing sections of the SP's local roundhouse walls with a cable and yanking them to the

Bowie 1958: it's just not the same. (A.T.Lewis collection)

ground. As the historic structure crumbled before the sword of progress, day roundhouse foreman Joe Wagner recalled the "Out Our Way" cartoons of J.R. Williams. Syndicated nationwide, the former Arizona cattleman had begun his pinpoint drawings in 1922, at the age of thirty-four. Williams worked as a fireman on the railroad but, vowed Wagner, "any railroad machinist will tell you, Williams must have worked in a machine shop to have drawn such real-life cartoons." Shop foreman Wagner and shopman B.R. Bradley, who started in the Tucson shops in 1917, noted that the machine shop in Williams's comics illustrated a disappearing age. "Railroad machinists are a vanishing race and are being outmoded by electricians, at least in diesel repair and maintenance shops," said Wagner.

The foundation of rails' social structure lay upon the company's facilities, equipment, and daily operations on the local division. Within this framework, consistent expectations of co-workers' behavior grew implicit among local rails. Adherence to procedure, decorum, and a common purpose characterized relationships on railroad jobs. As the material infrastructure of the SP evolved, spectacular waves of change crashed upon the social dynamic of her people.

Embedded in the nation's dramatic social change as the 1960s approached, the great steam locomotive's swan song came as SP pressed forward toward modernity. Rail electrician and Armory Park resident Frank Hutcheson explained, "I think it was just a general disturbance of the lifestyle. People started moving a lot. The big aircraft plant came into Tucson [Hughes Aircraft]. Davis-Monthan [Air Force Base] built up. The railroad was no longer the number-one

industry in Tucson." Airplanes and automobiles strangled railroad passenger volume. "In the old days, graded back roads were the only way to get to Tucson, so everybody rode the train," remembered ninety-year-old Gordon "Nose" Manning.

The Argonaut returned as the Nos. 5 and 6 and ran as one of the last regular SP passenger trains on the Tucson Division. "That was the only train we had on the north line, and we had none on the old EP&SW south line along the border," said Manning. "We had four passenger trains at one time, but after Interstate 10 came, we just about lost all of our passenger trains. There was plenty of business, but the company wanted to get rid of them. They had all the freight service they could handle." Labor chieftain Perkins asserted, "Getting rid of passenger trains was for the company's benefit. It was interfering with their freight traffic where most of their money was being made. Because passenger trains had to

---

ARGONAUT

Lounge Car
(Air-Conditioned)

Lounge Car for Standard Pullman Car passengers, periodicals and newspapers, market reports, writing room, barber, valet service, bath, ladies' lounge and bath.

Dining Car
(Air-Conditioned)

Breakfast from 7:00 A.M.   Lunch from 12 Noon

Dinner from 5:30 P.M.

PERSONAL SERVICE

Barber Shop—Men

Hair cut	$0.50
Shave	.25
Beard trimmed	.35
Facial Massage	.50
Facial Massage (Boncilla)	1.00
Hair Singe	.25
Plain Shampoo	.50
Shampoo (Egg, Oil or Tonic)	.75
Hair Tonics	.25
Bath	.50

ARGONAUT

Barber Shop—Women

Hair bob	$0.75
Hair bob-trim.	.50
Neck clip	.25
Plain Shampoo	1.00
Shampoo (Egg, Oil or Tonic)	1.25
Hair Tonics	.25
Bath	.50

Valet Service

Trousers (pressing)	$0.35
Vest	.25
Coat	.65
Suit	1.00
Overcoat	1.00
Woman's Skirt	.75
Woman's Coat	1.00
Woman's Dress (One Piece)	1.00
Woman's Suit	1.25
Woman's Dress (Silk)	1.50

Valet service from 6:30 in the morning to midnight. The porter of the sleeping car will arrange for this service. Please advise at what hour you desire to have clothes returned.

The Argonaut maintained a fine array of services during 1937. (Kalt Collection)

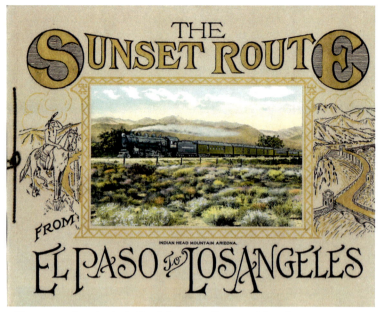

From premiere train to food from vending machines in twenty years. (UASC)

have the right-of-way over freight trains, they slowed them down and the SP wanted to get rid of them. The mediator let the company do away with the Argonaut. Then they originated Amtrak. Now, there's only one passenger train every three days through Tucson." Amtrak rerouted its No. 1/21 and 2/22 trains over Southern Pacific's Gila Subdivision between Tucson and Yuma, effective June 1, 1996. The railroad no longer directly served Coolidge, Tempe, or Phoenix. The move left the Arizona capital as the largest city in the United States without intercity passenger rail service.

During 1967, SP lost an estimated $2.69 for every mile it ran a passenger train. Company red ink totaled more than $19 million. SP's "varnish train," the Golden State Limited, made its final run

SP advertising portrayed a space age rail yard of the future at Colton, California. (UASC)

Cleveland Clyde worked at the depot when the SP limited its dining service to vending machines early in 1966. (Sid Showalter Collection)

through Tucson, February 22, 1967. Conductor V.R. McClain and his crew of sixteen, including engineer M.E. Shad, fireman D.W. Keplar, and brakeman H.H. Harvey, took 107 travelers west to Los Angeles. *The Tucson Daily Citizen* captured the dreary nighttime scene: "Here and there the orange points of cigarettes cut through the darkness. Up in the combination club car, the porter yawned and said he wondered how the company would get him back to Chicago at the end of his last run, his white jacket with brass buttons stained from the day's work, his tie a limp, shapeless clump of black. A lone club-car customer sipped a beer while the porter sat at a table and tried to stay awake."

Quick-witted and gracious, former division superintendent J.J. Tierney recalled the full-blown changes in railroading at the kitchen table in his comfortable Tucson foothills home in early September 2002. "Most railroad operating people never had any assigned

days off except in the yard," Tierney explained. "If you worked a switch engine in the yard, you'd work the job five days and have two days off. Otherwise, engineers, brakemen, and conductors didn't have assigned days off. They were at the mercy of the telephone, and whenever it rang, they were expected to go on duty."

When Tierney started with the SP in 1954, he said, "You were thankful to have work. It was a good job and you could lay off once in a while. People didn't like to lay off, though, because they couldn't afford to. They didn't have any money in their pocket. You hurt yourself to lay off. It had to be a special occasion, somebody's wedding, funeral, or death in the family. Men usually laid only off when they were real sick." As times changed, "people started to call up at any time and asked to be laid off for personal business or anything," Tierney said. "Then they started always laying off on Friday afternoons. It was a terrible time 'cause

(l-r) Switchmen Danny Bryne, Gordon Toncheff Jr., and Roy Boltz, fireman Nick Weber, and engineer Art Schupback stopped for a photograph at the Twenty-Second Street yard during 1966. (Sid Showalter Collection)

Yardmaster R.E. Crehan oversees local operations from the Tucson tower in 1973. (Rudy Benitez Collection)

everybody always wanted to be off for the weekend. Today people don't want to work because they get so much pressure from the home. The wife says, 'By God, that railroad can go to hell! I want you home for the weekend. The kids are out of school and you haven't been with them.' In olden days that didn't happen because the breadwinner was the ruler of the house. That's the railroad industry, and people don't want to do that anymore."

Abuse of the privilege of laying off only worsened, Tierney recalled. "It got to where we said, 'We can't afford to let you lay off for personal business because we don't have any people and the extra board is depleted.' Then a guy would try, 'Then lay me off sick.' We finally resorted to demanding a doctor's release. They'd have to spend the time to go get it, but it was really no problem because we had company doctors that would give it to them."

The SP replaced its dining and lounge cars in February 1966, rendering vending-machines its trains's only food source. Detractors accused the railroad of deliberately dropping its food services to drive customers away. The railroad reported that its best train averaged only seventy-two passengers and ran at a loss of

$980,700 during the first quarter of 1967. The American public "deserted passenger trains in favor of planes, buses, and private cars," avowed company officials. "The business traveler has been lost to the jets and when he left us it spelled the end of long-distance luxury service."

Almost 300,000 people lived in Tucson when SP's Nos. 39 and 40 passenger trains made their final runs, during late August 1967. The local depot played "host to the ghost of the Southern Pacific's 'Golden Empire' era," explained young *Citizen* staff writer David Carter. "The 'Empire' is mostly freight nowadays. Cattle, cucumbers, and cantaloupe are the prime bill of fare, passengers are passé. Today the lobby and baggage center have been cut in half; freight offices have taken over." By the spring of 1968, five western states, including Arizona, demanded SP restore its crumbling sleeping and dining car service on the once-elegant Sunset Limited. Now called simply the Sunset, the train's downgrading eliminated six conductors, twelve brakemen, and two train baggagemen from Tucson Division rolls.

In May 1968, federal examiner John S. Messner ruled SP violated the Interstate Commerce Act by not providing sleeping and eating facilities. The company also assessed "special service charges without offering special services." Messner declared the decline in rail travel need not be permanent. Much traffic could be gained "if the defeatist attitude of the rail carriers could be overcome," said Messner.

Through the years electronic "hotbox" and drag detectors had replaced brakemen. Computers replaced conductors, and remotely-monitored "end-of-train" devices allowed engineers to set the brakes from the rear of the train. William Crowell, whose father began as a local boilermaker in 1919, polished the finer point: "It got to be a young man's field. The trains were high speed and long. It got to be different. It got to be sort of a new world, really."

Gone were the days when hundreds of workers danced to the SP hustle and bustle. Herman Blythe worked until age sixty. "When I retired in 1982, there wasn't a single boilermaker on the payroll," said Herman. "That's how much we have changed over the years. I took reduced pension to get away from it. It got to where you'd just go to work and start pushin' buttons. At the end, they had me workin' with long-haired hippies. It got frustrating. Nobody knew how to show up on time, work hard, or bring a lunch to work. Everybody wanted to go out to eat. There was no fun in the railroad anymore."

If ever one thing proved "all it was cracked up to be," the SP filled the bill. Inside, outside, up-ways, down, the railroad earned every trait and moniker credited to it. The rosy and the raunchy, the generous and the usurious, the proud and the pitiful, all owned a place among the state's most memorable railroad tales. Standing tallest—the good-hearted people of southern Arizona who lived and worked during the days of steam when Tucson was a railroad town.

Truly, a new age had come upon the nation, but SP men and women remained loyal to each other and the railroad. *For-*

tune Magazine captured the core: "The Southern Pacific is men, and to these men it is not just a railroad. It is the Southern Pacific. It is a shining track that leads back into their boyhood. It is a thing they love, an intensely romantic thing that carries them ceaselessly from place to place, and hoots through the night. A railroad man is an organization man by reason of the tracks; for the tracks are to him what the sea is to lovers of the sea; an excitement yet a discipline."

As life passed him by during the late 1970s, locomotive engineer Carl Ball Sr. ran a steam engine back into his boyhood. No longer speaking much, Carl draped his right arm "out the window" over his wheelchair's arm rest and used its brake lever for a throttle. Then, beaming full-tilt, the beloved old engineer streaked over SP's shining track one last time. Now, that's a railroad man!

Carl Ball Sr. posed with his sons Elgin and Carl Jr. on the San Simon helper ca. 1919. (Elgin Ball Collection)

THE RAILROAD MEN

Let's sing a simple ditty for the hero of the rail, whose name and deeds grace the page of any song or tale; the stalwart son of honest toil with limb alert and strong—let's give to him our honor for he is many in Tucson.

And while the winter hour is cold and tardy is the dawn, and while you turn in broken dreams your downy cough upon, while through the skies contending hosts prevail—the wind and rain—he finds no shelter from the storm, the man who runs the train.

And when at night you sit at home and watch the fire glow when out beyond the city's walls you hear the whistles blow, be sure that at the very heart of those vibrations long, he stands prepared to do or die, the hero of our song.

And He who rides on every road, unceasing, to and fro, and by the side of every man is ever said to go—be sure that on the last long run His hand the train will guide, and "Heaven" will be the station and finished be the ride.

Arizona Star January 19, 1910

Rudy Benitez captured sunset over the Tucson yard during the mid-1980s. (Rudy Benitez Collection)

References

Endnotes are organized in sequential order for each chapter. In an attempt to facilitate future research, without cluttering the text for the casual reader, endnotes are referenced by the essential words of a quote or factual statement.

Introduction

1. "The train rolled [rocked] as it ran along the tracks," John C. Etchells, *Arizona Daily Citizen*, March 17, 1955. Born in 1873, Etchells grew up playing around his father's blacksmith shop near Pearl and Congress streets.

2. "The engine of the work train puffed and snorted," *Arizona Daily Star*, January 11, 1901. When it arrived in Tucson, engine No. 41 pulled thirty-nine flat cars, thirteen boxcars, eleven construction cars, and two water cars in the work train. *Citizen*, March 17, 1880.

3. The railroad warned Tucson parents, *Citizen*, March 18, 1880.

4. "There was rejoicing in Arizona last night," *Phoenix Enterprise*, March 23, 1880. Years later, The *Legislative Blue Book of Arizona* noted, "It fell to John W. 'Jack' Bruce to pull the first train into Tucson."

5. "People don't celebrate like we did in the old days," Leonard E. Romero, *Star*, March 20, 1955.

6. company's large turntable, *Citizen*, March 23, 1880. Several carloads of buggies and carriages arrived on March 25.

7. "Such is the effect of enterprise," *Citizen*, March 25, 1880. By April 13, company workmen had finished the local depot's foundation and begun laying flooring.

8. *Los Angeles Herald* reported, *Citizen*, April 15, 1880.

9. lack of clerical supplies forced agent A.J. Finlay to close his freight office, *Citizen*, April 15, 1880.

10. "The [passenger] depot now being built will not be large enough for Tucson," T.M. Cash, *Citizen*, April 20, 1880. George C. Hopkins took charge of the freight department and William H. Better, telegraph operator, *Citizen*, April 30, 1880.

11. "In reality, Arizona was such a lone, alien, orphan thing," F.C. Lockwood, *Pioneer Days of Arizona* (New York: MacMillen Publishing, 1932), p. 311.

12. Terrorized the southwest since the late 1600s, Thomas E. Sheridan, *Del Rancho al Barrio: The Mexican Legacy of Tucson* (Tucson: Mexican Heritage Project, Arizona Heritage Center, Arizona Historical Society, 1983), p. 9.

13. "reduced the trip to Los Angeles from five days to less than one," *Star*, October 20, 1898.

Chapter 1

1. Half of the population, Thomas E. Sheridan, *Los Tucsonenses*, (Tucson: University of Arizona Press 1968), p. 126. Spanish surnamed people represented 54.7 percent of Tucson's 7,531 residents.

2. "Take them as a class," *Star*, October 20, 1898.

3. "I can take the average ten-year-old boy," J.D. "Jack" Boleyn, January 6, 1898 letter in *Citizen*, January 10, 1898; *Star*, February 25, 1898; *Citizen*, February 28, 1898.

4. "While our chemical engine is a thing of beauty," Henry Buehman, January 3, 1898 letter in *Star*, January 5, 1898. Chemical fire engine, for $2,234, *Star*, January 7, 1898.

5. "didn't scare the flames a bit," *Citizen*, February 28, 1898.

6. "saved large amounts of property," *Star*, September 18, 1898.

7. SP Fire Brigade, *Star*, March 6, 1898.

8. "Had it not been for the heroic work," *Star*, September 18, 1898.

9. "Streaked with black smoke," *Star*, September 19, 1898.

10. Sunset Telephone and Telegraph, *Citizen*, September 19, 1898; *Star*, October 1, 1898.

11. Colonel William F. Herring's library, *Star*, October 1, 1898. P.B. and Albert Zeigler had purchased Bradley's New Candy Kitchen in March 1898, *Star*, April 1, 1898.

12. "Good Lesson for the City," *Citizen*, September 20, 1898.

13. City council disbanded its volunteer fire department, *Citizen*, September 20, 1898.

14. New volunteer fire department, *Citizen*, October 3, 1898; *Star*, October 4, 1898.

15. F. J. Villaescusa's wagon shop, *Citizen*, October 17, 1898.

16. Denied exemption, *Citizen*, May 18, 1898.

17. Made the SP shop brigade a separate division, *Citizen*, January 27, 1900 and *Star*, January 10, 1907.

18. "Tucson is not a 'fire town," *Citizen*, February 28, 1898.

19. Well dug north of town at Stockham Station, *Star*, September 2, 1898. The company discontinued its Stockham Station pump during June of 1903; *Citizen*, May 27, 1903.

20. "Our condition is deplorable in the extreme," Epes Randolph, *Star*, March 5, 1898; SP proposal by Epes Randolph, letter to F.E. Russell January 4, 1898 in *Citizen*, January 12, 1898.

21. "I do not believe in building a furnace and letting the other fellow," Sam Hughes, *Citizen*, March 4, 1898; *Star*, March 5, 1898.

22. Insurance man H.D. Underwood proclaimed, *Star*, March 4, 1898.

23. Doubling the capacity of the Stockham pumping plant, *Star*, September 2, 1898.

24. C.L. Sonnichsen, *Tucson: the Life and Times of an American City*, (Norman: University of Oklahoma Press, 1892), p.134.

25. Eugene W. Waterbury, *Star*, April 9 and May 18, 1898. Alexander Brodie asked men in towns around the territory to serve as recruiters, including Waterbury. Author Charles H. Herner, January 4, 2006.

26. 300 stands of arms to Bisbee, *Citizen*, April 27, 1898; *Star*, May 17, 1898.

27. William O. "Buckey" O'Neil led the territory's fighters, Charles H. Herner, *Cowboy Cavalry: A Photographic His-*

tory of the Arizona Rough Riders (Tucson: Arizona Historical Society, 1998), p.2. O'Neill was reportedly the first soldier mustered into the nation's troops.

28. "These quick movements have brought Arizona the recognition of the United States," *Phoenix Republican* May 17, 1898. That July, Tucson troops named their little Skye terrier Miss U.S. Crowley, *Citizen*, July 7, 1898.

29. "The people of Arizona are all shouting for our American heroes," *Star*, June 28, 1898.

30. "After a series of years of alternate panic and stagnation," *Bradstreet's* in *Star*, January 1, 1898.

31. "gold bonanza" near the Fresnal, south of Tucson, *Star*, August 13, 1898.

32. Miners' first convention, *Star*, January 26, 1898.

33. Tucson Sampling Works reopened, *Citizen*, June 29, 1898; *Star*, August 30, 1898.

34. agents of capitalists, *Citizen*, October 11, 1898.

35. Pima County taxes had dropped, *Star*, August 23, 1898.

36. Tucson Ice and Cold Storage, *Star*, January 23, 1898.

37. Paul Moroney, *Star*, March 12, 1903.

38. "every dollar is home capital," *Star*, January 23, 1898.

39. City council condemns the Wedge, *Star*, January 24, 1898.

39. "The city wanted to become more up-to-date," *Star*, May 1, 1902.

40. Tucson Electric Company, *Star*, January 26 and September 10, 1898.

41. Arizona Press Association, resolution, in *Star*, March 12 and 13, 1898.

42. "Its plodding motive power-not at all responsible for its grizzled appearance," Estelle M. Buehman, *Old Tucson: a Hop, Skip, and a Jump from 1539 Indian Settlement to New and Greater Tucson*, (Tucson: State Consolidated Publishing, 1911), p. 64-65.

43. Henry Clews, *Weekly Market Letter*, August 20, 1898 in *Citizen*, August 30, 1898.

44. "with suave manners," *Star*, April 8, 1898.

45. T. Seddon Bruce, *Star*, September 3, and September 11, 1898; *Citizen*, September 12, 1898.

46. "Tucson is a heavy loser each year," *Star*, November 22, 1898.

47. Rents half of those in Phoenix, *Star*, August 20, 1898.

48. "This will be the first (in all its details) really modern," *Citizen*, February 16, 1899.

49. "No one thing will improve our streets so much," *Star*, September 15, 1898. As late as 1903, the north-side gutter west of the Arizona Club filled with foul water from a nearby restaurant that had no connection to the sewer.

50. "It becomes no less our duty to care for Tucson's moral well being," Henry Buehman, letter January 3, 1898, *Star*, January 5, 1898.

51. "Tucson can never reach that proud distinction," *Star*, February 13, 1898.

52. "underlying spirit of progressive conservatism," *Star*, November 16, 1898.

53. "Tucson has never been," George Oakes, "*Star*, June18, 1898.

54. Tucson: Mountain States Telephone and Telegraph Company, 1949), n.p.

55. "The year which has gone into eternity," *Star*, January 1, 1899.

Chapter 2

1. "The advance of a railroad into any region," *Star*, January 22, 1902.

2. Cost-cutting edict, *Citizen*, April 6, 1898.

3. "After that Tucson began to open up in a business sort of way," "Reminiscences" (1875-1899), manuscript, Mose Drachman Papers, AHS-T. MS 0226, p. 44. Drachman provided "easily the most enlivening incident in municipal history since the close of Ben Heney's administration" when he and fellow city councilman D.S. Cochran staged a fist fight at the council's November 7, 1910 meeting. "The conflict was remarkable for the number and intensity of the blows exchanged and for their exceeding harmlessness," *Citizen* reported, November 8, 1910. The SP granted operating rights to the Santa Fe over its 242-mile Tehachapi Pass line from Mohave to Needles, California. Erle Heath, *Seventy-five Years of Progress* (San Francisco: December 1945), p. 201.

4. William C. Hood, *Globe Silver Belt* in the *Citizen*, February 15, 1898.

5. "People of every age and color," *Globe Times* in *Star*, December 3, 1898.

6. "Never failed to happify the railroad boys," *Citizen*, January 31, 1899.

7. "down to the baby and the favorite canine," *Star*, December 22, 1906.

8. In its safe, $42,700, *Star*, August 2, 1898.

9. A.J. Taylor, *Citizen*, August 2, 1898.

10. "I've gone in that ditch once and I probably will again," *Citizen*, December 20, 1909.

11. seven-tenths-of-a-mile arc near milepost 1028, *Southern Pacific Bulletin*, February 1921, p. 4. Tucson Division superintendent, William W. Wilson explained that a "recent line change had eliminated six ten-degree (thought to be very difficult arc to negotiate) curves." The SP had rebuilt .7 of a mile at Pay Car curve in 1917; D.F. Myrick, *Railroads of Arizona, Volume I: The Southern Roads* (Berkeley: Howell-North Books, 1975) p. 108.

12. "Trainmen raced to the engine," *Star*, August 2, 1898.

13. "Yesterday, in the blackness that precedes the morning's dawn," *Star*, December 20, 1909.

14. Forty instruments, *Citizen*, April 12, 1910.

15. "covered themselves in glory," *Star*, April 28, 1898.

16. Mariner to stand a $1,000 bet, *Star*, November 26, 1898.

17. Mariner relinquished direction, *Citizen*, January 26, 1900.

18. Boilermakers 40¢, machinists 38¢, and helpers 25¢, *Citizen*, September 9 and 17, 1901; *Star*, January 18, 1902.

19. Band members, *Star*, January 18, 1902.

20. Naco bullfights, *Star*, February 1, 1902.

21. "Tucson had all the road shows like Madam Schumann-Heink," Norman Wallace Papers AV 0366, p.33, AHS-T.

22. "Baseball was early Tucson's only major sport," Roy P. Drachman, *From Cowtown to Desert Metropolis* (San Francisco: Whitewing Press, 1990), p.6. By May 1909, Phoenix had abolished liquor in even social clubs, while Tucson remained "wide open." With the railroad's cheap fare, Phoenix fans found double reason to come south for their baseball.

23. Tucson's first catcher's mask, *Tucson Daily Citizen*, August 23, 1910. The *Arizona Citizen* became the *Tucson Daily Citizen* on December 16, 1901, Don Schellie The *Tucson Citizen: A Century of Arizona Journalism* (Tucson: Citizen Publishing Company, 1970), p. 72.

24. Prize monies-$750, $350, and $250 to the top three teams in one early Tucson tournament, *Star*, November 3, 1907.

25. "It was the team," *Star*, July 18, 1907.

26. "an old time fan," Beuhring, *Star*, February 28, 1903.

27. Levi H. Manning donated land, *Citizen*, May 26, 1900.

28. Thanksgiving Day battle at Carrillo Gardens, *Citizen*, November 27, 1903.

30. "jar loose several thousand nuggets of copper," *Star*, July 13, 1907.

31. 'If the wicked party is found by irate fans he will stretch a rope," *Star*, July 13, 1907.

32. Veteran engineer Dennis Ryan, *Star*, July 16, 1907.

33. "We'll Hand them a Package of Lemons," *Star*, July 13, 1907.

34. Connie Mack, *Citizen*, December 15, 1909.

35. "Baseball is officially declared dead," *Citizen*, October 6 and 19, 1910; *Star*, October 7, 1910.

36. No suitable city-maintained baseball ground existed, *Star*, January 21, 1921.

37. Tucson Baseball Association, *Star*, January 9, 1921.

38. "Local fans have seen both in action in high school circles," *Citizen*, May 18, 1922.

39. "Crash of willow against horsehide," *Citizen*, January 14, 1922.

40. First-ever series, *Citizen*, August 5, 1922.

41. "The game was marred by dirty baseball," *Citizen*, August 7, 1922; *Star*, August 4, 1922.

42. "vote of thanks," *Southern Pacific Bulletin*, November 1926, p. 27.

43. Cresceus, *Star*, December 18, 1901; *Citizen*, December 17 and 20, 1901. Ziegler purchased his partner Charles DeGroff's interest in Union Park ca. 1899, and bought the adjacent Bullock acreage in 1905.

44. "Almost everyone who knows or cares about God's greatest creation," *Star*, December 18, 1901.

45. "Nothing appeals to the visibilities of man like a good horse," *Citizen*, December 17, 1903.

46. 1902 territorial record, *Star*, April 12, 1902.

47. "injurious effects and dangers of the sport," *Citizen*, February 21, 1903.

48. Garigan spearheaded merriment on Sonoita Creek, *Star*, May 15, 1921.

Chapter 3

1. "brought (in) on a stretcher," *Star*, January 30, 1903.

2. "Traveling has become so dangerous," *Los Angeles Times*, February 1, 1903. 1901 ICC records indicate 53,339 injured and 8,455 killed in railroad accidents.

3. "Clough telegraphed the "signature" of conductor Parker to the dispatcher before the train arrived." Robert B. Shaw, A History of Railroad Accidents, Safety Precautions, and Operating Practices (Potsdam NY published by the author 1978) p. 146.

4. Some took risky chances, *San Francisco Chronicle*, February 1, 1903.

5. John W. "Jack" Bruce, John S. Goff, Territorial Officials, Volume 6, Members of the Legislature A-L, Cave Creek, Arizona; Black Mountain Press, 1996; David F. Myrick identifies George Bailey and Martin Wetzel as the first engineers to run a train into Tucson. Vol. 1: *The Southern Roads*, p.54.

6. "Jump! Save your life!," *Star*, January 31, 1903

7. "his heroic chieftain," *Citizen*, January 29, 1903.

8. "McGrath would have been living today," *Star*, January 30, 1903.

9. "The scene beggared description," *Phoenix Enterprise*, January 29, 1903.

10. "the ironwork of the cars was red hot," *Citizen*, January 29, 1903.

11. "Is anyone killed?" E. Frank Clough, *Star*, January 31, 1903..

12. Oscar Marion Stewart, Nyle Leatham interview, November 14, 2004.

13. W.B. Kelly, editor of the *Bisbee Review*, threw his coat over Donahue, *Arizona Republican*, January 30, 1903; *Citizen*, February 9, 1903.

14. African-American porter, *Citizen*, January 31, 1903

15. Maynard Flood, *Star*, November 15, 1962.

16. Katie Dusenberry, phone interview, August 5, 2003.

17. George Bruce, *Star*, November 15, 1962.

18. "Parker, you have left one of your orders on the counter," *Star*, February 1, 1903.

19. "believed there was a wreck," *Star*, January 30, 1903.

20. "You will not see Clough in this part for a long while," *Los Angeles Times*, January 31, 1903.

21. "Clough arrived on Wednesday afternoon," *Citizen*, February 5, 1903.

22. "came into the meeting with some display of bravado," *Arizona Republican*, January 30, 1903.

23. "Clough's deliberate absence is accepted as a plea of guilt," *Star*, February 1, 1903.

24. Willard reportedly "derived some amusement," *Citizen*, January 31, 1903.

25. When a *Citizen* reporter requested a passenger list, *Citizen*, January 31, 1903.

26. "IT IS HORRIBLE!" *Star*, January 31, 1903.

27. "The railroad company will attempt to cover up the facts," *Citizen*, January 31, 1903.

28. "It seems they [the *Citizen*] want the responsible head," *Star*, January 31, 1903.

29. "A squabble, in which is instilled no little bitterness," *Citizen*, January 29, 1903; *San Francisco Chronicle*, January 29, 1903.

30. Conductor Parker admitted under oath, *Star*, February 20, 1903.

31. Long letter from Mrs. Clough, ibid., February 10, 1903.

32. Hugh Mackenzie, *Star*, December 4, 1903.

33. Train Agent on all passenger trains, *Star*, April 9, 1903.

34. Captain J.H. Tevis, *Arizona Bulletin*, Solomonville, Arizona, February 13, 1903.

35. G.A. Parkyns, *Los Angeles Times*, January 31, 1903.

36. "On the tablets of memory, anguish, suffering and death," *Star*, January 30, 1903.

37. Nyle Leatham, interview, November 14, 2004.

Chapter 4

1. "Police galloped through the various streets," *Star*, June 18, 1909.

2. Whalen put forth his version, *Citizen*, June 18, 1909. The Whalens first moved to the Santa Rita Hotel and then to SP physician Dr. Hiram P. Fenner's home on June 21, 1909.

3. "most dastardly and cowardly crime in the history of Tucson," ibid.

4. Inspector Dickerman, *Star*, June 22 and June 29, 1909.

5. Tom Northern, *Star*, June 22, 1909.

6. "sent his fist crashing against one of Walker's optics, *Star*, July 14, 1909.

7. "Had I known that you was goin' to fine me $20," *Star*, July 14, 1909.

8. Walker swore, *Citizen*, May 12, 1910.

9. Miss Nellie Hazel Turner, *Star*, May 12, 1910.

10. Minnie L. Pierce arrested, *Star*, May 10, 1910.

11. Bragg testified, *Star*, May 13, 1910 and First Judicial District Court of Pima County Papers, Case No. A2187, October 1, 1909.

12. "broke down utterly," *Citizen*, May 14, 1910.

13. not a single enemy, *Citizen*, June 18, 1909.

14. "Old man Whalen was the guy," Norman G. Wallace OH, March 21, 1975, Sidney Brinkerhoff, AV-0366, p. 33. AHS-T.

15. Porter Hotel, *Citizen*, June 29, 1903.

16. Ran them to the company's desires, for a nominal fee, *Citizen*, September 28, 1901.

17. Raised three feet above the building, Myrick, Vol. I, p. 74.

18. A heat test one June day, *Citizen*, June 24, 1899.

19. "the most painstaking, polite," *Citizen*, August 15, 1898.

20. L.J.F. Iaeger bought the San Xavier Hotel lease for $13,364, *Citizen*, December 21, 1901; *Star*, January 29, 1902.

21. The move cut eighteen hours off the SP's run from New Orleans to San Francisco, *Citizen*, December 31, 1901.

22. Leaped into the ceiling above the San Xavier's kitchen range, *Citizen*, June 29, 1903. Hotel guests included: Frank Ditmar, Cincinnati; J.H. LeRoy, Ogden; Thompson and wife, Nogales; G. Ewinger, Los Angeles; H.E. Cooper, San Francisco; John B. Farrish, Denver; F. Hayes, West Virginia; H. Burnham, Philadelphia; Joseph M. Locke, Cincinnati.

23. "One of the quickest fires on record," *Star*, June 30, 1903.

24. Alex Rossi agreed to accept meal tickets, *Citizen*, June 29, 1903.

25. "a prince of good fellows," *Star*, June 30, 1903.

26. Hotel operator Iaeger "seemed to take the situation good humoredly," *Citizen*, June 29, 1903.

28. "guard the city's interests before railroading," *Star*, January 7, 1902.

29. "As the *Star* has frequently stated," *Star*, January 27, 1904.

30. "The small boy and his father," *Star*, January 26, 1902.

31. "initial luster did not last long," Tom Peterson, *Arizona Republic*, September 23, 1979.

32. "Flonzaley Quartet of shoestring promotion," *Fortune Magazine*, November 1937, p. 98.

33. Storekeeper's department, *Star*, August 23, 1907.

34. Clubhouse and reading room, *Star*, September 4, 1898, and April 18, 1899; *Citizen*, April 24, 1922.

35. San Francisco earthquake, Erle Heath, *Seventy-five Years of Progress* (San Francisco: December 1945), p.22; *Southern Pacific Bulletin*, June 1996, p. 12.

36. Headquarters at 65 Market Street, *Fortune Magazine*, November 1937, p. 95.

37. "rich rare colors," *Star*," July 24, 1907.

38. "Are they all hand-painted?" Donald J. Haggerty, *Desert Dreams: The Art and Life of Maynard Dixon* (Salt Lake City: Gibbs-Smith, 1998) in Doug Kupel, *Tucson's Southern Pacific Depot: Trials, Tribulations, and Triumphs*, unpublished manuscript, p.10; *Star*, September 24, 1907.

39. New division freight house, *Star*, July 18, 1907.

41. Personal record, *Star*, October 20, 1907.

42. Every piece of property, *Star*, May 16 and 23, 1907.

43. Long-time merchants relocated, *Star*, September 26, 1906.

44. "Watch Tucson grow, especially in the warehouse district," *Star*, September 26, 1906.

45. Publish all the details of accidents, *Star*, July 10, 1907.

46. Largest single blast for ballasting material on May 14, 1909 *Star*, May 19, 1909.

47. Pedestrian subway 1910, *Citizen*, July 15, 1910.

48. "gaudy uniforms of scarlet (with) gold buttons," John Heidel, Sandra Heidel, *John Heidel-Pioneer Arizona*

Hotelman, unpublished manuscript, January 27, 1966; *Star*, January 15, 1910.

49. "with two prancing horses and a driver in a silk hat," ibid.; *Star*, February 24, 1910.

50. "Phoenix will have to wait a little longer," *Star*, July 25, 1909.

Chapter 5

1. "There must be something inspiring," *Star*, December 11, 1903.

2. M.B. Bulla, *Star*, February 23, 1904.

3. William S. Kengla, *Star*, February 10, 1903. Kengla worked as an SP car inspector 1897-1898, *Tucson City Directory*, 1897-1898.

4. Joseph B. Corbett, *Star*, June 24, 1904. Corbett led the fight to establish the position or railroad policeman in Arizona.

5. Yuma SP Settling Tanks (Tucson: AMEC Engineering Global Solutions), unpublished report, 1999, p.5. The SP also piped water to its hotel just below the tank and later converted to a steel water main.

6. Water Basin Tender's Log, 91.74, AHS-Yuma; *Arizona Professional Engineer*, July 1980, p. 23.

7. Dr. B.F. Wooding, *Star*, November 11, 1906; U.S. Patent Department Records, San Diego.

8. "Many in Washington believe it is more valuable than train control," Wooding to Stockholders, September 1, 1925, Papers of M. S. Franklin, 1873-1927, AZ 336, UASC.

9. Fruitless investments, "to the extent of millions of dollars," Mary S. Hartman to attorney Selim M. Franklin, October 14, 1935, Papers of M. S. Franklin, 1873-1927, AZ 336, UASC.

10. The first evaporative coolers in Arizona, *National Register of Historic Places Inventory Iron Horse Expansion*, Continuation sheet 35, item 8, p.17. District Nomination Form, continuation sheet 35, Item 8, p. 17.

11. "So far Tucson has been spared," *Citizen*

March 18, 1880.

12. Three weeks ago, *Citizen* March 29, 1880. The road was Meyer Street on Sanborn Insurance Company on fire maps in 1880, Myers in 1901, Meyers in 1909, and back to Meyer Street by 1933. In 2007 the road bore the name Meyer Avenue.

13. "Isla De Cuba," National Register of Historic Places Inventory Nomination Form, Iron Horse Expansion District, continuation sheet 23, item 8, p.5.

14. "Silverlocks," H.V. Siedenberg, *Citizen*, January 27, 1899; *Star*, March, 2,4, and 9, 1899.

15. Walk to El Paso, *Citizen*, March 9, 1899.

16. Overheard talk beneath a water tank of sabotaging a railroad trestle, *Citizen*, April 25, 1899.

17. Passing coal, *Citizen*, April 26, 1899.

18. "The big engine...turned in the twinkling of an eye into a fearful agent of destruction," *Citizen*, April 24 and 28, 1899.

19. "If the brakemen on the SP trains did not have the tramps to look after," *Citizen*, April 26, 1899.

20. Fire at Tucson Lumber, *Citizen*, January 3, 1900.

21. "Said to be the best type of the real tramp article," *Citizen*, February 21, 1900. In 1910, the *El Centro Free Lance* chastised those that believed "that tramps were victims of the world of misfortune and inherited tendencies." The paper also blasted those who felt "hobos were part of an economic system designed to act as a governor on the machine." *El Centro Free Lance* in *Yuma Examiner*, December 23, 1910.

22. "They selected dark clothing to make it more difficult for railroad, "Steam Train" Maury Graham, *Tales of the Iron Road: My Life as King of the Hobos*, Paragon Press, New York, 1990, p. 19; *San Francisco Chronicle*, March 20, 1904.

23. Hobo "Professor" John J. McCook, *Citizen*, April 27, 1899; and April 10, 1902.

24. F.C. Welch, "Penn the Rapid Rambler," *Citizen*, February 19, 1902.

25. Hobos reported their harshest treatment, *Citizen*, April 25 and 27, 1899.

26. F. Hunter, *Star*, December 19 and 23, 1903.

27. "the 'bos took full control," *Star*, December 1, 1903.

28. "Hobos seem to know intuitively," *San Francisco Chronicle*, March 20, 1904.

29. "Dr." Ben L. Reitman, *Star*, July 13 and 14, and September 10, 1907.

30. Charles E. "Desert Charlie" Drumgold, *Tombstone Epitaph*, September 8, 1907; *Star*, June 28, 1909; *Citizen*, June 26, 1909. The *Citizen* reported Drumgold's name "Arizona Charley."

31. "Pestiferous American Hobo in Old Mexico," *Star*, May 1, 1909.

32. "a multitude of good horses... and at the end the inevitable calliope," *Citizen*, September 27, 1910.

33. "all suspicious characters who cannot give accounts of themselves," *Citizen*, September 26, 1910.

34. Railroad police set a record, *Star*, October 9, 1921.

35. "The rider of the brake beam is a menace," *Citizen*, June 29, 1922.

36. Robert E. Echols, *Star*, July 12, 1934.

37. Only hobo who ever hitched a ride on the railroad superintendent's private car, *Star*, July 12, 1934.

38. Hobo Joe Bentley, *Star*, November 19, 1946.

39. "Probably the most brilliant hobo," Steam Train Graham, p. 72.

Chapter 6

1. "harmlessly hoodwinked," *Citizen*, May 27, 1910.

2. Essayist, satirist, and historian Thomas Carlyle (1795-1781).

3. Born to William Eston Randolph, Harold F. Lane, Ed., *Biographical Directory of Railway Officials of America* (New York: Simmons-Boardman Publishing Company, 1913), p. 47.

4. "When you can do as much work as Epes Randolph," *Trains Magazine*, July 1950, p. 46.

5. "If the question should arise," Collis P. Huntington to H.E. Huntington March 3, 1887, Collis P. Huntington Papers (1856-1900), microfilm Series II, reel 18, vol. 101, University of Arizona Library (UAL), Tucson.

6. One of Huntington's cadre of bright, Richard J. Orsi, *Sunset Limited: the Southern Pacific Railroad and the Development of the American West (1850-1930)* Berkeley: University of California Press, 2005, p. 31-32.

7. "As you know, much depends on your own care and vigilance," E.G. Johns to Epes Randolph, June 11, 1888, Collis P. Huntington Papers (1856-1900), microfilm (UAL).

8. "You have done well," Collis P. Huntington to Epes Randolph, August 4, 1888, (UAL).

9. "New timber was obtained," George W. Lewis to editor *Cincinnati Sun Times*, April 28, 1931, (UAL).

10. "his swarthy complexion aglow," James Thorpe, *Henry Edwards Huntington, A Biography* (Berkeley: University of California Press, 1994), p. 83.

11. "If the parties are strong," Collis P. Huntington to E.G. Johns, August 4, 1891, microfilm Series II, reel 18, vol. 109.

12. Bridge collapse, *Cincinnati Enquirer*, June 16, 1892.

13. Indio, California, Mose Drachman, "Reminiscences, (1875-1899)," Mose Drachman Papers MS0226, p. 49, AHS-T.

14. "feared having a man in their midst," Epes Randolph to H.E. Huntington, May 24, 1894, H.E. Huntington Papers, Huntington Library (HL), San Marino, California.

15. "twenty-five [more] years of crowded, glorious life," Mose Drachman, p. 49.

16. Paymaster general of the Arizona militia, Arizona State Librarian Mulford Windsor to Gustave H. Schneider February 16, 1949, "Randolph Veterans Papers" (RVA-GSP), Gustave H. Schneider Papers, MS 0715, AHS-T.

17. "pioneer prophets" and "oracles of the desert," Sally Wright, "El Chamizal: Ramblin' River's Rendezvous with Pioneer Tucsonans," *Citizen*, June 7, 1964.

18. "I don't think there is any better way," *Star*, March 1, 1898.

19. "The cost was $50!" Mose Drachman, p. 60.

20. "Why, there is Ed," Newsclippings-1900, C.P. Huntington Papers, Series IV, reel 2, (UAL).

21. "Randolph was happy; he certainly liked to fight," Mose Drachman, p. 51.

22. "Randolph contributed as much as any man," Nat McKelvey, "The Indomitable Epes Randolph," *Trains Magazine*, (July 1950), p.45.

23. "For the rest of the Colonel's life," Mose Drachman, p. 52.

24. "Mr. Huntington...did not want to authorize work," Los Angeles Inter-Urban Railway, lai-gerwww.erha.org.

25. "Out of a host of men important in Harriman's service," Frank A. Vanderlip, "From Farm Boy to Financier: the Stories of Railroad Moguls," *Saturday Evening Post*, February 9, 1935, p. 24.

26. Headquarters in the Cameron , Charles E. Walker to Gustave H. Schneider August 14, 1940, RVA-GSP, AHS-T.

27. "That was the really remarkable thing," Professor H.T. Cory, *Imperial Valley and the Salton Sink*, (San Francisco: J.J. Newbegin, 1915), p. 1315.

28. "Very rarely, if ever before," ibid., p. 1316-17.

29. "Practically every engineer," ibid.

30. "It will be a matter of such importance," *Star*, December 21, 1906.

31. Netting $3,867, Cory, p. 1389.

32. "waited so long," Randolph to George W. Lewis, August 11, 1914, Cincinnati Historical Society.

33. "The returning of the Colorado to its channel," *Weekly Tribune* (Tucson), January 23, 1909.

34. Mexican Revolution in 1910, Clipbook No. 523, AHS-T.

35. Randolph "took charge of several small," Mulford Winsor, *The Legislative Blue Book of Arizona* (1913), n.p. The rails that entered Globe at the end of 1898 weighed only fifty pounds to the yard and lay on ties purchased from a defunct New Mexico railroad at 10¢ apiece; Randolph operated the Phoenix and Eastern Railroad independently from March 13, 1907 to March 1, 1910 when the Arizona Eastern ran it under a lease agreement, *Southern Pacific Bulletin*, August 1921, p. 5 and 7.

36. Tucson Realty in March 1905, "In Old Tucson," *Star*, March 7, 1925.

37. Two KofA dividends paid in 1906 totaled almost $45,000, King of Arizona Records, MS 1236, AHS-T. The town o0f KofA arose and a post office opened in June, 1900, after H.W. Blaisdell found water five miles south of the mine. The mill's capacity rose to 250 tons but ore played out in 1910. The town endured until the post office closed in late August 1928. Today, KofA is located on private property within a military bombing range. http://www.ghosttowns.com/states/az/az.html.

38. "would seriously disturb," *Los Angeles Times*, October 28, 1906.

39. "This apparently very rich mine looks," *Los Angeles Times*, October 28, 1906.

40. "Mr. Lindsay and myself are arranging," *Star*, October 26, 1906.

41. "Randolph was not a charter member," E.S. Ives to R.C. Lovett, president of several rail lines, December 7, 1905, Eugene S. Ives Papers, AZ 143, UASC.

42. "in order to obscure the line's ownership," E.S. Ives to R.C. Lovett, president of several rail lines, December 7, 1905, Ives Papers, UASC.

43. William A. Grauten, D.F. Myrick, *Railroads of Arizona: Phoenix and the Central Roads, Vol. II* (San Diego: Howell-North Books, 1980), p. 541.

44. "We couldn't if we would," *El Paso Times*, in the *Star*, October 16, 1910.

45. "the lapse of concessions," Courtney DeKalb confidential memorandum to Mr. Kennedy, January 1920, MS 1176, AHS-T. DeKalb and Randolph's disagreements blossomed into a public feud before the U.S. Bureau of Foreign and Domestic Commerce, April 23, 1919.

46. Interstate Commerce Commission subcommittee on banking and currency, *Money Trust Investigation of the Financial and Monetary Conditions in the United States under House Resolutions OS. 429 and 504 before the*

Subcommittee of the Committee on Banking and Currency (Washington, D.C.: Government Printing Office, 1913), Exhibit 134-A.

47. "Whatever his title, Colonel Randolph," *Star*, August 24, 1921.

48. "Forty-five years I have labored," Randolph to Arizona Senator Carl Hayden, August 18, 1921, printed in *Los Angeles Times*, August 24, 1921.

49. "I am not in a class with you 'Nabobs'," Randolph to Charles Weir, November 7, 1911 (Huntington Library).

50. Baby *alacranes* (scorpions), Randolph to Hayden in *Los Angeles Times*, August 24, 1921.

51. Arizona would have 1,000,000 more acres of fertile land, ibid.

52. A Federal Power Commission approved, *Southern Pacific Bulletin*, February 1921, p. 8.

53. "If Epes Randolph had been," Edward Hungerford, *Wells Fargo: Advancing the American Frontier* (New York: Random House, 1949), p. 242.

54. "He was intensely human and very charitable," Mose Drachman, p. 61.

55. "limp, lifeless at half-mast," *Citizen*, August 24, 1921.

56. "Caballeros bajen sus naipes," McKelvey, p.49.

57. "The most widely loved and respected America," *Los Angeles Times*, August 28, 1921.

58. "He passed the time of day," Tucson patriarch and former mayor Gustav A. Hoff to W. N. Cummings, August 27, 1921, MS 1243, Hoff Family Papers, ca. 1858-1962, AHS-T.

59. "He played the 'lone, long game'," *Star*, August 24, 1921.

60. "When Epes Randolph died," Roy P. Drachman, *From Cowtown to Desert Metropolis* (San Francisco: Whitewing Press, 1990), p. 113.

61. All the wheels in all the shops and on all trains, Dan Lewis, curator Huntington Library, interview September 9, 2002; *Star*, August 26, 1921.

62. SP president William Sproule, *Citizen*, August 25, 1921.

63. University of Arizona president Rufus B. von Klein Smid, ibid.

64. "Nearly prostrate from the shock," *Citizen*, August 23, 1921.

65. "Mr. and Mrs. Randolph were a handsome, elderly, gray-haired couple," Lovell Gunter Welsh interview by her daughter Lovell Bonnie, March 27, 1906.

66. "There is no question but that Randolph," Mose Drachman, p. 49.

67. "one of us, but our superior," *Citizen*, August 17, 1939.

68. "All the material," Oney Anderson Jr., Randolph Veterans Association historian, preface, August 15, 1940, RVA-GSP, AHS-T.

69. In Cincinnati, Ohio, Mike Bezold phone conference August 1, 2005.

70. Globe branch of the Arizona Eastern, Daniel Palmer, phone conference, August 1, 2005.

71. "What a colorful life was his," Mose Drachman, p. 49.

Chapter 7

1. Division superintendents, Subjects-Transportation-Railroads-SP-Personnel, AHS-T; *Star*, June 1 and 7, 1907.

2. "Something of a surprise, even to Mr. Averell," *Star*, June 1, 1907.

3. "Wilson some time ago realized," *Southern Pacific Bulletin*, October 1919, p.7.

4. "The SP yards in Benson present a very vacant appearance," *Star*, April 12, 1902. EP&SW charged rates at $5/ton less than SP, *Star*, February 15, 1902. That rose to $8/ton by the following January, *Bisbee Miner*, January 15, 1903. In 1902, J.S. Douglas built a $50,000 gymnasium, complete with a reading room, library, and natatorium for swimming. Douglas also donated $25,000 for construction of a gymnasium at the University of Arizona, *Star*, February 1, 1902. The SP completed a ten-room adobe building for its workers use at the east end of the Benson yard in September 1907, *Star*, September 17, 1907.

5. The SP locked horns with EP&SW in July 1907, *Tombstone Epitaph*, July 21, 1907.

6. EP&SW owners took good care of their railroad, ibid.

7. "To the Mexicans, we paid $5,000 and $6,000," Epes Randolph, *Star*, July 23, 1907.

8. Began tearing down buildings *Star*, July 17 and August 25, 1907.

9. By mid-September, the two rail giants had reached a truce in Naco dispute, *Star*, September 11, 1907.

10. On November 17, 1924, the SP closed the EP&SW passenger station, *Star*, November 12, 1924. That year, the SP began a group life insurance program for its employees.

11. Whitman Metals Reduction Corporation leased the EP&SW roundhouse on Twenty-Fifth Street, *Citizen*, August 27, 1930.

12. "The Celebration of the opening," *Citizen*, special edition, May 5, 1910. The SP began running its Mexican Express through Calabasas on November 20, 1910, leaving Nogales at 7:30 A.M. and returning at 6:30 P.M., *Star*, November 22, 1910. Milwaukee mayor D.S. Rose's Twin Buttes Railroad ran its first train into Nogales on July 4, 1906, Myrick, Vol. I, p. 308. As various interests took control of the mines, they also controlled the railroad. Banner Mining Company assumed ownership in 1950, Myrick, p. 12.

13. "Every bad-order locomotive is a Prussian soldier," McAdoo, *Southern Pacific Bulletin*, October 15, 1918.

14. Third Liberty Loan, *Southern Pacific Bulletin*, November 1, 1918.

15. "You could hardly get through town," Tom Collins, Ephemera Collection, Southern Pacific 1950s, AHS-T.

16. Peter B. and Mary A. Ziegler, *National Register of Historic Places Inventory Nomination Form, Iron Horse Expansion District*, continuation Sheet 31, Item 8, p. 13-14.

17. Rails comprised 60 percent of the Iron Horse neighborhood, National Register of Historic Places, Pie Allen Historic District Registration Form, Section 5, p. 1.

18. Tong warfare surfaced in the Chinese quarter, *Citizen*, May 14, 1922.

19. As the steam era faded, Chinese ownership of city markets fell to just forty stores, *Tucson City Directory* 1922, 1936, 1950, p. 47. A. Martin "Marty" Ronstadt remembered tht in the late 1930s, "Papago Indians came into my grand-uncle Andy Martin's drugstore with big balls of dried mesquite gum. It was really sticky if you touched it with sweaty hands, but we shipped hundreds of pounds of it a year to England. They used it as an emulsifier in cosmetics."

20. summer bachelor's club, *Star*, June 26, 1903.

21. "A piano player named Darling helped with quartettes," Gustave Schneider, February 16, 1949 (RVA-GSP), Gustave Schneider Papers AHS-T.

22. A list of sixty-nine tainted tarts, ibid.

23. Floodwaters and quicksand in the Gila River made crossings perilous, *Arizona Republic*, September 30, 1923.

24. "Epes Randolph, longtime head of the system," *Star*, January 5, 1926.

25. "Lady of the Rails," nineteen-year-old queen Lovenia Hegelund, *Arizona Republic*, October 11, 1926.

26. Passenger train on November 14, 1926, *Southern Pacific Bulletin*, November 1926, p. 10.

27. "I now ask, if the Southern Pacific is going to abide," *Arizona Gazette*, November 30, 1926.

28. Phoenix "threw open the gates to the city and told the corporation," Judge Frank H. Lyman, *Arizona Gazette*, December 8, 1926.

Chapter 8

1. The Tucson shop workforce grew from fifty men under Charles E. Donnatin's charge in 1886, *Citizen*, February 5, 1902.

2. Fred Ronstadt sold forty acres in Reicker's Addition, *Citizen*, January 23, 1900.

3. C.C. Sroufe, "in a very short time," *Citizen*, December 24, 1901.

4. Harriman 1902 visit, *Star*, March 23, 1902.

5. The SP initiated a pension system for its employees, *Star*, January 3, 1903.

6. "It can easily be seen that the very life of many communities is absolutely dependent upon the Southern Pacific railroad," William W. Wilson, *Star*, October 2, 1921. Five thousand people attended the Steinfeld's fashion show that month.

7. "The public at large has rights," *Citizen*, May 22, 1903.

8. SP completed a thirty-stall roundhouse southeast of its existing twenty-five-stall frame structure in May 1905, *Star*, June 24, 1904. The SP had enlarged the old roundhouse from twenty-four to twenty-five stalls ca. 1902.

9. "Risky business ," *Star*, July 19, 1907.

10. Began paying its local workers with paychecks, *Star*, July 27, 1903.

11. "Each individual attired in jeans or old clothes," *Star*, 1909.

12. In the spring in 1910, SP surveyors laid out a site for brand new Tucson shop facilities, *Star*, October 2, 1910.

13. the 55,000-gallon oil tanks, *Star*, May 20, 1902 and October 1, 1910.

14. "The effect of the fire on the men who depend upon their work there for their daily bread was pathetic," *Star*, October 1, 1910.

15. "There was great gloom in business circles," *Star*, October 2, 1910.

16. Epes Randolph, "It (Tucson) is the place geographically," *Citizen*, October 8, 1910.

17. "The community should take immediate steps," *Citizen*, October 7, 1910.

18. H.V. Platt "came in with blood in his eye," *Citizen*, October 17, 1910; *Star*, October 9, 1910.

19. Good Government League, *Citizen*, November 8, 1910; *Star*, November 23, 1910.

20. "with flying colors and every engineer in his place in the cab," *Citizen*, June 28, 1922. 4-6-0, Ten Wheel Locomotive No. 2277.

21. "no doubt be wielding a country-wide influence," Secretary Morgan, *Citizen*, April 1, 1922.

22. "the minimum amount found to maintain a worker," B.M. Jewell, *Citizen*, July 4, 1922.

23. "I had hoped I would never see the day," W.G. Lee, *Citizen*, November 14, 1921.

24. Compressed-air tank No. 109 cut loose a riotous explosion, *Star*, July 2, 1922.

25. "Due to the heat generated," railroad board of inquiry report, ibid.

26. Special commissions deputizing seventeen local SP guards, *Citizen*, July 2, 1922.

27. "practically deserted, the roundhouse," *Citizen*, July 2, 1922: *Star*, July 11, 1922.

28. A dynamic campaign, *Citizen*, July 2, 1922. Rail officials denied the intent to recruit Negro men, *Citizen*, July 5, 1922.

29. "When you took up for your livelihood," William Sproule, *Star*, October 25, 1921. Men began in the SP shops as apprentices, learning the rigor of strenuous work firsthand. The hands-on training system continued, but, by 1917, the also SP ran a formal shop apprentice training school in Oakland, California. Sixteen to twenty-one-year-old students earned 15¢ to 27 1/2¢ an hour during their coursework, depending upon their craft. *Southern Pacific Bulletin*, November 1, 1917, p.8.

30. "The strike is over, as far as the Tucson Division of the Southern Pacific is concerned," Otto B. Schoenky, *Star*, July 4, 1922.

31. "frank relation of the circumstances," Oscar. L. Pease, *Citizen*, July 9, 1922.

32. "There has been a failure to act when action has been needed," Gustavo Couret, *Star*, July 11, 1922.

33. Six shots fired, ibid.

34. U.S. Postal Service ready to mobilize 50,000 motor vehicles, *Citizen*, July 13, 1922.

35. Boxing card, *Star*, July 28, 1922.

36. Caleb Houston, "It does a fellow good to work for different railroads," *Citizen*, January 20, 1939. Herman Blythe explained that dangerous sparks meant a welder might expect to go through a set of overalls in three to four days. Men took engine "storm curtain" canvas, used by engineer's to

keep the cab warm in winter, and sewed welding aprons to protect their clothes. More than once a fellow welder inadvertently burnt a man's eyes while his helmet's hood was up. Men used a poultice made with Irish potatoes to ease the pain.

37. "I have it on reliable authority," William W. Wilson, *Citizen*, July 9, 1922.

38. Shopmen nurtured a "Civit cat," *Star*, October 8, 1910.

Chapter 9

1. "Robert H. Paul, one of the really brave," "Reminiscences" (1875-1899) manuscript, Mose Drachman Papers, MS 0226, page 72, AHS-T. "If Paul is beaten he can thank the Republicans who fixed in the rear for his defeat," J.S. Mansfeld, owner of the Pioneer News Depot, to C.R. Drake November 6, 1884.

2. "Mr. Huntington believed in himself first," *New York Free Press*, Newsclippings-, C.P. Huntington Papers, Series IV, reel 2 (UAL).

3. "I could not call it [a special session] without someone would pay for it," A.P.K. Safford letter to C.R. Drake, January 19, 1881, MS# 0228, AHS-T. The S.P. of Arizona incorporated August 20, 1878.

4. C.R. Drake came to Tucson in 1872, *Star*, June18, 1928. The U. S. military abandoned Camp Lowell, whose site became known as Military Plaza, and established Fort Lowell 7 miles to the northeast in March of 1873.

5. "Drake was one of the most prominent political leaders," *Citizen*, August 15, 1936. The paper reported that Drake held the labor supply contract when the SP first built its southern route.

6. in "every way inimical." C.S. Masten to C.P. Huntington, March 21, 1893.

7. "This game has been played before," *Sacramento Bulletin*, Newsclippings-1900, C.P. Huntington Papers, Series IV, reel 51, January 13, 1893 (UAL).

8. Sixty years after Huntington's death, his papers were rescued from a barn in Westchester County, New York. D. F. Myrick, renowned rail historian and author, volunteered to serve as the tenth "university" demanded in an archival agreement, saving Huntington's missive for the research community.

9. "It is notorious that the SP's," *San Francisco Chronicle*, April 6, 1904.

10. Used "demonstrations of corporate hostility," *Citizen*, January 3, 1902.

11. "The Southern Pacific Company, we presume from lack of knowledge," *Star*, January 5, 1902.

12. "There will be no more railroad building," May 15, 1902, *Globe Record* in *Star*.

13. In the fall of 1906, the "66 to 44" movement swept across Arizona, *Star*, October 22, 1906.

14. "the tax dodgers, the copper looters of Arizona," *Star*, October 12, 1906. "It can not be denied that these great corporations," *Star*, October 22, 1906.

15. W.F. Ellsworth explained that "many commodities" arrived in Tucson for less, *Star*, September 27, 1909.

16. "They crush the industries," *Star*, October 27, 1906.

17. J.C. Stubbs, *Star*, December 20, 1906.

18. "The Republicans had lots of money and paid well for brass bands," Gustave H. Schneider to Professor Charles Leo Hunley, undated No. 47, Schneider Papers MS 0715, AHS-T.

19. "Your Bowie to Globe rate is...thirty times greater on sugar," M.O. Bicknell report of the Arizona Railway Commission, July 19, 1909; M.O. Bicknell to Epes Randolph, June 29, 1909, Arizona Railway Commission records, State of Arizona Archives, Phoenix.

20. Before papers could be filed, Annual Report of the Arizona Railway Commission, 1910.

21. Arizona Railway Commission instructed the Interstate Commerce Commission on July 24, 1909, Records of the Arizona Railway Commission, Arizona State Archives.

22. "A more amazing piece of bossism," *Citizen*, October 14, 1910.

23. "Gigantic corporations," *History of the Arizona State Legislature, 1912-1967* [microform] J. Morris Richards, p. 70.

24. Buchanan 1912 House's only Democrat, Mulford Windsor, *Legislative Blue Book of Arizona*, 1912?, n.p, AHS-T.

25. J.W. "Buch" Buchanan, "Those were fighting days when the state was still a baby," *Star*, August 19, 1936.

26. Fred O. Goodell, *Benson News*, November 11, 1927; *Citizen*, July 24, 1928; March 26, 1935; May 8, 1956.

27. William G. McAdoo, "It was a matter of common report," *Southern Pacific Bulletin*, September 15, 1918.

28. "The railroads of Arizona are escaping taxation on millions of dollars worth of valuations," "Capital City News" from the *Citizen*'s Phoenix News Bureau, February 2, 1922.

29. "All trainmen, enginemen, switchmen, and enginemen are piece-workers," Donnelly, *Star*, December 3, 1931.

30. "Big Irishman, veteran railroader," *Arizona Republic* January 20, 1951.

31. In the fall of 1922, Collins squared off, *Citizen*, October 11, 1922.

32. "Taylor violated all ethics," *Star*, December 31, 1944. Despite Collins's tirade, well-respected Homer Boyd served multiple terms on the board.

33. "These trucks are causing much damage to the highways," Tom Collins to C.E. Addams, Arizona Highway Commission chairman, May 12, 1951, Collins Papers, MS 0164, AHS-T.

34. William C. Joyner, Clipbook No. 310 AHS-T, *Star*, April 2, 1927.

35. J.S. Hardwicke, Clipbook No. 238, AHS-T.

36. Tom Collins, "We are willing to cut our hours during the term of the depression but," Collins to Senator Carl Hayden, May 10. 1933, Collins Papers, MS 0164, AHS-T.

37. Limiting trucks to thirty-five miles an hour on state highways, Section 1589, Revised Code Arizona 1928, Chapter 15, Session Laws 1931-1932, First Special Session.

38. "I am sorry to leave," *Star*, December 5, 1944.

39. Judge Fred Fickett's commendation, Fickett to Tom Collins, January 31, 1933, Collins Papers, AHS-T.

40. "In you, Mr. Collins, I feel," an-old ex-railroader to Tom Collins, undated, Collins Papers, MS 0164, AHS-T.

41. "Hey, Happy! The governor's been trying to reach you," KVOA radio transcript, Tucson, March 1, 1942.

42. "I don't have to look up to anybody now," *Star*, June 13, 1950.

43. "He took to city hall a dynamic character," *Citizen*, June 13, 1950.

44. Betty Houston Crawford, "My father loved Tucson and loved being its leader," interview, March 20, 2006.

45. "Houston was probably the first 'full-time' mayor Tucson ever had," *Star*, June 13, 1950. The next day the *Citizen* added, "He lived a good railroader and he died a good railroader."

46. "He lived a good railroader and he died a good railroader," *Citizen*, June 14, 1950.

47. "I decided that any city with such a mayor must be one of the world's best places to live," reporter Bob Campbell, *Citizen*, June 13, 1950.

Chapter 10

1. After three years of fruitless exploration," *Citizen*, September 12, 1898.

2. The company tried using refined oil in a 4-4-0-type engine in Los Angeles during 1879, *Railroad Lore: From and About the "Friendly Railroad,"* undated SP publication, n.p.

3. Oil-burning engine in Yuma, November 1897, Myrick p.124.

4. Only two engineman instructors worked on the Tucson Division, *Star*, August 25, 1901. Five Tucson engines burned oil by then.

5. Twenty-eight locomotives burned the new fuel, *Star*, February 1, 1902; Wilbur F. Schoonmaker mid-January 1902, *Star*, January 10, 1902. By 1910, the "burro" made the 80 mile roundtrip between Benson and Nogales at 11.5 miles per hour, taking over seven hours.

6. Penwer Steel and Iron Works, *Star*, February 1 and May 20, 1902.

7. Mexican president Porfirio Diaz, *Star*, May 22, 1903.

8. The company recognized firemen, *Southern Pacific Bulletin*, August 1921, p. 27.

9. "the greatest find of all times," W.H. Whalen, *Citizen*, December 27, 1910.

10. An eyewitness said Hostler Woods, *Star*, December 16, 1902.

11. Under a shower of dazzling sparks, James E Boynton, *The 4-10-2: Three Barrels of Steam* (Felton, California, Glenwood Publishers, 1973), p.86. Many other facts of the accident were gleaned from Mr. Boynton's brilliant account.

12. "For many years after the locomotive blew up," C.D. Murtaugh, phone interview, July 9, 2005.

Chapter 11

1. Pima County Supervisor Charles F. Richardson, Judson Estabrook, and Wood Walker, *Star*, July 2, 1909.

2. "In 2006, the basic day is 130 miles," Dennis Simmerman, national director of research for the Brotherhood of Locomotive Engineers, phone interview June 8, 2006.

3. "Connie took a lot of heat," David Devine, interview March 4, 2003.

Chapter 12

1. Harry Stewart, *Citizen*, April 21, 1922. Tom Dugat's wife explained that her husband owed money to no one, but felt mortified that she had to return to work because his goats were not selling.

2. Two "aeroplanes" came from a San Diego military base, *Citizen*, May 18, 1922.

3. moonshine, *Citizen*, May 28, 1922.

4. The U.S. Marines stationed armed guards, *Citizen*, November 16, 1921. As national anxiety grew, the Air Transport Command named Tucson a control center in the event it had to take over the delivery of mail and high priority cargo items during the strike. When union leaders capitulated, the drastic plan proved unnecessary. The *Star* had stopped publishing hotel guest lists October 14, 1921, ending more four decades of tradition.

5. Authorities exonerated expressman Harry S. Stewart, *Citizen*, May 18, 1922 and adjudicated George Jr. Winkler, Jr. as a juvenile. Frank W. Jirou admitted his guilt in Judge S.L. Pattee's courtroom on July 27, 1922. Arrested in Albuquerque, Edward Winkler was convicted along with his father; George Winkler Sr. Judge Kirke Moore sentenced each to ten years and postponed the son's sentencing date ten years, as long as he avoided further legal troubles. Reports placed goatherd Santiago Valdez in Mazatlan.

6. $1,000 reward, *Citizen*, July 12, 1922.

7. Rumors of a knocking nature, *Star*, May 28, 1909.

8. "Many ambitious schemes for north and south and other branch lines came to naught," F. C. Lockwood, *Pioneer Days of Arizona* (New York: MacMillen Publishing, 1932), p. 312.

9. Spentazuma Gold Mining and Milling Company, *Engineering Mining Journal of New York* in *Star*, March 31, 1899.

10. "Look for gold, prospect for gold," the *Star*, January 22, 1904.

11. Ajax No. 1 and No. 2 mine papers filed July 18, 1907 in Pima County Book M.M., p. 688 and 689.

12. "a well known miner here and in Gila City," *Citizen*, November 11, 1919.

13. February 1889, the Arizona & South Eastern Rail Road Company completed, Myrick, Vol. I, p. 183.

14. Copper Queen, *Star*, November 18, 1898.

15. May 1903, when the Imperial Copper Company paid Albert Steinfeld and partners $515,000 for the "Old Boot" mine, *Star*, May 5, 1907.

16. By January 1902, Greene boasted a payroll of 7,000 workers, *Star*, January 25, 1902.

17. Randolph writes $1 million check, Mose Drachman, p. 54.

18. Several large mining enterprises helped Arizona produce 22 percent, *Southern Pacific Bulletin*, August 1921, p. 7.

19. General time inspector of the SP Time Service Webb C. Ball, *Southern Pacific Bulletin*, July 1920. p. 5.

20. 1891 and 1892, killing 40 to 60 percent of southern Arizona cattle, *Arizona Weekly Star*, January 23, 1904.

21. Alma "Jack" Bryce, No. B9791, A721, Vol. 2, (UASC).

22. One eager Midwestern buyer, *Star*, March 25, 1898.

23. "his moustache was frozen off and people [took] him for a Philadelphia lawyer," *Citizen*, February 7, 1899.

24. Eastern brokers offered, *Star*, May 27. 1899.

25. Rather than capitulate, *Star*, April 1, 1899.

26. "I am very sorry that I have to go into Mexico to buy cattle this year," R.G. Brady, *Citizen*, March 22, 1899.

27. "Nothing can faster deteriorate and (more quickly) give a bad name to our cattle," Colin Cameron, *Citizen*, March 31, 1899.

28. Texas Fever ticks, *Star*, May 17, 1898.

29. Greene had purchased some of that nation's oldest existing land grants, *Star*, December 28, 1901.

30. Colonel H.C. Hooker's Sierra Bonita Ranch, *Star*, February 15, 1902.

31. Fred Ronstadt sold forty acres in Reicker's Addition, *Citizen*, January 23, 1900.

32. New stockyards, *Star*, April 22, 1902.

33. Skinned at least forty victims of drought," *Tucson Weekly Star*, Thursday June 23, 1904.

34. "Loco weed," *Star*, July 10, 1907.

35. The insidious weed slaughtered two hundred horses, Tombstone Epitaph, July 14, 1907.

36. John Tyrell, *Star*, January 29, 1907.

37. last of 8,000 head, *Citizen*, March 31, 1899.

38. Willard Wright received 5¢ for head he inspected cattle for disease, *Star*, June 10, 1909. Wright, the son of local Judge C.W. Wright, also owned the Willard Hotel and went on to serve as a city policeman.

39. Miller & Lux, *Star*, March 31, 1909.

40. "Depopulated the country," *Citizen*, March 29, 1917.

41. Hignio B. Aguirre ran the Tucson Meat Market in 1903, *Tucson City Directory*.

42. the company battled thirty-three $500 lawsuits, *Tombstone Epitaph*, October 27, 1907.

43. A cow "should be a first-class rustler," *Star*, February 2, 1921.

44. Amos A. Betts, *Brewery Gulch Gazette*, October 14, 1932.

45. relocated cattle pens 1943, *Citizen*, February 3, 1972.

Chapter 13

1. "The railroad was phenomenally dangerous," William Deverell, *Railroad Crossings: Californians and the Railroad, p. 3*.

2. Seventy percent of all westward colonists, *Star*, February 25, 1902.

3. "Publicity for the attractions and advantages of the Western Empire," *Sunset Magazine*, Vol. 1, No. 1, May 1898, p. 1.

4. *Sunset Magazine* reached its peak circulation, *Memorandum from Southern Pacific Public Relations: The Role of the Central Pacific and the Southern Pacific in Developing California and the West*, 1966, p.9.

5. ibid., p.11.

6. "The boom...wiped out, undated Southern Pacific memorandum, n.p.

7. "To break the monotony of life is to live longer and better," *Southern Pacific Sunset Route* (New York: Liberty Printing Company, undated), n.p.

8. "Recall what Arizona was before their [limited trains] advent," *Memorandum from Southern Pacific Public Relations*, 1966, p. 17.

9. On April 22, 1902, however, the SP canceled its "combination rate," *Star*, April 20, 1902.

10. In June of 1900, the SP added a daily "mixed" train from Nogales, *Star*, June 16, 1900.

11. "The American public is a luxury loving people," *Southern Pacific Bulletin*, November 1, 1917, p.1.

12. "Composite" car, called the "smoker," as its first car, *Star*, December 1, 1898.

13. "As toothsome and savory a meal as was ever served up at Delmonico's or Marchand's," *Star*, December 1, 1898.

14. The car carried President Abraham Lincoln's body burial in 1865, *The Railroad Story, Association of American Railroads*, Wesleyan University, 1944, n.p.

15. Philadelphia Book Lover's Library, *Star*, April 18, 1902.

16. Named one sleeper the Tucson in May 1909, *Star*, May 14, 1909.

17. Allan Pollok, *Southern Pacific Bulletin*, February 1, 1918, p. 1.

18. A "two-application," *Southern Pacific Bulletin*, May 15, 1917, p. 7.

19. "Said to be hotter than a crematory," Kansas Senator John J. Ingalls, *Star*, March 7, 1901. Senator Ingalls died the year prior to the *Star*'s article but the paper continued to run his comments. The SP first installed air-conditioning in dining cars during 1932 and, by 1936, had the largest fleet of air-conditioned cars in the West, *Southern Pacific Bulletin*, September 1996, p. 5.

20. Clark's crew, *Star*, June 6, 1909.

21. Yardmaster James Griffen's crew, *Star*, June 27, 1909.

22. Conductor John Seamands, *Courtland Arizonan*, December 28, 1918.

23. A 1916-1917 company study of 65,019 cars, *Southern Pacific Bulletin*, July 15, 1917, p. 2.

24. May 1, 1917, 145,449 cars, *Southern Pacific Bulletin*, July 1, 1917 p, 2.

25. In September 1918, seventy-three white-flagged "special" SP trains, *Southern Pacific Bulletin*, November 1918, p.2.

26. "Sailing Day," ibid.

27. "better car loading, consolidation of terminals," ibid.

28. Suffered almost $5 million in passenger revenue losses, *Southern Pacific Bulletin*, May 1, 1917, p. 2.

29. "Low freight rates had not caused," Paul Shoup, *Southern Pacific Bulletin*, November, 1926.

30. auto-truck, *Star*, May 19, 1909.

31. Tucson's first auto park, *Citizen*, May 6, 1921. By November 1922, twenty-five cars arrived at the auto park each day, *Citizen*, November 28, 1922.

32. April 1922, the company collected only $413 in freight receipts, *Citizen*, July 14, 1922.

33. Felix Miller's application denied, *Citizen*, July 14, 1922.

34. "Now the battle cry of 'no more motor freight,'" ibid.

35. Laguna Dam, inverted siphon, *Southern Pacific Bulletin*, February 1921, p. 5. The Yuma Main Canal crossed underneath the Colorado River near Yuma in the inverted siphon. Today, it supplies to supply the West Main, Central, and East Main Canals Division, which flow south and irrigate land toward the Mexican border.

36. Ashurst-Hayden and Sacaton diversion dams, www.gilariver.com/lessons/Water%20Settlement%20Chapter%205.doc. Indian farmers received water for 35,000 acres of land and American farmers 27,000. Inequities in water distribution resulted.

37. "the most remarkable sale of public lands ever held in the United States," William W. Wilson, *Southern Pacific Bulletin*, February 1921, p.8.

38. The Post Project irrigated 5,500 of its 22,000 acres between 1918 and 1921, ibid., p. 8. Investors sold the project to creditors in October 1921, for $86,457.

39. Tucson Ice & Cold Storage, *Star*, June 15, 1899; *Citizen*, April 12, 1898.

40. Lettuce centered at the SP stations at Eloy and Toltec, *Southern Pacific Bulletin*, February 1921, p. 8.

41. PFE's Tucson operation expanded in 1922, *Citizen*, April 23, 1922.

42. Tucson fire chief Joe Roberts, *Citizen*, April 23, 1922.

43. In 1926, PFE introduced a forty-foot car, *History and Functions of the Pacific Fruit Express Company* (San Francisco: July 1, 1967), p.3; *Star*, February 14, 1902.

44. Men hung blue flags on a refrigerated train, "Fresh Produce Aided by PFE Plant," Ephemera-Railroads-Southern Pacific-1930s, AHS-T.

45. "Now the building is a hollow echo," *Citizen*, May 22, 1931.

46. SP opened its local company hospital, *Star*, August 20, 1931.

47. Denied SP's application to stop running its Nos. 107 and 108, Southern Pacific ephemera-1930s, AHS-T.

48. Downtown ticket offices in the southwest corner of the Pioneer Hotel, *Star*, July, 13, 1932.

49. "Get the Business Clubs," *Citizen*, May 19, 1922.

50. First "steel-sheathed" cars in 1936, doing away with wooden siding, *History and Functions of the Pacific Fruit Express Company*, (San Francisco: July 1, 1967), p.3.

51. By June 1937, Tucson Division payroll stood at $448,396, *Star*, July, 9, 1937.

52. "Speedy overnight freight train," *Citizen*, July 30, 1939 and February 23, 1940. The SP inaugurated the "Overnight" between San Francisco and Los Angeles August 5, 1935; Erle Heath, *Seventy-five Years of Progress*, (San Francisco: December 1945), p.37.

53. Overnight special tied up at the SP freight depot at 10:00 A.M. sharp, *Citizen*, July 30, 1939.

54. A shipper of perishables on the SP, *History and Functions of the Pacific Fruit Express Company*, (San Francisco: Pacific Fruit Express Company, July 1, 1967), p. 26.

55. A 1935 study showed that shippers diverted 64 percent of all, *Fortune Magazine*, November 1937, p. 186A.

56. First mechanically cooled cars, *History and Functions of the Pacific Fruit Express Company*, (San Francisco: July 1, 1967, p. 4.

Chapter 14

1. "The railroad forced individuals to make room for it in their lives," William Deverell, *Railroad Crossings: Californians and the Railroad*, (Berkeley: University of California Press, 1994, p. 2.

2. "With the coming of the 'Octopus'," Chas. A. Dinsmore to the *Star*, May 23, 1909.

3. "Railroads and their great trains, are the compulsory school masters," *Citizen*, January 22, 1902.

4. "The state government came under the spell," *Fortune Magazine*, November 1937, p. 103.

5. "Railroad corporations are the most rapacious," *Star*, October, 22, 1906.

6. Pima County Assessor John Bogan, *Star*, July 21, 1907.

7. "The SP was not the master of the public but its prey in California," *Fortune Magazine*, November 1937, p. 103.

8. "These railroads are 'soulless creatures'," political candidate C.A. Dinsmore in *Star*, October 23, 1910.

9. "The policy of courteous treatment of complaints," O.E. McCormick, *Memorandum from Southern Pacific Public Relations: The Role of the Central Pacific and the Southern Pacific in Developing California and the West*, 1966, p. 16.

10. George R. Brown, *Southern Pacific Bulletin*, May 1, 1915, p. 5.

11. The SP promoted an average of six conductors each year, Southern Pacific seniority list, January 1, 1932. Ninety-eight year old Tucsonan William F. Knapke published *The Railroad Caboose* in June 1968, after working for 32 different railroads during his career. *Citizen*, June 13, 1968.

12. "No man of phlegmatic disposition," *Southern Pacific Bulletin*, August 15, 1917, p. 2.

13. "be equipped with a common school education," *Star*, October 11, 1907.

14. "Tucson rail yard's grades of almost one percent", SP track profile provided by Windle C. Shue Jr. and Dan Tracy within minutes of an inquiry at www.trainorders.com.

Chapter 15

1. "Doing what boys did," *Star*, October 4, 1984.

2. By 1932, six men in the nine-member engine hostler crew, Tucson Division Seniority List, January 1, 1932.

3. Federico Sayre, March 20, 2007.

4. McIntyre family, *Star*, November 6, 1949.

5. "The railroad brought Tucson's frontier days to an end," Dr. Thomas E. Sheridan, *Del Rancho al Barrio: The Mexican Legacy of Tucson* (Tucson: Mexican Heritage Project,

Arizona Heritage Center, Arizona Historical Society, 1983), p. 17.

6. During 1903, Mexican citizens filled ten, *Star*, December 2, 1903.

7. "A thing of beauty," *Citizen*, September 17, 1910.

8. It is an undisputed fact that Mexican people are a music loving people," *Citizen*, May 24, 1898.

9. Conductor H.J. Temple, *Citizen*, November 23, 1898.

10. Cowboys "feeling ugly," *Citizen*, September 12, October 24, and 26, 1899.

11. "fighting jag" at Eve Blanchard's, *Star*, September 8, 1899.

12. "The Peon Scourge," *Star*, May 6, 1906.

13. "It was the wild part of town," H.T. Getty, *Interethnic Relations in the Community of Tucson* (New York: Arno Press, 1976), p. 48.

14. "most Tucsonenses lived sober, industrious lives," Thomas E. Sheridan, ibid., p. 126.

15. "places of refuge and vitality," Thomas E. Sheridan, *Del Rancho al Barrio: The Mexican Legacy of Tucson* (Tucson: Mexican Heritage Project, Arizona Heritage Center, Arizona Historical Society, 1983), p. 125.

16. "As early as 1860," Thomas E. Sheridan, *Los Tucsonenses* (Tucson: University of Arizona Press, 1968), p.5.

17. "Una cosa que no nos honra en mucho por cierto," *El Mosquito*, October 28, 1922.

18. "el anti-Mexicano (Orville S.) McPherson," *El Mosquito*, October 28, 1922.

19. "la hypocrita y artera Compania de Vistas Paramount," *El Mosquito*, January 23, 1923.

20. Employment office kept two separate lists, Spanish American Democratic Club, Raul Samaniego notes, June 13, 1959.

21. Mexican parents accounted for 54 percent of the births in Pima County in 1935, *El Tucsonense*, January 14, 1936.

22. Joe M. Lovio, "Voice of the People," *Star*, August 25 and 26, 1936.

23. Mr. Moore, *El Tucsonense*, September 23, 1936. Latin American Club president Ed Jacobs wrote the president of S.H. Kress to protest, *El Tucsonense*, August 25, 1936.

24. "slant-eye celestials," *Star*, May 11, 1899. The *Star* proposed that the term "celestial" originated from the ancestral practice among many Chinese of making offerings to Man in the Sky and Earth Grandmother, *Star*, November 12, 1900.

25. Wong family opened the OK Restaurant, Tucson Chinese Collection ca. 1879-ca. 1960, MS 1242, n.p., AHS-T.

26. In 1878, Low Tai You began the first Chinese vegetable garden, ibid.

27. Tales of bribery, *Star*, April 25, 1909. A New Mexico federal jury found Highland D. Maynard guilty of bribing immigration officials to smuggle Chinese workers into the United States.

28. "The wagon loads of fine vegetables," *Citizen*, April 25, 1899; *Citizen*, April 25, 1899; *Star*, May 7, 1902; Tucson Chinese Collection (ca. 1870-ca. 1960), MS 1242, n.p.,

AHS-T; *Chinese Digest*, April 1938, p. 9; Lim P. Lee, *The Chinese in Tucson, Arizona*, April 1938.

29. The 1880 U.S. census showed 158 Chinese men, ibid.

30. Chinese Laundry Protection, *Star*, May 7, 1902.

31. Clerk J.B. Ritter and a "megaphone man," *Star*, May 22, 1909.

32. Tucson's Chinese community re-developed, Chinese Chamber of Commerce formed, ibid.

33. Hatred roamed Tucson in the 1940s, Esther Don Tang, Chinese in America, 1996 KUAT video production, Celeste Gonzalez producer.

34. "Their duties will be to assist passengers in every way possible," *Star*, March 13, 1901.

35. Colored Men's Railway Mercantile in Chicago, *Citizen*, January 2, 1902.

36. "I am sure he has joined Abe Lincoln," Gillie Scott, *Star*, June 3, 1909.

37. International Brotherhood of Sleeping Car Porters, A. Philip Randolph, Larry Tye, *Rising from the Rails* (New York: Henry Holt & Company), p. 113.

38. "Whatever you had [to do for recreation] when this town was small was a tremendous pleasure," Abe Chanin, *Tucson Memories*, 1995 KUAT video production, Rudy Casillas producer/director.

39. "That's just the way it was," Olivia G. Smith, ibid.

40. "One other Mexican engineer was hired after William Sayre," Henry Zappia phone interview, June 14, 2005.

Chapter 16

1. "Turn that train's headlight out," The threat of night-time air raids forced SP trains to run with hooded lights for signals on the Pacific Coast until military restrictions ended early in 1944. The Federal government took nominal control of all U.S. rail lines for three weeks, beginning December 27, 1943, when a wage controversy threatened to interrupt rail service. Erle Heath, *Seventy-five Years of Progress* (San Francisco: December 1945), p.47-48.

2. SP began a projected $68,000 repainting and enlargement of the Tucson depot in the spring of 1941, Doug Kupel, *Tucson's Southern Pacific Depot: Trials, Tribulations, and Triumphs*, unpublished manuscript, p.19. Air-conditioning first found a commercial home in Tucson when Los Angeles engineers designed and installed a $60,000 system atop the roof of the Fox Theater during 1933.

3. "About 150 juniors and seniors in the ROTC program," Herb Bloom, *Tucson Memories*, 1995 KUAT video production, Rudy Casillas, producer/director.

4. "Great billows of black smoke could be seen rising," Schneider to Professor Charles Leo Hunley, undated No. 42, f.3, Schneider Papers, MS 0715, AHS-T.

5. The killing of prisoners Kobata and Isomura, http://www.manymountains.org/lordsburg/.

6. Almost 21,000 company employees served in the armed services, *Southern Pacific Bulletin*, December 1956, p.3.

7. No longer presented "the enjoyable affairs they once were," Southern Pacific publication, May 5, 1943.

8. Post-war gain of three million people in the eight states, *Southern Pacific Bulletin*, September 1996, p. 8.

9. "One of the auspicious signs of the times," *Star*, March 18, 1898.

10. "In asking her to step down," T. Seddon Bruce, *Citizen*, February 17 and 21, 1899.

11. Tucson election board for the second time refused to allow taxpaying women their right to vote, *Star*, May 7, 1898.

12. Women owned more than one-quarter of Tucson's taxable property, *Star*, May 8, 1898.

13. "Many of the members who voted for the bill did so as a joke," *Citizen*, February 14, 1903.

14. "Avowedly antagonistic to the principle of equal rights," *Star*, March 20, 1903.

15. "The saloons in Phoenix were a scene of the wildest joy," *Star*, March 21, 1903. Governor Brodie reportedly denounced such vulgar displays.

16. "She's a little lady," *Star*, August 9, 1900.

17. More than thirty women in Tucson, *Star*, May 25, 1909.

18. Judge Fred Fickett's commendation, Fickett to Tom Collins, January 31, 1933, Collins Papers.

19. "I was told if a girl is going to work for the SP," Jennie Morales Benitez, *Star*, February 28, 1990.

20. "There was the mystique of the old west," Roy P. Drachman, *Tucson Memories*, Rudy Casillas.

21. "The small town we grew up with ceased to exist once the war affected Tucson," Norma Stevenson Grove, ibid.

22. "Tucson grew up with its unique fragrance," Barbara Amos, ibid.

23. "I miss walking down the street and knowing everybody," Herb Bloom, ibid.

24. "That was when it started to change," Alba Torres, ibid.

25. "The war years changed the type of clothes," Cele Peterson, ibid.

26. sixty-five-position switchboard, Tucson: Mountain States Telephone and Telegraph Company, 1949, n.p.

27. "The town shut down at noon for siestas," George W. Wallace, *Tucson Memories*, Rudy Casillas.

28. "We'd go to the mountains and leave doors unlocked the whole time," Morton Solot, ibid.

29. "I hope all the newcomers appreciate it," Abe Chanin, ibid.

Chapter 17

1. The first diesel motor, *Star*, April 11, 1903.

2. "Tucson never missed a step," Herb Bloom, *Tucson Memories*, 1995 KUAT video production, Rudy Casillas producer/director.

3. Diesel freight engines debuted on the Southern Pacific Railroad main line during 1946, *Southern Pacific Bulletin*, September 1996, p.9. Diesel switch engines first appeared on SP lines in 1939. By the end of the war, the company employed a fleet of 130 diesel switchers. Erle Heath, *Seventy-five Years of Progress* (San Francisco: December 1945), p.45.

4. "I, too, care little for the modern type of railroad train," Gustav H. Schneider to Joseph Reed, July 14, 1948, "Randolph Veterans Papers" (RVA-GSP), Gustave H. Schneider Papers, MS 0715, AHS-T.

5. "You deplore Dieselizing of our motive power," Gustav H. Schneider to Reed, December 17, 1950 (RVA-GSP).

6. El Rapido, *Citizen*, November 24, 1950.

7. Gila Tomahawk's final run, *Star*, December 31, 1953.

8. Firms began to abandon desirable warehouses near the railroad, *O'Dowd Plan: Railroad Relocation Study: Fifteenth Street- EP&SW Alignment*, p.3.

9. Charles R. McGowan Sr. ran locomotive No. 1629 on the last steam engine run from Phoenix to Yuma, Charles R. McGowan Sr. SP time book, Betty Nowell Collection, May 9, 1956.

10. Consolidate its fast Argonaut into the Imperial, *Star*, September 24, 1957.

11. "The jet plane will spell the end," D.J. Russell *Southern Pacific Bulletin*, March 1996, p. 9. "Old-school," President D.J. Russell asked all male employees to follow his lead by always wearing a felt hat in the winter and one of straw in summer.

12. The SP purchased engine No. 4294 as its final steam locomotive in 1944, John B. Hungerford, *Cab-in-Front: the Half-Century Story of an Unconventional Locomotive*, (Reseda, California: Hungerford Press, 1959, p. 34.

13. A $17,000-per-mile CTC system revolutionized communication, Southern Pacific undated publication. The SP completed its first CTC installation on the Pacific system between Stockton and Sacramento, California during April 1930, *Southern Pacific Bulletin*, September 1996.

14. President D.J. Russell ordered agents to begin selling United Airlines tickets October 1, 1958, *Southern Pacific Bulletin*, September, 1996, p.13.

15. "Salute to Steam," Official Program, October 19, 1958, Sacramento, California, Stanley M. Houston Collection.

16. Steve Reibel's Acme House Moving & Wrecking Company, *Star*, December 21, 1959.

17. "Any railroad machinist will tell you Williams must have worked in a machine shop," *Star*, December 21, 1959.

18. The SP lost an estimated $2.69 for each mile it ran a passenger train, Ephemera Collection, Southern Pacific 1970s, AHS-T.

19. "Here and there the orange points of cigarettes," *Citizen*, February 23, 1968.

20. The public "deserted passenger trains in favor of planes, buses, and private cars," *Citizen*, September 12, 1969.

21. "The business traveler has been lost to the jets," *Wall Street Journal*, May 22, 1968.

22. "host to the ghost of the Southern," David Carter, *Citizen*, August 23, 1967.

23. "special service charges without offering special services," John S. Messner, ibid.

24. "The Southern Pacific is men," *Fortune Magazine*, November 1937, p. 94.

The Value of a Dollar

Cost is mentioned throughout the book. In the more than 100 year span of the story, the value of a dollar has changed greatly. The value of a rail's labors proved difficult to calculate. The chart below demonstrates changes in relative cost of an item that costs $1.00 in a standardized "consumer bundle" of goods during 1900: That item cost:

$1.44 in 1910

$2.69 in 1920

$2.49 in 1930

$2.22 in 1940

$5.10 in 1950

$7.68 in 1960

$11.55 in 1970

$22.08 in 1980

$38.72 in 1990

$51.90 in 2000

$63.31 in 2005

Samuel H. Williamson, "Five Ways to Compute the Relative Value of a U.S. Dollar Amount, 1790 - 2006," MeasuringWorth.Com, 2007.

Oral History Records

Text references to "attractive eastside home," etc., reflect the pride emanating from many rail families in having surmounted long-ago prejudices and economic limitations. As in many towns, "south of the tracks" was Tucson's "bad side" during the steam age. School children especially, felt the sting of insults and rebukes from "high-rollers," who lived "up on the mesa," north of the imaginary barrier. The obstacle took a harsher form for minority citizens, who faced real impediments to housing, etc. and endured ugly personal encounters. In addition, though many rails enjoyed steady employment expect during times of low traffic, the life style left little room for extravagance.

With apologies to all the wonderful rail families not included herein.

Available at Southern Arizona Transportation Museum after January 1, 2010:

Auslander, Edith Sayre, February 21, 2004.

Ball, Carl A. Jr., April 24, 2002.

Ball, Elgin, June 13, 2006.

Barnes, James A., June 30, 2005.

Blythe, T. Herman, April 17, 2002.

Bradley, Emily Rinkleib, November 13, 2002.

Butler, David, May 13, 2002.

Caballero, Eddie, April 24, 2002

Coltrin, Ralph, June 24, 2005

DeHart, Louise, 2-3-2004.

DeHart, Robert, December 21, 2002.

Elwood, James W., October 11, 2002.

Fitzpatrick, Dorothy Kengla, May 23, 2002

Garigan, Elizabeth, June 1906.

Hinton, Alice Hanson, 6-1-2005.

Houston, Hazel, July 27, 2005.

Huffman, A. E., June 27, 2005.

Jackson, Harold, February 18, 2005.

James W. Nugent, May 5, 2002.

Lee, Raymond and Louise, July 21, 2005.

Lundquist, Clarence George "Boots", May 3, 2002.

Mackaben, Geraldine "Maudie" Hammonds, July 3, 2002.

Manning, Gordon, May 5, 2002.

Manning, Ruth, May 5, 2002.

Marlar, Harlin, February, 18 and March 4, 2005.

Mendez, Francisco "Frank", June 27, 2002.

Moreno, Ruben, May 16, 2003.

Newman, Julia A., April 24, 2007.

Pain, Armando, May 19, 2005.

Payne, Harlan, September 30, 2002.

Pecktol, Eddie, July 15. 2004.

Perkins, George R., July 8, 2004.

Roberts, Floyd, November 8, 2002.

Ronstadt, A. Martin "Marty", February 21, 2004.

Sabala, Annie, April 17, 2004.

Salsbury, Hamilton, April 24, 2007.

Showalter, Sid, November 9, 2002.

Speer, Leon, June 23, 2006.

Stapp, Richard Sr., January 28, 2003.

Starliper, Helen, November 11, 2002

Stoddard, Charles, June 26, 2002.

Tierney, J.J., September 5, 2002.

Webster, E.C. "Moonbeam", October 10, 2002.

White, William H. Jr., April 18, 2007.

Tucson Railroaders Project, Arizona Historical Society-Tucson:

1. Jackson, Harold, AV0001-12, June 6, 1984.

2. Weinzapfel, Constant "Connie", AV 0406-11, January 17, 1984.

3. Alfaro, Vicente, AV0001-01, June 12, 1985.

4. Juanita Villegas Bernal, AV001-03, May 18, 1985.

5. William Crowell, AV0001-06, May 29, 1984.

6. Frank Hutcheson, OH, AV001-11, May 15, 1984.

7. Adelberto Langston, AV0001-14 June 5, 1985.

Index

Photo Index

A

Amec Infrastructure-66
Arizona Daily Star-36,43,46
Arizona Historical Society-iii,iv,v,vii,x,2,6,8,11,14,20,22,23,24,2
6,29,32,35,37,38,39,45,47,50,51,53,54,55,
58,59,61,64,101,106,108,115,116,117,118
,121,122,125,126,127,128,146,148,149,16
1,162,165,169,170,180,192,194,197,201,2
04,205,207,213,222,227,234,242,273,282,
294
Arizona Republican-40
Auslander, Edith Sayre-256

B

Baker, Stephen-335
Ball, Carl A. Jr.-258
Ball, Elgin-73,76,105,110,111,150,159,166,170
,171,172,183,191,196,208,222,262,289,30
5
Ball, Gene-246
Barnes, James A.-134,269,271,272,275
Bays, Arnold-34,179,248
Benitez, Rudy-304,306
Benjamin, Stan-49
Blythe, T. Herman-80,110,135,164,166,167
Bradley, Emily Rinkleib-182
Brundick, Eleanor Bonorden-39
Burke, Jason-80,164,166,167
Burke, Nicholas Lowell-102
Bushnell, robert and Elizabeth-195
Butler, Carolina Castillo-252,253,264
Butler, David-249

C

Caballero, Eddie-139,265,297
Calabasas, Arizona-ix
California State Railroad Museum-211,215,226
Cananea, Sonora-24
Cincinnati Museum-Historical Society Library-84,85
City of Tucson Planning Department-295
Colossal Cave Mountain Park Research Library-154
Coltrin, Ralph-105,288,290,293
Coltrin, Ralph Jr.-246
Crawford, Bettie Houston-109,152,156,157,158,174,178,299

D

DeHart, Robert and Louise-245,246,260,285

E

El Zariba Shrine Temple-Phoenix-99

F

Fitzpatrick, Dorothy Kengla-65,66,109,143,147,185,279
Florence, Arizona-167

G

Gallardo, Manuel-135
Garigan, Mary Annabelle-30,31,132,274,281
Grodt, Gaylon-9

H

Hammonds, Al and Maude-ii,17,27,79,133,141,143,168
Hanson, Ray-1,55,104,129,131,136,138,142,212,2
35,236,240,299
Heidel, John-28,48,62,70,235
Houston, Stanley M.-93,94,95,122,134,198,201

Huntington Library-7
Hyatt, Michael-160

I

Imperial Valley Irrigation District-83,87,90,91,92,213

J

Jackson Family-232

K

Kalt Collection-ix,2,18,34,44,67,68,69,71,74,80,86,1
03,112,137,144,177,186,196,200,216,217,
218,255,261,269,277,278,298,301,335
Kerby, Tom-199,259

L

Leatham, Nyle-37,42
Lee, Raymond and Louise-113,114,115,267,268
Lewis, A.T.-300
Lordsburg, New Mexico-165
Los Angeles Times-43
Lundquist, George-38,71,164,250,251,259

M

Marlar, Harlin-233
McCelland, Robert-172,283
McIntyre, Donald-140,262
Mida, Al-60,334

N

Newman, Julia Peters-254,286
Nowell, Betty-173,239,296
Nugent, James W.-57,165,167,176,184,186,187,189,202,
274

O

Oman, Joe-x

P

Pain, Armando-219,220
Pantano, Arizona-251
Pecktol, Eddie-165,243
Perkins, George-155
Pfersdorf, Jim-157,283

R

Roberts, Floyd-178

S

Sabala, Annie-124,142
Salsbury, Gilbert L.-184,257
Salyer, Barbara-175,283,296
San Francisco Chronicle-41
San Francisco Examiner-145
Sanborn Insurance Company-46,51
Showalter, Sid-81,182,189,225,231,244,284,291,303
Smith, Howard-168
Southern Pacific Bulletin-15,190,221
Speer, Leon-187,188,247
Stapp, Richard Sr.-106,107,109,129,151,210,238,241,243
,289
Stein, Betty-224,229
Steins Pass, New Mexico-169

T

Tierney, J.J.-237

U

Union Pacific Museum-172,298
United States Geological Survey (USGS)-34
University of Arizona-vi,12,19,24,48,52,90,94,96,107,119,
196,212,249,292,302
Arizona Live Stock Board Brand Book-206

W

Wallace, Harold-82
Welsh, Lovell Gunter-54,88,97,214,280,290
Wherry, Charles-89
White, Thomas-33,203,215
White, William-193

About the Dixon Lunettes

Maynard Dixon painted four lunettes in his San Francisco studio, under commission by the Southern Pacific Railroad in 1907, to fill arches in the newly-built depot's western waiting vestibule. Prominent museums and large private art collections featured Dixon paintings throughout the nation during the next three and a half decades. His reputation grew and many recognized the self-taught San Francisco native as his era's Dean of Western artists. Maynard and his wife, well-known artist Edith Hamlin, moved to Tucson in 1939, while maintaining their summer home in Mt. Carmel, Utah. He died at his home on Prince Road in 1946.

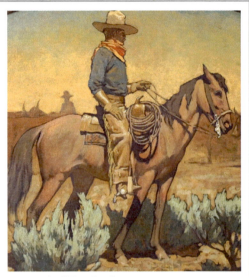

Detail of The Cattleman.

The railroad sent the three repairable paintings to San Francisco for cleaning, restoration, and framing. Local superintendent H.R. Hughes and rail historian Gustav H. Schneider called it, "fitting that the paintings should be given to the people of Tucson," when they donated them to the Temple of Music & Art at 330 S. Scott Street, on behalf of the SP November 11, 1942. Shown at first, the treasures retired beneath layers of dust in the Temple's basement, until secretary-treasurer Ernest Hoffman found them during a general clean-up in August 1969. Clay Lockett purchased the lunettes and, after cleaning and restoration, displayed them, "to preserve a valuable part of Tucson's heritage," during June 1971 at Catalina Savings & Loan, 201 N. Stone Avenue.

The original Dixon lunettes demand perpetual public display in a prominent local facility capable of their archival restoration and maintenance, for "the people of Tucson" to appreciate. Prints of the three originals will soon hang in Tucson's Historic Depot thanks to donors: Tucson-Pima Historical Commission, Joe Kalt and Judy Gans, Mark Sublette-Medicine Man Gallery, Dr. Kenneth Karrels, Dr. James B. Klein, and others, and to cooperation between the Southern Arizona Transportation Museum, the Tucson-Pima Historical Commission, the Arizona Historical Society Southern Division, and the City of Tucson.

Detail of The Miner. (Photos by Al Mida)

Detail of The Apache.

About the Author

     The grandson of a Tucson SP accountant, William Kalt, grew up in a proud pioneer Arizona family. History lessons began early for the career public educator, as relatives shared tales of the rough and tumble days of their youth. Smitten with stories of life in the southwest, Kalt began his studies of the SP in pursuit of family history. The quest soon evolved into a broader search for the railroad's role in Tucson during the steam era. Bilingual in English and Spanish and imbued with a passion for history, Kalt sought out people of every heritage, who lived the glory days of steam. Capturing oral histories of Tucson's railroad men and women, in combination with archival research across the southwest, he found deep and lasting friendships, amusing accounts, and a cherished understanding of the people who called themselves "rails." Kalt's "I'll Meet You In the Cornfield: the Tragic Train Wreck of 1903" appeared in the winter 2004 issue of the Journal of Arizona History. His story, "Epes Randolph: Railroad Man of the Southwest," won the society's James F. Elliot II award for the best article by a non-professional historian during 2006. In December 2006, the Tucson Corral of Westerners elected Kalt deputy sheriff. (Stephen Baker photo in Kalt Collection)